# Boarding
# Out

# Boarding Out

*Inhabiting the American Urban Literary
Imagination, 1840–1860*

✦

David Faflik

NORTHWESTERN UNIVERSITY PRESS
EVANSTON, ILLINOIS

Northwestern University Press
www.nupress.northwestern.edu

Printed in the United States of America

10  9  8  7  6  5  4  3  2  1

**Library of Congress Cataloging-in-Publication Data**

Faflik, David, 1972–
    Boarding out : inhabiting the American urban literary imagination, 1840–1860 / David
Faflik.
        p. cm.
    Includes bibliographical references and index.
    Revised version of the author's dissertation, University of North Carolina at Chapel
Hill, 2005.
    ISBN 978-0-8101-2838-5 (pbk. : alk. paper)
    1. American literature—19th century—History and criticism. 2. Boardinghouses—
History—19th century. 3. Boardinghouses in literature. 4. City and town life in literature.
I. Title.
PS217.C57F34 2012

2012001461

∞ The paper used in this publication meets the minimum requirements of the American
National Standard for Information Sciences—Permanence of Paper for Printed Library
Materials, ANSI Z39.48-1992.

*For Philip F. Gura:*
*Seer. Sayer. Believer.*

CONTENTS

ILLUSTRATIONS

# ACKNOWLEDGMENTS

A labor of love, this project has been years in the making, and I have hardly labored alone. Teachers, colleagues, friends, family, and professional acquaintance have lent their varied, vital support along the way. I would be remiss if I did not acknowledge their contributions.

*Boarding Out* began as a dissertation at the University of North Carolina–Chapel Hill. If the book before you has evolved much since then, my thinking about boarding still owes a deep debt to the members of my committee. Joy and John Kasson helped shape my American Studies mind even before I became their student in 1999. The subsequent years that I spent learning from them directly were formative. If I have found my way in academic life, it is as a result of their unfailing intelligence, kindness, patience, and encouragement. In the Kassons I have been doubly lucky. Bob Cantwell and Tim Marr were similarly supportive in helping me shape this project at its beginning, and challenged me to think well past the early boundaries that I had drawn for myself. My mentor Philip Gura receives the final mention here. *Boarding Out* would not exist without him. This book's dedication only begins to suggest what he has meant to me—what he will always mean to me.

My debts are not only doctoral, but personal. Loving my labor, I have been head over heels for my wife, Kari, since the sunny day in Seattle when we met. She sustains me in all my good works. We have more to come. Friends Mike Keller, Paul Baggett, Julie Barst, Jason McEntee, Kathleen Donovan, Grant Farred, Kate Gentry, Bob Gupta, and Bill Rorabaugh were there when being there was needed. They know where there is. Where I would be without the original Faflik five only they know.

I have been institutionally supported as well. At the dissertation stage, I received invaluable funding through a Gilder Lehrman Fellowship at the New York Public Library, in addition to an Andrew W. Mellon Foundation Fellowship at The Library Company of Philadelphia. Jim Green at the latter library invested time and attention in me during my month of research there; I am still flattered, and this book has only benefited from him. The members of the research staff at the American Antiquarian Society are an institution unto themselves. Harvard's Houghton Library opened their archives to me. With their permission, I quote in chapter 3 of this study from the unpublished family papers of Oliver Wendell Holmes. The Missouri Historical Society likewise grants permission for my citations from the manuscript diaries of Englishman Thomas Butler Gunn. Short stays at the Massachusetts Historical Society and the Historical Society of Pennsylvania complemented early research at UNC-Chapel Hill's Davis and Wilson libraries. Interlibrary loan staff at the University of Arkansas and South Dakota State University extended my research much further than it otherwise could have gone. Several professional journals, furthermore, played host to my preliminary boardinghouse perspectives before this book's completion. With their permission, chapter 3 reprises portions of "Community, Civility, Compromise: Dr. Holmes's Boston Boardinghouse," *New England Quarterly* 78, no. 4 (December 2005): 547–69, while chapter 1 expands on "Boardinghouse Life, Boardinghouse Letters," *Studies in the Literary Imagination* 40, no. 1 (Spring 2007): 27–47.

That brings me at last to Northwestern University Press. Assistant Director Henry Carrigan Jr. showed great faith in this project from day one. I owe him everything, and more. Peter Raccuglia helped me past obstacles great and small. Gianna Mosser oversaw proceedings with an expert's eye. Paul Mendelson lent his deft editorial hand. I thank you all.

The University of Rhode Island's Center for the Humanities met a portion of the production costs for this book. I thank the Center for its generous support.

# Boarding
# Out

Introduction

# The Forms and Functions of Modern American Metropolitan Literature

> But . . . [insert city of choice] is an immense ocean. Drop in
> your sounding line and it will never reach the bottom. Have a
> look, try describing it! No matter how carefully you try to see
> and understand everything, to describe everything, no matter
> how many of you there are, trying hard, all of you exploring
> that great sea, there'll always be places you never get to,
> caverns you never uncover, blossoms, pearls, monsters, quite
> incredible things that every literary diver overlooks.
>
> —Honoré de Balzac, *Le Père Goriot*, 1835

A curious work, Mortimer Thomson's *Doesticks; What He Says* (1855)
typifies a shift in America's literature during the middle decades of the
nineteenth century.[1] Modern architects might say that its form follows
its function. For as contemporary America underwent radical changes in
size, scope, pace, and identity as a result of the nation's momentous urban
turn before the U.S. Civil War,[2] writers like "Doesticks," to borrow the
popular humorist Thomson's pseudonym, helped articulate an author's
equivalent of infrastructure with an urban literary form whose versatility
and adaptability were suited to a society in transition.

With the cities around them emerging and evolving as never before,
Americans of "Doesticks's" day sought literal and figurative ways to
inhabit the New World metropolis. Period literature gave shape to that
search in close correspondence with a signature city shelter, the boardinghouse. Surplus populations and rising real estate prices (the two trends
were mutually reinforcing) had rendered the traditional stand-alone
household increasingly obsolete for all but the era's wealthiest urban
dwellers. Boarding ranked foremost among the measures taken to resolve

that problem by assembling non-related peoples under one roof to partake of food, shelter, and paid-for domestic services that approximated the idealized comforts of "home" within the confines of the city. Held loosely beneath the roofs of these structures resided something other than a venue for human habitation, however. Also present was the human habit of storytelling, manifested through a set of boardinghouse-inflected literary conventions that were as flexibly mixed and mobile as boarders themselves. Boarding's store of symbols, tales, tropes, and points of view, its recurring patterns of images, characters, and suggestive settings recurred so frequently in print as to become a fixture in the pages of antebellum newspapers, magazines, broadsides, and books, not a few of these last now considered classics of the American Renaissance. In boarding the era's readers and writers alike secured an imaginative capacity to settle into metropolitan environs that, at the time, must have seemed as unfamiliar as urban initiates like Doesticks perceived them to be. Accompanying the country's urban turn, in short, was a concomitant literary turn that similarly hinged on boarding. The former ushered Americans into the protoindustrial city; the latter brought the city into the nation's literature. This study resides where the once widespread social practice that was boarding intersects with the discursive praxis from the past to which it was inextricably linked. If the precise causes and consequences of that overlap are not quite quantifiable, they do permit in retrospect the kind of qualitative description and analysis of antebellum *literary* boarding that this book offers.

But to return to *Doesticks:* here we find one representative author's playful meditation on American urbanization not as social problem, but literary possibility, with the modest residential landmark that was the boardinghouse standing as a central fact and foundational metaphor for his musings. In the self-reflexive commentary "To the Reader," Thomson implies in the introductory pages of his assorted "sketches" the theme that emerges in the course of his own work as well as in the writings of many of his immediate peers (v). To wit, the author-narrator conflates his comical adjustments to city life—the picaresque episodes of which comprise *Doesticks*'s fragile storyline—with his closely wedded attempts to construct a literary form that would lend itself to the chronic crowdedness, hurriedness, and sensory excitement of his urban milieu. It was but recently, Doesticks relates, when the "eternal sameness of a country village" instilled in him the "roving fever" that has brought many before and since to his chosen destination of "Gotham" (34–35). Following his "metropolitan advent" he turns his attention in two directions at once (40). On the one hand, and coinciding with his entrance into Manhattan,

Doesticks soon becomes "haunted perpetually" by an urge to "write a book! write a book!" (15), to preserve his initial urban impressions. A clear conception of what *kind* of book to write eludes him, however. On the other hand, and as he explains in some detail in a subsequent chapter on "Model Boardinghouses," Doesticks early in his urban career also recognizes the necessity of tending to domestic matters. "As soon after my arrival as I could collect my senses," he writes, "I deemed it advisable to search for lodgings" (50). Two searches, then—one for "lodgings," one for literature—coalesce into a *common* effort at finding suitable forms for communal city settlement. Each search not only informs but codepends on the other. Both begin and end in the boardinghouse.

Of the pair, Doesticks's domestic quest would seem the more straightforward, but like the literatures it inspired, it was implicated in the complexities of a "crisis" in urban modernity often associated with the lives and literary texts of the early twentieth century. Thomson accordingly positions his antebellum "Gotham" on the cutting edge, where it belongs. He foregrounds city experiences that were entirely new to the United States, as did dozens more authors of the day who contributed to a general outpouring of boardinghouse writings. He furthermore predates by some fifty years what many consider to be the modern period proper.

The hallmarks of the cultural condition that Thomson evokes are familiar, if boarding's role in its unfolding is not. There remains no consensus on when modern America dawned, but commentators tend to agree on modernity's main contradiction: a permanent social and perceptual state of instability. The modern meant fluidity. It meant the constant disruption of change-in-the-making. Modernity in its American, nineteenth-century, early industrial incarnation—after its commercial beginnings in sixteenth-century Europe, but before its later descent into predictable rituals of consumerism—meant movement, not stasis; noise, not silence; anxiety, not equanimity; diversity, not uniformity.[3] Intensive immigration and accelerated native migration were two of the factors that set this modernity in motion. Each of these developments brought a crush of new arrivals to urban centers like New York, Philadelphia, and Boston, which by midcentury saw their polyglot populations swell by the hundreds of thousands. Continuing revolutions in transportation, technology, and communications meanwhile moved these peoples into, around, and out of America's cities at once unthinkable speeds, and in unprecedented numbers. Links by road, turnpike, canal, telegraph, railroad, streetcar, and transatlantic steamship challenged—in modern fashion—the very notions of geographic distance and the time previously needed to bridge it.

Transient peoples required an improvised residence, in regions where the national demographic surge provided visible evidence of American modernity. Both at city center and in peripheral urban districts, recurring housing shortages necessitated the close-quartered accommodations that made boarding as much a cause as an effect of an area's incorporation into the metropolitan nexus. Throughout much of the country's northeastern corridor, as well as at selected sites further inland and south, rental, communal living proved an attractive option for urban transplants like Doesticks, simply because the spike in local real estate prices that attended runaway demand for limited housing stock argued against independent home ownership. Boarding was not the only form that urban occupancy took. Nor was it exclusive to the United States. Indeed, Europeans boarded, too, or, as was more often the case in growing urban centers overseas, they lodged in single-room "communal" quarters without sitting down to the three daily shared meals that for many observers constituted the boardinghouse's chief attraction.[4] But, if it was not peculiar to the New World, and impacting as it did both city and suburb, boarding was for a short historic interval the most popular form of city domesticity in the United States. It was resorted to by urban Americans at higher rates, in greater numbers, and with a certain hurry-up attitude measured in rental arrangements lasting weeks and months but seldom years that eclipsed boarding in alternate contexts.

In their prime, urban America's boardinghouses effectively replicated in miniature the very cities whose existence they foretold and confirmed. Each of these "structures"—city as shelter, and boardinghouse as domicile—maximized occupancy and thus the frequency of contact between inhabitants; each minimized personal privacy and the spatial prerogatives that went with it; each intensified an already brisk mode of city living by encouraging an unprecedented residential itinerancy. In antebellum boarding lay the seeds of a fractured modern lifestyle that most have come to associate with the twentieth century and beyond. What boarding for many came to signify, then, during the 1840s and 1850s were the great transformations in outward behavior and basic human organization that distinguished America's decisive metropolitan moment. Georg Simmel says of the metropolis per se that the "deepest problems of modern life derive from the claim of the individual to preserve the autonomy and individuality of his existence in the face of overwhelming social forces."[5] By this standard, the steady stress of big-city living—a strain surely compounded by boarding among a faceless aggregate of strangers—would have seemed a "problem" offering few, if any, solutions.

No less modern were the ways in which Americans registered their nation's epochal urbanization at the level of consciousness, or "*urban consciousness,*" as Betsy Klimasmith says (my emphasis),[6] in an effort to "preserve subjective life" amidst what Simmel again calls "the overwhelming power" of the metropolis ("The Metropolis and Mental Life," 411). With the influx of job-hunters, pleasure-seekers, and those motivated by hopeful relocation came changes not only in the external signs of U.S. cities; citizens' *internal* responses to the urban as a distinctive cognitive category likewise underwent revision, and prompted a specific literary reaction. Here is where the literature that took the form of works like Thomson's assumed their true function. Whether writing by private reflection, or for print publication in an expanding metropolitan press, the would-be urban authors of this generation seized upon the "problems" of modernity as an opportunity to impart literary shape to a full spectrum of ideas, inclinations, and emotions that redounded back to cities, and which otherwise might have gone unuttered. These same authors, not incidentally, often located in boarding both a serviceable city residence, and a reliable discursive framework, for giving expression to metropolitan thoughts widely shared among the masses of readers (many of them former, current, or future boarders) for whom cities had become as much an inescapable social fact as they were a viscerally felt phenomenon.

It is precisely this balance between objective fact and subjective response that characterizes Doesticks's hunt for a home, much as it does his and other authors' search for a set of literary strategies by which to map the cities refracted inside them. The visiting nineteenth-century New Englander Ralph Waldo Emerson might dismiss New York in his journal as all "surface in a world of surfaces."[7] His friend Margaret Fuller might concur, contrasting as she did the intellectual "*depths*" of small-town Massachusetts with her brief "abode . . . in the shallows" of 1840s Manhattan.[8] Yet, there is sufficient testimony from Doesticks and others to suggest that the search for the "real" city was no superficial endeavor; it was coextensive with a drive toward formidable "*depths*" which even Fuller, in her socially conscious municipal newspaper coverage for the nationally circulating *New York Tribune,* would concede belonged to the city. Thus a newly arrived Doesticks, after deeming it "necessary to search out a fit habitation, wherein I might eat, sleep, change my shirt . . . , and attend to the other comforts of the external *homo,*" also states his concern for "the inner individual" (50). His "search" is not just an exercise in the mundane, an ordinary instance of daily routine; it is a "voyage" of "discovery" endowed with a significance commensurate with the unofficial rite of passage that midcentury city habitation had become (51).

True, the metropolitan episodes imparted by a single "external *homo*" hardly generate more than topical interest, if that. But, when taken in tandem with hundreds, perhaps thousands, of similar stories, and when shifted from the "external" realm of observable domestic data, to the intangible dimensions of the urban dweller's "inner individual," works of the order of *Doesticks* begin to suggest the outlines of a legitimate literary genre in their own right. It is a genre equipped with the necessary *furniture* to achieve something other than mere mimetic effect, despite the deflating subtitle *What He Says* under which Thomson collects his smiling persona's badinage. Like countless short prose pieces from the period, as well as the many poems, plays, and full-length novels that addressed themselves (whether directly or indirectly) to the antebellum nation's new urban world, *Doesticks* not only records and then relates Emerson's "surface" details of the city by way of the urban boardinghouse. It climbs inside that physical construct to explore the range of its imaginative, metaphorical meanings. What *Doesticks* "says" is one thing. What *Doesticks does* is to interrogate what it originally meant in America to *habitate*—in the developing metropolitan sense of that word—an elusive urban mindset that might have been built upon the outer trappings of city residence, but ultimately inhered in interior responses to conditions whose demands upon "the inner individual" reached well beyond "wherein I might eat, sleep, [and] change my shirt."

This is not to deny the importance of the actual city in the period or the seminal place that it occupies in books such as Thomson's; it is to redirect attention from the city's literal to its literary properties. More than a simple setting, the urban boarder's topography that figures in *Doesticks* and comparable works often provides them with a focal seat and conceit of sustained action and psychological development, becoming at once the arbiter of sequenced incident, complication, duration, and (ir)resolution for the overall plot and character insights that tenuously take shape by volume's end, as they do here. The boardinghouses on offer in these and like pages also, and more important, provide the primary source of stimulating response from boarder-narrators, supporting characters, and by consequence readers, at psychic levels that remain unprobed by many of the era's more matter-of-fact fictional and nonfictional domestic texts.

Restated, the majority of American boardinghouse narratives pitch plot on a middle ground somewhere between material fact and internalized "fictions." Situated along an unstable city continuum, befitting a nation in urban transition, literary boarding remains to this day in a perpetual state of motion; it continually shifts its focus from the reportorial mandate of late-century realism to the ethereal realms of romance. This middle boarders' realm did not belong by exclusive right to contemporary U.S. authors, but it does emerge in a critical survey of historical urban writings as something of a proprietary place apart. In his superb study *Imagined Cities*, scholar Robert Alter groups European writings from the mid-to-late nineteenth century up to the modernist experiments of the 1920s under the heading "experiential realism."[9] Alter names by that phrase a pervasive effort among period British and Continental novelists to channel into their works the metropolis as it was sensorily *experienced* through the flickering consciousness of individual narrators. Alter's urban moderns lack "the certitude of realist representation," and so dispense with the kinds of pedestrian details with which works like *Doesticks* abound. Their uncontrolling consciousnesses also regularly descend into epistemological "confusion, fantasy, and fragmentation," and so cast the boardinghouse romance's prior reliance on a more confident brand of introspection as a naive substitute for representational "reality" (*Imagined Cities*, 20–21). Inasmuch as Alter is careful to distinguish the objective experiences of urban modernity in Europe and America, and by extension the respective efforts on either side of the Atlantic to transmit that experience to language, subjectively, within separate cultural contexts (ibid., xi), he begins to suggest what it was that made the city in literature different (if not "exceptional") in the antebellum United States than it was elsewhere in the West.[10] The boardinghouse is the difference that this study proposes. In boarding unadorned fact meets processed image, ingenuous delineation greets artful interpretation, and transparently "public" houses adjoin "private" homes that have passed through the alembic of literature. All are conveyed in an *accommodating* discursive form whose twin socio-literary functions derived from cognate projects to inhabit the modern American metropolis in life no less than letters.

✦

If city settlement was the common plot of American literary boarding at the mid-nineteenth century, then modernity itself was perhaps the genre's consensual protagonist. Boardinghouse writers like Thomson composed ostensibly unassuming anecdotes of the city even as they managed to materialize two of modernity's defining forces—time and space. An altered sense and experience of these same forces underwrote the rise of the antebellum metropolis in the United States, much as it did (and does) when and wherever urbanization occurs. Boarding, too, depended on quintessentially modern temporal-spatial conditions; the quickening clock of the capitalist city, combined with its sanctioning the competitive search for that most prized of urban commodities, living space, reappeared in the boardinghouse's high turnover rate among tenants and the limited lebensraum that occupants who lacked alternatives usually accepted without protest, if not without complaint. Concurrently, and not by coincidence, urban versions of time and space equally informed boardinghouse writing, lending literary boarding a particular city feel. On one side of this dialectic, the boardinghouse narrative drew its variable forms and functions from the up-tempo rhythms and densely settled terrain unique to modern cities. There is a foreshortened feel to the discourse of boarding, the urban domestic sources of which add a touch of verisimilitude to their local coloring, and in fact comprise the basic building blocks from which this literature is raised. On the other side of the equation, boarder-authors gave as much as they got from the metropolis. By converting time-space into text through boarding, they extended to modernity the particularity not of personhood but of a readily identifiable communal place. In this place they engaged and elaborated the era's consuming discussion of home, whose reassuring features rebutted the city's alienating abstractions.[11]

*Doesticks*'s formal literary properties illustrate boarding's reliance on city time and space *as* forms. As did many other boarder-narrators, Thomson's eponymous first-person protagonist innocently pens his initial urban encounters for any value they might possess as instruction or diversion, whether for his own or others' sake. The often unlooked-for result is just what readers receive here: an object verbal lesson in the city's temporal-spatiality. Shortly after his arrival in Manhattan, for example, Doesticks learns firsthand of temporal rhythms that differ sharply from the rural rising and setting of the sun to which he is accustomed. Not only is the city alive with possibilities; it is alive with busy urban people, whose bustling activities recall the "restless wave" that Doesticks invokes in his opening pages (vi). Undeterred, his response to metropolitan time is emulation, rather than resignation. Although he allows that it takes, in most instances, "some considerable time" for country folk to adjust to urban customs (120), he nonetheless resolves "to make myself ever-present" in an effort to absorb the city's sights and sounds as soon as possible—a resolution that also serves as a fitting description for the high velocity hypertense of the boardinghouse text. "In a literary point of view," the narrator announces at the start of his volume, the written thoughts that he has mustered amount to "airy nothings" (vi). But, if "nothing" aptly identifies the content of this or some other boardinghouse narrative, then "nothing" must pass as a rapid transaction (v). Scenes, peoples, and settings move determinedly forward in discursive boarding, with all the propulsive energy of a city wide awake.

That momentum is built into boarding. As Doesticks discovers, a hurried, anxious search for proper lodgings often marked the arriviste's introduction to city life; that search in turn ranked among the genre's favorite set pieces, and frequently lends the texts in question a characteristic air of hastening. What Lloyd Pratt names the "complex universe of time" flies in boardinghouse writings,[12] and this compression of clock and calendar works to redirect narrative trajectory away from digression, even as it condenses events into proverbial New York minutes. Doesticks demonstrates as much when he writes with impatience of his own and a newfound companion's experiences scouting the city for shelter: "To describe all the dilapidated gentlewomen, whose apartments we inspected—all the many quarters in all sorts of musty smelling rooms, and to recount how many promises we made to 'call again,' would take too much time" (51). Assuming that one could locate a home—and Doesticks does find several, in quick succession—tenants conspired with landlords, or, usually, land*ladies,* to normalize a life led in the short term, rather than one adjusted to the *longue durée.* Brevity was the rule of most boardinghouse leases, and literary boarding mirrored the frantic to-and-fro traffic flows of the city's otherwise unpredictable inhabitants. Witness Doesticks's lasting but one night at his first boardinghouse (bedbugs drive him away), and nine days at his second (a mysterious meat dish served ad nauseam sends him packing), before he establishes the tentative routine that holds for some months following—a week's stay, but no more, at a series of residences. It was a "variegated existence," this, as Doesticks says (148). It was a frenetic one as well. As a result, the texts that host the Doesticks of the antebellum literary world unfold at a breathless double-time rate. To read such works is to enlist in a page-turning race that reenacts the discernible movements of modern urban boarding.

As with time, so with space: boardinghouse discourse collapses the physical and conceptual coordinates within which narration occurs. Squeezed on the one hand by overcrowded cities, and confined on the other to cramped quarters in rented rooms, at communal dining tables, and inside boardinghouse parlors, boarders were no less pressed by whichever text they should happen to inhabit. Save for the *perceptual* freedom allowed the occasional omniscient narrator, print forms of boarding obey a downsizing trend toward *spatial* limitation, by restricting action to a circumscribed urban field. Boarding existed at all because the nation's cities grew big; boarding translated to page, however, in accordance with the system of scarcity that informed urban residential practice. The greater the metroplex, the smaller the living space—and so it was with the genre's writers, too, who reinscribe in their boardinghouse works dramatic boundaries narrowed by the realities of urban domesticity.

Once more Doesticks's case is instructive. After spending only a fortnight in Manhattan, he enjoys a veritable lifetime's worth of urban entertainments that run the length and breadth of the island's lower precincts. He attends the opera "with detestation," the theatres "with approbation," and Christy's blackface minstrels "with cachinnation," in addition to visiting P. T. Barnum's Museum of exotic oddities and "almost all the other places of amusement in the city" (121–22). It is an ambitious itinerary, inasmuch as it telescopes—temporally and spatially—Manhattan's famous grid into a circumambient playground on which Doesticks bestows the modifier of "Modern," capital "M" intended (120). As representational reportage, Doesticks's account might seem an anachronism, a throwback to the days when the American city not only was knowable but literally walkable. As a sequence of plotted action, it warrants the "Modern" label he gives it, since Doesticks's "play" transpires in narrative space that is as clipped and curtailed as the quarters afforded by most of the boardinghouses to which he had access. Trawling the metropolis for lodgings, Doesticks elides the details of physical distance that would have filled the gaps, so to speak, between the interim episodes of his peripatetic existence. When not at domestic "work," which is to say, when not in pursuit of an acceptable domicile, he appears neither inclined nor able to inhabit the full array of urban spaces that were available to him. Doesticks makes the rounds of New York's "amusements," but he so internalizes boarding's concatenated condition as to neglect the sizeable narrative territory that is interval. Scenes shift in *Doesticks* with a frictionless ease that in the end proves spatially deceptive. Despite being constantly on the run, readers of boardinghouse texts, when spared the vigorous plodding of plot, well might mistake one urban way station for another. Like boarders they would seem to be moving, and often; yet theirs is the shared sensation of going nowhere, fast.

In structural terms, literary boarding reprises this paradox of unremitting traction/tethered inaction as its most recognizable form. And so it bids to be the generic sine qua non of cities—the genre, that is, without which readers would need to achieve a vastly modified interpretative understanding of the urban. It is true that scholars make convincing claims for several discrete genres in this respect. Of these the traditional choice for more than a century of both writers and critics looking to identify an Ururban literature has been the novel, due to its breadth of scope, and the diversity and depth of perspectives that it permits.[13] Yet, ranked alongside the novel are a number of worthy alternatives. There is the urban short story, whose very shortness allies it to boarding. Or there is the communally encoded subgenre of the serial novel. Walt Whitman wrote to "contain" New York's "multitudes" circa 1855 in free verse, while curbside journalism persists in recycling the vernacular of city streets, as it democratically transcribes what Edgar Allan Poe earlier called "the rush of the age." Even lyric bids to preempt boarding as a tautly "vertical," as opposed to loosely "horizontal," mode of writing, and as such qualifies for Ivy Schweitzer as a *non*-narrative genre specially attuned to the "intensity" and discontinuity of modernity.[14] Similarly adapted for urban representational purposes, however, boarding arguably conducts its business with far greater efficiency than any other literature. Subsequent chapters will demonstrate that the genre I call "boardinghouse letters" was not mutually exclusive to the novel, short story, sketch, epic, serial, lyric, newspaper, advertisement, or magazine piece, necessarily. Boarding encompassed these and related forms, on occasion causing them to merge in ways that shape our literary understanding of the modern American metropolis. Renouncing the novel's diffusion, boarding prefers urban compaction. City time reappears there as narrative truncation, *un*timely anticlimax, and breakneck pacing, while boarding's metropolitan spaces adhere to a less-is-more paradigm that few novels can match. In addition, by making much of little, and integrating at least a semblance of the recurrence that marks periodical production and consumption, literary boarding also surpasses short print forms and antebellum serials in relaying for readers the vicissitudes of urban experience. This is not a question of page count. Instead, boarding's conveyed *suggestion* of limitation, not unlike the trade periodical's formatting concerns over column length and paragraph breaks, summons a contemporary "board today, gone tomorrow" philosophy that invites boardinghouse letters to be read as a revolving door: random characters come and go; narrators alternate, retreat, and return; images mix and multiply; and discursive communities coalesce, and perhaps founder, in and around conditional intertextual connections, in keeping with the changeable nature of ties among boarders. Having sprung from the city, boarding as a representational strategy remains true to its roots and bears unmistakable fruits.

Like the cities with which they sympathized—structurally, thematically, temporally, spatially, and imagistically—boardinghouse letters assumed their mature form as part of a process that reached its peak stages of development over the several decades preceding the Civil War. Once found, boarding's generic form was not final, however. City, modernity, and discourse all evinced an unstinting state of renewal that resisted terminal completion. As with the urban domestic search, then, discursive searches of the order of Doesticks's were an ongoing enterprise. Doesticks himself rehearses this search for readers as a metanarrative gesture. Previously new to the city, and once a novice at writing, he reports having sought out upon his arrival in Manhattan "a lingual garb" that was "so quaint, eccentric, fantastic, or extravagant" that it would harmonize with his, the not-quite-metropolitan artist's, prior personal circumstances and authorial position. The alleged "new-found style" on which he tentatively settles, boarding, is not the literary breakthrough that Doesticks thinks it is. Other writers unknown to him had arrived there some decades before. But the "roving unsubstantial ink-brats" that he gathers "into their present shelter" do remain a kind of monument in their own right: they suggest the self-conscious resort to urban residence, real or imagined, made by many antebellum authors en route to a better subjective reckoning of the city. That migration, undertaken en masse, and in the name of literary representation, functions to this day as a metonym for composing the modern (*Doesticks*, vi).

There was, to repeat, nothing fated about boarding's emergence as a literary form. Like his predecessors, Doesticks accordingly considered his options when he sat down to write. He dismisses the "yellow-covered novel," "malignant biography," "pseudosentimental verse writing," and "fictitious narrative" as inadequate. "Novel writing is out of the question," he says. "Poetry has been overdone." Already he has "failed" "in the play-writing vein" (16–20). Also vexed is his occasion for writing. His needs, to begin, are "impossible to class as strictly . . . classic, scientific, historical, humorous, or descriptive." His subject, the city, is itself "extravagant" in the extreme. And his aims are divided, as he declares, being both to produce a book "of immense utility" and one that is "agreeable to the palate of the public." Doesticks thus reaches his "present shelter" (not, the implication is, his last) of boardinghouse letters in the fits and starts that readers would expect from an author who, if not still unfamiliar with his surroundings, inhabits urban environs that resist standing still (20–21, 23). Faint traces, fleeting moments, and abbreviated spaces are what his "Letters" yield, provisionally, transitionally, in the grain of modernity.

✦

Inhabitants of the mid-nineteenth century found in boarding a versatile brand of expression for metropolitan form, function, and city subjectivity; in the figure of the flaneur they found a modern embodiment for these same aspects of the urban Western world. The European-descended flaneur was the age's sidewalk connoisseur. A "strolling urban observer," in James Werner's fine phrase, he (with key exceptions, there are few female examples of flanerie) was the sometime discriminating theater critic and newspaper reporter, whose "mode of viewing and negotiating the complexities of the city" heralded a new epistemology fitted to the reigning (dis)order of time-space collapse.[15] The Parisian poet Charles Baudelaire gave this "mode" of negotiation a name when, in an eponymous essay from 1859, he called the flaneur "The Painter of Modern Life." By "Modern" Baudelaire meant "the ebb and flow of movement," "the ephemeral, the fugitive, the contingent"—the conditions of being that he associated with urban settlement. "To be away from home and yet to feel oneself everywhere at home," the Frenchman wrote, "to set up house in the heart of the multitude" was to be the roving resident that the metropolis required, and the "kaleidoscope gifted with consciousness" that defines flanerie to a tee.[16] In the flaneur's American incarnation, meanwhile, to accept the city on these terms was to become a boarder in fact, in feeling, or both.

On either side of the contemporary Atlantic, the flaneur was the modern metropolis's pioneer, the original resident of the city for its own sake. He was unwavering in his mission as a leisured, literary-sketch man, and partook of the sensations of commercially advanced city-living by yielding, without fully ceding, his public and private selves to his surroundings. So deeply immersed in the urban was the flaneur that he came to share an almost symbiotic relation with it. So studied were his reflections upon Baudelaire's "home" away from "home" that he resisted a more totalizing city dependency. In wandering through the metropolis, exploring its arcades, boulevards, and architecture, its citizens, hotels, and boarding-houses, the flaneur strode ever closer to the pleasurably painful loss of selfhood, of individual inhibition relinquished, that he but dimly expected would follow his near-absorption in the urban crowd. But no less purposeful was the flaneur in his pursuit of a seemingly contrary pleasure. Balancing his ardent, if undemonstrative, celebration of modern man in the mass, the flaneur paired his external excursions around the metropolis with internal deliberations. Inside the confines of his urban imaginary, the flaneur distilled the city's multiplicity into elements more manageable for the purposes of cognition. He thereby recovered a small part of the solitary autonomy that otherwise was denied by cities, and boarding-houses, teeming with "alien" peoples.[17]

The rewards of these labors were not exclusive to the flaneur. Also benefiting from his ability to organize the modern metropolis as a habitable mental construct were the readers of his feuilletons, or printed newspaper sketches. From such writings emerged a genuine transatlantic discourse of flanerie. By electing the city as its overriding point of interest, not only did this literature establish a precedent for nineteenth-century writing;[18] it laid the base on which boarding's distinctive literatures were built. Emphatically of the city, then, the flaneur yet maintained in relation to his urban environs the critical distance that is the mediation of print. He parleyed metropolitan spectacle—perhaps as witnessed from some boardinghouse window, several stories above street level—into the Baudelairean "kaleidoscope" that was his "consciousness," and so enacted what Dana Brand calls the "privatization or domestication of public space."[19] "Domestication" in this context amounted to an act of communication, resulting as it did in a lingua franca for the metropolitan West that would reappear in boarding with much ambivalence. How to find personal urban space where it seemed there was none, how to be at "home" in cities that forever changed the meaning of the same, how to mingle with crowds without abandoning the sanctity of selfhood: these were the modern problems that the flaneur addressed in life and letters, and that antebellum boarders and boardinghouse texts would confront in their dialogic embrace of, and defensive withdrawal from, the urban.

England and France, respectively, were the European sources of the boarder-flaneur for readers and writers of the antebellum United States. Charles Dickens's flaneur-like alter ego "Boz" brought the London boardinghouse into print as early as 1834. The author's avowed purpose in utilizing this discursive resource was to transpose onto a motley group of English boarders "the noisy strife of the great boardinghouse, the world."[20] Many of Dickens's American admirers took note. They also would have been cognizant of Frenchman Honoré de Balzac's boarding-inspired oeuvre. That writer's famous Paris boardinghouse, the Maison Vaucquer, from his novel *Le Père Goriot* (1835),[21] gave at least several Americans (also famous) cause for thought. If Margaret Fuller, for one, initially searched in vain for meaningful "*depths*" upon reaching Manhattan, then she found revealed in what the prolific French novelist called the "immense ocean" of his beloved capital city a "sounding" mechanism that recommended flanerie as a model for substantive inquiry (*Le Père Goriot,* 15). Fuller shows her appreciation in a *Tribune* review from the mid-1840s, where she summarizes Balzac's boardinghouse as a skillfully conceived microcosm of modernity. Henry James, writing later, would extend to the Parisian still greater praise. Boarding, through Balzac, signified for the expatriate author a new urban ontology; in boarding he encountered not just "one of the most portentous settings of the scene in all the literature of fiction," but loftily saw there "a sort of concentrated focus of human life, with sensitive nerves radiating out into the infinite."[22] To judge from the state of the nation's literary affairs before an adult James arrived on the scene after the U.S. Civil War, not a few Americans shared his sentiments. These pertained not just to Balzac, whom James much admired, but to the sizeable range of boardinghouse writers and texts.

Far west of Paris, American boarder-flaneurs conducted their dialogue with the imaginative fact of the city with much the same sophistication as did their counterparts in the Old World, but with an urgency, tone, and "architecture" all their own. It might have arrived at a later date, and evolved according to different historical terms, but the modern metropolis was no less a reality for the United States during the first half of the nineteenth century than it was for Europe in the latter half of the eighteenth, and beyond. Functionally speaking, then, there was little to separate the experience of modern transience in the period. Authors from either side of the Atlantic were under a similar mandate to introduce the urban into their writings.[23] Metropolitan Americans, however, saw boarding become an engine and index of burgeoning urban growth in ways that Europeans simply did not. Thus, structurally speaking, the writers of the American metropolis in time had available to them a supply of boardinghouse materials that promised unique discursive forms. Before those forms were fully forthcoming, Americans laid claim to boardinghouse flanerie as a functional cultural import,[24] and saw it remain what it was at its origins—a local, *domestic* production for Europe's artists.

Thereafter, as the free trade in literary boarding began in earnest, the boarder-flaneur came to speak a dialect more recognizably native. What Janet Wolff describes as the "impressionistic and essayistic" quality of literary urbanism persisted throughout the Atlantic world,[25] regardless of the specific national contexts in which city writings and writers appeared. The "literature of flanerie," that is to say, by which Susan Buck-Morss would indicate the contemporary fad for urban character typologies, "novels of the crowd," and other related creations,[26] did not differ greatly along hemispheric lines, at least in the genre's most obvious features of temporal-spatial economy and interpretive urban "impressionism." What differences there were between European and U.S. flanerie reduced to the crucial question of boarding. Americans' resort to communal urban residence occurred on a scale unseen outside of the United States. It also required a mindset flexible enough to receive modernity's sensory assault on perception, like its unthinking insistence on change,[27] as the common city condition. Americans' fluency with such conditions suggested the familiarity of prolonged usage, something that Europeans would find it difficult, if not impossible, to replicate as their countries adopted alternate forms of urban habitation. More telling, American boarder-flaneurs joined their comparative appreciation for the essentials of everyday boarding to the modern's subjective gaze into a life inside the city of the mind. Europe's flaneur reveled in the isolating potential of that posture, and made of passive spectatorship, inward or outward, a virtual sport for the privileged elite. Boarding in such numbers as they did meant that few Americans could or would occupy flanerie in this, its most solipsistic phase. Rather, because of boarding's leveling tendencies, its practical denial of places and spaces of private privilege among proximate householders, in addition to the ideological overtones of equality that attached to public assemblage generally in the antebellum United States, the writers of boardinghouse letters in the American grain brought to the modern (self-) involvement with subjectivity a residual faith in phenomenological detail. External observation and internal contemplation stood on a level footing in antebellum America; so, too, did the majority of the nation's boarders, for whom the urban currency of domestic dollars in principle provided a medium of exchange neither better nor worse than that of their immediate neighbors, and secured for them along with their comparable living quarters a shared boardinghouse idiom and worldview. A culture—and literature—as beholden to boarding as was antebellum America's made of city necessity a "virtuous" democratic means of interpreting modernity. Literary boarding, the means under examination here, was a more-than-metaphor that the American flaneur, unlike his European cousin, could inhabit in keeping with the personal and national imagination.

Boardinghouse flanerie seems to have come readily to those of the era's authors based in the United States. Frolicking in the metropolitan "ocean" of Balzac's "literary diver" (*Le Père Goriot*, 15), an emblematic boarder-flaneur such as Doesticks can refer offhandedly to his personal, published thoughts on New York's historic *new*ness as nothing but "bubbles." That these same "bubbles," like boarders, "have been, for some time, floating on the sea of literature—the lightest froth on the restless wave," only belies their contribution to a serious artistic program to penetrate deep beneath urban appearances, and into the mysteries of the mid-nineteenth-century city (*Doesticks*, vi). Not all Americans were capable of such aplomb amidst the dislocations of urbanization. Certainly not many strike so relaxed an urban attitude in print. What's most striking in Doesticks's metropolitan (*cosmopolitan*, even) self-assurance is that it recurs regularly, if not so forcefully, in much of the literature that we now can classify as boardinghouse letters. The form's function, in other words—its collective attempt to *ease* the discourse's participants into modernity, to *settle* them, literally and figuratively, within the city—appears to have succeeded remarkably well (perhaps too well, we will learn). Flanerie's twentieth-century philosopher, the German critical theorist Walter Benjamin, deemed urban modernity itself a "shock experience" whose "particular impressions" called on "consciousness ... to be alert as a screen against stimuli."[28] But rare is the American boarder-flaneur for whom the "stimuli" of the city constitute cause for "shock," and one wonders why. After all, neither boarding by fact nor fancy could restore to the urban American in full the hypothetical loss of calm in "consciousness" that many before Benjamin feared must result from reiterative contact with the metropolis. For the American modern, in other words, as for his European counterpart, the psychological, social, and cultural stakes of city living in the period were much the same. What the former had that the latter lacked was boarding, in national proportions. A utilitarian residence turned urban American master trope, boarding as a cultural form achieved the status of an argot spoken throughout the contemporary United States. Those proficient in this language—and many Americans were, including some who were urban only by association, rather than residential location—almost by default were the New World's flaneurs. Self-possessed with metropolitan savvy, and "alert" as able itinerants to the contingencies of temporal-spatial change, America's boarders shared in their mercurial discourse a palliative for modern "shock."

✦

All of which brings us to the content of this study. Boarding, we have seen, meant many things to antebellum Americans. It was a functional residential form for the launch of the U.S. metropolis. It was a figurative bridge between the objective and subjective experiences of the new American city. It was modernity indoors, the urban condition made personal and domestic. And it was at once passport, transport, and base of operations for the New World's flaneur, that "painter of modern life" whom Baudelaire could not have suspected would become the archetypal boarder across the Atlantic. In the end, however, the boardinghouse achieved perhaps its most lasting impact as a framing device for period literature. To write with the city in mind during the middle years of the nineteenth century, or even to read and think urban thoughts within an enlarging metropolitan system of signification from which fewer and fewer Americans could consider themselves exempt, to some extent was to communicate by boarding. Not all of the era's urban literatures resort to boarding, of course. Readers, too, could experience the city textually in a variety of ways, at a once-remove from the world outside the text. But the boardinghouse stood at the forefront of Americans' contemporary *literary* efforts to negotiate the urban as a whole way of life, albeit an evolving one.

Given this emphasis on boarding *as literature,* the chapters that follow unfold as a collection of case studies, with each performing in turn a careful close reading of one or more particular boardinghouse texts, and with contextual support provided by supplemental texts. Holding these close readings together are the multifaceted boardinghouse representations of modern time and space that accrete over the course of the monograph. Accordingly, I have examined urban literatures from not just one, but all three of the era's principal metropolitan areas in the American Northeast—New York, Boston, and Philadelphia. This decision reflects my greater aim, which is to draw conclusions about antebellum American literature that might apply to more than a single U.S. city, even if my primary evidence does derive from the national region in which urbanization occurred most forcefully. Furthermore, I have organized chapters topically, rather than chronologically. Although this may seem to contradict my interest in the temporality of modernity, it is in keeping with the short historical duration under examination here. Boardinghouse letters found their most functional form in only several decades' time; thus, as a subject for scholarship, they resist a rise-and-decline narrative that otherwise might apply to period or century studies. Like the brief leases they figured, boardinghouse letters originated and terminated without ceremony (if not with total finality), and so welcome this comparably open-ended approach. Ultimately, in attempting to reimagine, and so reclaim, the early American metropolis as a literal-figurative construct, this study requires that degree of poetic license which sanctioned literary boarding during its most fertile years.

If we cannot imagine in full a bygone means of imagining, we can in part reconstruct a mindset that once situated the nation's cities and its biggest boardinghouses within the same mental grid, running from lived equivalence at one end, to well-practiced analogy at the other. Hence the structure of this study likewise pairs fact with figure. Chapter 1, "Boardinghouse Life, Boardinghouse Letters," undertakes a summary social history of boarding in America, before building on that foundation this book's central claim: that boarding was *psychically,* and not just materially, central in enabling modern urban American life for "we," a former boardinghouse people. This chapter opens with a synopsis of actual metropolitan boarding practices in the antebellum period. Also treated in passing are the semantics of contemporary boarding terminology, a discussion that could comprise a separate linguistic study of its own. A more complete account of "Boardinghouse Letters" follows; this latter section supplies the conceptual premise of the overall study. I begin with a sampled inventory of early American authors who either boarded out or at least wrote in and/or with a boardinghouse orientation, in the spirit of Doesticks. Proceeding from there, I establish the genre's literary properties and, most important, explain the role that this literature played within the wider culture. What *were* boardinghouse letters, and what did those letters *do* for writers and readers? These are the essential questions that this chapter asks and begins to answer.

It is worth noting the literary-historical implications of these queries. To begin, the attention paid here to boarding is of a piece with scholars' increased recognition for the literary city before the Civil War. Recent work has challenged the conventional belief that the realist and naturalist writers who appeared after the war's end in 1865 exercised an exclusive hold on urban writing in America. Popular antebellum genres like urban sensationalism, city-mysteries, working-class dime novels, and what one writer deems an outright New York discourse now form no less a subject of renewed academic interest than do the more arcane literatures of the charity-visit or crowd.[29] Boardinghouse letters belong to this same demotic discursive turn toward the urban, which encompasses both belles lettres and a sizeable body of nonfiction.[30] Yet, boarding was not solely an expressive epiphenomenon of the nation's pavements. As Adrienne Siegel explains, the new American city generated interest among those whom she designates "elites" as well, and it is their "intellectual energy" during the fifty-year window from 1820 to 1870 that she says directed the more general literary labors which the country conducted on behalf of the metropolis. My work on "Boardinghouse Letters" partially endorses this view, although it resists the top-down cultural hierarchy that Siegel's position assumes. Closer in kind to my argument is Janis P. Stout's earlier, post-Freudian contention that America's period authors, including its most respected romantics, testify to a fascination with the psychology of the city in their writings.[31] Boarder-authors, I believe, wrote in much the same vein. This I hope to demonstrate in the chapters to come.

Another of the assumptions upset by boardinghouse letters pertains to the abiding regional stereotypes of nineteenth-century American literature and culture. The revisionist conviction is spreading among the discipline's specialists that contemporary rural New England and the plantation South, no less than obvious locales like Manhattan, contributed wholeheartedly to oral and written assessments from the period concerning the impact that urban expansion was having in the United States. Boarding encourages this revision. Commercial cohabitation, we know, reached well beyond the mid-Atlantic coastal corridor into inland towns and every U.S. state. Citification thus would have been as manifest as the country's continental destiny in Doesticks's day, no matter where one resided. With, additionally, its heavy reliance on similitude, and its diversely metropolitan (and almost metaphysical) juxtaposition of opposed images, boarding continues to condition today's readers to interpret texts much as it did in the past. That is to say, it bids them to make, on the basis of even slight literary allusions to modernity—including abruptness of narrative time, uncertainty in space, heavy introspective investment, and diminution of place—the short imaginative leap required to reach the threshold of a self-conscious urban awareness. Boardinghouse writers often welcome such readings, practicing, as many of them did, an authorial strategy that resembles what Lawrence Buell denominates "minimization." By this Buell means the patterns of indirect reference in writings from the early national and antebellum eras to a then-nascent urban industrialization. The practice was not uncommon, he says, among New England's regional authors, who preferred providing city commentary as parenthetical asides rather than embedding direct urban encounters in their texts.[32] Nor was this sleight-of-hand strategy uncommon, I would add, among boarder-authors, whose metropolitan portrayals frequently include little more than a slice of urban life: a house, perhaps a home, and its rotating roster of inhabitants. Not even the still largely rural, preindustrial, prewar South, with its reigning pastoral-patriarchal mythologies, was immune to the city's insinuating itself in this way. As Jennifer Rae Greeson writes, urban gothic literatures imported from the North found much favor among readers in Virginia, Georgia, and the Carolinas, who responded to the genre's stock conventions of nocturnal urban danger and city women in distress with all the undisguised enthusiasm of local authors.[33] Whether and how the rise of a pre-Confederate boarding population influenced southern readers' responses to literary urbanism remains one among many city-mysteries worth studying.

To rethink America's regions, finally, is to remap the greater nation. Boarding instantiates metropolitan modernization not only as a near-universal occurrence on the domestic front, with "domestic" understood in its binary senses.[34] It also, in figures like the flaneur, suggests that Americans' urban sensibilities had grown accustomed enough to crossing and recrossing the Anglo-Franco Atlantic by midcentury as to expand the parameters of American literature well past their former provincial limits. Without even counting the swelling numbers of immigrant boardinghouses in the antebellum United States, we can say that boardinghouse letters did not so much go global over the course of their development as they did begin in transnational directions from the start of their first articulation as discourse.

However apt it may be that boarding, given its lasting impact on time-space narration, should prompt scholars to rethink their temporal-spatial claims concerning the chronologies and localities of nineteenth-century American literature, it is just as proper that a verbal form which in effect functioned as a heuristic on urban habitation should intervene in the ongoing debates over domesticity. Chapter 2 of this study, titled "Rhetorical Boarding and the Limits of Domesticity," duly engages these debates on boardinghouse terms. Of broad interest is the fate of those frequently idealized versions of *Keeping House and Housekeeping* (1845),[35] to borrow the title of one period offering, once boarding enters the discursive discussion. I pursue the matter by treating celebrity author Fanny Fern's *Ruth Hall: A Domestic Tale of the Present Time* (1854). The boardinghouses that appear in Fern's book, and in supporting texts that I inspect from her fellow authorities (not all of them female) on home, further refine our tentative understanding of how the nineteenth century's writers figured gendered domestic spaces in newspaper print, poetry, and prose. Feminist critics especially have accomplished much with their reevaluations of domestic texts in recent decades. Yet, their scholarship largely misinterprets or else simply misses boarding *from a literary point of view*.[36]

Fern's *"Domestic Tale"* is neither conventionally "domestic" nor a (rather lengthy) "tale" by any stretch of the contemporary literary imagination. As is self-evident in the text, the author interrogates a domestic ideology that valorized women's comparative dependency inside the "separate sphere" of the socially detached but lovingly tended household, apart from the independent "public" realm occupied by gainfully employed men. The central setting of Fern's interrogation is the urban boardinghouse, where her titular protagonist repairs under duress, and from where she equivocally departs by story's ambiguous end. This is no narrative of domestic bliss: Ruth Hall knows only briefly the comforts of rural middle-class home life, and city boarding becomes over the course of Fern's New York "novel" an occasion for authorial commentary on both the practical and ideological shortcomings of her culture's attachment to household arrangements that urban life increasingly rendered unattainable. Domestic time and space were ample, even abundant (or, at least, perceived to be) prior to modernity's midcentury emergence; they were at a premium during and after the decades in which Fern wrote. The author seizes upon boarding as an apparent epitome for modern America's temporal-spatial sacrifices. She nevertheless finesses the contrasts that she draws, so that boarding becomes as much a foil as it is a proposed replacement for her country's firm faith in "home." Not all of her original readers were willing to forgive this ambivalence. Writing by diary his reaction to *Ruth Hall,* one cultural conservative would dismiss Fern's *"Tale"* as but another of her "bad-hearted books,"[37] a response that reveals less about litera-ture than it does about his and other detractors' instinctive defense of domesticity's main tenets—tenets which, some believed, *Ruth Hall* sought to subvert.

Of far more importance to questions of literary form is how *Ruth Hall* reworks the art and occupation of storytelling by means of the board-inghouse imaginary. Notwithstanding its double devotions to what are here the related domestic arts of narration and household management, *Ruth Hall* proves boarding to be a genre most uncomfortable with itself, in decidedly undomestic fashion. Fern's *"Domestic Tale"* is in this respect not unlike that other generic misnomer we saw in Doesticks's *What He Says.*[38] Both are stories in search of a functional form. Composed primar-ily of short, staccato chapters that mirror the neophyte author Ruth's (and the seasoned author Fern's) own newspaper columns, *Ruth Hall* reads as a verbal version of the internalized metropolis: in distilling city experience into haltingly sequenced vignettes, and severely rationing her outlays of narrative time and space, Fern contrives to deliver a metanar-rative on the unsuitability of the novel form for so grand a subject as the subjectivity of urban modernity. The generic novel's very discursive-ness, its "roomy" capaciousness, ironically proves for Fern's purposes *too* full a form to encapsulate the realities of city living as a personally felt phenomenon.

*Ruth Hall* functions instead by maximizing what it most lacks. Spa-tially restricted, Fern's book *boards* its way into a generic realm that is no less real for being imagined, and that is large enough for her story to unfold. Perhaps contrary to logic, she accomplishes this feat by narrow-ing the structural base of her *"Tale"* to the city experiences of individuals, as opposed to spreading the narrative foundation of her account so as to "contain" the populist Walt Whitman's "multitudes," or to include what another New York author described as the "Boarding-House on a Large Scale."[39] Temporally challenged, too, Fern's *Domestic Tale of the Pres-ent Time* pushes irresistibly forward from its protagonist's pre-lapsarian (which is to say, non-urban) past. And yet *Ruth Hall* enjoys in the rush of events that it orchestrates, or the news of the day that it relates, time suffi-cient for even Ruth's speedy passage through the trials of urban residence to reach a narrative ground where time no longer matters. So complete is her initiation to metropolitan living, so balanced the urban equipoise of this female "flâneuse," to apply Janet Wolff's term for the nineteenth-century woman as city sophisticate,[40] that Ruth's final rise from domestic submission to mastery passes into the timeless mythology of boarders' lore. No "*Tale*" can tame her. No "novel" can "contain" her. Only in boarding does Fern locate a literature in which the very want of time and space seems agreeable, because it agrees with both the similar wants of the modern metropolis, and the predicament of so many antebellum women who had (or had *been*) domesticated without having and holding a "room" of their own.

Turning from Fern's "*Tale*" of the individual domicile, the companion chapters 3 and 4 reevaluate the collective aspects of boarding. They simultaneously transact a related turn as well, elaborating the creative interplay that *Ruth Hall* suggests between the "private" domestic sphere of the personal home and the "public" arena of civil society. Antebellum New England, and not Manhattan, provides the narrative location in both cases. And two of the region's native sons support a complementary discussion of the metropolitan boardinghouse as a civic-literary, rather than strictly domestic, institution. The boarder-authors featured here are Oliver Wendell Holmes and Henry David Thoreau.

Holmes provides a direct examination of urban boardinghouse life and letters in his popular *The Autocrat of the Breakfast-Table* (1858), which is the central text of chapter 3, titled "Boston's Boardinghouse Community." Although he presides in a midrange boarding establishment not far from Massachusetts's gold-domed capitol building, the author's formidable "Autocrat" persona remains tied to his less prosperous fellow residents and the surrounding city. So porous are the dividing lines—literal and metaphorical—between parlor, people, pavement, and plot in Holmes's subtly constructed story that the communal residence that holds proceedings together in his account of Boston's protobourgeoisie tilts noticeably toward a metropolitan polis that is rarely out of sight in these pages and so seldom out of mind. It is the conservative, cosmopolitan Autocrat's mealtime table talk, in fact, that converts his residence into a proxy town hall-type meeting, despite the faint protests of the lead talker himself to sharing discursive space with his housemates. Much of middlebrow Boston occupies a seat at the Autocrat's table, and the polyvocal majority they constitute resists the monologic tendencies of the most fluent conversationalist among them. One talker may dominate this text; no single boarder's words reign supreme when rebuttal and debate are the operative rules of colloquy, as they are here. Readers' own seats at table, meanwhile, extended to them by the tacit invitation that is print publication, effectively bring them to board as well. Thus, to read Holmes's work is not only to involve oneself in boarders' negotiations over questions of expressive precedence, which is to say, over whether and how a conversational hierarchy is to take hold at this fictional address. To sit down to *The Autocrat of the Breakfast-Table* is also to engage an openly participatory text whose boardinghouse form, premised on the everyday requirements of cohabitation, fittingly furthers one of literary boarding's latent functions: the creation of an inclusive interpretive community. In this case, communal inclusiveness becomes the principle from which much of the household discussion springs. The content, tenor, and tone of many of the Autocrat's running remarks reflexively return to issues of broad civic significance. And so the society of collective residence joins with a collective conversation on society to lead author, Autocrat, boarders, and readers away from their isolated domesticated selves toward an egalitarian urban pluralism.

The boardinghouse form chosen by Holmes complicates this process of socialization by letters, in a manner equally ironic. Written originally as a twelve-part serial sequence for Boston's *Atlantic Monthly* magazine, the author's *Autocrat* might have been communally conceived as a civic response to selfish domestic independence, but it was transmitted through a literary vehicle whose time-space restrictions figure the residential lease. And so the *Autocrat* underlines boarding's unsettling distance precisely from domesticity. Despite being the *Atlantic*'s greatest draw during its first year of publication, the "Autocrat," not unlike its boardinghouse source of inspiration, operated at the level of the text in systematic shortcomings. Readers were left to wait some thirty days in between installments. Each issue in turn provided only provisional conclusions. Neither novel nor sketch nor story, and lacking in continuity, conversational or otherwise, the *Autocrat* reveals a fugitive form that many American boarders would have recognized in their own personal residential predicaments. More disturbing still, the *Autocrat*'s fragmented style of narration, compounded by the storyline disturbance it suffered as a result of periodical serialization, structurally underscores but another of boarding's unlooked-for implications—that the society of cities that the boardinghouse both predicted and effected was close kin to modern alienation.

Concord author Henry David Thoreau's *Walden* (1854) would seem an unlikely boardinghouse text by comparison, notwithstanding its close thematic involvement with the domestically suggestive relation between self and society. And yet in chapter 4, "Concord Board: Democratic Domestic as Urban Organic," I read Thoreau's iconic account of his two years' residence along the shores of a pastoral New England pond as a regional, if idiosyncratic, variation on mainstream literary boarding. Thoreau was no city-dweller, for he lived and wrote from outside downtown Boston. But he was acutely conscious of modernity, as were most urban boarders, and takes his bearings in *Walden* accordingly. Determinative seasonal rhythms supply the text with the natural temporal momentum of solar motion, even though the author strategically inserts into his much-revised manuscript such tableaux as his "Sounds" chapter to evoke an eternal arboreal stillness. For the purposes of narrative compactness, Thoreau furthermore has condensed his (already brief) sylvan lease on life from two years to one, and so undermines both his own and his book's inclinations to "settle." *Walden* in consequence possesses much the same calendrical regularity as a May Day moving ritual, which yearly event saw metropolitans up and down the eastern seaboard collectively electing in droves for a change in rental housing accommodations with the annual return of "Spring," also the title of Thoreau's penultimate chapter. Similarly resonant of cities are *Walden*'s narrated spaces. From the "Former Inhabitants" whose fate he meditates, to the "Winter Visitors" with whom he keeps company in Walden's woods, Thoreau was seldom, if ever, alone in his handcrafted cabin. Nor was the actual boardinghouse that he left behind at his parents' address in town isolated. Both residences were by design a kind of domestic palimpsest, insofar as they spatially facilitated the virtual overlap of boarders past, present, and future on Concord's reusable common ground. However timeless its themes, then, however cosmic its claims,[41] *Walden* thus erects not only a semi-rural monument to individual self-consciousness; it raises a figurative city as well, the organic form of which the author has patterned on the far-reaching effects of city boarding. *Walden* itself is a city, in fact, and Thoreau its discursive craftsman.

An intricate urban construction, *Walden* betrays no elitist aesthetic. Thoreau, rather, like Holmes, was in a boardinghouse frame of mind when he composed his opus. He harnesses a written conceptualization of the domestic indoors with a sincere concern for the surrounding civic environment, so that there is always someone at home in his house, and a society to be attended to when- and wherever readers are within reach of the author-narrator's organizing voice, whether in or out of doors. Our Concord artist can pretend to no more than mock isolation as he delivers his disquisition on modern New England living. Boarding, moreover, was a civic institution in its own right; it belonged by virtue of its public-spiritedness to the interlocking network of improvement enterprises, including local lending libraries, state-sponsored schools, and lyceum lecture halls, which metropolitan Boston had spawned during the middle decades of the nineteenth century. As such the boardinghouse endows Thoreau—himself an exemplary "connected" social critic, as Richard Teichgraeber writes[42]—with a literal frame by which to figure *Walden*'s "urban"-style domicile as a constituent member in a larger civilizing endeavor then underway in what was by far the region's most densely populated commercial-residential zone. Because Concord had drawn ever nearer to an encroaching Boston metropolis since at least the days of the American Revolution,[43] it afforded for Thoreau the city-*like* experiences that his peripheral urban outpost continues to offer even today. More important, because greater post-Puritan Boston, at urban center and edge alike, had all but made the personal and institutional ethic of connectedness into a requisite test of citizenship, the antebellum city's centripetal, participatory pull was strong enough to exert itself on the author's text. *Walden* offers page after page of politico-philosophical engagement, as evidenced by the layered mutual exchanges that the book's "boarders" conduct with a host of neighboring communal institutions, of which the author's boardinghouse is but one.

These same institutional exchanges are the ties that bind Thoreau's text together. Because they promote the public welfare, and by extension endorse a classical understanding of *communitas,* the concerted acts that went into the building of greater Boston's cultural edifice differed little from the social trends that originally gave birth to boarding. Each and all were at their core democratic. At the same time, *boardinghouse* time, the pains that Thoreau takes to improve the modern household fruitfully coincide in a not-so-rustic *Walden* with the labors of his neighbors to raise new civic institutions. The net result of that coincidence is this: the discourse of the urban domestic begins to suggest itself to the author as a possible formal solution for how best to write his way toward a characteristically American vision of an open society. Holmes's *Autocrat* conducts a similar experiment, while reserving the right to preserve sociocultural distinctions. The arch-democrat Thoreau expresses no such misgivings in making the boardinghouse as dwelling place into a nationally liberating literary form.

Boarding's sociopolitical potential intersects with literary experimentation in chapter 5, "Class Mapping the Literary Metropolis." The centerpiece of discussion here involves a residential reading of sensational author George Lippard's scandalous city-mysteries novel *The Quaker City* (1844). Interest in this commercially best-selling text to date has dealt with the romantic excesses of its narration, character development, and imagery, all of which Lippard exaggerates to ideological effect in relating what he believed to be the antagonistic class relations of his home city, antebellum Philadelphia. Pivotal to the author's working-class critique, and indicative of the avant-garde, stylistic heightening that he employs throughout his enveloping story, is the household setting of much of the novel's plot—the urban Gothic mansion Monk-hall, a convenient, if implausible, microcosm of contemporary Philadelphia's social structure. The merchant princes, degraded prostitutes, and common criminals who inhabit Monk-hall recall the class lines of the larger city, as is well known. They also constitute an unusual assortment of urban boarders, a group who, while gathered under the single roof of a singularly wicked Philadelphia shelter, provides a stark metonymic figure for the city's general social gradations on the one hand, and its particular *residential* hierarchies on the other.

Lippard, like many American writers, resolved upon the metropolitan domestic as a favored literary form by which to indite urban modernity. The wide range of urban housing options that the author's romance both documents and describes in its evocation of a fictional cityscape thus contains a certain discursive logic from which the boardinghouse genre as a whole usually partakes. So systematic is Lippard's *literal* survey of the physical, architectural city, however, that his novel reads well beyond the mass average of boarding's normal generic bounds. *The Quaker City* reads, rather, as a veritable class map of the modern metropolis, as Lippard closely keys his sprawling tale of urban seduction, murder, and intrigue to the stark material differences that were endemic to Philadelphian habitation. Overall, the text's workers endure a deplorable domestic situation; high costs and low comforts are for them the substance of area housing. By contrast, the city's well-to-do enjoy all the residential refinements that their ill-gotten (in Lippard's estimation) dollars can buy. Even boarding has lost all traces of communal compromise at the upper end of the local housing market, and promises instead guaranteed purchase on the luxurious lifestyle that many of the book's characters covet. America's middle classes, meanwhile, are largely missing from Lippard's residentially inflected account of the urban American class dynamic. Absence is irony in this instance, since it was the metropolitan bourgeoisie who, historically, boarded most; they board little or else not at all in *The Quaker City*, an omission that is testament to the author's polarized view of the city. Here, class divides not only reappear as socially encoded "domestic" distinctions, but inhere in what the author believed to be the pernicious discrepancies between different brands of urban habitat.

In revising, by revisiting, literary boarding's already tenuous literal-figurative equilibrium, *The Quaker City* also tests the genre's temporal-spatial norms. As we have seen, conventionally unconventional boardinghouse letters pioneered the urban narrative practice of time-space curtailment, so that boarding's written figurations of city "when" and "where" regularly, and reliably, demonstrate pronounced involutive tendencies. The literary turn effected by boarding revolves in many instances inward and not outward, inclining toward the lesser and not greater, just as boardinghouse poetry and prose rhythmically unfold sooner and not later in recording worldly fact and invented fancy. Not so *The Quaker City*, which by generic comparison runs in reverse.

Spatially, Lippard's novel runs amok. Although much of his romance centers on the above-mentioned boardinghouse, the sinister criminal hideaway Monk-hall, the author also conducts readers on a prolonged walking tour of Philadelphia through the twists and turns of an antic storyline. The centrifugal force behind this mode of narration resides not solely in its implied contrast between boarding and the relative stability of domestic autonomy. Much boarder literature proceeds from a similarly inspired juxtaposition. Rather, to read *The Quaker City* is to some extent to subscribe to the well-traveled life of the antebellum working class, and so partake of the same daily odyssey that saw urban workers traverse their respective cities from boardinghouse to workplace and back again, perhaps before heading out on the town for further movement across the metropolis. For all their literal-mindedness, so great are the *figurative* liberties that the author takes in surveying his city that his suggestions of urban space grow wildly distorted. Lippard might shine the delineating light of the documentarian on his subject, the city, but he ultimately predicts the disorienting literary vision of a perplexed inhabitant of the "vertical city," which site of settlement later would confound Americans of the next century. His dichotomous worldview grounded squarely in the material residential inequalities of his time, Lippard anticipates the vertiginous perceptual/aesthetic, temporal/spatial experiments of twentieth-century modernism as an art form.

Temporally, *The Quaker City* likewise defies urban discursive expectations. Like Holmes's *Autocrat,* Lippard's novel debuted in serial installments, and so by default internalizes the same upsetting speed of the city that one detects in many such publications, with their regular tacit reminder of time's passing. *The Quaker City* is in other respects the temporal opposite of the *Autocrat* and other boardinghouse works. Whereas the latter typically figure modern acceleration, the former brings boardinghouse time to a virtual halt: running in its current reprint format to some 600 pages in length, *The Quaker City* ekes out over the narrative course of only three days enough hairbreadth escapes, emotional crises, and violent confrontations for any one particular city's entire recorded history. Lippard's novel is as a result more saga than serial. It is also, for this very reason, a novel not only of proletarian protest, but of urban laborers' resistance to the demands of modernity. Purchased upon its appearance in copies totaling in the tens of thousands, *The Quaker City* as a cultural artifact was once complicit in a kind of collective work stoppage that denied the modern urban commercial co-optation of time. Whether casually consumed by legions of producer-readers en route to their respective sites of wage labor, or else gleaned on the sly on the job, or maybe perused back at whatever modest boardinghouse establishment these perennial employees happened at that moment to inhabit in between shifts, Lippard's *Romance of Philadelphia Life, Mystery and Crime* afforded contemporary workers not a permanent "domestic" shelter, but temporary imaginative refuge.

Chapter 6 marks a return to more conventional literary forms, but with a boardinghouse difference. "Boarders, Brothers, and Lovers: *The Blithedale Romance*'s Theater of Feeling" conjoins the imaginative space of boardinghouse letters with the emotional space of a dominant contemporary discourse, antebellum sentimentalism, to propose a hybrid genre of "boarder" romance. *Blithedale*'s author, Nathaniel Hawthorne, wrote with several decades' worth of socio-literary precedent behind him when he himself crossed the above genres in his much-discussed book from 1852. His ostensible satire of the rural utopian Brook Farm community is in many respects a novel-length meditation on a subject that had become a mainstay of the print marketplace—urban boarding as an occasion for modern feeling. On the one hand, the close domestic contact attendant on cohabitation encouraged a physical proximity that served as a solvent on the alienating anonymity of modern urban existence, the affective distancing of city life, and the conservative strictures of Victorian sexual mores. Boarders, in short, would and often did forge close personal bonds, whether of a homo- or hetero- variety, and both social and sexual in nature. On the other hand, estrangement between co-occupants was also not uncommon, sometimes creating a strained interpersonal atmosphere inside communal domiciles like the author's fictional "Blithedale." Thus, Hawthorne's domestically close-knit cast of characters endures but one of the familiar perils of shared residence as the individual members of his suburban Boston boardinghouse suffer by exposing their most private sensitive selves to their housemates. No matter what the terms of boarders' relations with one another, however, mere physical compensation for genuine sentiment was not infrequently the eventual outcome. Boarding afforded a convenient arena for sexual pairing otherwise proscribed by antebellum society; as such it provided an ideal, if not idyllic, venue for renters who were unable (or unwilling) to cultivate feelings for their fellows. Nineteenth-century literature is rife with just such instances of boarding presenting a barrier to the open exchange of human emotion. *Blithedale,* then, is only one of many period examples of a fundamentally metropolitan literary tradition in the making. It, alongside a number of contemporary boardinghouse texts, challenges the generic category of the "sentimental" by reimagining a literature shorn of all feeling.

*Blithedale* also unveils what is in effect the theatrical core of boarding, and so suggests still another component of the genre's essentially hybrid form. Hawthorne's fourth novel takes pains to *dramatize* what should be (but has not been) obvious: with flagrant effect, the boarders of his book *act out* in spoken pantomime many of the varied motions of emotion, but with such melodramatic posturing that they run the risk of making a farce of affection in fiction. *Blithedale* as a book is hardly farcical, considering the keen thrust of its social critique and the disturbing arc of its storyline. Although Blithedale's brethren might feel vehemently, however, they do not feel deeply, judging from their recurring communal feuds and the never-quite-realized sexual encounters that move the book forward (without "moving" readers, necessarily) before bringing proceedings to a tragic close. In boarding, the author suggests, there inhere sentimental distortions so inhibiting as to make the "real" thing of lasting feeling all but impossible. In cities, he observes, anticipating a now much-rehearsed cultural lament, affect itself amounts to little more than a spurious performance *staged* by urban dwellers for the faceless spectators of the metropolitan crowd.[44] In boardinghouse discourse, finally, Hawthorne demonstrates a storytelling form so permeated by the impersonal, unpredictable rigors of the urban as to nullify the subjective lives of its main fictional *players,* and to make of the human aloofness of modern cities mere objective spectacle. A drama of emotional disunity, *Blithedale* resides far from the classical Aristotelian stage tradition of unified time, place, and action. A modern compromise, boarding itself reads in *Blithedale* as both a prelude to love lost and as an aftermath to a society that collectively has willed home without heart.

The "Epilogue," finally, retreats from the subject of urban love only to raise the specter of death, in and of the boardinghouse, before concluding with a cursory overview of boarding's lively afterlife in recent American popular culture. Antebellum literature is littered with the bodies of boarders found dead or dying in their chambers. If we needed reminding, surely this motif reminds us that all American lives must pass. Boarding's many casualties figure as well the virtual (but never fully completed) extinction of one of the nation's particular urban domestic forms. To that bitter end, several tales by writer Edgar Allan Poe center a summary discussion of boardinghouse death. Poe's fiction instances scores of haunted houses; it peoples those houses with boarders. Lacking the boardinghouse per se, Poe's work nevertheless might be read as an indirect commentary on what the author felt were the horrors of urban habitation generally. The many deaths and emotional trials in Poe's houses speak to his and his readers' recorded fears not just of dying in a big-city boardinghouse, but of having to live in one at all.

Following the Civil War, such fears were more and more obsolete, as the American boardinghouse itself began a steady decline. Apartment houses by that time had opened their doors to the increasingly receptive middle classes, while immigrant labor in the main had embraced the densely settled tenement house, save for those recent arrivals who still found room at what former U.S. President Theodore Roosevelt scornfully described in 1919 as urban America's "polyglot boarding house."[45] Progressive reformers, meanwhile, recommended stand-alone homes in the suburbs as a solution to what many among them believed to be the rampant disease, vice, and crime attendant on crowded city living. As a result, boarders proportionately were far fewer in number by the last years of the nineteenth century.

And yet the boardinghouse remains. Closing this study is a brief examination of boarding's late cultural renaissance. The *situation* of communal living that was implicit in an earlier national habit of boarding reappeared first as early twentieth-century folklore and folk art, and later as a staple of the transatlantic sitcom and "real-world" TV from the 1950s forward. If sizeable numbers of former boarders fled to America's suburbs in the post–World War II era, then suburban dwellers continue to board by proxy courtesy of mixed media like music, print literature, and video image. In particular, evening TV programs, which again and again treat close-quartered living in equal measure as sociological case-study and sensational entertainment, allow viewers to migrate in their minds to a city center that they otherwise have left behind. The U.S. boardinghouse did not die. It lingers. Some might say it thrives in prime time.

✦

As this range of topics and texts suggests, America's antebellum boardinghouse letters are very much in accord with a renewed interest in the literary city,[46] and so welcome simultaneous reflection on the urban past and present. Current concerns within the academy over nation,

race, class, and ethnicity, as well as a continuing postfeminist commitment to interrogate the modern engendering of domesticity, combine to
make boarding not only an integral part of any discussion of nineteenth-
century metropolitan discourse development, but a likely starting point
for any historically informed consideration of the global ascendance of
the urban that is underway today.[47] Although my primary aim in this
study is to retrieve from cultural memory the discursive forms and imaginative functions of American boarding during the decades before the U.S.
Civil War, I grant the timely political-literary concerns of world cities
secondary status in these pages. Immersed as we are in the metropolitan,
familiar as we have become with cities, few among us well-read cosmo-
politans realize the close correspondence that pertains between an earlier
brand of urban habitation and our own. I want to prompt such a realization. Indeed, renters and owners everywhere have much to learn from
their boardinghouse forebears' attempts to domesticate under limited and
limiting conditions of time and space which, if now normative, were once
shockingly unfamiliar. My hope is this: that even a partial appreciation
for America's boardinghouse letters shall enable us to see the city anew
with inquiring eyes rather than assume so much, or expect so little, of
urban modernity.

Chapter 1

# Boardinghouse Life, Boardinghouse Letters

Now having a night, a day, and still another night following
before me . . . , it became a matter of concernment where I
was to eat and sleep meanwhile.

> —Ishmael, from chapter 2, "The Carpet-Bag,"
> in Herman Melville's *Moby-Dick,* 1851

In March 1842, a 22-year-old New York journalist named Walter Whitman declared the "universal Yankee nation" a "boarding people." He provided as proof of his claim what would become, in the following decade, a characteristic catalog description of his United States. For this early Whitmanian gesture, the future poet employed simple city arithmetic, calculating his country's distinguishing features by adding together the domesticating peoples and residential places that then comprised an urbanizing America. "Married men and single men," Whitman wrote, "old women and pretty girls; milliners and masons; cobblers, colonels, and counter-jumpers; tailors and teachers; lieutenants, loafers, ladies, lackbrains, and lawyers; printers and parsons—'black spirits and white, blue spirits and gay'—all 'go out to board.'"[1]

Almost two centuries later, Whitman's pronouncement reads as something of a riddle, given the current comparative neglect of that once representative American domicile, the boardinghouse. Indeed, as editorial prophecy, Whitman's remarks might strike the retrospective observer as incomprehensible, since boarding long since has relinquished the kind of self-evident (and largely self-explanatory) status that it formerly enjoyed both as a topic for periodical commentary, and as a wholesale symbol of a young United States. As contemporary newspaper reportage, however, Whitman's words well capture the state of the United States prior to the Civil War. For Americans of his day in fact were "a boarding people," drawn as they were to boardinghouses in numbers large enough

to constitute a sizeable national constituency. One might expect a certain hyperbole from the author of the country's first free-verse rhapsody,
*Leaves of Grass* (1855). But even the Long Island–born poet-turned-
newspaperman's subsequent claim that three-quarters of Manhattan's
adult population had lived or even then were living in boardinghouses
as of 1856[2]—this at a time when the vast majority of U.S. residents still
favored the stand-alone dwelling—matches recent estimates of the central place the boardinghouse held in mid-nineteenth-century American
life.[3] Quite simply, it is neither statistical inflation nor poetic license that
threatens to distort the historical importance of boarding in America's
past. It is, rather, the opposing risk of understatement, of denying the
boardinghouse its proper due, that bids to prevent a faithful measure of
antebellum America. The spirit of Whitman's remarks is not only telling,
then, but socioculturally accurate as well, inasmuch as they suggest the
extent to which a former "boarding people," by the time of his writing,
had managed to transform the boardinghouse itself into a habitual habitation—and self-identifying shelter—in the modernizing West. It is the
purpose of the opening section of this first chapter to inquire into what
boarding was, precisely, and how it achieved outsized proportions in the
United States.

Such an inquiry is fraught with complications. Foremost among them
is this: despite boarding's early prominence among Americans, contemporaries could be as imprecise as they were inconsistent when they
referenced a trend that was once widespread enough to qualify as a veritable national pastime. Just one consequence of this general abstraction
is the question of classification. There is no simple schema, let alone a
reliably scientific taxonomic system, by which to highlight the boardinghouse out of a whole spectrum of improvised midcentury housing
practices. Two of the more familiar residential options from the period—
boarding and lodging—not infrequently constituted a distinction without
a difference in the desperate minds of renters, at least semantically speaking. Amid the ascendance of urban America, few metropolitans were
inclined to care that an evolving domestic vernacular could turn a term
like "apartment," for instance, or the phrase "going a-boarding," in multiple (and perhaps meaningless) directions.[4] Outweighing the subtleties
of colloquial taxonomy was the more pressing necessity of finding, and
keeping, suitable city shelter.

Yet, neither the strong demand for adequate urban housing, nor the
precariousness of city-dwellers' living predicament, could long obscure
the fundamental difference between boarding's communal living-dining
experience and the comparatively solo (and supperless) enterprise that

was lodging. Moreover, if the varieties of metropolitan habitation differed in nature, they also differed by number: there was much to separate the private household that received the occasional boarder from the commercially operative boardinghouse whose roster of non-familial inhabitants was likely at any given moment to exceed that of the "original" occupants. The difference in this latter instance inheres as much in the economics of house-holding as in matters of household economy. Especially during difficult financial periods, the rent received from paying boarders could help determine not only the cold calculus of family income, but also the social capital of class status that came with it. When, where, and how a person boarded carried practical implications, in other words, as did the occupancy of a boardinghouse, lodging house, or a house by any other name. Set against the requisite search for a domicile in a new modern America, the nomenclature of "home" thus must have seemed a secondary concern. All of which combines to frustrate the cultural historian of boarding today. To begin to apprehend the full diversity of the antebellum urban domestic is first to learn the loose grammar employed by the nation's original metropolitan renters.

Loose, but not lax: despite the slippage, linguistic or otherwise, endemic to city residence, there were and remain recognizable limits within which boarding can be said to have occurred. Historian Kenneth A. Scherzer proposes several such limits, seemingly contradictory, that help frame this discussion. Scherzer writes first of the "formal" boardinghouse, which he characterizes as "a place in which inhabitants—particularly young males—received food, laundry, and upkeep" in exchange for a specified fee, paid individually and periodically among groups of not less than five or more non-related coresident householders.[5] Boarding by this somewhat restrictive definition consisted of a communal housing package of bed, bread, and domestic services for a clientele of moderate-sized assemblages of (mostly) men who often, but not always, marked their arrivals at early adulthood in the American metropolis by entering their names into the growing lists of boardinghouse registries to be found among the country's burgeoning cities. A select few of these same urban newcomers related their experiences in print, and it is their collective body of writing (on the collective conditions of cities) that partially informs this present study.

Extending outward from Scherzer's somewhat narrow domestic parameters are the myriad informal instances of boarding that inform his and others' attempts at strict definition. These ad-hoc arrangements often existed beyond the purview of the "formal" boardinghouse, but many American metropolitans depended on them all the same—whether in their everyday lives, or in the urban literatures that a culturally conscious minority of them (both male and female) produced. Fixed domestic categories were for these historical boarders an unattainable luxury; residential fixity itself was a rarity among the mass of America's urban migrants, a plural population whose transitory housing behaviors have rendered it as elusive in our day as it was in its own. Some of these peoples appear to have boarded along the classic lines of cohabitation that Scherzer outlines. Others may or may have not lodged, depending on the residential standards by which we measure their respective domestic conditions. Considering, however, the fine line that many antebellum renters tread between boarding and lodging, or the fact that both men and women often mingled at the same shelters, or even, again, the nuanced distinction that held (or not) between the professional boardinghouse as a place of business, and those American households that casually accepted a few extended kin, with or without the exchange of cash payment for services rendered and received, it is no wonder that "boarding" as it existed under these circumstances continues to resist easy classification. A highly variable social practice, boarding not only located many urban peoples perennially in between, and on the run; it recapitulated their provisional lives as an urban domestic vernacular that resisted definitive semantic limits with respect to city residence. Fittingly, these same people would go on to produce a polymorphous boardinghouse literature, the loose generic forms of which for a time provided ample conceptual shelter for the seemingly irreconcilable diversity of early metropolitan America.

Antebellum boarding, in short, never achieved a "pure" form, literary or otherwise. It instead evolved from approximate and improvised domestic patterns, imprecise naming conventions, and interlocking systems of written and oral communication that were as imaginatively rich as they were unsystematic. Kenneth Scherzer accordingly writes of the family-*like* living on which boarding as a means of social organization hinged. Boarders, he explains, "were free from the authority and constraints of parent[s]" since busy boardinghouse keepers often were too busy to keep more than token tabs on the many inmates who resided under their respective roofs. The more boarders, the less personal was the living arrangement, in other words. Hence the "semiautonomy" that Scherzer says characterized most boardinghouses. Not a few of these nineteenth-century establishments recalled the comfort and contact of traditional domestic settings, but without the too-close emotional ties and familial obligations that went with them.[6] A boarder could receive as much of this quasi-family condition as he wanted, for a fee. For however personal communal living might feel, however warm the relations across the landlord-tenant divide, boarding was a hybrid activity that tethered the human demand for housing to the cold calculus of economic logic. Weekly rent payments alone were enough to remind boarders and keepers alike that the domestic economy of boarding involved at bottom an impersonal transaction for saleable home-space. Boarders for the most part accepted—thrived on, even—this novel modern living arrangement. Unlike lodgers, those non-kin household residents who skipped common meals, urban America's boarders sought, received, and paid for a special brand of half-freedom that at once facilitated their will to roam even as it reified the cultural category of "home." In the words of a contemporary, boarders could be as "promiscuous" as they pleased in joining a table full of messmates, yet without suffering the "perfect isolation" of lodging.[7] At sittings for breakfast, dinner, teatime, and supper, they could also return for second helpings, gratis, provided the "family's" provisions lasted.

Although synchronous with the rise of the city in the United States, and thus belonging to the modern period proper, boardinghouses were an integral part of the American experiment from its inception. As long as there had been New World inhabitants, there had been New World boarders. Dutch merchants enjoyed the temporary shelter afforded them by boarding as early as the seventeenth century. Drawn by the previously untapped markets of the West, they quickly replicated in New Amsterdam an American variant of phased changes already underway across the Atlantic, where the rising population centers of early modern Europe long since had begun to convert traditional inns and taverns into fully operative boardinghouses. Boarding out thus abetted enterprising Dutch designs during a period of intense imperial competition. English colonists eventually supplanted their Dutch rivals, and fared even better by boarding. Assisting the successive waves of new arrivals from Albion's shores—young males, for the most part, as unattached in their persons as were their prospects uncertain—were the by-now familiar circulars and newspaper notices that advertised for "gentlemen" boarders both in private families and a small but growing number of boardinghouses. Immigrants from all nations needed to secure work before they could board, of course. As in the Old World, one's residence in America was inseparable from one's place and status of employment. Well into the early national period, apprentice and journeyman artisans and mechanics resided by default in households headed by their masters—sustaining a traditional boarding behavior well past the threshold of U.S. independence. Up and down the Atlantic seaboard, moreover, eighteenth-century sailors and port workers patronized boardinghouses that catered to their peripatetic needs as the hired subalterns of global mercantile capitalism.

None of this was new. Boarding, in fact, was new to America only insofar as "America" itself was "new."

Yet, postcolonial boarding did break with historical precedent on at least one count. Numbering in the hundreds of thousands, the early European transplants who settled in America over the course of several preceding generations had helped to transform the country's "wilderness" into a comparatively dense network of populated settlements. It was this same seismic population shift that spawned America's cities, and that furthermore spelled radical domestic change for urban inhabitants there. In port cities like New York, where many new arrivals first made landfall, housing densities crept and then leapt upward as masses of visitors and immigrants vied for residential space. Boarding in its mature, modern incarnation emerged from this landmark demographic development. With surplus housing stock in America at a premium by about 1790, many households increasingly looked to boarders as an added (and sometimes necessary) source of revenue. It was simple supply and demand: independent householders, women included, had domestic space to let; the homeless needed homes. Homeowners and would-be boarders yielded to the seeming market logic of this situation, creating what historian Elizabeth Blackmar calls a "cash nexus for household relations" that was centered on living space as an exchange commodity.[8] More boarders meant more money for landlords, and so the lure of boardinghouse dollars—like the lure of boardinghouse pounds and pence just a few years earlier—made the path from casual to professional boarding a well-trod one at this time. A brief Manhattan advertisement from the period speaks volumes in this regard. Promising board "in a private family for six gentlemen on Greenwich [S]treet," it suggests a more-boarders-is-better trend that found private homes with only a few boarders becoming full-fledged boardinghouses with increased frequency.[9]

So, too, did master-worker relations reinvent themselves by the end of the eighteenth century, courtesy of boarding. With high rates of immigration holding steady in this period, not a few business operations in the new United States purposefully began targeting émigré needs; many of these same businesses experienced a boom in trade as a result, even as the success of their primary commercial endeavors encouraged a secondary entrepreneurial investment in the lucrative urban housing market. With a watchful eye on their labor force, employers in expanding industries like shoemaking and carpentry were willing, when able, to build boardinghouses for their sizeable pools of employees. Owners and operators deducted rent from wages in an old-fashioned (and self-serving) gesture at patriarchal authority. Boarding nevertheless redistributed rather than reinforced traditional allotments of workplace power. Boarding by now, in short, had become a form of barter, an impersonal market relation between two interested parties. Boarders to some extent were empowered as buyers in a modern economy of boarding; they were not to be dictated to in dealings with the retailers of domestic space, even when retailers doubled as employers, perhaps as their own. Furthermore, by residing at establishments that were not connected with the boss—sleeping five or six to a room in the process—journeyman boarders could substitute the oversight of a master, while away from the workplace, with the soft supervision of a boardinghouse keeper. When enough like-minded journeymen boarded at the same address, they in effect formed industry-specific trade houses. This shift in boarding practices fell short of a working-class housing upheaval. If, however, these disparate bands of workers were not quite the class-conscious fellow travelers that a nascent cadre of union organizers would have them be, then their late-century status as fellow boarders in common recalled a still-recent civic change: following the War for Independence, an ever-larger and thus more formidable population of boarders emerged as a genuine force to be reckoned with in American society, the country's economy, and also in its politics.

A proverbially transitional state, boarding achieved the peak of its popularity and influence in close correspondence with the adolescence of a young United States; not by coincidence did it nurture and sustain the similarly liminal condition that was the American modern. Urbanization, industrialization, breakthrough improvements in transportation, and accelerating trends both in immigration and cultural production—all of these pivotal changes were underway during the decades when the American boardinghouse reached its prime, years that span the late early national period and extend up to and through the Civil War.[10] Precise figures are scarce, and census data misleading,[11] but the current best estimate gives the number of American households with boarders and/or lodgers by 1860 at about one in five.[12] Strictly speaking, boardinghouses reached their maximum national capacity in the 1890s. It nevertheless was during the antebellum period that observers first began to recognize that boarding had begun to achieve outsized significance in the United States.

In its American context, boarding was both a reflexive index and a contributing cause of epochal transformations that were then remaking the U.S. city. "Urban" and "boarder" no longer served within this environment as discrete identifying terms for an America that at once was becoming metropolitan and modern. Increasingly, the two terms worked in tandem; if they were not quite synonymous, then they did function symbiotically at the level of shared national experience. American manufacturers inadvertently had begun to make plain the connections between the encompassing country, its cities, and boarding out as early as the 1830s, when they laid the foundations for less-than-bucolic mill towns like Lowell, Massachusetts.[13] The exciting assortment of peoples, points of view, and expanding consumer options collected together at these planned light-industrial locations, together with the tightly packed boardinghouse dormitories that many textile operations hosted on site, made the suburban manufacturing town a good approximation of city life for a resident workforce that was still by and large rural in its upbringing and orientation. In the words of one of Lowell's most recent historians, "This *was* city life" (emphasis added).[14] "This" was, that is to say, the requisite mix of urbanizing peoples, complex economies, and dynamically crowded spaces from which the American metropolis emerged. "This" was also the backdrop against which boarding became an enabling corollary to modernization. It was not long before boarding as a sociocultural phenomenon assumed proportions that were large enough to affect the country's residential landscape on a wide scale, and conspicuous enough to create a pervasive fascination with the cities to which the U.S. boardinghouse was tied.

With an American variant of the Industrial Revolution well under way in the United States by at least the 1840s, boarding no longer merely anticipated or approximated the urban; it truly *was* urban. Bypassing, for the most part, the industrial excesses of Europe's dreary manufacturing towns, which emphasized heavy industrial production of coal and iron, America's big cities—New York, Philadelphia, and Boston, in particular—embraced mass production, the division of labor, and new workplace technologies in relatively friendly form. The antebellum American metropolis specialized in the manufacture of consumer goods (shoes, cheap apparel, furniture) and on finishing trades (slaughterhouses, tanning, sugar refining) that made life for traditional craft workers difficult and often unpleasant without necessarily subjecting them to the occupational hazards and residential horrors of a Manchester, England.[15] America's brand of metropolitan industrialization did expose, however, the severe housing shortages attendant on the rapid growth of the urban-industrial showplaces that were then on offer in the United States. American manufactures required workers en masse. Migrants from the countryside and immigrants from abroad were ready to oblige. During the 1840s alone, the two groups together raised the rate of urban population growth by three times what it was for rural areas by pouring into the nation's largest cities.[16] This new economic order required operators, suppliers, and professionals. A protomiddle class, eager to capitalize on that requirement, carved out an urban niche for itself as its aspiring members took up middle-management positions and opened stores in those city centers that most needed their services. Housing starts lagged far behind the resultant increased demand for, and escalating price of, urban domestic quarters. Only by squeezing more and more bodies into already crowded home space did antebellum citizens avert an outright housing crisis. Measured as the number of persons per household, house density for New York alone reached 14.7 by 1855. That doubled the figure seen at the close of the eighteenth century and gave proof positive that metropolitan industrialization was under way in America in earnest. Boston, meanwhile, kept pace at 9.3, and Philadelphia registered a snug 6.5. True, fourteen out of fifteen Americans still lived in single-family households at this time.[17] Yet, urban residents, long since settled or not, saw the writing on their cities' walls: rather than deny obvious demographic change, and rather than (re)rusticate out in the country, they stood their urban ground and boarded out as never before.

Although no complete list of antebellum urban boarders exists, the constellation of data that is available provides partial indication of boarding's impact on city life before the Civil War. Walt Whitman, we remember, made a compelling case for boarding's prominence in metropolitan America when he claimed three-quarters of Manhattan's sons and daughters as boarders. Another writer from the 1860s made the same claim, and so corroborated Whitman's figures.[18] If his numbers seem high, then the one thousand boardinghouses listed in *Trow's New York City Directory* for 1854–55 underscores boarding's immodest proportions. No American city could match New York for boardinghouses, of course. Yet, city directories elsewhere boasted substantial totals of their own: there were some 122, 150, and 12 of Scherzer's "formal" boarding establishments in Boston, St. Louis, and New Orleans, respectively, with only the periodic outbreaks of yellow fever along the Gulf coast discouraging there the close human contact that came with a life lived in common. Of special note back in climates more favorable to boarding was Boston's South End, where fresh supplies of newcomers raised the local total of boarders to an impressive 25 percent of area inhabitants. That leaves only Philadelphia unaccounted for among what were formerly the nation's three largest cities. Despite its reputation as a "City of Homes," the City of Brotherly Love boarded out with the rest of urban America. The small commercial grid surrounding Independence Hall serves as a suggestive illustration in this respect. Within the space of just a few city blocks, four professional boardinghouses, all located on major streets, saw a brisk traffic of boarders paying the $4 to $7 average weekly bill for plain board, or the $12 to $15 charged the upwardly mobile for a more sumptuous brand of boarding.[19] After we reckon for "informal" boardinghouses as well, we can estimate that almost half of the households located in central Philadelphia—by nostalgic association, the very cradle of American democracy—contained one or more boarders. There is, accordingly, little reason to wonder at Scherzer's calling boardinghouses a "symbol of community change."[20] Like the cities that housed them, America's mid-nineteenth-century boarders knew little *but* change as they adapted to modernity with the rest of the urbanizing West. Theirs was the era that forever altered the meaning of "community," and made "change" itself into a watchword.

Boarding's modern pedigree did not reside solely in cities and industry, however. Modernity meant more than workshops, sweatshops, and crowded urban neighborhoods. It was also a feeling, a state of mind, an attitude and worldview that left moderns temporally suspended in between what Michel de Certeau calls an "opaque" past and an "uncertain" future, and spatially forsaken of solid ground (figurative and domestic) on which to stand.[21] Boarding in its main features encapsulates this, the uncertainty of modernity. Like most moderns, boarders were a transient population of resident-exiles. Unmoored and unattached, they were not unknown to change jobs, boardinghouses, or even cities on a moment's notice. They learned the requisite etiquette of boarding quickly, or else not at all. Were they to survive in the city, the first and last lesson that they would have to absorb involved the necessary extemporaneity of modern urban life. It was a message that suitably reached them, if at all, through the volatile medium of happenstance exchange. For the chance human interactions of boarding amounted to a crash course on the metropolis, with possibly many an unlooked-for benefit to be derived from this piecemeal education: these included, among others of boarding's boons, the helpful hints on local employment opportunities that circulated at "home," the emotional support networks established among household peers, no matter how wayward one's actual housemates proved to be, and ready boardinghouse tips that boldly spelled out the city's chief perils and pleasures.[22] Newlyweds, widows, bachelors, and, less frequently, couples with children were among those who enrolled in boarding's American course. Most of them boarded for brief spells. "Long-term" boarders were an anomaly (and an oxymoron) by comparison, since even this rare breed of resident tended to relocate on an annual basis, if not more often. Within the metropolitan paradigm typified by urban boarding, time had come to be measured in quantities as small as the rented city space that served more and more moderns as a makeshift domicile. Indeed, the short-term lease, by which boarding legally bound renters-in-common to some unspecified amount of scant square footage, remains a fitting metonym for an entire age.

Enhancing boarding's modern credentials are boarders themselves, perhaps as heterogeneous a people as any assembled in antebellum America. From boarders' diversity came the variegated colors that marked the nation's cities, and in part comprised the disorienting multiplicity that is modernity. The list of influential American moderns who boarded their way into the country's consciousness is thus as unlikely as it is long. Urban entertainment impresario P. T. Barnum, for example, operated a rather unremarkable New York boardinghouse before he achieved international celebrity after opening his infamous American Museum of oddities on Broadway. Another sometime New York boarder, the self-appointed prophet Robert Matthews, occupied a Battery boardinghouse where he found few converts, despite his divinely inspired pronouncements at the tea table. Back in the nation's capital, meanwhile, the District of Columbia was teeming with boardinghouses that expedited metropolitan development along the Potomac, even if it catered to creatures less curious than Barnum's, or Matthews himself. Hundreds of U.S. congressmen boarded out during federal legislative sessions. The decided regional orientation of Washington's houses—with all of the boarders at any given facility haling, to a man, from a single American region like New England— would appear to contradict the more sweeping mid-nineteenth-century move toward pluralism.[23] As integral component parts of Washington's advancing civic infrastructure, capital boardinghouses nevertheless endorsed modernity, since they contributed to make out-of-towners (and what proper modern was not from "out of town"?), in this case political officeholders, feel at "home" in what was still a rapidly urbanizing environment. In any case, whether they boarded out by entrepreneurial choice, spiritual conviction, geographic affiliation, or simple convenience, boarders formed a crazy patchwork of unsettled strangers whose improbable threading together seems a tangible, if partial, expression of what modernity meant in the United States before the Civil War.

Sociologists describe a life cycle for boarding, the seemingly arbitrary, transitory nature of which suggests just how twisted was the fabric of modernity. As we have seen, boarding was but a phase through which thousands of young men (and women) passed after they left the protection of the nuclear family, but before they managed to establish families of their own within the cities toward which many of them gravitated in early adulthood.[24] Boarding as a model of social behavior therefore reveals rather tenuous ties. By internalizing conventional domestic standards that equated the independent family with the independent (which is to say, freestanding) household, the familiar rite that was boarding valorized precisely what circumstance in the main had denied boarders. Thus did boarding in effect arrest the "normative" development of a large segment of the American population, and so reinforce the fragmented quality of modern life. A similar fate of frustrated expectations awaited boardinghouse keepers. Keepers by and large were widows, many of whom struggled to meet basic living expenses once they were deprived of the income of a breadwinning husband. Boarding offered an alternative to penury. Or, at least, it provided a momentary stay against what otherwise seemed an inevitable loss of socioeconomic standing: keepers who accepted boarders into their homes could hope, with some justification, to retain the status of small proprietors, and thereby halt their immediate slide into the working classes.[25] In other words, if boarders began life in the boardinghouse, then keepers ended it there. Neither group boarded from birth unto death. But neither seemed able to describe a life trajectory of its own. Boarding interrupted—often critically, and maybe fatally—the destinies of both landlord and tenant alike.[26]

No less modern were the physical household structures that brought boarding into being. Like boarders, these, too, had come to figure into America's unwritten urban plan less by design than by a selection process that must have struck contemporaries as random. Cities in their irresistible spread excluded virtually no home from this process, by which "normal" houses became boardinghouses with a frictionless ease that almost suggests the consent of their ostensible owners. Urban workers were in many cases the catalysts behind a structure's (or, more likely, a whole neighborhood's) boardinghouse conversion, but they were not the cause. The city grid, like the modern economy, was subject to larger market forces of supply and demand; so, too, were urban accommodations and the assorted peoples whom they housed influenced by socioeconomic conditions that were mostly beyond their control. Because many metropolitan laborers could not afford the cost of daily round-trip transportation between their respective places of residence and employment, legions of these, boarding's foot soldiers, relocated to city centers to be near the manufacturing and mercantile concerns that employed them. As workers moved in, businessmen, professionals, and class-conscious non-manual laborers such as clerks moved out. Depending on the city in question, they and their families relocated uptown, to another part of town, or out of town altogether to begin life anew in the expanding suburbs.

Pockets of inner-city respectability remained, nonetheless. Some among modern urban America's emergent petty gentry were unwilling to sacrifice proximity to the workplace, despite the financial strain they faced from rising real-estate prices that rendered single-family dwellings in city centers beyond their reach. The more well-to-do among these, the resolute middling classes, elected to reside in downtown boardinghouses where weekly rents were high enough to exclude the hordes of invading workers. Pockets of prosperity appeared when- and wherever upscale boarders settled together. The occupants of these bourgeois comfort zones primarily sought compensation not for their white-collar labors, but the discordant urban experience that was sometimes to be found just a few blocks distant from fashionable domestic quarters. If maintained properly, the antebellum boardinghouse conceivably could function as a buffer against an unseemly city. Boarding even became a status symbol of sorts for some urban dwellers, provided the accommodations met the refining pretensions of this particular breed of boarder.

The steady surrender of whole portions of downtown business districts to commercial cohabitation continued so long as businessmen themselves subscribed to a nineteenth-century domestic ideology that, on principle, separated workplace from "home." As the midlevel managers of modern urban capitalism relinquished their increasingly unaffordable (or simply unsustainable) city mansions, they left behind them a residential infrastructure that was ideally suited for boarding: in their early postprime, many of these edifices remained ornately imposing enough to attract would-be renters; they were also commodious enough to allow for the creation of enclosed individual apartments inside houses. Boarders who paid for the privilege slept solitary in these latter enclosures, which comprised the "room" component of boarding's combined room and board package. Others slept multiple persons to a room, even perhaps sharing the same bed when board money was especially tight. Entire downtown districts entered into decline with the spread of these and similar cost-saving measures. For in the absence of domestic "guests" who could afford a few residential luxuries, boarding in its most elemental form was apt to take its toll on the houses, the fading splendor of which accelerated amid the midcentury increase of boarders and the parallel flight of the middle classes to the metropolitan perimeter. The pattern repeated itself when boardinghouse keepers of means followed the tide of fashion and likewise relocated, in a collective bid to maintain the reputations and rent levels of their (mobile) homes.

Hence the life *cycle* of boarding—for the city's inhabitants, if not its houses—could involve a circular journey into modernity that, for some, was fraught with practical hardship, periodic anxiety, and the psychological strains attendant on runaway urbanization. Referring to Manhattan in 1845, the city's former mayor Philip Hone spoke to the destabilizing condition of the modern metropolis when he declared for New York the maxim, "Overturn, overturn, overturn!"[27] It was no disturbing street protest that prompted Hone's remarks. Nor was there something peculiar to his birthplace that drew forth his comment. Indeed, he might have said the same of any metropolis in antebellum America, given the speed at which cities across the country were altering the face of the continent. Hone's was the participial predicament of a metropolitan boarder, for whom the "overturning" modern city never rested. Another contemporary, who, unlike Hone, made a serious study of antebellum boarding, later restated his observation when she euphemistically spoke of New York's "butterfly condition." It was an appropriate phrase in its day. And it retains its relevance now, when the unrelenting impetus for change that brought boarding to prominence in the nineteenth-century United States finds new form in the malleability that is *post*modernity.[28]

Among Westerners, Americans were not unique in attempting to adapt domestically to modernity. Nineteenth-century France, for example, made the modern apartment building its preferred habitat for the metropolitan capital at Paris. Apartment-living here at its French inception recalled in part the obvious features of boarding, minus the trappings of the close-knit household "family" that boarders hypothetically enjoyed. Evidence suggests that Parisians were quick to turn what many Americans might have deemed residential hardship into a generally accepted and socially acceptable practice, one whose appeal crossed urban class lines. Metropolitan London, meanwhile, made a reluctant yet inexorable migration to lodging. By century's end, urban developers in England had subdivided the mass of the Anglophone capital's independent dwellings into a downsized aggregate collection of rental housing stock. The Victorian ideal of the Englishman's "home" as his "castle" did persist, resisting as it did the alternate model of urban habitat that was on offer in Paris. London builders, for instance, were prepared to go so far as to devise separate entranceways, even staircases, for individual residences within a single structure. Theirs was a nostalgic architectural gesture aimed at preserving the nation's vaunted English liberties, both political and domestic. In the end, however, not even the unbroken façades that remained among London's elegant terraces through the 1830s could conceal an undeniable urban fact: as in America, inner-city congestion required that the once proudly independent households of England be partitioned into saleable home space, and so join with the rest of the northern urban Atlantic in a timely modern compromise.[29]

The United States was unique in at least one respect, domestically speaking. American boarding had become so egregious in the eyes of midcentury European travelers that it suggested all the noisy dislocations of modernity in one unstable location. Upon landing in Manhattan in 1831, the visiting French dignitary Alexis de Tocqueville was struck by the democratic leveling of New York's boardinghouses, where even the state's governor had taken up residence. Tocqueville afterward secured (with considerable trouble) a room at a Broadway boardinghouse of his own, and so received the short instruction on U.S. domestic arrangements that impacted his understanding of the nation writ large. By boarding, Tocqueville fancied to discover that the average American citizen was "continually in agitation, so that he is always changing his abode." To boarding, then, can we trace Tocqueville's now-famous assessment of American "restlessness," a conclusion that dozens of subsequent visitors reached by a similar residential route. Among them was the English-woman Mary Duncan, who sensed that boarding typified what she called Americans' "migratory habits." She regretted these "habits," fretting that "however useful and pleasant an accommodation they [boardinghouses] may be to strangers," such temporary residences would "become all the 'home' Americans know." Duncan's compatriot Charles Mackay voiced a similar concern when he compiled for publication the U.S. travel notes that he took on behalf of John Bull "old-fogyism." Boarding was in his mind "peculiar to America" and that country's "fast" inhabitants, and yet he clung to the hope that the more "reasonable" among them would retire a "system" that he considered pernicious. Contra Mackay, H. F. Fleischmann found nothing like the free and easy urban American board-inghouse in his native Germany. Openly accessible, and conveniently arranged, boarding seemed less a modern problem than a metropolitan triumph. Another sturdy Englishman, Alfred Bunn, nevertheless penned a growing consensus among European outsiders when he dismissed board-ing in its American context as morally suspect. "The Americans live more out of their private houses than in them," he wrote, "families, as well as individuals, 'boarding' at all the principal hotels."[30] Bunn and his fel-low Europeans hardly could pretend to be *pre*-modern immaculates, since they had been touched by an Industrial Revolution that brought them knowledge of urban modernity earlier than it did their American counterparts. Still, they had modernized for the most part without the boardinghouse as a "home" base. On this crucial domestic difference did they stake their expressed regret for boarding's supposedly corrosive effects on an impressionable United States—even though, in the end, they, too, like the majority of American boarders whom they observed, largely had seen the nation's modern cities in the flickering images of transit, and so in the imperfection of passing.

In his indictment against American boarding, Bunn returns us to the problem with which this chapter began: namely, the inherent difficulty of defining the boardinghouse at all, let alone explaining its importance to the wider culture. Bunn's accompanying brief against U.S. hotels, for example, inadvertently conflates two related domestic situations from the urban American 1830s. Both hotels and boardinghouses, after all, were residential venues where "boarders" were welcome for extended stays. Indeed, the American maestro of antebellum boarding, Thomas Butler Gunn, like Bunn begged the question of boarding's exact features and functions when he wrote in his *The Physiology of New York Boarding-Houses* (1857) that "the most magnificent of our palace hotels are *but* Boarding-Houses, temporary or permanent."[31] It was during these same years, furthermore, prior to the U.S. Civil War, when working-class tenements began to appear in the slums of America's cities. They, too, qualified as a kind of boarding establishment, although they were not "formal" boardinghouses as sociologists understand that style of domicile today.

This present study reconstructs boarding as antebellum Americans encountered it. Receiving special emphasis are the literary ramifications of this encounter, the means by which boarding became at once an urban muse and strategic mindset for U.S. authors as they learned to conceptualize nation-changing urbanization on "home" soil. In a country that had "gone to city" even as it went to board, boarding was less the debilitating national idiosyncrasy that some European observers believed it to be than an institution that enabled innovations in period American life and letters. This was true despite the definitional confusion suggested by Bunn, Gunn, and others. Strict definitions aside, the reflections on boarding that appear in this account amount for the most part to serious self-reflections by the people to whom boarding mattered most. This study likewise focuses specifically on the peak years of boarding's cultural prominence in America. If the boardinghouse today subsists along the outer urban reaches of a quaint American subculture, it occupied a seat at or near the very center of American culture during the middle decades of the nineteenth century. Only then, at the dawn of the American modern, was boarding close enough to the country's core consciousness that it could inspire a unique genre of literature. This book depends on that genre, much as the antebellum nation depended on boarding.

Contemporaries wrote of the "boarding-house," hyphen intended, in accordance with former orthographic standards of written English, but boarding figured for them as more than the compound sum of its related parts. The boardinghouse, rather, was an inescapable and indispensable facet of their nineteenth century. As such boarding multiplied the meanings of modernity, both practically and imaginatively, and in turn left its imprint on antebellum literature. Having forever altered the material lives of urban Americans, boarding changed their interior selves as well. The results of that change found expression through a nationwide urban imaginary that was indebted to boarding for its various forms and frequent appearances in print. From boardinghouse life sprang boardinghouse letters.

✦

Boarding out in the antebellum period inspired no few self-appointed poets laureate of boarding. Dozens, hundreds, even thousands of the age's boarders reflexively recorded their experiences with the itinerant tenancy of city living by means of the boardinghouse as a literary form. Some wrote for themselves, recording by diary and personal journal their own initiations into urban America. Others penned boardinghouse missives for friends and family, in the process providing an epistolary perspective on the metropolitan domestic. Still others besides, urged on by some combination of art, literary ambition, and the selfless pursuit of cultural knowledge, wrote for a general audience of interested readers. None of these last would have been surprised by anything they read about boarding. The boardinghouse was often already the controlling fact of their everyday lives, and it was just as frequently the all-too-familiar theme for much of the popular literatures that an expanding urban print marketplace made available to them.

Boarding's strong literary currency was based in part on numbers. America's mid-nineteenth-century authors self-consciously wrote about boarding, in other words, because a seeming disproportionate number of them boarded. There is evidence to suggest that the nation's authors from the era boarded out at least as much, if not more, than did their countrymen. This would go some way toward explaining the content of antebellum publications, page upon page of which bears the unmistakable shades of an urban boarding ritual that many an American author, and reader, knew firsthand.

The challenge for literary historians today is to face the conundrum posed by boardinghouse demographics. If boarding was once so conspicuous, then what has become of the body of literatures that American boarder-authors presumably produced? If boarding was once as common as it was across all ranks of society, and among authors in particular, then how might we best uncover boarding's discursive ties to modernity? Of course, to parse boarding's manifold forms may simply be to split generic hairs over a literature that in the end amounts to little more than a literary curiosity. Or, perhaps the close bond proposed here between boarding and authorship is nothing more than an illusion, a consequence of certain writers' having taken the trouble to articulate for a less expressive (or less egotistical) public a boarding experience that was by no means peculiar to literary professionals. The sheer weight of the evidence at stake nevertheless should trouble even the healthiest of skeptics. Americans formerly boarded out at rates that were high enough to astonish virtually anyone with an interest in the nation's past. Writers in turn once wrote about the boardinghouse often enough to give pause to the scholar not otherwise impressed by boarding as a strictly social phenomenon. What, then, has become of a literature that captured contemporary culture on the page when it took the American boardinghouse as its subject? The latter half of this chapter begins to account for this, one of the great vanishing acts in U.S. socio-literary history.

A quick inventory of antebellum boarder-authors is a likely starting point in the effort to reclaim the boardinghouse as city discourse. The results of this survey are revealing. Already with the emergence of America's so-called Renaissance writers at midcentury, there would appear to have been forged an uncommon bond between the literary life and the national pastime of boarding. Transcendentalist Ralph Waldo Emerson boarded out on the lecture circuit during his early career as a celebrity intellectual. He also accepted his disciple, Henry David Thoreau, as a boarder in his own household, before the latter's fabled residence at Walden Pond. Thoreau, too, shared domestic space with boarders back in Concord proper inside his family's home; his doing so was not the whim of a younger son, but a mother's sage response to shaky domestic finances. Thoreau boarded as well with one of Emerson's brothers on Staten Island during a short-lived trip to New York in 1843. Novelist Nathaniel Hawthorne also boarded out for extended periods at least three times in his adult life: once in 1839, while working as a customs officer in Boston; for a second trial two years later, at the reform-minded Brook Farm commune in nearby West Roxbury; then again in 1850, and again in Boston, just before author, wife, and children moved to a red farmhouse in rural western Massachusetts. Man of letters Edgar Allan Poe boarded for several spells in New York. He despised the city but enjoyed the ample provisions of the boardinghouse tables where he stayed. The poet Emily Dickinson's is a fittingly ambiguous case of boarding. She "boarded" briefly at Mount Holyoke Female Seminary, where communal quarters for girls were the norm. She likewise spent some seven months in the Cambridgeport boardinghouse of her Norcross cousins late in the Civil War. It was here, not far from cosmopolitan Harvard and Boston, that she made her last extended residence outside her parents' Amherst home. A young Herman Melville boarded out in Liverpool, Washington, D.C., and New York as a consequence of his early, and enforced, transatlantic roving. Even in later years, with his wife Elizabeth away visiting friends and family, the aging former sailor swapped stories and shared meals at the Harnett sisters' boardinghouse on Manhattan's East Twenty-Fifth Street.[32] Walt Whitman similarly made his "house" a "home" while boarding out from his early teens until after the Civil War. Long would he cherish the memory of Mrs. Chipman's fine New York boardinghouse in lower Manhattan, where, during the early 1840s, he deepened his appreciation of all things American—boardinghouses included—before he finally declared the United States a nation of boarders.

Boarding looms still larger under an expanded antebellum canon. Much as historical boarding exceeded the statistical limits of domestic moderation, boarding's discursive component impacted the ongoing development of a wide array of American literatures. One of the main claims of this project is that the literary arm of boarding touched more than a small sampling of authors, most of whom wrote their major works within the span of a couple of compressed decades. Rather, although the nation's writers achieved by boarding their climactic encounter with the American metropolis at midcentury, they had begun the preparations for that encounter decades earlier. Consciously or not, they continue to this day to confront the city on authorial terms long ago established by the boardinghouse. The African American poet Phillis Wheatley, to begin, all but literally closed the door on early American letters when she died as a domestic servant in a Boston boardinghouse at the late colonial date of 1784. Another sometime boarder was Charles Brockden Brown, who, as arguably the nation's first indigenous novelist, wrote works that span the eighteenth and nineteenth centuries. More American boarder-authors followed. The poet and newspaper editor William Cullen Bryant boarded in New York before his family joined him from New England. Fellow newspaperman Horace Greeley *found* a family (a wife, at any rate) in a boardinghouse not far from Bryant's. Leisured man of letters Sidney George Fisher boarded in between episodes of dilettante authorship in Philadelphia, while the dandified poet and editor Nathaniel Parker Willis spent some months boarding at New York's expensive Astor House hotel—where he comfortably conducted research for his widely read sketches of metropolitan high society. Another African American writer,

escaped slave Harriet Jacobs, commenced a life of freedom, as well as a
narrative documenting her hardships, in a New York boardinghouse on
Sullivan Street prior to the literary-historical dividing line of the Civil
War. Like Wheatley before her, she shut yet another door on another
chapter in American letters.[33]

Others boarded "informally," as Kenneth Scherzer might say. The
influential critic, poet, and *Atlantic Monthly* editor James Russell Lowell
*lodged* in a private room on Boston's Court Street. It was there that he
made a feeble attempt at a legal career while turning with artistic intent to
the writing of verse. James Fenimore Cooper, America's best-selling frontier novelist, knew hotel boarding in this life, and post mortem boarding
in the next. While New Yorkers prepared a memorial in the departed
writer's honor, "upholsterers and plasterers," wrote *Harper's* magazine
editor George William Curtis in 1853, had "ransacked" Cooper's Hudson
River Valley estate in order to convert it into "our wonderful American
metonymy, . . . a 'Cooperstown Boarding-house,' " for visiting tourists.[34]
Beneath the American Renaissance, meanwhile, the popular sensational
author Ned Buntline performed his part in keeping the nation's boardinghouses filled to capacity. Out on the road in search of topics to write
about, Buntline made a habit of hotel boarding in the nation's frontier
cities. He boarded by proxy back home in Manhattan, where he kept
up to six mistresses out of harm's way and under cover from his wife at
boardinghouses scattered about town.[35] From its canonical heights, then,
to its subversive depths, antebellum boarding stretched across the period's literary landscape as scores of the country's authors elected to board.

Notwithstanding the dryness of such data—and the spuriousness of
any "realization" that America's authors, like all their countrymen everywhere always, managed to eat, drink, sleep, bathe, and seek shelter from
the elements—the plain fact of boarding's literary affiliations reveals
much about the creative process in the period. Viewed as an isolated
act, boarding is but a footnote in American literary history. Viewed as
it relates to the mechanics of writing, to the logistics of bringing written work to print, boarding assumes extraordinary importance in how
we understand the metropolitan context of antebellum literary-cultural
production. Helpful in uncovering this context is the scholarship of print
historian William Charvat. Recent practitioners of the history of the book
in America more or less have recycled Charvat's 1959 account of antebellum publishing. Charvat and his followers define the parameters of
authorship in this period as decidedly urban.[36] During the years under
investigation here, 1840–1860, Americans as a whole massed together
in and around the nation's three biggest cities—Boston, Philadelphia,

and New York—making possible an unprecedented concentration of citizen-readers. Publishers, printers, and periodicals also gathered in metropolitan centers. Taking full advantage of the easier urban access to financing and transportation networks, industry entrepreneurs invested heavily in plant and equipment infrastructures, creating a capital base that in turn streamlined the production and distribution of literary commodities. Local consumption fueled the whole process, as the expanding pool of city readers provided the primary demand that warranted an enlarged productive capacity in the first place. Capital cities thus created the conditions for an urban print revolution, while city capital underwrote that revolution.

The biographies of the above boarder-authors indicate a parallel mass migration of literary labor to the metropolis as writers became city-settlers and moved to the largest markets for their wares. Fed on the meager profits from their writings, when they were paid at all, starting authors like Hawthorne, Poe, and Whitman, even Thoreau, were often just one step ahead of the starving-artist stereotype that had crossed over from the artists' garrets of London. Keen competition among writers ensured that literary supply outpaced demand, great as that demand was. It also ensured that many an antebellum author, having relocated to the new metropolis to write at all, scrimped and saved on living expenses so as to *remain* in the city. As any urban laborer knew, or as the strapped middle classes might confess, boarding was perhaps the only way to stay: widely enough practiced to be convenient; cheaply enough furnished to be affordable; and flexible enough, given the short boarding-terms and high turnover rates for boarders, to accommodate the unpredictable paydays of writers-for-hire. *Putnam's* magazine might decry the myth of American authors' hand-to-mouth existence all it wanted. For the twenty literary notables whom its sometime editor, Charles Frederick Briggs, profiled in January 1853, making much of their elegant (and paid for) homes, the magazine overlooked some 3,000 starvelings who were boarding and writing in the nation's biggest cities. "Double insignificance" was how one of these 3,000 described his plight in retrospect, conjuring up at once the precarious employment and housing prospects of the urban American boarder-writer.[37]

To summarize, if writers boarded out in higher percentages than most Americans, then it is the urban orientation of publishing that must account at least in part for their doing so. Were writers to write, they had to do so in the city. At the very least, they had to work out the terms of a professional relationship with the urban-based producers and consumers of print.[38] Were they in consequence to abandon the metropolitan periphery of a place like Concord, say, and tend to that relationship face-to-face in a hub like Boston—to work on site, as it were—then surely modernity had concrete consequences for authors. They needed cities in the worst way, as cities presupposed the people and profit margins that made authorship available as a trade. They also needed industry, and industry again meant cities, since metropolitan purveyors of print provided the dollars and technologies that underwrote publishing as an enterprise. They needed, finally, the affordable city-shelter that the boardinghouse alone offered. Would-be antebellum writers in the main became authors, moderns, and boarders all at once. To the city they went; in the city they stayed; and to the boardinghouse they must at some point go unless possessed of independent means of support.

The ties between boarding and authoring are more than circumstantial. This study claims causality, in other words. Antebellum writers wrote the way they wrote *because* they boarded. On the one hand, they portrayed boarding and boarding-*like* experiences often enough to make the boarder-author's urban trials a familiar set piece of contemporary literature. Boarding accordingly impacted such obvious formal variables as plot and setting in a wide range of works. On the other hand, and more important, boarding-authors ensured that boarding not only shaped their works formally, but controlled them functionally as well. So closely does boardinghouse life overlap with boardinghouse art in the texts that many of the era's authors produced for print that boarding finally rises above the mere surface-level features of any given piece. The very language, themes, images, and anxieties found in boardinghouse texts derive from the urban domestic frames—literal and figurative—in which writers conceived them.

Preventing the critical assessment of boarding's role in writing is the boardinghouse's literary-historical lineage. Boarding's working-class associations long have eclipsed its deservedly recognized presence in the field of U.S. letters, much as the laboring lives of many of the country's working men and women were all but lost to America's romantically inclined nineteenth-century writers. Notwithstanding the proletarian credentials of a Melville or Whitman, precious little actual *work* appears in the literature from a period that concerned itself more with the psychological and emotional lives of Americans than with their workaday world.[39] Boarding's hard-luck associations, then, warranted or not, seem to have sentenced it to a life of semi-obscurity, this despite the frequent appearance of boardinghouse pieces in antebellum publications. Compounding this problem is the dismissive tongue-in-cheek treatment that antebellum authors often reserved for urban boarding. As we have seen, both professional boarding and professional authoring, exact contemporaries, owe a heavy debt to cities for their existence. Given the pedestrian struggles that often attended that existence, many a boarder-author came to belittle the boardinghouse, poking fun in print at the inner workings of an urban literary life that fell far short of the traditional subject matter for belles lettres. What transpired behind low-end boardinghouse doors in effect became a formulaic tale for the city-initiate writer. The self-effacing nature of that formula all but ensured the young literary artist's disappearance even as he tried, in a literary way, to bring boardinghouse life to light.

Some examples help to illustrate the ways in which boarder-authors willed themselves and their fellow boarders to the margins of both antebellum life and the pages of the many books, magazines, and newspapers that they otherwise littered with the literary figure of boarding. A generic boardinghouse plot, with its predictable urban orientation, runs as follows: green country youth comes to city; youth seeks out suitable boardinghouse shelter in said city; close metropolitan contact and a house full of fellow boarders educates youth in the best instances, corrupts it in the worst; and, finally, fledgling youth stands on his own two feet, having abandoned the boardinghouse for the comparative independence of a separate household. Serial author Charles Frederick Briggs set the American pattern with his *The Adventures of Harry Franco* (1839). Whitman rendered a sobering imitation of Briggs in his temperance tract *Franklin Evans* (1842). And travel writer Bayard Taylor rehearsed a personal tale of urban migration in the highly autobiographical *John Godfrey's Fortunes* (1865), in which he looks back twenty years at the New York boarding of his early adulthood. Each of the fictional boarders presented in these works leaves country for city, and each in turn lives and learns in a metropolitan boardinghouse whose low rent is its chief attraction. The rite of passage described is at once one of self-discovery and economic maturity.[40] Growing up translates here as moving out—out of the boardinghouse, and into a career and home of one's own. A feminine version of the boardinghouse storyline more or less preserves this pattern. To cite but one example, the little orphan Gerty from Maria Cummins's best-selling novel *The Lamplighter* (1855) *begins* life in a dilapidated Boston boardinghouse instead of arriving there from rural parts. Her sentimental journey from rags to riches runs its course only after she leaves boardinghouse, landlady, lodging, and then city (in that order) to start life anew in the country. Boardinghouses anchor not only the works of Cummins, Briggs, Whitman, and Taylor, however. They also ground many more works like them. Yet, the stories that these works relate consistently sever their boardinghouse ties. An occasion for writing in the first place, the working-class boardinghouse also seems to have been a fictional obstacle for both writers and their protagonists to overcome.

Not by coincidence, and with no small touch of irony, boarder-authors often plot an escape from the boardinghouse parameters of their works (and lives) by having their fictional boarders either turn author or else begin boarding *as* authors. The underlying idea is that authorship itself will be profitable enough to make the boarding lifestyle that normally accompanied it unnecessary. Moreover, given the urban imperative of both housing and writing in this period, the boarder-as-author plot line—like its more general country-to-city cousin—betrays the metropolitan bias one would expect. It also betrays an additional irony, one based on writers' actual experience in the city: authorship seldom paid in the ways that would-be writers had hoped, thereby sentencing them to more boarding.

As common a tale as this is, the very premise of down-and-out boarding has made the boarder-author as much a hidden figure in print as in real life. That is to say, the boardinghouse vanishing act is mutually reinforcing: both the boarding literary man (women boarder-authors were the exception) and his fictional counterpart lived on borrowed time at one of the new nation's lowliest urban places, the cheap boardinghouse. Bayard Taylor's *John Godfrey's Fortunes* provides a prime example of the boarder-author's auto-erasure at the antebellum boardinghouse. An aspiring writer, Godfrey leaves rural Pennsylvania for New York. A chapter title from his account makes clear the outcome of that move: "In Which I Go to Market, But Cannot Sell My Wares" (179). By dashing off what he calls "moral and millinery tales" for female readers (200), Godfrey narrowly escapes the "Poet's . . . poor-house" of which a friend warns him only to land in the kind of cheap boardinghouse that had become a familiar feature of urban working-class neighborhoods before the Civil War (169). Godfrey's landlady is thoughtful enough to supply for his room a small writing table, "with one shrunk leg" (195). Her tenant nevertheless suffers no delusions about his home environment. Across the street sits a row of foul tenements. Said street seldom gets cleaned, and the smell of garbage piled curbside does little to offset the depressing effects of a boarders' neighborhood marked by "quiet and decay" (194). Dependable pay for his writing, like even the shabbiest gentility, eludes Godfrey. In his telling, the boarder-author's initiation into boarding is sadly lacking, and literary work itself unwise.

After exposure to several such predicaments as Godfrey's, readers of the hard-luck school of boardinghouse letters might decide his case was typical. On the one hand, the modern, "vagabond life" that he describes fits many a boarder-author's unmoored condition to a tee (200). On the other, vagabondage comes at a high cost: trapped as they often are in incipient urban boardinghouse ghettos, boarder-authors go the way of the working-class neighborhoods in which they reside—ever downward, fading more and more from a mainstream middle-class view.

Boardinghouse texts reveal just this pattern. N. P. Willis goes slumming as a hard-pressed writer in a boarding piece that he wrote for the *New Mirror* newspaper. The "small money" in his persona's pocket confines his "low-priced brain" to a cheap boardinghouse like Godfrey's. Boarder-author Twitter enjoys high-priced houses by skipping out before rent comes due. Advances from his publisher, Harper's, keep him regularly in between residences. The "penny-a-liner" Mr. Bob Jenkins fends off an all but inevitable socioeconomic slide at Mrs. Kolltater's Snob House boardinghouse, this despite his "seedy coat and calamitous countenance." And a self-identified "poor-devil author" from Manhattan slaves away at sensational tales in one Mrs. Screwby's Bleecker Street boardinghouse. His fellow boarders, also tormented by "the Demon of Starvation" in unheated rooms, include "Brown, the unpublished poet in Number Three," and Jones, of Number Eight, whose "inky fingers and untidy aspect" announce at once his occupation and housing condition. Today's recognized literary masters, meanwhile, wrote down their own renditions of the disappearing boarder-author. Melville's *Pierre* (1852) is perhaps the most famous. His fictional literary enthusiast, Pierre Glendinning, toils away at a never-to-be-realized masterpiece in a strange domestic setting that one contemporary reviewer called a "modest boarding-house chamber." Doomed to a retired life in an out-of-the way corner of the city, which the narrator deems "rather secluded and silent" during business hours, and "remarkably . . . depopulated" from dusk 'til dawn, Pierre eventually instances the perverse logic of literary boarding by vanishing altogether in an untimely death. As a colleague of Melville's said in reference to his own fictional lament of boarding-writing, boarder-authors like Pierre were bound to be "Bored to Death."[41] Suffering not only from "double insignificance," the author as boarder was also at risk of being doubly silenced—through the choice of urban authorship as a career, and the working-class, boardinghouse self-exile that was so often a corollary of that choice.

Neither boarders nor their respective "houses" were all alike, however. Boarding as a discourse did not depend on a single working-class formula. Equally implicated in big-city boarding were *middle*-class people, *middle*-class housing, and a *middle*-class literary response to the metropolis. Like its working-class counterpart, a sturdy urban bourgeoisie more often than not boarded out because circumstances required its members to do so. Inner-city housing was often too costly for all but the outright rich and upper middle classes. Yet, because even the smallest domestic amenities made for marked gradations among boardinghouses, and, of course, in the asking price for rent, boarding's patrons occupied as full a spectrum of class status as there were a range of boardinghouse choices a cut or two or more above the cheap variety. True, big-city workers resided at low-end houses in higher numbers than did the middle classes at more well-equipped ones. It was to the midrange houses that even workers aspired, however. Middle-class boarding set the general *tone* for boarding before the Civil War and thus matched low-cost boarding in importance.

It was likewise to the middle-class boardinghouse that writers moved if and when it was within their means to do so. Any boarder-author who was not strapped for cash—and there were enough of them to prove an important exception to the general Grub Street rule—could qualify as a candidate for a more reliably middle-class boardinghouse experience, and in turn translate that experience into sketch or short-story form for high-circulation journals like *Harper's* and *Putnam's*. Once in print, pieces on middle-American urban boarding complemented for these magazines' by and large middle-class readers the down-and-out boarding material that simultaneously retained its place in month after month of publication. The weekly edition of *Harper's* explained what all the boardinghouse fuss was about, stating that "every body," at least among its New York readers, "has had, has, or will have" a personal trial with "one of the most striking institutions of this metropolitan city," the boardinghouse.[42] Thus, the middle mass of urban boarders in some respects provides a representative case of antebellum boarding practices as a whole. Middle-class boarding might have been out of reach for many urban mechanics, artisans, day-laborers, and upstart authors, but it was on average just that—an average experience to which most boarders, boardinghouses, and boardinghouse letters tended.

Despite its greater exposure in real life and in print, however, even middle-class boarding would appear to have left but the faintest of traces in the literary-historical record. Literary boardinghouses should be obvious, but they are not, and with good reason. The first of these concerns the actual domiciles around which boarding as a discourse revolved. Run-of-the-mill accommodations denominated themselves with a brash "BOARDING" sign that made no pretense as to what transpired inside. With little investment in the social graces, the landlords of these establishments also advertised aggressively for boarders in metropolitan dailies.

**Figure 1.1.** Building nos. 35 and 37 (at center) share this stretch of New York's Broadway with other townhouse structures. All but identical in outward appearance with their neighbors, nos. 35 and 37 are distinct in that they are boardinghouses—run by proprietresses Mrs. Davy and Mrs. Ballard, respectively. From *The Illuminated Pictorial Directory of New York* (Jones, Newman, & J. S. Newbank, 1848). Courtesy of the Eno Collection, New York Public Library, Humanities and Social Sciences Division.

**Closeup detail of 1.1.**
Pedestrian traffic at Mrs. Davy's Broadway boardinghouse, New York, 1848.

By contrast, middle-class houses took pride in making a muted public appearance. They seldom, if ever, revealed boarding's bourgeois secrets openly, since the dominant domestic norm proscribed the "genteel" home in the "genteel" neighborhood from bearing even a single external marker that would indicate its being a place of business (see figure 1.1). An understated brass plaque inscribed with the landlord's name replaced the vulgar boarding notice. Middle-class landlords, moreover, often held themselves to entirely different standards of decorum than their working-class peers. Rather than advertise for boarders, for example, they secured them by word of mouth, expecting and receiving letters of reference from applicants who already inhabited "respectable" social circles. Savvy management by landlords in part explains this strategic self-concealment.

Operating in what historian John Kasson calls a "marketplace of appearances," sharp boardinghouse owners had a vested interest in making no appearance whatsoever. In a culture that prized the stand-alone home, all the more so as that style of dwelling became increasingly rare in the nation's cities, a house that *looked* like a boardinghouse reduced its own asking price for board.[43] Middle-class boarding remained inconspicuous for another reason as well. Given the nineteenth century's changing notions of civility, it was simply downright rude to make public those forms of behavior that urban communities more and more urged be kept private. "Rudeness," says Kasson, involved singling out "for special attention that which should remain inconspicuous," and nowhere more than in the inner sanctum of an ideal domestic life did this inconspicuousness apply with greater force.[44] The best middle-class boardinghouse looked for all the world like what it was not. To expose the work that went on behind the domestic façade would be indiscreet. As conspicuous as antebellum boarding was, the middle-class boardinghouse was anything but.

There is, in addition to boarding's human forms and functions, another contributing factor behind middle-class boarders' deceptive invisibility in American letters. This is Michel Foucault's "author function," a theory that readily applies to the boarder as author. By "author function," Foucault would indicate the limited rights of ownership that a writer enjoys for any material that he creates, in his own name, for the capitalist marketplace.[45] The more successful boarder-authors relayed their work into high-circulation print venues at a steadier rate than those of more obscure boardinghouse backgrounds. In this one respect, middle-class boarder-authors enjoyed *more* name than plebeian members of the brotherhood. They were *more* functional by Foucault's terms, and so held greater rights of proprietary ownership and authorial image.

In their non-literary lives, however, boarder-authors were renters, not owners, and so to some extent had no name, no author function, even within those rooms that they occupied when they wrote the literary boardinghouse into being. Whatever partial, individual identity boarder-authors did possess was subsumed by the city household group that constituted their immediate surroundings. Washington, D.C., boarders provide a case in point. Known about town by their landlords' surnames—"Downson's crowd," for example, or "Coyle's family"[46]—capital city boarders, authors or not, blended with the "crowds" that were to be found indoors at their domestic residences. Like city-dwellers generally, they also adopted a virtual anonymity in a faceless urban context, where pedestrians' well-calculated public profiles amounted to little more than masks.[47] If non-authors were subject to this kind of city-specific loss of selfhood, then identity *theft* might not be too strong a word for the dis-ownership felt by boarder-authors, who had been left bereft of a home of their own, forsaken a personal name, and denied an identifying stamp for their completed works.

Boarder-authors in effect reattribute their texts to the houses where they were produced, leaving boardinghouse texts unattributed. This is no theoretical vacuum: so often do antebellum boarder-authors, even the middle classes among them, make boardinghouses the substance of their work that author, boarder, house, and text frequently blur. What emerges from this menage is as much a literary act as it is a finished literary artifact. As dispossessed boarder-authors themselves fade from view—joining the elusive modern act of boarding and the receding middle-class boardinghouse in an urban netherworld—boardinghouse texts seemingly begin to speak for themselves. Relying as they do on a narrator, narrative situation, and narrative setting that are all absent, boardinghouse letters become a kind of transparent commentary on big-city life. Seldom in boardinghouse texts is there on offer for readers a stable, definitive image of a believable big city; nor are the most basic of literary conventions reli-ably in place, so as to navigate readers through what little hint of a city there is. Obscuring the boardinghouse in print, then—and the archives are full of such imagined residences—is the comparative *dys*function of the middle-class boarder-author's author function.

Middle-class boarder-authors become one with their boardinghouse texts and contexts in three representative works on boarding from the period. These are Donald Grant Mitchell's (Ik Marvel's) *The Lorgnette, or, Studies of the Town by an Opera-Goer* (1855), Thomas Butler Gunn's *The Physiology of New York Boarding-Houses* (1857), and Oliver Wen-dell Holmes's *The Autocrat of the Breakfast-Table* (1858, discussed at length in chapter 3). Middle-class boarding, like working-class boarding, follows a standard script in writings devoted to boardinghouse life. The three works above provide the general outline of that script: well-read male (women, again, are rare) evinces a literary bent; said male begins boarding or continues to board, *by choice;* author-boarder situates him-self in city by turning his writer's eye to the very boardinghouse(s) that he occupies, commenting on its distinguishing features; boarder-author, boarding, and boardinghouse become indistinguishable, as disembodied writer retires from the foreground of his own account to a background that is predominantly occupied by the house itself.

Both the boarder-author and boarder-narrator are evicted as a result of this process, in what amounts to a human deferral of volition to the over-riding urban domestic interest that governs these texts. With time on their hands, and money in their pockets, fictional middle-class boarder-authors have arrived on the boardinghouse scene with few obligations save those that they might have to themselves. Boarding by choice, and not by necessity, they are not inclined to worry about next week's rent—or much anything else, for that matter—and so quickly, perhaps inevitably, deflect their otherwise unoccupied attentions from the relative predictability of self to the engaging distractions of society. "Society" in this case consists of an immediate metropolitan environment constructed for them by boarding. It is to these enveloping boardinghouse surroundings that they in turn devote themselves in the shape of casual literary exercises, which the middle-class boarder-narrators under discussion here submit to undertake on behalf of boarding. Written *in* a boardinghouse, their verbal renderings of a leisured boarder's life reverse the conventional roles of subject and object. The writer writes, but an ostensibly inanimate home assumes narrative control, inasmuch as readers must refer to whichever residence(s) impinges upon them for the ultimate source of character development, subtle shifts in perspective, and the larger arc of action. Lost in this narrative unfolding is the storytelling boarder-narrator, whose secondary domestic status is finally exposed by the controlling textual consciousness of boarding.

Mitchell's Ik Marvel persona relates such an exposure. Marvel writes of a well-to-do country gentleman acquaintance, who while wintering in New York wiles away the hours of his metropolitan residency by recording his impressions of town life in a mock correspondence with another friend named Fritz. Despite the oversupply of local authors, the acquaintance in question hopes to publish his account for the amusement of the public. Any amusement that he does manage to muster is attributable less to the condescending cleverness of his epistles than to the very boardinghouse where he decides to stay. Thinking "it would be a quiet place for my work," he earlier had decided upon a certain fourth boardinghouse that he inspected, and yet in due course he grows fixated with the activities of the other boarders who are present at his selected address.[48] Quiet enough, apparently, for him to lose himself in his "work," the boardinghouse that he chooses is also lively enough to unseat him from the center of his account. Specifically, the marital spats of the couple rooming next to him, the fashionable prattle of the landlady's female charges, and the free advice on town life from bachelor boarders all enter into our boarder-author's letters and gather a momentum of their own. City life outside the boardinghouse receives some treatment; so, too, does the opera of Mitchell's subtitle. But the opera glasses, or "lorgnette," of the main title might as well apply to the drama indoors at this particular boardinghouse: that is where our gentleman turns his telescopic gaze in between city-sketches, and this is where he focuses his attentions so long as no other business presses, which is to say, often. To settle upon a protagonist in Mitchell's "study," then, is to try to choose between a boardinghouse, a boarder-narrator, and a general assemblage of boarders that are to some extent inseparable.

Thomas Butler Gunn also collapses the gap between author and narrator in his adamantly first-person, nonfiction *Physiology*, with much the same result as Mitchell. The houses and boarders of his telling together assume the starring role that is normally reserved for such an able raconteur as Gunn's "I." Gunn predictably relates that it was the itch of authorship that first brought him to board. Like Marvel's man, he has passed through a preliminary phase in which his literary labors compel him to find a "quiet abode" where he can concentrate on his work. Unlike Marvel's opera-goer, he undertakes a variety of work best described as hackwork: "Parisian correspondence for two Sunday papers," serial romances, "testimonials for patent medicines, rhyming advertisements for a puffing tailor, and also . . . tracts for a religious Society" (148). Gunn is well past the mercenary stage of his career now, however. Thus, he opens his account with a dedication "To All Inmates of Metropolitan Boarding-Houses, . . . By an Ex-Member of the Fraternity." That "*Ex*-Member" status is the key to the account that follows. Gunn informs readers with these words that he currently lives and writes among the non-boarding middle classes, suggesting that he no longer needs to board and probably does not. That is not to say he can live without the boardinghouses that appear in his work. As a home owner, he has shed his dependence as boarder. As a literary professional, Gunn is all dependence, since he would cease to exist as author, or at least as a first-person narrator, without the boarding material that he parlays into print.

Gunn's "Ex-Member" status has another effect as well: there is real first-person authority in his varied snapshots of urban boarding, an immediacy that paradoxically sacrifices his very person to his greater subject, the modern city as experienced domestically. Gunn surveys the full range of New York boardinghouses and so elides himself from his own narration. He indiscriminately tastes boarding at its best and worst, from the "mean" and "cheap" to the "tiptop" house—something that neither Marvel's status-conscious observer nor Holmes's fastidious "Autocrat" would ever dare do. Gunn earns his authority through due diligence, then, and converts his wealth of boardinghouse experience into an aesthetic of overwhelm. That aesthetic relies on an unrelenting taxonomy of type after type of boardinghouse that occludes the typecaster in a roundabout way. There is, for example, the "Hand-to-Mouth Boarding-House," as well as the "Fashionable Boarding-House Where You Don't Get Enough to Eat." Gunn visits the "Artists' Boarding-House," the "Medical Students' Boarding-House," the "Serious Boarding-House," the "Vegetarian Boarding-House," and the "Boarding-House Where the Landlady Drinks." The list is almost endless. Gunn has inspected all of these establishments in quick succession, having made comprehensive inclusion the principle on which he proceeds. The end result is that Gunn displays much of a modern Manhattan that readers otherwise might spend a lifetime exploring, even as he manages to hasten himself out of a text that is finally too crowded for its own creator. Irretrievably trapped between houses—his is, he reminds us, a modern, "mutable generation, . . . unwilling to pause, ever jostling onward, considering nothing final"—he cedes first-person narrative privileges to the boarders and boardinghouses whose staggering multiplicity hampers the narrator in the competition for readers' attention (12).

It is an untoward outcome for a flaneur, for whom proper cognitive management of the modern metropolis is a (largely unpaid) profession. Gunn's *Physiology* indeed does derive from the flaneur tradition. The author was aware from his time on the Continent of serial newspaper feuilletons, which when collected together in full-length book form constitute the kind of flaneur's *physiology* that we have here. Rather than reward him with active perceptual mastery, however, the sheer bulk of Gunn's urban boardinghouse observations situates him in a passive epistemological position, and so denies him the close narrative control to which flanerie ideally aspires. Gunn might insist, then, that most boardinghouses are "sui generis," inasmuch as they take on the unique characteristics of their individual proprietors and occupants (15). But the jumble of houses and characters that he narrates suggests an urban domestic milieu where identity itself is less individual than interchangeable. As an ambitious boarder-narrator, Gunn is everywhere and everyone inside the pages of his *Physiology*. He achieves virtual omniscience in his exhaustive chronicle of all variety of boardinghouses. Not unlike the "generic" boarder, however, he is no one headed nowhere in particular, his glimpsed impressions of the city betraying too much of the fluster of a whirlwind urban tour to convince as a feuilleton. Gunn provides a visual corollary for the buffeting about of the anonymous modern metropolitan with an illustration from his book (figure 1.2).[49] His is a disturbing cartoon sketch of urban deracination, incarnate: a portable big-city boardinghouse is radically reduced to scale to fit inside a wheelbarrow; pushing forward headlong "To Posterity" with his load is a ridiculous grim reaper figure—a city rendition of Fate, for all practical purposes. "Home" has been diminutized, so that the omnipotent resident of Death dwarfs his domestic cargo. Yet,

**Figure 1.2.** Modern portable boarding. Both boarders and boardinghouses are diminutized in Gunn's *Physiology.*

the drawing intimates another dwarfing as well. Hovering over all of us, from the cradle to the grave, is the subordinating presence of metropolitan residence. Houses may be small in this picture, but boarders such as Gunn are even smaller.

It is no exaggeration to say that Gunn was but a minor player in the transatlantic drama of modernity. *Boardinghouse* drama more accurately describes the uncoordinated performances in which urbanization actually appeared as a dramatic spectacle for theatergoers in the English-speaking West. As a discrete literary genre, boardinghouse drama did in fact exist, and it was formative in the development of American boardinghouse letters both before and after the U.S. Civil War. From about the War of 1812 up through the end of the century, this generic subspecies allowed English and American audiences to enjoy at a once-remove a boarders' world that distilled to its essentials both the good and bad of urban experience. Boardinghouse dramas made light of the foibles and frustrations of boarders and boarding. They were farcical by default, and they found a large audience among pre-vaudevillian people who, because they most likely boarded by necessity, were eager to make light of their domestic travails with minimal psychic risks to themselves. There were no few selections from which playgoers could choose. These were mixed in terms of media, and fairly predictable in the prevailing message they disseminated: that the proper response to boarding's trials was laughter.

Entr'acte songs performed by the likes of the London stage actor Charles Mathews helped to condition boarder-spectators for such a response. Mathews's rollicking "Mrs. Bradish's Boarding House" invited listeners to consider what was risible in urban residence; their favorable response allowed the comedian to make repeated tours of the United States in the 1820s and 1830s, while he no doubt deepened his personal knowledge of urban itinerancy. The nation's immigrant beer halls and social clubs, meanwhile, provided an early, if temporary, home for the development of a rudimentary boardinghouse skit. Boarding even evolved into a full stage production when it took the form of the comic theatrical afterpiece. Englishman Samuel Beazley, to take the leading example, filled the seats of theaters for more than two decades with his *The Boarding-House; or, Five Hours at Brighton. A Musical Farce in Two Acts* (1811), which succeeded in humorously dramatizing boarding on both sides of the Atlantic. For their part, audiences responded to these divertissements with glee, and made boardinghouse productions a staple of playhouses in England and the United States well into the antebellum period.[50]

It is easy to see why boarding enjoyed such popular success as a dramatic art form. The years of boarding's ascendance, to begin, saw the rise of an urban genteel culture that transformed middle-class life itself into a series of self-conscious performance rituals. With class anxieties on the increase amid the ongoing reorganization of commercial markets and a developing industrial revolution, the precarious class status of a protobourgeoisie depended in no small measure on the middle-class aspirant's *acting* the proper part, only without the benefit of floodlights. The requisite props of bourgeois performance might include everything from "respectable" standards of dress and etiquette to the contemporary fad for stylish mourning rites and parlor theatricals.[51] In any case, whether at home, in city streets, or perhaps at the actual theater, modernity meant keeping up appearances and so implied a daily regimen of strategically crafted theatrics. With the equally dramatic growth of the metropolitan West, however, urban residents from across the hemisphere no longer could depend on the freestanding shelter as a performance space for gentility. Boarding was instead the stage on which many modern metropolitans performed "respectability," having cast themselves in their most coveted role. These years also witnessed brisk business generally at theaters in Europe and America. Historian Lawrence Levine goes so far as to name this period a golden age of democratic entertainments, with theaters drawing hundreds, even thousands of people from different class backgrounds to the same playhouses.[52] Many theatergoers were urban people eager to take advantage of the city's cultural resources; many urban people were boarders who had been drawn to city centers by the socioeconomic forces that governed the mid-nineteenth-century workplace. Thus, the playhouse and boardinghouse to some extent led a mutually sustaining existence. The audiences for the former were often the inhabitants of the latter, and vice versa, notwithstanding the fact that the leveling tendencies of the one seldom appeared as forcefully in the other.

With equal, convenient access to local theaters, city boarders not only frequented urban playhouses; they were a core constituency for period dramatic productions. The simple logistics of domesticity in part brought boarders to the stage. Considering how often they relocated from house to house, the transient, heterogeneous masses of boarders in places like London, Paris, New York, and Boston already had one collective foot out the door. These "poor undomesticated animals," as the New York playwright William K. Northall called them, not surprisingly took repeated refuge from their domestically challenged condition in theaters, where an evening's dramatic spectacle (and a de facto rented roof over their heads) substituted for the creature comforts of home. On any given night, boarder-theatergoers might even encounter a straightforward staging of an urban domestic world that they knew only too well, since the theater's paid players (often itinerants themselves) regularly performed pieces in which boarding at once provided the subject, setting, and pacing, as well as the formal organizing device for the drama on offer. Boarders also sought at contemporary playhouses something less tangible than a surrogate shelter or scenic dress rehearsals of their real lives. Hoping, said Northall, to stimulate what he presumed to be the deadened senses of their hearts without "homes," boarders often turned to the genre of drama for whatever affective rewards of human fellowship it might afford, no matter how contrived. Lacking access to the conventional setting of family feeling, in other words, boarders experienced their emotional lives *on the boards,* where they could exchange all or part of a day's wages for a dramatic rush of theatrically induced sensation.[53]

Contemporaries were explicit about boarding's dramatic possibilities, as the example of boarder-author Thomas Butler Gunn again illustrates. Before emigrating to America from London in 1849, Gunn apprenticed as a draughtsman under the esteemed architect and playwright Samuel Beazley. Beazley was also, we recall, the force behind that premier boardinghouse farce of 1811, *The Boarding-House; or, Five Hours at Brighton.*[54] However prolific he was, Beazley's motives for writing drama were chiefly mercenary: it was the means by which this designer of English theaters gainfully employed himself when not on architectural assignment. And yet something more than money led the man who was credited with the

creation of London's Lyceum (or English Opera House), and with reno-
vating its renowned Drury Lane Theater, to alternate between building
houses of drama to dramatizing, in his very first production, the promising
dramatic material of boardinghouses. Beazley's instincts proved instructive for his protégé, Gunn, who devoted a full chapter to the "Theatrical
Boarding-House" in his *Physiology*.[55] There, the younger boarder-author
reports that the New York actors of his acquaintance manifest an ardent
enthusiasm for boarding; specifically, these professional exhibitionists
domesticate with great satisfaction at a boardinghouse located not far
from Broadway, where the landlady's daughter "never closed doors," and
the landlady herself made no attempt "to screen the system—or rather
want of it" that characterized life inside her shabby establishment (76–
77). As Gunn and company realized, the domestic *was* dramatic, all the
more so in settings that practically lacked a curtain of concealment. There
were, in effect, no curtains in the cramped city-spaces of the boardinghouse. Set out on semi-public display, boarders enrolled themselves by
circumstance in a dramatic mise-en-scène, as an anonymous columnist
observed in 1843:

> If you have a desire to study man in all his varieties, throw away
> Shakespeare and put down stakes in a boardinghouse. More life—
> real genuine scenes—may be witnessed at one of these places during
> a period of twenty-four hours than at a tavern or other place of
> promiscuous resort.[56]

In open acknowledgment of contemporary drama's indebtedness to
the urban domestic, the writers of Gunn's metropolitan milieu sustained
a Beazleyan tradition when they conflated playhouse and boardinghouse.
To take but one example, the English actress-turned-playwright Anna
Cora Ritchie located her novel *Evelyn* (1845) at a fashionable New York
boardinghouse. Her female narrator accounts on cue for her choice of
residence by confessing to a "fondness" for the intensive "study of human
nature."[57] Donald Grant Mitchell's principal *Lorgnette* boarder undertakes a similar "study" by dividing his time between a boardinghouse in
Manhattan and an opera box that presumably stands but a few blocks
distant from his home address. Gunn also cedes center stage in his work
to an assemblage of boarder-players; their self-aggrandizing presence
within *Physiology* reduces the author-narrator Gunn to the occupancy
of a supporting role in his own text. Again and again in boardinghouse
letters, boarding itself—and the city it figures—is at once the *donnée* and
the very source of the drama.

Oliver Wendell Holmes's urbane "Autocrat" is a veritable master in the urban art of boardinghouse drama. A consummate monologist, and a tenured metropolitan, the Autocrat is not as easily overshadowed by the theatrical surroundings of his Boston boardinghouse as are the comparably unseasoned city-dwellers in works by Mitchell and Gunn silenced by domestic Manhattan. The Autocrat does not completely dominate the proscenium that is his text, however. Both complementing and countering his forceful expression are the unsolicited comments of his breakfast-table messmates. Their verbal assertiveness is the conversational equivalent of boarding, a vox populi response to the physical-cultural phenomenon (whether a larger-than-life housemate, or a whole metropolis) with which they must learn to coexist. Holmes began his popular "Autocrat" series in the early issues of the new *Atlantic Monthly* magazine in 1857. By the time he collected his sketches—all of which revolve around a late middle-aged, first-person narrator's extended residence at a midrange Boston boardinghouse—he had assumed immense stature in the literary and intellectual life of antebellum America for his contributions to both medicine and belles lettres. His Autocrat is fittingly big as a result: learned, literary, wealthy, opinionated, and inclined to hold forth at common meals on the most esoteric of subjects, even if his fellow boarders often vacate the dining room unnoticed during his rhetorical performances. The Autocrat's fellow boarders will have their say, and do. As one of Holmes's recent critics argues, they prevent the most seasoned speaker among them from monopolizing table talk by repeatedly interrupting his abortive monologues with impertinent questions or digressions. A divinity student, a female schoolteacher, a waggish young clerk, and an improbably named Ben Franklin, the landlady's precocious ten-year-old son, thus contain the Autocrat's loquaciousness, while also ensuring that the conversation at their household flows in fluid modern style.[58] On a lark, the gentlemanly Autocrat has resorted to boarding merely for a change of domestic scenery; he requires not room and board, but a desired change in the conversational content of his life. This, too, eludes him in the end, because the lower-middle-class boarders with whom he resides are at best a reluctant audience for his daily narrations. Boarders and boarding once more prevail in the running contest for readers' attention. As with many an individual boarder-narrator before him, the Autocrat is less a controlling presence in his text than a notably vocal member of a boardinghouse collective. He has words enough, but lacks an autonomous will of his own.

Notwithstanding their dramatic attributes, then, and despite the voluble confidence of their comparatively prosperous narrator-creators, popular middle-class accounts of metropolitan residence from the period suffer from much the same silencing as their boardinghouse protagonists. Boarding by its very nature positioned antebellum practitioners in a state of cohabitational codependence beyond the pale of a midcentury domestic ideal that celebrated single-family occupancy. This was the case at the upper echelons of urban domestic gentility, where even boardinghouses that were well-appointed and amply provided contradicted the consensual understanding of "home." It was also true at the lower register of run-of-the-mill establishments, where writers more residentially challenged than the likes of Gunn, Mitchell, and Holmes wrote of common modern domestic woes. Urban America's domestic dreams having been deferred indefinitely, boardinghouse texts regularly function without a central, acknowledged consciousness from which readers can receive fully rendered, "proprietary" representations of the city in literature. In other words, because boarding as a social practice postpones the literal-legal ownership of "home," boarding as a literary form naturally gravitates toward a grammatically passive position from which the figurative apprehension of the city as a cultural construct is regularly frustrated. It was a frustration born of relative deprivation. Since few but a domestic elite would ever hold unencumbered title to freestanding urban households of their own, it stands to reason that many boardinghouse texts should structure themselves around the very structure whose glaring absence was the precondition of boarding. What's missing from most boardinghouse texts is the narrative coherence and control that had been omitted from the lives of many boarders, who, as urban object-occupants, and not subject-owners, to some extent had been left to the mercy of the city environs that surrounded them.

Dependent and deprived, middle-class boarder-narrators nevertheless inhabit texts in which chronic domestic dissatisfaction rarely acquires personal urgency. Gone in most instances from the middles-class account of urban adaptation is the hungry search for food, shelter, and literary dignity that not infrequently imparts to boarding's working-class discursive form the immediacy that would attend narrations of first-person struggle. Middle-class boarder-authors such as Mitchell, Gunn, and Holmes do share their reflections on urban residence, but, as complacent members of the bourgeoisie, they long since have ceased to struggle. They instead supply for their semi-autobiographical boardinghouse texts first-person narrators who have reached that stage in an author's life where material concerns over basic human necessities no longer constitute pressing questions. Their narrators are comfortably enough situated that they can afford to abandon the proverbial search for bread and butter, and so entertain more abstracted investigations into the complexities of the metropolitan condition. This abstractedness does not cause middle-class boarder-authors to turn irretrievably inward, however. They utilize the learning and leisured resources of their unhurried narrators as a storytelling convenience: to observe, for observation's sake, any boardinghouses and boarders that offer themselves for inspection; and to assemble, for art's sake, enough running commentary on the urban domestic scene at hand to warrant boarding's becoming a legitimate basis for literature. Much of this commentary is subordinate to boarding, of course. With seemingly so much to say, and with such deep economic and intellectual resources at their disposal, middle-class boarder-authors cannot escape the literal and figurative city confines from which they, like the majority of renter-writers, must compose urban prose and verse. Many boarder-authors appear as a result as little more than afterthoughts in the tales they tell. Their shadowy figures remain in most boardinghouse texts; otherwise, the imposing figures of a house, housing, and the housed combine to remove them from narrative view.

Hence the literary-historical problem with which this section began. Because boarders and boarding assert themselves so forcefully into the antebellum discourse of urban modernity, one would expect them to have had a noticeable impact on contemporary literature. Boarding did transform American life and letters during the middle decades of the nineteenth century, but it did so in ways that are not so easily detected. On the one hand, conventional courtesy bound houses to genteel standards of humility. Any house, boarding establishments included, that pretended to inclusion in polite society was expected to conceal its everyday domestic operations from the watchful eyes of the public. Propriety bid the boardinghouse to hide. On the other hand, and as we have seen, boarder-authoring itself was an exercise in self-concealment for the scores of urban peoples whose respective subjectivities necessarily deferred, both practically and dramatically, to the cities that enveloped them. As a nondescript landmark of the larger urban landscape, or else as an inconspicuous platform for personal discursive commentary on the city, the boardinghouse has lost its deserved spot on the modern metropolitan map. Lacking the grandeur of the panoramic "bird's-eye" views so common in antebellum writing, wanting the visceral appeal of "mole's-eye" examinations of subterranean street life,[59] the more mundane boardinghouse has been absorbed into the city in literature. Despite, or maybe *because* of, the intense scrutiny expended on urban America as it stood during the two decades prior to the Civil War,[60] the boardinghouse dissolves into the larger literary city.

As a vantage point for external observations of that city, and as an internal stage on which to act out the drama of urban close-quartering, the boardinghouse permits close conceptual management of a modern metropolis that otherwise has proved resistant to simplification through literature. Donald Grant Mitchell's boardinghouse distractions, Thomas Butler Gunn's boardinghouse crowding, Oliver Wendell Holmes's boardinghouse intrusions all suggest the city, but without the grit and grime of the city per se that postbellum writers later would bring to a subsequent realist urban aesthetic. Upon meeting such domestic suggestions in print, readers could and can take the short figurative step that allows one small part of the antebellum city, the boardinghouse, to represent synecdochally the city as a whole. Just as the horizons of boarder-authors (or their narrators) sometimes extend no further than the boardinghouse door of their rented rooms, the boardinghouse often becomes a complex substitute for the real city outside those doors: setting, metaphor, figure, trope, point of view, and more, and all at once.

Returning to the literary-historical record, then, one might say that the metropolitan boardinghouse, in print, performed its intended cultural work all too well. After summoning the city, the figure of boarding enacts a discursive version of the bait-and-switch: having attracted our attention, it recedes behind the cover of a seductive distraction, in this case the self-advertising sensations of the urban as recorded in writing. To invoke another analogy, one might say that readers of and for the antebellum city in literature fall victim to an urban reversal of the forest-for-the-trees scenario. They lose sight of the figure of boarding by shifting their attentions to the greater metropolitan context within which a truly modern residential mindset originally occurred. Sign and signifier are where they should be. It is the would-be reader of the boardinghouse who is amiss. Only by adjusting our critical lenses can we properly evaluate boarding on its own expressive terms.

In the end, boardinghouse letters form an American mythology in their own right. It is by way of the boardinghouse that the original U.S. urban archetype, Mose, the Bowery b'hoy of antebellum print and stage, brought city streets into the nation's folklore. It is the boardinghouse where New York's German immigrants, seasoned New World boarders, set their amateur beer-hall farces in a smiling celebration of *volk*-life. William Dean Howells, spokesman for American literary realism, unveiled the nation's Gilded Age city at a mother-daughter–run boardinghouse in his novel *A Hazard of New Fortunes* (1890). More recently, twentieth-century playwright Tennessee Williams added a touch of tragedy to boarding in plays that remind his countrymen that we are all, in a sense, American boarders, a people passing through. It is also the boardinghouse, doubling as a haunted house, where Nobel laureate author Toni Morrison sets her second full-length work, *Sula* (1973), updating a national discourse on race with a revival of an American obsession with boarding.[61]

To acknowledge the importance of literary boarding is not to recast the canon, necessarily. Yet, such an acknowledgment should encourage scholars to clean academic house, as it were. Some thirty years of accumulated scholarship on the domestic sentimental has revealed much about the contemporary discursive conventions of home. There nevertheless remains much work to be done in explaining the relation between "home" and "house," or boardinghouse, to be exact. Beyond house and home, moreover, there remains another critical connection to be drawn as scholars rethink the forms and functions of mid-nineteenth-century American literature—namely, the extent to which readers and writers of the age cognitively collapsed the categories of boarding, the urban, the modern, and the metropolis. This project marks the start of that collapse, and it proceeds by restoring to literary boarding some small share of its former glory.

Chapter 2

# Rhetorical Boarding and the Limits of Domesticity

> I left a home, a peaceful home,
> With every comfort stored,
> Thinking no troubles e'er would come
> If I but went—"*to board!*"

However close was their connection, boardinghouse life and letters had another near neighbor in mid-nineteenth-century domestic convention. The pervasive idiom and ideology of "home," by which contemporaries reified their greatest residential expectations, touched not only the style and content of the period's orthodox domestic literatures; they influenced the terms of reception accorded boarding in its early metropolitan context, and continue to this day to set the parameters by which we read the boardinghouse. Impeccably kept, closely knit, prosperous but not luxurious, built less for market production than home consumption, and graced with a narrowly conceived maternal presence devoted to light housework and the raising of children—the model midcentury home of domestic discourse represented for many Americans, boarders among them, what Richard Brodhead calls a "new middle-class paradigm ['emerging'] in the decades around 1830."[1] Represented as well by this "paradigm" was an idealized focal point for much of antebellum literature.

Notwithstanding home's wide cultural reach, the discourse of boarding complicates Americans' comfortable understanding of the domestic. Boarder-authors did not necessarily bridge the obvious distance between the undomestic trials of boarding and the idealizing strains of domesticity—this, despite the domestic trappings of numerous boardinghouse texts, and regardless of the close dialectic connection that pertains between boarding as a social behavior and as a literature. Nina Baym rightly reminds us that there is no "preexisting domestic scene" to which readers of even the most cogent domestic texts might have returned in their discursive canvassing of the antebellum residential landscape. Rather, the function of period domestic thinking, and writing, as manifested in what she styles *Woman's Fiction* for the years 1820–1870 was to "theorize" and so "create" an imagined household space into which poured the explanations and consolations sought by a citizenry that was undergoing the tense consolidation stage of urban-industrial class formation.[2] If the popular expressions of domesticity that were to be found in period fiction and home-management manuals were wanting in the way of verisimilitude,[3] they did provide safe reassurance for readers that a particular bourgeois brand of domestic sanctuary was available. The discourse of boarding by contrast seems calculated to highlight the residential obstacles that many more Americans faced en route to their longed-for attainment of home.

Indeed, for all its thematic overlap with the domestic, discursive boarding finally shifts its interests away from home altogether, and reveals assorted narrative strategies quite out of keeping with the mollifying tenets and tendencies of a resilient domestic faith. At a glance, boarding suggests the inverse image of a home that many nineteenth-century authors (whether prescriptively, optimistically, half-heartedly, or skeptically) attempted to write into being. A closer inspection of rhetorical boarding, however, reveals a discourse with designs upon readers neither the cause nor effect of which meaningfully involved the domestic at all. Boarding's forms and functions were oriented toward the cities of the then-future, not the homes of the impossible present or past. Boarding's designs, that is to say, were modern, metropolitan, and comprise not an enthralled response to the domestic but a separate conversational sphere. With federal census data for Manhattan alone revealing a national boarder population that, by 1850, was large enough to have surpassed in size many an actual city,[4] it is only natural that Americans should have participated in the development of a discourse that was so closely attuned to the shared manners and mindsets of hundreds of thousands of urban itinerants for whom a socially sanctioned and safely settled mode of inhabitance was unavailable. As we have seen, discursive boarding spoke both directly and indirectly to the interests of the nation's boardinghouse peoples. Boarding accordingly flourished in the American popular press, on stage, and in books bound for commercial publication. Despite their similarly compounding (in the domestic tradition) material facts and verbal fictions, then, these respective boardinghouse expressions of the changing metropolitan meanings of home together amount to something more than a mere subgenre to literary domesticity. Boardinghouse letters are not simply a negative measure of Americans' capacity to adapt to a new urban habitat, despite the chorus of concerns that arises in an admittedly large body of boardinghouse writing over matters deceptively domestic: inflated rental rates, insufferable housemates, and shifting standards of middle-class respectability in the emergent cities of the United States, to name but a few. Boarding, rather, with its straitened city conceptions of narrative time and space, represents a distinctively untraditional literary tradition. As a discourse, it occupies an urban place apart from the comparatively prolix domestic novel, and subverts rather than supports the contested separate sphere that legions of house-bound women therein occupy.[5]

Embedded in the domestic, literary boarding challenges the basic premises of domesticity, and signals the American beginnings of a modernity that mandated radically different urban dimensions for the human temporal-spatial condition. Practically, by securing such vast self-reflexive descriptive space on page and stage, boardinghouse letters in effect legitimated a behavior, boarding, that not a few contemporaries deemed anathema to their vision of an inhabitable United States. No doubt it is tempting to read boarders' constant complaints of the domestic shortcomings that they endured as an endorsement of precisely what boarding was not—an elusive household refuge, sole title to which many residential renters could not and would not achieve in their increasingly urban lifetimes. Yet, the poetry and prose of boarding, like the words reserved for boardinghouse accommodations in the era's city directories, newspaper advertisements, private journals, and personal correspondence, in part rebut the socially constructed prize of private home ownership that so many of the day's Americans struggled to secure. Perceptually, boarders endured struggles all their own. Modern urbanization met them with an immediacy that was unknown by many of their countrymen. Boarders, in turn, began to interpret their new urban world in ways that must have been almost unimaginable for independent home owners, rural dwellers, and those who otherwise opposed metropolitan change. Rhetorically, boarders found ample expression for their alternate experience of cities with a literature that, by the antebellum period, had assumed a tone and texture distinct from the forceful conventions of a never dominant domestic discourse. Superficially domestic in its external features, literary boarding possesses forward-looking forms and functions that reach well beyond the discursive norms of domesticity. This chapter explores those forms and functions at the peak of boardinghouse letters' popularity during the heavily domesticated decades before the U.S. Civil War.

✦

To restore boarding to its rightful place among the language and
literatures of the antebellum United States is first to confront what contemporaries themselves signified by that all-important term, "home." It
was a word fraught with competing meanings throughout the nineteenth
century. Richard P. Horwitz, for example, in his study of early industrial
life at Lowell, Massachusetts, finds that residents of metropolitan Boston
during the late first half of the nineteenth century suffered much cognitive confusion in attempting to relate their tentative understanding of the
domestic to the surrounding built environment. Locals used labels like
"structure" and "establishment" interchangeably to designate buildings
of a public nature: factory, church, city hall, courthouse, school, and jail
all fall under this rubric. Meanwhile, the private "dwelling house" signified as a unique category of its own, since it often implied a degree of
privacy, permanence, and familial comfort that generally was thought to
be missing from other area "structures." The question of domestic terminology involves more than a simple public/private dichotomy, however.
Boarding, after all, brought public and private into close correspondence
in its daily operations, in the process creating the semi-private spaces by
which boarding was widely known. It was also the case that the supposedly private "dwelling house" passed in New England parlance as a
catchall phrase for everything from country homes and urban townhouses
to mechanics' quarters, communal-style factory dormitories, and Irish
shanties.[6] Such loose domestic vernacular provides evidence that naming a "home" could be almost as difficult as owning or occupying one.
What this brief verbal survey likewise suggests is that regional Boston's
domestic/linguistic indecision was no anomaly. It was indicative of an
unsettled domestic condition endemic to the new metropolis at America's
mid-nineteenth century. On this shaky foundation was built a set of literary conventions that we now identify (with equal, increasing uncertainty)
under the domestic label.

Much as antebellum Americans stumbled upon the nomenclature
of "home," scholars, too, have continued in recent decades to interrogate basic domestic terms, chronologies, and taxonomies. At stake in
their competing socio-literary accounts of the timing and temper of an
alleged nineteenth-century nationwide triumph of evolving middle-class
household norms are the matters of whether, when, and why a generation of U.S. women was tied physically, emotionally, and socially to a
home over which it held sovereign feminine sway. Closely related to the
domestic debate is the question of sentiment, the posited *–ism* of which
has sustained lively commentary over a supposed revolution in feeling
that contemporary women may or may not have staged in a separate

domestic sphere reserved for them (by choice? compulsion? necessity?) beyond the pale of male supervision. Framing both debates, domestic and sentimental, is the complex relationship of gender and power. Critical consideration of what domesticated women were free to accomplish—or, conversely, prevented from venturing because of their sexual identification as homemakers—has yielded a range of opposing viewpoints which, in the current academic climate, are unlikely to harmonize anytime soon.[7]

This domestic-sentimental impasse carries implications for the field, and for boarding. On the one hand, the ongoing debate over domesticity has led scholars to reassess the literary-historical discourses of home in refreshing ways. Nineteenth-century metropolitans' loss of habitational security has been our own interpretive gain in this respect. On the other hand, a general climate of domestic questioning permits this study to depart in purposeful ways from the domestic altogether. So redundant has the domestic question become that it is now possible to reject a formerly serviceable heuristic like separate spheres, as did the contributors to a special number of the journal *American Literature* some years ago.[8] In the continuing absence of an accepted replacement paradigm for home, it is in other words an opportune moment to shift the scholarly discussion of the antebellum United States. Boarding affords such a paradigm shift. However implicated it is by the domestic, however dependent it may be for its distinctive qualities, conventions, and contradictions on the lived experience of city cohabitation, the discourse of boarding alters the very nature of the debate that is domesticity. Under a boardinghouse analysis, antebellum America emerges from the shadow of home's limited conceptual context. This same boardinghouse perspective reveals the nation's defining ties to modern urbanization, a whole congeries of cultural forces that extend beyond home to indicate far larger changes underway in the Western world.

Committed as the academy is to revising the semiotic system of home, even the most informed commentators have assigned boarding a marginal place within the reigning, if internally riven, domestic paradigm. Boarding rarely receives mention in the scholarship on domesticity; if treated, it has been misread as a mere inflection of domestic discourse.[9] This chapter proposes that boarding in its modern rhetorical forms carries none of the features that we associate with domestic orthodoxy, and so disqualifies itself from participating in an abiding conversation on home. At the very least, boardinghouse letters underwrite the willingness of revisionist scholars to entertain a more open view of the American nineteenth century's domestic and discursive practices. Not all antebellum boarders, authors, and readers renounced domesticity outright. Some of them persisted in trying to harness a parochial understanding of home to whatever residence they could find and afford. Yet, the domestic of which boarders usually discoursed referenced something other than the home that previous Americans had known. What boarders thought and spoke and wrote about contributed to the construction of an idiom designed specifically for cities. Boarding to this extent helped to image forth the nation's early metropolis.

Americans' literary interest in the city did not begin with boarding; boarding simply elaborated a nation's earlier halting attempts through the medium of words to grapple with urban changes so profound that they stretched existing discourses to their limits. Boarding as an art form does indeed mark a point of departure from the domestic. But boarding-house letters also suggest how closely the cultural categories of city and domesticity were already bound even before the period upsurge in modern metropolitan writing. Author Maria Cummins's *The Lamplighter* (1854) provides but one illustration of the domestic's regular attempts to confront (rather than deny) the city in literature. As Nina Baym writes, Cummins's best-selling novel is at once "domestic" and "metropolitan," since it features a female protagonist who navigates social "relations" and "spaces" that include both idealized evocations of home and the most forlorn of working-class Boston's urban boardinghouses.[10]

Classic domestic texts such as *The Lamplighter* nevertheless pursue narrative paths that finally lead away from the city. No matter that more than a few of the young heroines who feature in these works are urban-born and bred; their sentimental passage into responsible adulthood often substitutes the specificity of the city with a kind of placeless abstraction. The general trajectory of these characters' moral development tends toward a quasi-utopian pastoral middle ground, and suggests a cyclical city-country movement that Susan Warner's equally best-selling *The Wide, Wide World* (1850) epitomizes. That novel's young heroine, Ellen Montgomery, finds herself upon story's opening in Manhattan. From there she literally heads for the hills to reside with relatives in the country, making the occasional trip to the nearest small town or to visit friends off in locations still more obscure than her own. By novel's end, she has landed across the Atlantic in Edinburgh, where she resolutely awaits her return to American rural parts. Mirroring Warner's own life, Ellen's city-country migrations replicate those of many fictional domestic women besides. The genre might recognize social phenomena like urbanization.[11] It might accumulate sharp descriptive detail ahead of a later local color literary tradition. Yet, the antebellum domestic novel shows none of the timely treatment of external society that we find in boardinghouse writings. Domestic letters face inward, not outward. They distinguish themselves by the strength of their commitment to emotional interiority—of authors, narrators, characters, and readers, for whom the relation of home's poetry and prose to the city was often little more than an afterthought. Cities typically figure an antithetical image in the domestic canon, since domesticity itself was as much an antidote to the dislocations attendant on market revolution, full-scale urbanization, and class formation as it was a mimetic attempt to faithfully represent the "real" conditions of the mid-nineteenth-century United States. Thus, the lack of urban icons in the pantheon of period domestic texts is no coincidence. From the Kentucky slave cabin of Harriet Beecher Stowe's Uncle Tom, to New England village life as rendered by authors Catharine Maria Sedgwick, Lydia Maria Child, and Sarah Josepha Hale, and on to the eponymous Gothic mansion from Nathaniel Hawthorne's Salem-based *The House of the Seven Gables* (1851), the home of antebellum narrative seldom had much use for cities, save as a convenient storytelling foil for would-be ex-urban peoples.

Boarding accordingly evolved its own store of literary conventions apart from (and in opposition to) those of domesticity. On the one hand, given that boarding as an urban discourse was so close an outgrowth of boarding as a behavior, it had behind it the hard facts of history that other genres lacked. Domestic letters, at least in their formulaic phase, never enjoyed such consistent material support. On the other hand, domesticity held no monopoly on interiority. Not a few boarders and boarder-authors evince a complex psychology of the city derived from their collective encounters with urban residence. To be sure, there was little romance in the stressful ritual of near-simultaneous renting and relocating, and yet that ritual just as surely touched boarders personally, and deeply. Pressed by a relentless quest for adequate, affordable housing, practitioners were subject to a psychic state that gauged time, space, and human action in urban fractions that figured modernity. This very serial instability reappeared in the scattered discussions that boarders conducted, in print, on their unsettled metropolitan existence. That existence differed markedly from conventional household aspirations, as boarders' vagabond forms of expression demonstrate. For many Americans, some boarders among them, the discourse of home held happiness to be the successful pursuit of a restrictive conception of habitat. Boarders by and large pursued a different rhetorical route, one decidedly urban. As an alternative genre of residential writing, boarding was therefore brief where domestic letters were long. It was rushed when domesticity was dilatory. It was formally varied—"novel" as an adjective, not a noun—when and where literary domesticity in the main favored expansive prose narration. Boarding, above all, was the grammatical tense of tomorrow's cities, while home was an anachronism of untenable domestic perfection from the past.

By crystallizing certain modern compromises that we now associate with city living, boardinghouse literature defined a strange new urban experience for hundreds of thousands of mid-nineteenth-century Americans. These people may or may not have actually boarded, but enough of them resorted to *literary* boarding to imaginatively inhabit a U.S. city whose historical emergence at once left everything and nothing to the imagination. Compounding this paradox was one that masses of boarders resolved through rhetoric: rather than aspire to be *At Home in the City*, to borrow the title of Betsy Klimasmith's study of the domestic literatures of modern urban consciousness, Americans during the middle decades of the nineteenth century followed the example of the boarder-flaneur, and warmed at once to the tangible, psychological, and literary possibilities of a modernity that, when it arrived in full, fundamentally altered Western culture's understanding of settledness. As they moved along a continuum of urban residence, Americans once had tried to apply an ascendant domestic discourse to the cities that surrounded them. That effort failed because of a poor rhetorical fit: home was simply not adaptable enough a conceptual category to encompass the metropolis. Later, with the 1860s arrival of multistoried apartment buildings, boarding was no longer the likeliest route for many Americans to the food, shelter, and related domestic necessities that they required to survive in the city.[12] With that evolution in shelter came a change of discourse as well. *Apartment Stories* is Sharon Marcus's identifying phrase for the urban literatures from this subsequent period, years that saw Europeans, especially, develop expressive correlatives for habitational circumstances that earlier had given rise to boarding. But it was during the antebellum period proper, a protracted escalation stage of urban development in the United States, when boardinghouse letters found their own unique form. In the process, boarding broke ground on which high literary modernism eventually would rise, and where an ever-more outdated domestic discourse would falter, if not fall.

✦

Boardinghouse letters superficially suggest an almost pathological domestic pessimism among Americans of the age. Indeed, not a few contemporary householders speak as if some cherished residential essential were being irretrievably lost at midcentury. It is, then, tempting to read boarding as less a literature than a compound domestic question: do boardinghouses qualify as homes at all, and, if so, how? Many an American boarder would have responded with a vague but popular notion that a fortunate few of the nation's home owners thrived in a way that they never would. The sometime boarder Walt Whitman revealed the morbid core of these fears in a New York newspaper piece from 1856. There, he states that "it is in some sense true that a man is not a whole or complete man unless he *owns* a house and the ground it stands on." Where that left women, Whitman does not say. Where that left renters, as distinct from the domestically independent, he summarizes in the response that he supposedly received from a "little girl" when he asked her where her parents lived. "They don't *live;* they BOARD," she declares, nonchalantly recalling an urban America sadly lacking in single-unit homes but boasting boardinghouses in abundance.[13]

Boarding in the above passage, and in countless comparable examples from the period, has become a kind of vacant mise-en-scène, with Whitman almost resigned like his specious child to the approximate death-in-life to be had there. It is a grim diagnosis for a romantic poet, and an uncharacteristic moment of analytic detachment. But for readers on the receiving end of Whitman's bleak editorial, it would have represented a familiar strain of domestic discourse: the writer contains the apparent threat of boarding by subjecting it to a predicate position within his own grammar, and assigning it inferior status within the narrow residential limits of his own worldview. True to the discursive form of domesticity, home exceeds its allotted space in Whitman's column, despite its being in absentia. Home must be all or nothing in his account. Even the pursuit of an elusive household ideal has been abandoned here, since our writer prescribes as a cure for residential sickness precisely what boarders wanted, in the negative sense of that word—"a house and the ground it stands on." What Whitman has done is to redact into the mouth of a "little girl" the common literary posture, and predicament, of a domesticity that by and large disapproved of the mature urban boarder. Whitman provides two of these latter residential types in the persons of the girl's parents. Rather, he lends boarding voice only by proxy, in the juvenile shape of a daughter whose parents are as absent as the "home" they presumably cannot afford to purchase. Their very words, it should be noted, represent less an urban boarder's sensibility than a meek simulation of domesticity. Domestic time, meanwhile, improbably stands still in the parents' interminable urban boardinghouse interim. They would "live" if they could, but, like so many of their modern metropolitan peers, they are fated to wait and so "BOARD" on nondescript "ground." Trapped as much in residential exile as they are by domestic rhetoric, the boarders of Whitman's world know only a cold domestic comfort.

Perhaps no writer better captured the general dread of boardinghouse malaise than Sarah Josepha Hale. As the well-known author of a series of domestic manuals and moralizing fictional works like *Keeping House and House Keeping* (1845), the conservative Hale had made a national name for herself as editor of the successful women's magazine *Godey's Lady's Book*. Hale knew America's cities, having lived and worked both in Boston and Philadelphia. She had boarded briefly. And, in her novella *"Boarding Out": A Tale of Domestic Life* (1846), she portrays a model home whose antithesis is, in her narrator's estimation, the very boardinghouse that Hale long since had forsworn. Her "Tale" opens in Boston a few days before Christmas. Husband and wife Robert and Hepsy Barclay sit in their stand-alone home discussing an "experiment" in boarding that Mrs. Barclay has conceived after a domestic "flare up" between Polly and Sally, the cook and chambermaid, respectively. A mother of three, Mrs. Barclay sees two benefits to boarding: one, she estimates boarding to come to half the cost of maintaining one's own residence; and two, she envisions boarding as a remedy for what she calls the "annoyances" occurring underneath her own roof. For his part, Mr. Barclay has no delusions. The "economy" of boarding is a myth, he says, boarding being *more* expensive than housekeeping by his calculations. He also suspects that his wife naively looks to boarding as a "panacea" for all that ails a middle-class housewife of her standing (7–9). He rhapsodizes in defense of home:

> And so you feel no reluctance, wife, to giving up this convenient house, with its finely-warmed apartments; the bathing apparatus; the library, with its shelves so laden with books ... ; the conveniences of good closet-room, and those spare chambers, where your friends are so well accommodated; the commodious yard, the fine prospect of the surrounding country, and all the many advantages which this residence possesses, and which you were so anxious I should procure? (13)

Next comes the anticipated diatribe against boarding, which a particular strain of the domestic genre had made de rigueur. Mr. Barclay describes a boardinghouse as follows:

> where the house is another's, where you are circumscribed in room, where the children are apt to be kept in one apartment, and, instead

of hospitality, no friends can or will more than call; besides, the . . .
dire uncertainty of getting apartments where a comfortable home and
a pleasant landlady, and agreeable boarders are all combined. (13)

Despite these warnings, Mrs. Barclay prevails. The family sells its house
and boards out.

The outcome is predictable. Events unfold, in fact, as an irresistibly tragic didactic rite by which readers might release themselves from
boarding through so many tears shed, or worse, so much blood spilt.
Plot complications threaten at the outset as the Barclays scramble in
their search for suitable boardinghouse quarters. Heavy foreshadowing
obtrudes onto a compressed residential narration which, under rhetorical
circumstances more receptive to (and favorable toward) the urban, would
yield happier results. This is not a boarder-flaneur's story, however. Thus,
the Barclays locate their first boarding establishment with much difficulty.
Once found, this home proves insufficient; so the family (what's left of it)
breaks up house and moves again, finally relocating to an expensive hotel
as "permanent" boarders. Adding irony to injury, Hale has the Barclays
leave their two sons with a relation in the country, so as to minimize the
impact of several internal urban migrations that already have taken their
toll. The Barclays never settle: wife grows idle and vain, developing a taste
for fashionable suppers and balls in the hotel lobby; husband neglects
work, avoids meals in, and spends more and more time at the bar downstairs;[14] and the youngest Barclay, a three-year-old "homesick little girl,"
intones throughout, "Mamma, I want to go home" (102). Fatally, no one
heeds the youngest child. Boardinghouse life has Mr. and Mrs. Barclay
too distracted to listen. Mr. Barclay's career then founders.[15] The child
sickens and dies. Mrs. Barclay repents, as a scolding narrator admonishes
middle-class matrons "to find 'domestic happiness,' in the old-fashioned
sense of the word . . . at one's fireside," not at a modern metropolitan
boardinghouse (103).

Hale's is a familiar antebellum formula, in which home is less a fully
realized literary depiction than an abstract conception of "domestic happiness." Hers is a formula, moreover, that registers urban habitation as a
species of trauma: home for Hale can hurt those who transgress a certain
vaunted residential values structure. To read *Boarding Out* as a written
record of those values is to encounter an antebellum domestic imagination
in which boarding possessed the literal capacity to kill, and in which the
conventional alternative to boarding was worth dying for—so long as the
final laying to rest was suitably "domestic," and occurred "at one's [own]
fireside." Not all of the authors who defended the domestic on anything

remotely resembling these terms were prepared to write to such extremes. Walt Whitman, for one, generously spares the lives of his boardinghouse protagonists, despite situating his parent-boarders in a terminally neutral residential zone. Hale's suggestion, by contrast, is at once more grim but less pessimistic: in her reckoning, the modern American homesteader at least has a home to return to after passing through the worst of boarding, even after surviving the horrors of the morgue. Hers was not a consensus view, necessarily. Yet, the many literary texts that match the pattern of *Boarding Out* do capture the dire tenor in which discursive, domestic deliberations over urban boarding once occurred. In answer to the perennial domestic question, "Do boardinghouses qualify as home?" such texts respond with a resounding "no."

However prevalent, these and similar expressions of contemporary domesticity misrepresent boarding as a functional literary form. Boarding as it appears in the examples from Whitman and Hale has been enlisted to perform the rhetorical duties of what, within an antebellum American context, is in effect a rival residential discourse. When assigned a subordinate place on the page beneath the domestic, then, boarding is denied the proper means of self-expression, and so ceases to be boarding as that discursive form should be understood. When granted equal discursive status, boarding reads precisely as what it was—a separate rhetoric of cities. Functionally urban, and defiantly undomestic, boarding as literary form enabled contemporary Americans to make meaning of the metropolis.

✦

A domestic indignity for some, boarding was for others neither a dangerous malady nor a national tragedy. The discourse of boarding in fact encouraged an epochal imaginative freedom for many antebellum authors and readers. Through boardinghouse letters, Americans finally were able to formulate a metropolitan storyline wherein to entertain the possibilities and problems of city living, while lending full expression to urban attitudes, idioms, and perspectives well beyond the rhetorical limits of domesticity. By residing outside a period ideal of household independence, boarders by definition departed from most normative valuations of home. With that departure—a literal domestic leave-taking—rhetorical boarders migrated in their minds to a discursive environment where domestic convention by and large had been abandoned. Replacing domestic letters was the genre of boarding. The cities of the United States figured differently here: urban America pressed with comparative ease against residents' imaginations; Americans, in turn, inscribed their unchecked urban impressions on the nation's literature. They did so freed from the dictates of domesticity, and with all the openness of modernity.

Boarding achieved its full discursive potential in American author Fanny Fern's New York "novel" *Ruth Hall: A Domestic Tale of the Present Time* (1854).[16] The pseudonymous, celebrity writer Fern sets a "bad" boardinghouse at the heart of her book; but, whereas the average domestic discourser might have recognized in that storytelling structure only narrative limitation, Fern discovers there a platform on which to craft a hybrid literary genre that is fully metropolitan in its functions, and qualifiedly feminist in its portrayal of antebellum urban women. Not all readers were pleased with the literal-figurative city that is Fern's text. Among the most outspoken critics of Fern's urban figurations were members of the mainstream American press. "As a work of art," opined one of these, an anonymous reviewer for *Putnam's* magazine in 1855, *Ruth Hall* was "extremely imperfect." Indeed, only a "charitable hypothesis" could move this same reader to grant *Ruth Hall* the status of "a novel, and nothing more nor less." For, the admonishment continued, the working journalist Fern suspiciously culled the "staple" materials of her books from recycled "newspaper paragraphs" that she had composed previously for various periodical publications. The "sketchy, scrappy, and unsubstantial" nature of these writings typified for this commentator "the very last degree of flimsiness."[17] Writing from his "Editor's Easy Chair" in *Harper's* magazine, meanwhile, American man of letters George William Curtis issued his own dismissal. "Is there any story at all?" he asked of *Ruth Hall,* before condemning its "pictures" as being as little "like life as the portraits of an itinerant painter," and possessing "no point, no moral, no interest."[18] Undeterred by such warnings, and apparently undaunted by Fern's adopting an impressionistic, "painterly" narrative posture that the French flaneur Charles Baudelaire would employ several years later in his seminal essay "The Painter of Modern Life," a silent majority of *Ruth Hall's* original readers reportedly purchased some 70,000 copies of the book during its first year of publication.[19] Such sales figures were not unprecedented, but they were high enough to suggest a sizeable audience of contemporaries who were ready to explore the literary city with Fern on her own terms. Hers were boardinghouse terms that saw the author proposing significant urban revisions to the novel tradition in Western literature, even as she audaciously orchestrated fictional debate in her book over antebellum America's gendered status quo.

Like the city of Manhattan that it surveys, *Ruth Hall* is a veritable beehive of the kind of busily "itinerant" narration that writers like Curtis deplored. Much as the urban masses were on the move in the metropolis, the inhabitants of Fern's text maintain what Hayden White calls the constant "to and fro" motion of discourse (etymologically derived from the word *discurrere,* to run back and forth) between assimilated experience and "the clutter of phenomena which refuses incorporation into conventionalized notions of 'reality.' "[20] Here, it is the contingency of urban life that resists discursive encoding. Not one of *Ruth Hall*'s main characters settles domestically during the course of the novel; each in his or her own way leads a peripatetic existence best exemplified by (and often realized in) boarding. Simultaneously, none of the core thematic issues that structure Fern's "*Domestic Tale*"—life, death, city, country, love, home, work, words, print, profit, and womanhood, among others—reaches anything resembling final resolution; each remains as unresolved, or unsettled, as the city itself. *Ruth Hall*'s balanced *im*balance results in a controlled narrative tension that recalls the aesthetic of "connectedness" that scholar Betsy Klimasmith finds in nineteenth-century urban literature generally. "Connectivity" in this instance involves the close ties between cities, city peoples, and densely networked infrastructures that necessarily multiply inside a boardinghouse book like *Ruth Hall.* Joined with "connectivity" at the boardinghouse base of Fern's text is the related literary principle of "openness." As Klimasmith writes, the insistent overlap of persons, places, and spaces in the nation's early modern cities—especially in its early modern urban literatures—did not simply anticipate "the alienated, fractured subjectivity" of the modern period proper during the first decades of the twentieth century. Urban interpolation marked as well a psychological and social opportunity for "characters, authors, and readers." Contingence, "connection," unsettledness, and "openness" represent here an avenue through which Fern herself, protagonist Ruth, and readers of *Ruth Hall* can "learn to navigate a complex environment that nevertheless opened new possibilities for growth, change, and progress."[21] *Ruth Hall* is in many respects a novel of hardship and loss. It is also, in its "open" boardinghouse design, and its formal reliance on "connectedness," an antidomestic testament to the rewards of urban adaptation.

As author, Fern could attest with firsthand authority to the demarcated limits of domesticity, as well as the discursive opportunities afforded by urban American boarding. Like so many women writers of the time, Sara Parton, better known by her pen name, Fanny Fern, had a personal knowledge of boarding that stretched back into her teens. Fern attended boarding school as a girl in Hartford, Connecticut, and took lessons there alongside many of the other middle-class daughters whose educations had been left to a growing number of female academies in the United States. Boarding continued into the young Sara's adulthood. After a first marriage ended in her husband's illness and early death, and a second dissolved in a scandalous divorce,[22] Parton (née Willis) and her two daughters found themselves refused support by relations. It was at this stage when Fern and her family entered into a protracted phase of boarding. Leaving their suburban Boston home for what third husband James Parton (another ex-boarder) later would call "a third-rate boarding-house" in the city,[23] mother and daughters were able to do little more than subsist during a period that saw the female family provider in turn earning wages by sewing, school-teaching, and then writing conventionally domestic-sentimental sketches for northeastern newspapers. Sara Parton wrote under the pseudonym Fanny Fern, and her collected *Fern Leaves from Fanny's Port-folio* (1853) became an instant best-seller. Written *in* a boardinghouse with her children at hand, a number of Fern's sketches— those already penned, as well as those yet to be set to type—were also *about* boardinghouses. Highlights from her boarder's portfolio include the profile of a well-to-do, hotel-boarding widow, a smiling reflection on boarding bachelors who, Fern writes, "miss half their duds, moving from one boarding-house to another," and Fern's retelling of her own eventual migration away from boarding. This last, titled "My Old Ink-Stand and I; or, the First Article in the New House," recounts the author's moving from Boston to New York in search of higher prices (which she secured) for her writings. It recounts as well Fern's transition out of hard times, from boarding "in the sky-parlor" of that "hyena-like" landlady Mrs. Griffin into what she describes as her own "bran-new pretty house" on Brooklyn's Oxford Street.[24]

Fern survived her trials by boarding, and internalized urban occupancy as an art form. The "*Domestic Tale*" that is her first full-length narrative thus to some extent reinscribes the boardinghouse life of its author: *Ruth Hall* opens with an ostensibly domestic frame, only to vacate that literary structure for a form best termed metropolitan. Compared to the domestic novel that it is not, *Ruth Hall* literally reads as a boardinghouse brief. Its short, staccato chapters prove favorable to sharp scene-shifts and the condensed collapsing of action, as opposed to the fluid movements and leisurely gait of conventional domestic prose narration. Its temporal-spatial patterns replicate at the level of the text the vibrant energy and volatility of Fern's contemporary Manhattan—where domesticity squarely met the modern logic of impermanency, a logic figured in period literatures like *Ruth Hall* as the boarder's short-term lease. In *Ruth Hall* meet the respective arts of antebellum urban life and nineteenth-century writing, a merger that moves Fern's text far from the typical formulations of home, and out from beneath the category of the novel as a genre. Such is the paradox of a work that marshals readers to and through a sequence of household interiors, each dramatically preparatory to the next, only to propose a conception of residence that leaves readers on the "outside" looking "in," at least by the domestic standards of the day. In lieu of stationary shelter, *Ruth Hall* substitutes a metropolitan model of residence as reiteration—of ceaseless adjustments in social station, habitational location, and psychic orientation—that urban Americans well might have greeted as "real," and rural dwellers might have glimpsed as a prediction of living conditions to come. Fern was more than ironic when she chose a *"Domestic"* subtitle for her work, then. So compromised is the integrity of the domestic within her volume's shifting urban context that home here is not only the most unstable of constructs; it is a structure that Fern's text does not seriously imagine inhabiting.

The author begins her dismantling of residential convention by granting the domestic a substantial share of the narrative space in *Ruth Hall's* opening pages. It is hardly a gesture of largesse by Fern, since she in effect contrives to make domesticity complicit in its own undoing. She apportions normative residence room enough to prove itself out of place in *"the Present Time"* and metropolitan context in which much of her book unfolds. A neat territorial dichotomy consequently characterizes the text. Early chapters reveal a free and easy country life for Ruth (like the author, graduated from a boarding school) at the start of a traditional stay-at-home marriage. This is the only stage when this young, motherless mother of two serves as mistress of a generously proportioned independent household.[25] Later chapters, by contrast, create a pervading sense of confinement after Ruth's youthful husband unexpectedly dies. With him dies whatever hope that readers might have harbored for a neat domestic climax to this *"Tale,"* for Fern's work reverses the usual arc of the domestic genre. Moving inside-out, instead of outside-in, the forsaken widow Ruth enjoys habitational happiness early, only to relinquish the rural prerogatives of real estate for a series of temporary shelters in the imposing city while she searches for work to support her girls. The author, by design, situates Ruth upon her arrival in an unnamed Manhattan at a busy metropolitan boardinghouse. Here, in this conventionally spaceless space, where urban dwellers kept occupancies high and landlords counted empty beds as so much untapped inventory, Fern has home confront the practical spatial restrictions of the city.

The urban ingénue Ruth initially bridles at boarding. Only gradually does she develop the metropolitan mindset that allows her to occupy in full *Ruth Hall's* boardinghouse frame. Her spatial perspective, that is to say, remains residually domestic well into the early adventures of her urban life's journey. Readers can witness this lingering resistance—at once residential and ideological—as the author leads Ruth (and through her, readers themselves) on an ambulatory tour of tight city spaces which, by metropolitan necessity, function as dwelling places in the novel's central chapters. The net effect of sights revealed to Ruth during this, her early urban itinerancy, is sheer discouragement on the one hand, and utter discursive dissonance on the other. To a woman reared amid the social and psychological expectations of home, the city seems the meanest of habitats. Ruth's introduction to boarding begins when she and her nuclear family relocate to the Beach Cliff hotel. At the hour of their arrival, some months prior to her would-be convalescent husband's passing, this holiday resort is crowded with "the usual number of . . . fashionable mothers" from the city center (55). Ruth's ailing husband (who had boarded before their wedding, some eight years before) spends his final days here, and so casts a pall upon boarding even as he drives his surviving wife and daughters still closer to the city. Denied the support of her unloving father-in-law, a widowed Ruth subsequently visits a succession of makeshift shelters in Manhattan as she fights to stave off indigence by searching for gainful employment. Home to urban poor like Ruth, the city's almshouse beckons without ever actually claiming her as one of its inhabitants. Sweatshops full of seamstresses, closed-door New York counting houses, and the dungeon-like chambers of a city insane asylum (where Ruth is "employed" emotionally in voluntary support of a stranger, a literal madwoman in the attic)[26] round out the author's fictional landscape. Then follow a number of more likely residential addresses that Fern conjures in a survey of the dense human habitations awaiting urban dwellers like Ruth: the boardinghouse on a "narrow street" that she originally moves into, the "heated air" of a lodging-house attic that follows not long afterward, and the depressing tenement—its every "tier above tier" occupied by "careworn faces"—that looms until Ruth finds a professional, if not residential, niche in her newfound calling as writer-for-hire (87, 143, 111). There is little lebensraum in Fern's city.

Ruth's decision to domesticate at what the author calls "one of those heterogeneous boarding-houses" only compounds the apparent problems faced by an untried urban hand like our heroine; now she must compete for a precious short supply of residential space with a virtual city indoors, consisting of "clerks, market-boys, apprentices, and sewing-girls," not to mention "the maid-of-all-work" (87). The city's spatial limits, in short, have shaped a pinched "*Domestic Tale.*" Ruth's early struggles—for health, happiness, and a habitat equal to her hopes and needs—cause her to canvass an entire city in search of shelter, but without securing anything more than a running page count in the process. "Hotel Life" (chapter 25) fades with such abruptness to "Ruth's New Lodgings" (chapter 37) that these and the similar urban spaces in between them all but overlap, even as a weary Ruth paces city streets on a circular journey: holding close to her domestic dreams, she reinvests her meager wages in the best home that she can buy, with each and every rent payment made returning her to the pavements in order to secure further work. It is, all the while, not the topography of the city that she learns. She knows only the tedium of ceaseless travel, since Ruth seemingly has been everywhere but finally remains nowhere in her Manhattan. So compressed is the narrative account of Ruth's physical New York movements, and so severely reduced her allotment of household space in the temporary shelters that she halfway inhabits, that the foundational days of Ruth's arrival in the city read as an impossibly short excursion around the discursive urban block.

There is a ready explanation for *Ruth Hall*'s walled-in feel: "one is necessarily circumscribed in a boarding-house," as the beleaguered Gertrude complains in Fern's follow-up volume, *Rose Clark*.[27] As this and the above remarks from Whitman, Hale, and others indicate, many period authors deemed city shelter anathema to home and discoursed accordingly. Lydia Maria Child, for instance, after having boarded for a season at Boston in 1837, recalled that "suffocating" spell with much melodrama, begging, "Take the fetter off, I pray you—restore me the 'free air.'" In her published *Letters from New-York* (1843), meanwhile, the product of Child's time in Manhattan, she goes on to record an array of New York's incidental domestic spaces—Sing Sing penitentiary, a filled-to-capacity orphans' asylum, police watch-houses that serve as dorms for vagrants, and "the lowest and dirtiest boarding-houses"—as if they were on the verge of overpopulated collapse.[28] Catharine Maria Sedgwick seconds Child's emotions, making crowded urban space a motif of her domestic fiction from the 1820s and after. Schooled and boarded in her youth at Manhattan, Albany, and Boston, Sedgwick wintered as an adult with her lawyer-brothers in Manhattan, just as she later claimed boarding as the theme of her entire life when she wrote that she had "'boarded round' so much, had my home in so many houses and so many hearts . . . that I seem to have no separate, individual existence." That was no boast, judging from the fate of her fictional boarders. One, the title character from the short story "The City Clerk" (1850), moves from a country farm to a New York boardinghouse to a cell in the Tombs, or city prison, in short order. Another, the miser Smith from Sedgwick's fourth novel, *Clarence* (1830), resides in a boardinghouse garret (not unlike Fern's) "tucked so close under the inclining ceiling, that he seemed hardly to have breathing space."[29] At the masculine margins of the domestic spectrum, sensational writer (and former boarder) George Thompson fills his novel *City Crimes* (1849) with an entire back catalog of claustrophobic city spaces. Others' renditions of metropolitan residence look pleasant by comparison. The characters who appear in Thompson's work inhabit such unlikely urban quarters as sewers, wine cellars, the locked safe of a Wall Street insurance office, even a wooden crate—this last location holding a wholesale shipment of household cabinets and a convicted house-breaker, no less.[30]

From a domestic perspective, the "*Crime*" implicit in a work like Thompson's *City Crimes* was not the lack of residential space but the "*City*" itself. Harriet Beecher Stowe's aforementioned *Uncle Tom's Cabin* (1852) in fact makes a virtue of "snug" domestic "territories" in a novel where the eponymous, humble Kentucky cabin of the author's telling can accommodate, with room to spare, a slave husband, wife, infant, children, furniture, and kitchen utensils, plus the requisite "company" of the surrounding plantation.[31] Antebellum writers breached household etiquette not by downsizing home, then, but by adjusting an abiding construction of shelter with city revisions. In the minds of many, these revisions threatened to undermine sacrosanct notions of domestic economy, or *how* to keep house, and domestic geography, or *where* to keep it. Boarder-authors such as Fern committed a still-worse transgression as well. They challenged the shibboleth of home by outright withdrawal from its supporting rhetorical system. Domestic writers responded to the effrontery of the city either by excluding the urban from their literatures, or else by exposing the socio-spatial shortcomings of city living, as Fern would appear to do in *Ruth Hall*'s preliminary pages. The changing face of modernity made it difficult to maintain such rigid domestic dichotomies, however. Even a rurally inclined writer like Child, the veteran author of antebellum cookbooks, unwittingly nudged her readers toward a post-pastoral conception of habitat when, echoing Thompson, she reflected on "the great prison-cell of a city." She states, "What I love is to have a *home*, and *stay* in it, even if it be a bottle or pickle-jar."[32] In days gone by, it would have been unthinkable that "city" and "*home*" should inhabit the same sentence. With boarding's ascendance, cohabitation became both a syntactic necessity and the spatial mandate of the metropolis.

✦

If the defenders of domesticity equated the city with captivity, Fern entertains a spatial paradigm in which modern urban residence breeds personal discursive redemption. Such is *Ruth Hall*'s spatial paradox. Gillian Brown writes that nineteenth-century domesticity "inflects" contemporary Americans' vaunted individualism with "values of interiority, privacy, and psychology." Private home ownership, that is to say, is construed as having afforded the residents of independent households the corresponding "interior" space required for an emotionally mature selfhood.[33] Fern bids open defiance to this traditional conflation of home with "heart." In the congested spatial conditions of boarding she instead allows Ruth Hall to discover room enough for what Catharine Sedgwick calls her "separate, individual existence." Indeed, Fern's heroine experiences her most profound period of self-development in the metropolis, in accordance with the pluralist terms of urban co-occupancy. Thus does Fern invert the typical pattern of domestic narration, in which boarding so often ends in arrested development. The author's "*Tale*" in other words borrows from boarding a setting suited to complex characterization, and thereby extracts from the spatially deprived city all the narrative license that she or her heroine could need. It is another boardinghouse irony: denied the autonomy of private residence, Fern's resilient female lead finds compensatory psychological space in the city. Expecting, in turn, to confront a metropolitan text packed with people, readers of *Ruth Hall* receive the double contradiction of an urban woman whose self expands in the improbable isolation of boarding.

Part of boarding's artistic appeal for Fern surely was personal. Like many of her contemporaries, the author thought of boarding as only a short-term solution to Americans' outsized demand for urban housing. Strange for a sometime practitioner of domestic letters, however, she also could attribute at least two of her major life's achievements to the city. The first of these was self-supporting motherhood, paid for in Fern's case by the opportunities for print publication that were available to a writer of her reputation in the antebellum metropolis. The second was Fern's successful Manhattan transfer from the psychic codependence of domesticity to the self-assured urban subjectivity of co-occupancy. Ruth's intrepid pedestrianism, like her rapid adaptation to boarding, is the character's behavioral equivalent of her author-narrator's famously sharp-tongued prose style: both suggest a sense of self strongly confident enough to withstand the pressures of the surrounding urban scene. The *character* of both women indicates a metropolitan mastery that bears all the hallmarks of flanerie, but in a female form that Deborah Epstein Nord names the "flâneuse."[34] Put differently, boarding was for Fern the author what it is for Ruth in fiction—a "Declaration of Domestic Independence," to borrow the words of another of Fern's semi-autobiographical narrators in *Rose Clark*.[35] Boarding in some respects helped liberate Fern from the conventions of stay-at-home domesticity. One might thus read *Ruth Hall* as the residentially inflected roman à clef that it is, so highly humanized a presence is boarding in Fern's book.

Unlike the boardinghouse characterizations made by many period writers, for whom urban occupancy was equally an occasion for observing human habitation, Fern spares her heroine the reductive treatment of stereotype. Ruth is as developmentally restless as the city itself—that is to say, Ruth *does* develop as a character throughout Fern's text. Shaping this development is the series of symbiotic exchanges that the author arranges for her protagonist at a succession of New York residences. Fern, in turn, duly records Ruth's growth as if it were simply the expected evolution of some downtown city district. Change is a foregone conclusion under the conditions of urban modernity. Change is also the driving interest of *Ruth Hall*. Impermanency accordingly makes compelling reading in these pages: no home remains unshaken in *Ruth Hall;* no character escapes plot complications; the forward march of narration never pauses; and there is no perceptible rest in this city of some half a million people. Domestic autonomy is not possible within this particular discursive environment, and yet *Ruth Hall* nurtures rather than hampers Ruth's personal and professional development.

Against the grain of a standard *"Domestic Tale,"* the city aids individuation in these pages. Urbanism actually underwrites the author's delineation of a protagonist who resists the homogenizing logic of the metropolitan mass average. Read domestically, *Ruth Hall* would appear to fall short of its imagined destination, since Fern's book abandons the idealized aspirations toward home that inform its opening chapters. Read novelistically, the text strains to fulfill generic expectations, since it lacks the introspection of romance and mostly omits the exterior details of literary realism. Afforded by boarding the psychological space of city fiction, *Ruth Hall* nevertheless finds a functional form in the genre of urban bildungsroman.[36] A consummate "itinerant" artist, a "painter" not of recognizable "types" but knowable city people, Fern populates her narrative space with a heroine whose relations with residence translate for Ruth into multiple levels of interior depth. The author's gloss on Manhattan's surface details is finally Ruth's gain, then. An abstracted physical city looms large and crowds constantly in *Ruth Hall,* but the book's primary urban spectacle is Ruth's own subjectivity.

Provisionally settled in conspicuous boardinghouse surroundings, Ruth endures the objectifying scrutiny of a watchful metropolis before she graduates to the status of integrated city subject. She must learn to look, and not just be looked *at,* if even the most sympathetic of readers is to experience Manhattan through her eyes. Meanwhile, the relentless gaze of the city sets its sights on Ruth at her very first boarders' living quarters in New York, and retains it there until Fern's heroine finally overcomes her initially disadvantaged position within the psychic hierarchy of urban perspective. Chapters 36 through 45 establish a pattern in which Ruth rarely speaks, is often spoken *of,* and figures a veritable display in the shop window of the city, arranged for the benefit of passersby. Ruth's fellow boarders Jim and Sam inaugurate her urban exposure when the latter asks, in Ruth's absence, "Jim, what do you think of her?" "Deuced nice form," is Jim's response, as his partner trains his admiring gaze on himself "in an opposite mirror" of the downstairs parlor. Jim adds, with a comment that caresses its objectified signified, "This little widow is porcelain" (87). A chapter-length exchange of only three pages in the original edition of Fern's volume, the conversation here is as short as Ruth's residential space is scant. Subsequent chapters, shorter still, unfold in much the same way. Ruth interjects every now and then with words of her own. Her anguished "tears dropping one after another" provide a silent substitute when words fail (92, 95). She is, however, more frequently and passively regarded by former friends, relations, and strangers as an object of gossip. Some of their comments express pity; some betray scorn. What holds much of their talk together is that it identifies Ruth with a communal brand of residence to which they claimed tacit rights of open urban access. At this moment, Ruth inhabits nondescript "lodgings" that socially locate her "down hill so far as this," as an incredulous female acquaintance remarks, and epistemologically situate her as something, or someone, that is readily available to be observed (99). Not all onlookers disparage the image that she figures. Yet, even random wellwishers like Tom Herbert, who had infrequent commercial dealings in the past with Ruth's departed husband Harry, speak of Ruth with the unearned familiarity of a paying spectator to a public performance. "I know her well enough," he says, unconsciously reminding readers of the extent to which Ruth's then-current domestic position left her vulnerable to being "known" (98). Outside the recognized shelter of home, Ruth was prone to such transparency. Indeed, judging from the treatment that she receives from the "maid-of-all-work" at her boardinghouse, the city could see right through the walls of her selfhood, so long as she continued to board. When a care package arrives one day for Ruth, the hired help of her house unthinkingly "opened the door" to Ruth's room after "omitting the ceremony of a premonitory knock" (103). There sat Ruth and her daughters, but "there" could have been anywhere, if anyone had rights of entry. Ruth might as well have not been there at all, if the key to her inner being was common property.

Ruth's urban epiphany—her defining moment of self-recognition, and thus self-realization—comes unexpectedly, "when every door of hope seemed shut" (112). After reluctantly but desperately sending her daughter Katy to collect a much-needed cash handout from her hostile father-in-law, Ruth "sat down at the small window" of her boarding-house chamber "to watch" for her elder child's return:

> The prospect was not one to call up cheerful fancies. Opposite was one of those large brick tenements, let out by rapacious landlords, a room at a time at griping rents, to poor emigrants, and others, who were barely able to prolong their lease of life from day to day. At one window sat a tailor, with his legs crossed, and a torn straw hat perched awry upon his head, cutting and making coarse garments for the small clothing-store in the vicinity, whose Jewish owner reaped all the profits. At another, a pale-faced woman, with a handkerchief bound round her aching face, bent over a steaming wash-tub, while a little girl of ten, staggering under the weight of a basket of damp clothes was stringing them on lines across the room to dry. At the next window sat a decrepit old woman, feebly trying to soothe in her palsied arms the wailings of a poor sick child. And there, too, sat a young girl, from dawn till dark, scarcely lifting that pallid face and weary eyes—stitching and thinking, thinking and stitching. God help her! (111)

Ruth's "prospect" here extends no further than the neighboring build-ings that front her own boardinghouse. So close are "those large brick tenements" across the way, in fact, that she almost might reach out her hand to comfort the "pale-faced woman" whose impoverished predica-ment and physiognomy recall her own. Her housemate, Sam, sat earlier before the boardinghouse looking-glass in smiling self-approval. Ruth, by contrast, sits and stares at the figurative mirror that is the metropolis beyond her windowpane, and so receives a predictive image of what, or who, she must become if residential trends continue as they have.

However hard her circumstances, Ruth finally comes to exchange in this instant her accustomed position among the urban observed for an urban observer's seat. The scene passes quietly, but it is for her a break-through of personhood that exemplifies what Lauren Berlant describes as the author's ability "to convert the meaning and value of female life in the quotidian," "the meaning, the pacing, and the spaces of everyday domestic life," into an assertion of "the sovereignty of subjective knowledge."[37] Ruth receives, first, a sad reminder that the grass is indeed always greener, even in the city. She considers herself fortunate that she does not reside "at one block's remove" in a "pretentious-looking house" frequented by "throngs" of "gray-haired men, business men, substantial-looking family men, and foppish-looking young men." The hyphenated suffix ending "-looking"—which is attached in this passage both to a "pretentious" "house" and multitudes of "men"—suggests that Ruth previously might have been deceived by urban appearances, but no longer. The "wan and haggard" face of "a woman" who on occasion "appeared at the windows" of the residence in question indicates all too plainly to a transitively *looking* Ruth how the object-prostitutes who reside just down the street from her own humble abode "could afford such things" as "damask chairs, satin curtains, pictures, vases, books, and pianos" in "such a neighborhood" as they shared. Yet, active urban observation entailed more than negative contrasts for Fern's protagonist. Ruth also begins to recognize true beauty in the "inhabited" city, as when she fittingly—fitting for a boardinghouse bildungsroman, that is—admires in the "upper" "window" of "a large but thrifty German family" a lovely "little pot of thriving foreign shrubs." This sight alone is visual testament for Ruth that a "love of flowers" may "take root" in the otherwise "sterile soil" of New York (112). More important still is Ruth's turning the full focus of her attention inward, not outward, at this the dawn of her urban awakening. As daughter Katy arrives back at her boardinghouse, safely returned from running her mother's errand, Ruth can say sincerely, "Dear child, I am so glad you are home" (113). "Home," in other words, with all its close contemporary associations with the personal "soil" of romantic self-cultivation, suddenly has become a genuine possibility amidst the domestic shortcomings of urban boarding. Inquiring of Katy if she were able to "see" her grandfather, Ruth has seen something, or someone, of far greater importance. Having at long last "take[n] root" in the city, Ruth can see herself *as* a self, which is precisely what Fern would have her readers do, too. Immersed in Berlant's "meaning" of everyday urban life, Ruth learns what we as readers learn, the significance of the city for subjectivity.

Unlike Whitman's disembodied boarders, Ruth possesses not only the capacity for introspection but vocalization. Much of the latter half of Fern's novel consists of foregrounded dialogue between diverse city peoples and an increasingly outspoken Ruth. The "space" of the narrative accordingly fills with Ruth's articulated movement from supplication, as a recent widow, to application, as a would-be seamstress or teacher, to publication, as a mother turned freelance writer. Under the pseudonym

"Floy," Ruth writes topical, thoughtful, or sentimental articles, as the mood suits her. She exercises as well her hard-earned commercial license by migrating as author between various print media outlets in the city. Declining further service to one of her original publishers, the aptly named "Pilgrim" periodical, for example, Ruth informs its resentful editor, Mr. Tibbetts, of her decision to leave his employ: "I have yet to learn that I am not free to go, if I choose" (202).

It is another irony of the city that Ruth's writing escapes the notice of *Ruth Hall*'s readers. For, aside from the above-mentioned conversations between assorted characters and Ruth, Fern narrates a sizeable portion of her novel's latter chapters within an epistolary frame that conceals Ruth's actual inscribed words from our view. Ruth's writings reach many a city reader. Witness the correspondence that she inspires from an audience for her columns that extends across an enthusiastic Manhattan in awe of her "genius" (234), as one among her many admirers writes, into the metropolitan hinterland. Letters arrive for Ruth not only from the city center, then, but from what historian William Cronon calls the "many small places"—in Ruth's case, the editorial office of a country newspaper, an untraceable "Hopetown College," and a rural, upstate scholastic academy for boys (234–35, 213–14, 242)—that naturally and necessarily "communicate" with the metropolis.[38] But, whereas Ruth's precarious position as the renter of urban residence earlier left her exposed as the most easily accessed of texts, her strengthened sense of self comes to frustrate our boardinghouse view of her every move and emotion. More to the point, it prevents our reception of Ruth's writings, both professional and personal. Now it is we who occupy the passive position. We learn only at a once remove, just after the fact of action, that "Ruth took up her pen," "wrote a long letter," "sealed and superscribed" said letter, "rose to go to the post-office," and then "carried the letter to the post-office" before "dropping it into the letter-box" without our having had the opportunity to examine its contents (186). *Ruth Hall* is alive with voices (including Ruth's, her neighbors, urban verbal eccentrics like her punster daughter Nettie, and the omniscient narrator) that Betsy Klimasmith likens to the aggregate sounds of cities generally.[39] If the city prompts Ruth to talk, however, in the end it also teaches her and Fern together to manage which precise words, if any, are fit for public consumption. City considerations of space prevent them from practicing conventional domestic economy. What they practice instead is an economy of verbal savvy suited to the scribal and printed spaces of the modern American metropolis at midcentury.

✦

As with space, so with time: much as *Ruth Hall* surprisingly finds roomy psychology in the narrow byways and boardinghouses of the city, Fern's novel pushes forward headlong from cover to cover of its contents, only to locate a temporal retreat in boarding. Literary boarding at once suggests the quickened condensation of city life and affords a momentary stay against the rush of the modern metropolis. A simple timeline for *Ruth Hall* belies this seeming contradiction. Running at one end from the protagonist's fleet passage through matrimony and motherhood, it concludes at the other with an itinerant widow's subsequent progress (or regress) through boarding, lodging, and authorship. "One o'clock!" the narrator interjects at one stage during an eventful interim, reminding Ruth and readers alike of time's conspicuous passing in the short, episodic arrangement of events inside this story (66). Even the most poignant personal moments terminate without sentiment in *Ruth Hall*. The book will not linger for feeling, and it does not indulge feelings that linger. "Don't loiter on the way" is how Ruth imparts so hard a temporal truth to Katy, before her daughter steps outside their boardinghouse chamber on an alms-seeking errand (107). It is a comment that might serve as a directive to readers. What the author calls "breathless haste" is not waste in these pages (146); it is a necessary corollary to narrative, the forward (or retrograde) movement of which depends as much on the internal contrivances of plot as it does on temporal pressures seemingly external to the text. In fact, *Ruth Hall* incorporates the ever-"*Present*" urban hypertense of its subtitle into its very structure. Metropolitan "*Time*" is thus the story's chronometer, the ephemeral temporal standard against which brisk fictional lives are led, residences fled, hearts broken, emotions mended, and serial literatures written.

If boarding is the central mechanism in this textual timepiece, it is also the improbable cause of *Ruth Hall*'s pregnant pauses. Fern literalizes modern temporal abstraction by setting her discourse to the quickened rhythms of urban domestic rental. Readers, as a result, share in a "restless spirit" that is as much an attribute of the "hurried" protagonist—Ruth passes her New York "days and hours," the narrator relates, with great "impatience"—as it is a descriptive indication of habitational Manhattan's tendency for "sudden change" (146, 142). The temporal consequences of admitting the city indoors are not wholly limiting; they are liberating as far as Ruth Hall is concerned. Her ultimate redemption is a product of urban rapidity. Her saving grace resides not merely in her maturation from marriageable young woman to dependent boardinghouse widow to independent author, but in the dispatch of a city that she internalizes as both boarder and as a participant in the recurring production cycle of metropolitan print. "How long" must she "wait!" Ruth exclaims with frustration from her lodging house chambers, during a critical scene when she renounces self-doubt and decides upon literature as a paying profession (146). She "had risen early" on this particular "sultry morning in July," "early" enough to achieve another city epiphany. "Just then," the narrator announces, "a carrier passed on the other side of the street with the morning papers, and slipped one under the crack of the house door opposite" (145). Within the slender "crack" of this "Just then" juncture, Ruth comes to recognize the productive potential of an urban industrial "sunrise." Although inexorable, time's diurnal passing in the modern metropolis yields time enough for creation. In a city that proverbially never sleeps, the laboring day fashions recurring opportunities for personal and commercial growth among "early" risers such as Ruth. "Morning" alone is brimming with city possibilities. It awakens literary demand at dawn in the shape of eager newspaper readers. It invites the purveyors of print to supply and circulate their wares among the "papers." And, in so doing, it enables boarder-authors such as Ruth to convert stray urban seconds back into residential, self-developmental space. Writing in installments, and living in city increments, Ruth's literary wages keep her installed not at "the house door opposite," but in rented rooms where she practices her serial craft. The poetry and prose that she comes to produce appear with clockwork precision, a timely reminder that she has learned to reside in metropolitan time with all the equanimity of negative capability.

Such is *Ruth Hall*'s rush that it relinquishes claim to the title of novel, even *urban* novel, but so complete is Ruth's self-development over the course of her story that the subtitle description of *"Tale"* is as much a misnomer for Fern's work as *"Domestic."* The strictures of city time compress narration here into chapter-length "glimpses" (chapter 64) and "peeps" (chapters 46 and 63) of the protagonist's variegated existence. Whatever desire we might have for prolonged exposure to her unfolding is thereby denied by a manic Manhattan that resists the suspension of animation, and foregoes the comfortable narrative expansion of the generic novel. It is with much irony, then, that chapter 77 announces in reference to a wearied, would-be writer Ruth that "Publication Day Comes at Last." There must be no long "at Last" in a work inscribed by boarding's temporal contradictions. Rapid urban turnover prevails in these pages, meaning that readers can scarcely "settle" into the text. Somehow time suffices, however, for Ruth to master the art of urban being simply by being urban. To read *Ruth Hall* is thus to inhabit hurriedness, in accordance with metropolitan convention; it is to retreat as well to the shelter of city subjectivity, wherein resides time enough for even the greenest nineteenth-century New Yorker to keep pace with the temporality of modernity.

Pressed by events inside the text, pressured by traditional discourses without, *Ruth Hall* ironically achieves a narrative leisure that is anathema to the efficient rhythms of city domesticity, and in fact recalls the privileged masculine position and casual promenade-pacing of flanerie. Contemporary domestic commentary from both sides of the Atlantic acknowledged no such nuance in interpreting the ways that metropolitan Americans such as Ruth kept time. Much of this commentary was an explicit catalog of the temporal transgressions—heedless hurry on the one hand, lazy delinquency on the other—that many believed boardinghouse Americans committed in accepting what seemed to be the compromised conditions of urban housing. Englishwoman Mary Duncan, for example, admonished Americans for the runaway clip of their boardinghouse lives in the nation's "busy cities."[40] Duncan and other observers particularly worried that boarding out accelerated and so disrupted American childhood in its innocent beginnings. Historically, boardinghouses catered mostly to single adult males, so that a boardinghouse upbringing would have been something of a rarity.[41] Duncan wrote, all the same, with a conviction that boardinghouse children grew far too forward, far too fast, in their social behavior. Ruth's droll young daughter Nettie comes to mind when Duncan laments that "the little creatures get the manners of grown persons" (198). Duncan's compatriot Charles Mackay similarly felt that city children reared in co-occupancy would "become prematurely old for want of fresh air and exercise." Another visiting Englishwoman, Harriet Martineau, likewise feared for the hotel-dwelling upstarts whom she encountered during her own short-term metropolitan residence in the antebellum United States. Martineau mentions with motherly regret the sight of city-dwelling urban youth overindulging on sweets served them "by a dozen obsequious blacks" attending at table.[42]

Their childhood truncated, urban American boarders arrived at adulthood with a seeming disregard for the bourgeois proprieties of time. Such, at least, was the opinion of many defenders of domesticity. From their perspective, boarding encouraged improvident marriages among couples who could not as yet afford the initial capital outlay required for a home of their own. Rather than bide their time and accumulate the combined cost of a mortgage, furniture, and household staff, the boardinghouse bride and groom entered matrimony much sooner than they otherwise could have. More disturbing, they thereby reduced the likelihood that their marriage would survive long. It was a domestic truism, moreover, that wives who were left alone among co-occupant strangers could not help but contract romances with male housemates while husbands were away at work. As the American minister William Henry Milburn noted, the circumstances of boarding necessarily led the young, undomesticated wife to wile away her weeks with "such acquaintances and associates as the common table may bring her into contact with." Mary Duncan supplied the logic behind such thinking when she explained that boarding, inasmuch as it relieved resident women of traditional household duties, left them with large stretches of idle time; the boredom of boarding, in turn, meant temptation among urban occupants who remained less than wholly occupied.[43]

Milburn's disturbing boardinghouse vision of marital collapse is typical of an implicitly temporal talking point on both sides of the American and European gender divide. He portrays female boardinghouse inmates, for the most part childless, lounging about with no housework to do, with no knowledge of the domestic arts at all, in fact, and developing a taste, in turn, for the welcome distractions of lax entertainments—newspaper coverage of divorce trials and, as another Englishman warns, "sensational literature." These same boardinghouse ladies, Milburn believed, dawdled away their afternoons by gossiping in each others' rooms, and sharing family secrets perhaps better left unspoken. His assumption was that the irresistible attractions of fashion (especially among hotel boarders, such as Sarah Josepha Hale's Barclays) eventually would take hold, leading the dissatisfied boardinghouse wife to regard her husband's "narrow income" as insufficient to afford all of the "expensive decorations which she deems requisite to show off her fine person." Milburn foresees a sad outcome already written by circumstance. He writes, "The chances are that she will begin by ogling and end with infamy; that her expensive tastes will be gratified by her husband's recourse to fraud, or her own more ignominious means." Such was his concern that he would conclude, just two years before the Civil War, "I cannot but regard the growing habit of boarding . . . as one of the most terrible dangers by which the domestic and social interests of our country are threatened."[44]

Harriet Martineau elaborated Milburn's concerns over boarding in terms that sustain his preoccupation with city space and time. For Martineau, boarding afforded metropolitan males but precious little of the former; she draws the unattractive co-occupant prospect of "public meals, a noisy house, [and] confinement to one or two private rooms." Nor did her "man of business" stand much chance of enjoying a sufficient share of the latter, since she describes the boardinghouse as "but a poor solace after the toils of the day." Boarding, in short, confounded for Martineau the very separate spheres on which domesticity rested, making much spatiotemporal trouble in the process. Itself a "noisy" "business," boarding eroded the domestic spatial distinctions between the public masculine world of work and the private feminine realm of home. Temporally, her version of boarding was just as upsetting. As Martineau's average boardinghouse man inhabits the intervals of the working week, his internal clock runs exclusively to the unflagging "toils" of "business." Martineau's boardinghouse woman, meanwhile, drifts by on the lost obligations "of the day" as her clock in effect stops.[45] The urban children of Martineau's account in other words surfeit themselves on sweets as her city women partake of too much time.

*Ruth Hall* resists such temporal dichotomies. In Fern's fiction, the regular flurry of urban activity comes to a deceptive boardinghouse standstill, and so engenders a romance of moments that permit city people to fulfill their personal metropolitan potentials. As we have seen, Fern telescopes Ruth's story. Her protagonist endures much domestic complication within the framework of a compact narrative that expedites Ruth's rapid transit through a mostly masculine New York world of money-making, financial management, and boardinghouse sociability. At the same time, urban time is on Ruth's side, in that the author recognizes and valorizes the temporal opportunities that attend what Michel de Certeau calls "The Practice of Everyday Life" in the city.[46] Ruth's moral-professional rise from indigent widow to literary noteworthy occurs not before or after her repeated residential migrations but *during* the unsettling episodes of her unconventional existence. Of course, with boarding as its temporal-spatial basis, *Ruth Hall* must render Ruth's quest for sustainable shelter incomplete; boarding figures for Fern only a provisional phase of residence. But, if the author rejects the uplifting household outcomes of domesticity, she nevertheless does endow the urban "Everyday" with a metropolitan faith in the here and now. Fern's text is optimistic testament to the in-between. It is precisely within this space—in between definable genres, staccato chapters, and permanent domiciles—and at this time—stolen metropolitan moments that transpire among the interstices of boarding, relocating, knowing, and growing—where and when the readers of *Ruth Hall* come to reside. Time and space suffice here for the title character to shape her sense of self, and for Fern to author an urban boarder's life outside the bounds of woman's expected separate sphere.

Perhaps the most important temporal truth revealed to Ruth in Manhattan is this: the modern city affords time for more than domestic sentiment. Fern instills this lesson during her protagonist's residential

interval at the Skiddys' boardinghouse, a husband-and-wife-run establishment that strains to maintain the external trappings of conventional
domesticity. Ruth and her daughters enjoy no household indulgences here,
dining as they do on "one plate [that] suffices for fish, flesh, fowl, and des-
sert" amid "soiled table-cloths, sticky crockery, [and] oily cookery" (87).
Nor do they enjoy much privacy, situated as they are among a townhouse
filled with fellow boarders. Landlady Skiddy's continuing quarrel with
her harried husband, moreover, has converted the couple's matrimonial
woes, in addition to their house-bound children, into the joint responsibility of the residents. The house itself advertises this shiftless state of
affairs. "From the first entry" of their address at "No. 50—street," in a
"dark" boardinghouse "quarter of the city," flows the less than genteel
"odor of cabbage." The household help, for its part, enacts a tacit demon-
stration of domestic unpleasantness. Seen "leaning out the front window
on her elbows" in "vulgar" display (87, 99), Biddy McFlanigan, the Skiddys' stereotypical "red-faced Irish girl," is conspicuous visual testament to
a comment made by Ruth's daughter Katy in understated reference to her
temporary home, "'Tis n't a pretty place" (92).

Boarding's temporal saving grace proves to be the book's implicit storytelling principle. All things—time, traffic, texts, and the itinerant lives
they touch—must pass quickly when the city impinges on domesticity, as
it does in *Ruth Hall*. That said, this non-novel's tenement-dwelling "poor
emigrants" admittedly register the negative effects of time's rapid passing.
The depressed poor who live next door to the Skiddys are "barely able to
prolong their lease of life from day to day" (111). By contrast, only one
household away, an increasingly confident Ruth enjoys the benefits of
urban hurry: nothing lasts, but nothing bad lasts, either, so that the *passage* of pain and pleasure involved in the rite of her New York initiation
ultimately qualifies the causes and consequences of her actual city condition. The short form of de Certeau's urban "Everyday" in this respect *is*
its function. As a foundation for narration, the city might seem spatially
constrained, but it promises a temporal means to personal freedom. The
above-named Biddy McFlanigan recognizes as much when, with the Skiddys' marriage on the verge of collapse, she unceremoniously packs her
trunk and abandons landlords and tenants. Ruth, too, realizes the opportunities of metropolitan time when she installs herself in Mrs. Skiddy's
absence as interim boardinghouse mistress. Her interregnum is brief,
since Mrs. Skiddy, convinced of her husband's contrition, soon returns.
Fern regardless has Ruth's reign last just long enough to remind us that
her improvisational domestic prowess represents a different order of time
both in- and outside this urban text.

Country-bred, and formerly the married keeper of a suburban home of her own, Ruth as if by instinct tries to impose familiar domestic practices on fractious urban circumstances that at first resist her ordering impulses. Her initial item of boardinghouse business in Mrs. Skiddy's absence is to tend to the unhappy couple's infant son, Tommy. The child earlier had responded to his father's clumsy attempts to feed him with "a milky *jet d-eau*" in Mr. Skiddy's face. More confusion follows when the father tries to "propitiate the distracted infant," as the narrator relates, but succeeds only in having "ladles, spoons, forks, dredging-boxes, mortars, pestles, and other culinary implements" "strewn" about the floor (115). Ruth attends to that mess and then to Tommy:

> Ruth took the poor worried baby tenderly, laid it on its stomach across her lap, then loosening its frock strings, began rubbing its little shoulders with her velvet palm. There was a maternal magnetism in that touch; baby knew it! He stopped crying and winked his swollen eyelids with the most luxurious satisfaction, as much as to say, there, now, that's something like! (116)

The "maternal" substance of the scene is conventionally domestic, with its "tender" depiction of the bond between mother and infant. The temporal timing of the passage is off, as it must be, since Tommy's "luxurious satisfaction" draws the forward (or backward) momentum of Fern's narration to a halt. Indeed, after Ruth ensures that boardinghouse tea comes "off quite swimmingly," and that "baby, thanks to Ruth's maternal management, lay sweetly sleeping in his little wicker cradle" (117)—while Ruth's own "sweetly" sleeping girls lie in their beds upstairs (119)—readers might think that a minor domestic "revolution" has occurred here in Manhattan (114). This is the city, however, and so even the pleasing still life of Tommy's boardinghouse "satisfaction" must be short-lived. Fern has boarders who are moving about the house and "shut" doors "hard." She further enhances the urban ambience of the scene with the occasional "knife or fork dropped on the table" in the dining room, and the sound of "a heavy cart rumbl[ing] mercilessly past" on the street outside (117). Tommy, in turn, wakes and cries. Mr. Skiddy coaxes and fumbles. A week later, Mrs. Skiddy reappears, her arrival equally upsetting to her husband, the other residents, and the family cat. Ruth's rule had brought momentary "tranquil and quiet" to the Skiddys'; it introduced heretofore unknown signs of domesticity, including a "neatly swept" hearth, "brightly polished" pewter, and kitchen items arranged on "their respective shelves" (130). It is a "Glimpse" (chapter 64) of what boardinghouse life might be, if urban time could stand still.[47] But time inside this text seldom rests, since it is measured by busy city people like Ruth who would rather reinvent home than wait for it.

What distinguishes Ruth from the urban crowd—and *Ruth Hall* from domestic discourse generally—is the practiced capacity of both character and text to negotiate the modern temporality of their shared metropolitan context. For many of Ruth's real-world contemporaries, peripatetic residence was but another urban paradox, as read by the short hand of the antebellum clock: restless domestic motion had become so predictable that it led many of them to accept an enervating sameness as their prevailing life condition. Unfazed by the perpetual moratorium of the lived metropolis, Ruth Hall thrives by the ironies of urban time. Not only does Fern's heroine think and act decisively under urban temporal duress; she secures her literary calling by writing in and of a quick metropolitan tense, the very short duration of which only serves to heighten her facility with words.

With Mr. Skiddy's sudden removal to California, and landlady Skiddy's subsequent conversion of her boardinghouse (room with meals) into a lodging house (room without meals), Ruth once more discovers herself in an out-of-house condition, but one that now pays artistic dividends. Her straitened personal finances require that she and her girls move to a more affordable and far less comfortable "room without board, in the lower part of the city" (142). There Ruth continues to face the weekly obligation of rent. But lodging proves a boon, since Ruth's deepening dependence on the short-term lease quickens the rate of her life's rise. On the one hand, her departure for "lower" Manhattan sets Ruth within easy walking distance to the dense collection of print publishers in the island's southern precincts. On the other hand, although "day after day chronicled only repeated failures" during Ruth's early search for work among these same publishing concerns (155), the shortened measure of a renting writer's New York "day" affords her opportunities for authorial employment. She might not find employment at the offices of "The Daily Type," the first of the city's newspapers to decline her services. Yet, she encounters there in the person "of a printer's boy, who was rushing down five steps at a time, with an empty pail in his hand," embodied indication of who and what she needs to be to secure hire (153). Urban readers' "Daily" demand for "Type" necessitates an industrial-like supply of literary content. And the "rushing" underlings whom Fern mentions in *Ruth Hall* represent the most pedestrian level of a production process designed to bring print to the reading public. Ruth joins the ranks of this virtual literary assembly line. Her first regular paid writing assignment

for "The Standard" newspaper in fact sees her embracing the temporality
of the literary city, as she literally burns midnight oil in her determination to compose her columns on hurried urban terms. As the narrator
relates, her typical "Morning" arrives "*so soon*" after many an extended
evening's labors: "Scratch—scratch—scratch, went Ruth's pen; the dim
lamp flickering in the night breeze. . . . One o'clock—two o'clock—three
o'clock—the lamp burns low in the socket" (160–61). It is the pressing
insistence of the "Daily" press, and Ruth's accomplished ability to produce
at pace, that enables her to turn copy into commodity. Without the rush,
there no doubt would be fewer personal worries for Fern's protagonist
as she struggles to support her family. Without the rush, there also would
be no city, and no need for "rushing" writers like Ruth. It is testament to
her maturing metropolitan sensibility that she can by live by urban time
as well as write by it. It is, in addition, indicative of Fern's commitment
to modern non-domestic discourse that she should have her heroine write
the way that she lives, and live the way that she writes—which is to say,
with all of the hurries, and many of the worries, that pertain outside the
ideological construct of home.

Ruth cannot control city time, but she does come to recognize over
the course of her authorial journey that she can turn urban temporality to her advantage. The long reach of New York's print publications
into the nation's interior practically collapsed the distance between metropolitan authors like Ruth and their far-flung readers. If some of these
readers resided in the city, others inhabited spaces that were peripheral to
the American metropolis, yet still within its interconnected reach. Urban
print shortened the time required for the hinterland to correspond with
the metropolis, and so, in due course, receive by rail and in the mails
the latest in the way of metropolitan reading materials. In Ruth's case,
country has much to say to city (and little time to say it) regarding "Floy,"
Ruth's nom de plume while writing for "The Standard." Her editor there,
Mr. Lescom, informs his soon-to-be star writer that Ruth's "very first
articles are copied" elsewhere in the United States, a "good sign," he says,
of her "popularity." He also receives a "letter from Missouri" of clam-
oring demand among new subscribers out West, who eagerly anticipate
Floy's contributions "for the coming year" (167). Although "a novice in
business-matters," Ruth is no naïf at this stage in her self-development
(168). She trades on her growing name recognition as an author to negotiate a contract with a competing publication. The peripatetically named
"Pilgrim" periodical pays the urban wayfarer Ruth the same low wage
as "The Standard." Time still flies for her, then. Or, as the narrator states,
"months passed away, while Ruth hoped and toiled" and "scribbled away

in her garret" with "rent-room to pay, little shoes and stockings to buy, oil, paper, pens, and ink to find" (170).

It is, however, "in the hurry of finishing her next article" for "The Standard" that Ruth experiences another urban awakening. This one, like times previous, is temporal. "Pushing aside her papers," says the narrator, interrupting a condensed recapitulation of "the exciting" stories that "Floy" has been writing of "The Wise Men of Gotham," Ruth "discovered two unopened letters which Mr. Lescom had handed her" (173). Both letters it turns out heap praise on the author "Floy." More important, both impart a revealing truth about Ruth's chosen medium of serial publication. Although she might wish for the "leisure to have pruned and polished" her periodical pieces, Ruth also realizes that "there is more freshness about them than there would have been" had they not been "tossed to the printer before the ink was dry," or before their author "had time for a second reading." The comparative dilatory freedom of monograph publication may be in Ruth's immediate future. "*I* write a book?" she soon asks, in mock-rhetorical modesty (174). But it is the short-term turnover of urban serialization with which this short-term boarder-author most readily identifies, and from which she stands most to gain. Financially, the industrial standardization involved in producing and consuming newspapers like "The Standard" provides Ruth with a regular return on her labor investment. The more often she writes, the more dollars she earns. There are also socio-aesthetic benefits to serial publication for Ruth. Not unlike the letters of praise that she receives from her readers, Ruth's hurried writings possess the spatiotemporal privileges of the epistolary form. What Elizabeth Hewitt says of formal epistles—that they "are written across the distance of time and space"[48]—applies equally to Ruth's popular newspaper sketches, which circulate widely, and appear with all the rhythmic regularity of modern urban industry. Ruth's letter-like serials, moreover, are of and from the city, and thus figure a form that matches their function. Fitting for a boarder, Ruth in effect "rents" the column space in which her writings reside. Her writings, in turn, appear with such high frequency that they replicate the incessant temporal "Standard" of the metropolis and a city-conditioned author like Ruth, both of whom seem forever wide awake.

✦

Outside the established parameters of the domestic, *Ruth Hall* constructs a literary alternative to the conventional antebellum home. Here, in the discursive space of boarding, Fern's protagonist discovers the romantic depths of her mature self. Here, too, does Fern demonstrate that a "*Domestic Tale*" need not restrict itself to generic formulae. *Ruth Hall* is, after all, neither domestic in the traditional sense nor conformable to the literary forms of "*Tale*" or novel. Here in *Ruth Hall,* finally, the author writes the urban tense "*of the Present Time*" into mass circulation. The rush of *Ruth Hall* inheres less in the best-selling stylizations of sentiment that we associate with contemporary women's literature than in the page-turning pace of itinerant residence that governs Fern's narrative. *Literary* boarding is for Fern what it is for Ruth personally. Her heroine's hard-won movement from lowly renter and aspiring author to literary fame and hotel dwelling frames an occasion for testing the modern meanings of time and space.

*Ruth Hall*'s boardinghouse base denies readers what Fern elsewhere describes as the "comforts and elegancies of a home."[49] That Ruth's professional fortunes turn on her work for the suitably named "Household Messenger" nevertheless suggests that the author was at best ambivalent about domesticity in the city. Fern the journalist sympathized with what a writer for *Harper*'s magazine called "republican methods of housekeeping." She wrote with a New York boarder's envious admiration of the "comfortable, cleanly, convenient, *small* houses" for single families reputedly enjoyed by Philadelphians further to the south of her own adopted metropolis—the kind of single-family dwelling to which Ruth Hall, Fern leaves unclear, may or may not retreat outside the city at her story's inconclusive end. Indeed, the author leaves her protagonist at the close of this non-novel once more in-between—in between houses, somewhere in between country and city, and in between a conventional literary conclusion of happily ever after. Readers take leave of Ruth as they found her, on a threshold. It is not marriage that Ruth now awaits with baited breath; it is a liminal metropolitan existence, which presumably will see her sleep with her daughters in the suburbs, while she commutes by rail and contributes by mail to an urban workplace centered in the city's periodical print industry. Fern would have demurred when *Putnam's* magazine, in 1853, depicted boarding as a tortuous "Inferno" of Dantean proportions. But perhaps she might have agreed with her sometime friend Thomas Butler Gunn when he wrote as follows in his *Physiology* of Manhattan habitation: "a Boarding-House is, emphatically, *not* a home."[50] Fern, in short, was no apologist for boarding. *Ruth Hall* stops far short of endorsing this period residential practice.

*Ruth Hall,* rather, shifts readers away from their ingrained domestic thinking toward a modern discourse of the metropolis. To parse the author's boardinghouse prose for its conceptual understanding of home is to restrict oneself to a literal reading of this *"Domestic Tale."* To explore with Fern the temporal-spatial potentialities of the city is to inhabit instead the full figurative designs of the text. Those designs were diverse, in the spirit of the author's Manhattan. *Ruth Hall* at once brings "the sentimental mode into doubt," as Susan Harris suggests, while forcing a gendered confrontation with what Lauren Berlant terms the inscribed "power" of the patriarchy. *Ruth Hall* is "modern," moreover, by one recent commentator's account, because of its frank female critique of antebellum society.[51] But, as the foregoing account has begun to demonstrate, *Ruth Hall* is perhaps most meaningfully modern in that it finds a functional form in the emergent urban sensibility that is boarding. That the boardinghouse was no conventional home has been the historical premise of the preceding pages. That the discourse of boarding occupies an urban place apart from the domestic altogether is the more significant literary implication of a work like *Ruth Hall.*

Chapter 3

# Boston's Boardinghouse Community

Institutions . . . do not merely continue, especially in America;
they have to be created, and they have to be kept alive.
—Martin Green, *The Problem of Boston*, 1966

To suggest that antebellum boarding was at once more and less than domestic is also to say that it occupied no private separate sphere. Boarding on the one hand enjoyed something of a privileged position within the popular consciousness. The very genre of boardinghouse letters indicates that the great uncertainties of contemporary residence shaped the material setting of the American home as much as they did the thoughts of tens of thousands of the nation's renters, readers, and writers. On the other hand, boarding did not just languish inside the American mind. The pressing national concern over cohabitation inspired a voluminous corresponding discourse, the long reach of which ensured for boarding an open forum of discussion and debate by a larger American public. Market merged with home inside this civic space. Men and women mingled. A sanctifying domestic ideology informed the everyday municipal activities, agencies, institutions, and ideas that continue to this day to maintain the metropolis. Boarding from this public perspective in part removes the question of urban residence from the exclusive conceptual category of privacy, and situates it instead within a wide-ranging conversation on modernity.

This chapter considers the politico-literary forms of that conversation. In doing so, it further distances urban boardinghouse writings like *Ruth Hall* from the domestic discourses against which they have been wrongly measured for so long. The work of one particular boarder-author receives extended treatment here, chiefly for the instructive lesson on public values that his writings bring to boarding. That work is Oliver Wendell Holmes's *The Autocrat of the Breakfast-Table* (1858). Holmes's contemporaries adored the *Autocrat* and so made it the most celebrated boardinghouse book of the era.[1] The fervor of their response hinged on the fictional middle-aged narrator—the rather fussy "Autocrat" himself—whom the author endows with a capacity for laughably bombastic monologues duly delivered in the dining room of his Boston boardinghouse. Crowding its way into the Autocrat's conversational space, however, and disrupting his pronouncements on everything from the "self-made" man to city-country rivalries, is a rainbow assortment of fellow boarders who represent in their persons and forcefully expressed opinions a formidable board-inghouse public that will not be silenced. In fact, notwithstanding the narrator's grandstanding, it is the very diversity and vocal vivacity of Holmes's boarders that center readers' attention in what otherwise must seem a random textual assortment of small talk, practical didacticism, and philosophical musing.

Holmes in effect gathers his boarders together as an object lesson on the metropolitan meanings of community, a lesson that they embody by virtue of cohabiting (with some complications) in the new American city at midcentury. Despite his devotions to decorum, the Autocrat does not conceal his reservations about the propriety of such mixed society. His impromptu lectures on this and related subjects might be said to consti-tute a primer in social conservatism. Yet, the society that matters most in these pages—and that effectively qualifies the Autocrat's condescending posture—is the New England cross-section of boarders who inhabit *Auto-crat*'s pages, among whom Holmes's kindred, sympathetic spokesperson is but a lone dissenting voice. In having to cede conversational space to his housemates, the self-satisfied Autocrat unwittingly becomes an ironic emblem of American democracy's leveling potential during these disrup-tive years of urbanization. As such, he demonstrates boarding's dialogic involvement with period political discourses. To read the *Autocrat,* then, is to extend boarding's literary designs beyond any strict valuations of the private, domestic, or aesthetic. Holmes's text endows boardinghouse letters with a public communal function, delivered in an appropriately colloquial narrative form.

Colloquial, but hardly cohesive: appearing originally in serial form in the *Atlantic Monthly* magazine,[2] Holmes's work comes no closer to achieving a seamless narrative construction than does the Autocrat in marshaling his housemates to conversational consensus. "The Autocrat" serial, that is to say, might make gestures toward a tight storytelling structure, but the inherent disjointedness of its monthly medium made the year-long run of "The Autocrat of the Breakfast-Table" something other than the sum of its installments. To begin, the Autocrat informs readers early in the series that each of the twelve consecutive breakfasts (spaced at thirty-day intervals, in between the *Atlantic*'s regular publication schedule) over which he presides in fact collapses multiple meals and colloquies. "The Autocrat" as a "whole" is thus less an integrated account of recorded conversations than a fragmented collection of selected utterances. Furthermore, although Holmes would have his persona speak timeless boardinghouse truths, his print mouthpiece heralds modernity with a rhetorical performance that recalls metropolitan life in its seeming incoherence. With so much to relate, but neither the time nor space to express it adequately—"I was just going to say, when I was interrupted" are the Autocrat's very first words[3]—our ostensible protagonist colloquially adheres to the same strictures of time and space that characterize boarding. In other words, author like narrator must modify his narrative form to suit the occasion: in this case, the early morning mealtime of a Boston metropolis of boarders. Presumably Holmes's self-important speaker shares the leisure of the *Atlantic*'s own readers. The one indulges dilatory talk; the other savors "periodical" pleasures. For the rest of the modern working world, the city beckons, however. And so this same city strongly "interrupts" the Autocrat's idle "Breakfast-Table" privileges, fracturing the already fleeting form of his reflections.

If the city inspired this serial, it also precludes its completion. "The Autocrat's" separate monthly sequences must coalesce to become the book that their author would have them be. But with their constant conversational breakdowns—occurring when various boardinghouse characters speak out of turn, when the narrator departs on digressions, or simply when individual serials reach their allotted page limit—each installment of "The Autocrat" is as regularly irregular, as predictably unpredictable, as the urban discursive context from which it derives. Not only are the pacing and linear plot expectations of conventional poetry and prose ill-equipped to function within this context; the Autocrat himself, unapologetically allied to convention, hesitates to undertake the innovations necessary to find a form that fits his modern surroundings. A succession of piecemeal narrations, "The Autocrat" consequently reads as deconstructive commentary on the challenges of metropolitan authorship. Politically, Holmes's theme is community. His writings enact an urban public held together by the slenderest of democratic threads. Formally, Holmes's Boston boardinghouse falls apart, inasmuch as the Autocrat's traditional conceptions of narrative coherence are functionally unsuited to a New England environs in flux. Many an *Atlantic* reader would have taken the serial's seriocomic conceit to heart: the narrator's reluctant embrace of boarding probably recalled their own. Many a contemporary writer would have recognized the rhetorical predicament made plain in these same pages—how to lend stable politico-literary structure to a city that will not stand still.

✦

As a cultural site, the antebellum boardinghouse transcends the private domestic sphere and satisfies the requirements that scholars following Jürgen Habermas attach to the public sphere.[4] Boarding might have occupied a position outside the jurisdiction of the state; it was nonetheless civic in its mission, and accordingly typifies the Habermasian paradigm of public. For example, although it was often no more than a matter of mutual convenience for landlords, private property owners, and itinerant tenants, boarding met the habitational needs of large segments of the American population. Indeed, it did so long before the availability of reliable public housing, and without the financial or administrative support of the government. Boarding, too, in its discursive form invited pointed cultural criticism, the kind of ritualized complaint made possible by democracy.[5] The regularly published grievances of boarding's perennial shortcomings are from this perspective a running renters' editorial on the state of the residential nation. The boardinghouse, in addition, and like other U.S. institutions, was ideally as capacious in its constituency, as open in its admission policies, and as expansive in its reach as the public that mandated its creation. Boarders, in short, were themselves a subsidiary public for whom the common bond of boarding was widely enough shared to lend the practice a kind of quasi-institutional status. Here in the *semi*-private space of the antebellum boardinghouse, a democratic life outside officialdom was quietly at work.

"The Autocrat of the Breakfast-Table" lends that life voice, while underscoring the institutional structure that boarding both practically and metaphorically afforded metropolitan Americans before the start of the U.S. Civil War. Although Holmes might have struggled to find in his serial a suitable literary form for the city, he identified in his Boston boardinghouse a symbolic, communal support structure for an entire nation that edged ever closer at the time of his writing toward violent sectional conflict. The full significance of that identification becomes clear in light of what at least one historian controversially concludes caused the war. Scholar Stanley Elkins claimed midway through the previous century that the bloodiest internal conflict ever seen in the United States was the result of a decades-long, North-South breakdown of the nation's civic infrastructure. "The power of so many American institutions," he explains, "had one by one melted away." Among these "institutions" Elkins includes a church suffering from disestablishment, weak legal and political systems, and an irresponsible capitalist economy. Society itself, in his estimation, became something of an abstraction, as even thinking men and women from the intellectual axis around Boston accepted self-reliance as the preferred philosophy for a modern, atomized age. Institutionally shaken, Elkins's American republic breaks along the fault lines of region, race, and ideology. Conservatively secure in his communal vision, Holmes's Autocrat resists Elkins's anomie and the outcome it implies. The Autocrat, that is to say, sustains his faith in both nation and tradition by ironically resorting to a non-traditional modern institution that Elkins never mentions—what a visiting Englishman described in 1859 as "the national institution of boarding-houses."[6] Boarding is "The Autocrat's" more-than-metaphor for the country as urban collective.

The individual installments of "The Autocrat" might not aggregate as a coherent text, but the fictional boarders who populate Holmes's improvised Boston boardinghouse demonstrate a residential capacity to congregate en masse, and thus constitute a workable model of an American community in miniature. As an institution, the boardinghouse of course normally would have brought its constituents together as a matter of chance, rather than choice, and for only short durations. Thus, one must qualify any discussion of boarding's potential institutional empowerment with an appreciation for the inherent limitations of so loose a form of association. By virtue of its pervasiveness, however, no less than its persistence throughout the antebellum period, boarding became a provisional means of alignment at precisely that historical moment when the nation seemed poised to come undone. Boarding assembled in admittedly haphazard fashion a disparate set of Americans who otherwise might have had little, if anything, in common. It is this civic aspect of boarding that Holmes recognizes, and that he sub-textually makes the informing political discourse of his "Autocrat" commentaries.

"The Autocrat of the Breakfast-Table," then, offers a split boardinghouse perspective on a critical period in the nation's public past. On the one hand, antebellum boarding as it appears here and in a related strain of contemporary literature embodied the nation's midcentury political instability. Recurring (and in "The Autocrat's" case, serial) print depictions of boarding often at once deplored the practice even as they helped normalize the built-in uncertainty of a certain urban lifestyle. On the other hand, a particular brand of literary boarding invited the era's Americans to imagine alternatives to national fragmentation in the form of a progressively communal conception of the modern metropolis. In sharp contrast to Elkins's institutional view, with its implied pessimism of a faltering nation, the "national institution of boarding-houses" as it appeared in period literature provided the more optimistic boarder-author with an opportunity to write the terms of patently more hopeful American prospects. Boarders themselves recognized, in writing, the antebellum boardinghouse as more than mere housing. Among the more sanguine, it was a potentially unifying institution that could serve to remind hundreds of thousands of reading residents (or resident readers) that Americans were and would remain countrymen because, if for no other reason, they were cohabitants.

Boarding was by no means a guaranteed knitting together of Americans as one man, under one roof. But as a practical matter, it did require many of them to set aside their differences to preserve domestic peace. Under the best of circumstances, it could even instill a communal mentality among virtual strangers—this, despite President Lincoln's speaking of an American "house divided," and subsequent portrayals by scholars of midcentury institutional decline.[7] It is not the historical boardinghouse's availability as a sustaining "little commonwealth" that warrants attention here, however.[8] Of greater interest is the enabling role that boarding played in literature for those authors who wrote less to deplore the boardinghouse's domestic shortcomings than to prevent national disunion. Whether representing a miniaturized model society, or else exposing trends that had impaired a larger American *sensus communitatis,* the literary boardinghouse served as a figure of hope at just this juncture. Readers and writers who were so inclined could conceivably locate in the print experience of boarding a metaphor for the country's circumventing its institutional impasse. As political compromise stalled, that is to say, a number of authors chose to salvage a sense of community through the boardinghouse as discourse.[9] If their deployment of this writerly device finally failed, they left behind them a largely unacknowledged monument to boarding's literary place in holding a once-fragile United States together.

The conservative Autocrat's participation in this essentially liberal enterprise may seem unlikely, but his creative commitment to the cause of community becomes far more plausible within the context of an interpretive view of Boston quite different than Elkins's history of American malaise. With a concerned citizenry epitomized by "The Autocrat's" own author, Oliver Wendell Holmes, nineteenth-century metropolitan Boston proved an important exception to Elkins's general rule that the nation abandoned its supporting institutions. Historian John Kasson portrays these same years as "a time of institution building as well as breaking." No doubt work and family remained the everyday preoccupations of most Americans. Yet, not a few of them added to these two features of private life a passion for voluntary association that actually strengthened public life. Stuart M. Blumin sees "something new and quite notable" in contemporaries' rush to join formal organizations that sought through specialization both self- and social betterment. It was in fact post-Puritan Boston, a city nursed on the seriousness of civilizing ideas, and the setting for perhaps the strongest institutions known in the nineteenth-century United States, that led the way in this development. Greater antebellum Boston aimed at creating what Martin Green calls "an ideal total community." By reforming old institutions, even as they created new ones, Boston-area residents thought they could rid their city of crime, vice, and disease, extend decent living conditions up and down the social ladder, and make, again on Green's terms, "good sense, good behavior, and good taste" the "norms" of New England culture. Harvard, the Perkins Institute for the Blind, Massachusetts General Hospital, the Historical Society and Athenaeum—there is little evidence of institutional collapse here.[10]

Nor could one find proof of institutional imperilment in greater Boston's boardinghouse letters. The work of area authors like Holmes, representative in this respect, suggests a New England populace that was prepared to reimagine and so reinvent some new civic apparatus that would restore, or perhaps remake, the United States. Literary boarding by such authors appears to have been a union-saving response to an imminent national crisis. Holmes and his literary peers peopled their writings with dynamic examples of American diversity. They then registered a (grudging, in "The Autocrat's" case) willingness to share discursive space with these American people, effecting through literature the kind of community that many among their audience might have interpreted as a plan for national reconciliation. Belletristic boarding was no substitute for tangible steps to avoid war. Neither the historical boardinghouse nor its literary equivalent was adequate defense against the violence unleashed in 1861. Yet, rhetorical boarding provides some indication of the public work that contemporary authors were prepared to perform, no matter how divided the American "house" might be.

✦

Literary boarding builds communities, as a negative example perhaps best illustrates. Unlike the positive institutional formations undertaken by Holmes or, as we will see in the next chapter, Concord's Henry David Thoreau, the boardinghouse of antebellum letters also provides textbook illustrations of communal rupture. Witness the work of the New

York–based Nantucket journalist Charles F. Briggs, whose novel *The Adventures of Harry Franco* (1839) realizes the boardinghouse's full fractious potential.[11] The title character of Briggs's text receives a hastened education in big-city institutions upon arriving at a Manhattan hotel from rural New England. Franco's experience with hotel boarding is a trial by fire, insofar as the dining room at his establishment proves to be a combative, unfriendly, uncivil environment. His crisis moment in communal residence unfolds as follows: the greenhorn Franco dines his first night at the same table as a stereotypical southern "gentleman," not knowing the rules of the shared public supper; the two come to fisticuffs over a cultural and regional misunderstanding. Physically and temperamentally recalling South Carolina's slaveholding Senator John C. Calhoun, Franco's antagonist is "a lank cadaverous looking personage," speaks "in a drawling effeminate voice," sports "long black hair" and a bow-knotted cravat, and spouts tobacco juice and invectives in the direction of "a stout negro man who stood behind his chair, and jumped at his command with the greatest alacrity" (1:38–39). Franco asks his partner at table if the decanter before them is filled with Madeira, only to hear in response, "I kind o' reckon it's sherry." Not understanding that he must order his own drink, Franco fills and finishes off his glass, prompting his tablemate to say, "That's right cool stranger." A knife appears. Fists fly. And above the din our southerner shouts, "You infernal son of a northern abolitionist, I will teach you to drink a gentleman's wine" (1:39).

It is a comical escalation of sectional tensions that borders on the absurd. Writing from Democratic Manhattan, however, the Whig author Briggs, who opposed the expansion of slavery outside the American South, well realized that his scene carried a political import that belied (at least for readers of his own generation, if not ours) its apparent silliness. The author sought to instill at least two serious lessons in this passage. For Franco, the first of these lessons is personal. Briggs's title character feels "abashed," as he relates, "in finding that I had been guilty of a gross breach of good manners" (1:44). For readers today, the lesson is less personal than public, since the playful pratfalls of a novel written in 1839 might seem in retrospect a prophetic warning of the obstacles to northern and southern "gentlemen" coexisting within the nation's institutions. In American social settings that ranged from hotels to boardinghouses to the halls of Congress, civility had become an early casualty of the intensifying U.S. debate over slavery and various related sectional grievances. One result of sacrificing civility was this: even the supposedly civic spaces that the nation had established as sociopolitical common ground were less and less able to prevent and contain the kinds of heated outbursts that Briggs not so whimsically depicts. Long before the Senate-floor caning of Massachusetts's Charles Sumner,[12] a statesman whose violent denunciations of southern intransigence were notorious for a disregard of decorum more flagrant than Franco's, boarding for the inhabitants of Briggs's fiction has become merely another excuse for a skirmish. There is no community within this author's ostensibly communal institutions. There is only uncommon ground. Boarding at once provides the setting, the temporal occasion, and the discursive terms of battle.

With his "Autocrat" serial, Oliver Wendell Holmes rehearses an altogether different outcome. He attempts to hold in check the divergent tendencies of his times with a running conversation that invites greater America to "the table." It is the table talk itself which, according to scholar Peter Gibian, models a workable, if not always amicable, ritual of community formation in these pages.[13] There is, then, a seeming rhetorical logic to the Autocrat's omnivorous talk: it is his mission to make morning colloquy the tie that binds the nation's many boarders together. Holmes duly examines the legitimacy of that logic over the course of multiple boardinghouse breakfasts, each appearing originally and serially in the *Atlantic Monthly* magazine. In the all-important interim—the time and space within and between the *Atlantic*'s separate installments—the author permits his semi-autobiographical Autocrat persona to expatiate on topics that range widely from life, love, and death to literature, society, and religion. A dilettante author himself, the Autocrat intends to publish his remarks, or so he says, at some unspecified date in the near future. Thus conscious of the posterity of print, he elevates the tone of his talk to the level of drawing-room politesse. This decision imparts a certain stuffy reserve to some meals. The conversational flavor of these breakfasts nevertheless does not derive entirely from a bland Samuel Johnsonian formalism; the pieces savor of an unexpected spicing. The final taste of these texts comes from an inattentive audience of messmates, who deflate the soaring rhetoric and defeated decorousness of their would-be preceptor. While the Autocrat's monologues—buoyed by what David Shields describes as an eighteenth-century faith in the difference-dissolving potentialities of "civil discourse"[14]—tend toward anticlimax, however, the sheer variety and audacity of interruptions they engender sustain an unpredictable forensic interplay that pays homage at least initially to the cultural liveliness of America. In the process, laughter becomes a common cause.

Despite his admitted tendency to monopolize talk, then, the Autocrat half-reluctantly proceeds on the assumption that his messmates will "take a certain share in the conversation" (1:48). And indeed they do, much to his chagrin. In conversations to come, the Autocrat complains that one boarder "abuse[s] his liberty" by contradicting him (1:48). Another boarder, bolder still, administers a mild but pointed rebuke when he asks the resident pundit, "Do not dull people bore you?" (1:50). A third sportingly interjects with a pun even as the Autocrat criticizes that practice, contending as he does that "political double-dealings naturally gr[o]w out of verbal double dealings" (1:53). By title, and in principle, the Autocrat claims conversational preeminence here. But the constant interruptions to which readers bear witness reveal that he falls far short of colloquial supremacy in actual fact. He might remark, in addition, that "just as a written constitution is essential to the best social order, so a code of finalities is a necessary condition of profitable talk between . . . persons" (1:52)—his analogy once more recalling his creator's own ideological understanding of boardinghouse discourse. Yet for the Autocrat, antebellum boarding remains less a forum for conversational dominance than a democratic laboratory for extemporaneous exchange. Those who can pay the boardinghouse price of admission may stay, notwithstanding the narrator's self-flattering comparison between "clever fellows," such as himself, and the "common" "mediocrity" that, by implication, surrounds him (1:49). Those who stay claim certain rights, chief among them the liberty to make private opinion public.

What we must recognize, finally, is that the tongue-in-cheek tone of much boardinghouse literature amounts to more than a creative lark. In the case of "The Autocrat," the text in question is as earnest in its agenda as the Autocrat himself is long in talk. Holmes insists from the start of his serial on the political tenor of his donnée.[15] Or, as his narrator avers, "This business of conversation is a very serious matter" (1:50). So, on one level, the author might have contrived a house full of boarders merely to dramatize their everyday affairs. On another, his strategic handling of the mundane masks deeper meanings.

It is also critical to realize that the collective manifestations of dialogic resistance in "The Autocrat" are not, by nature, simply another destabilizing component from an already formally compromised storyline structure. Within the larger rhetorical-institutional framework of boarding, they also create the sustaining conditions by which Holmes can demonstrate a conversational equivalent of negative capability on municipal, perhaps even national, terms. Choosing as he does an unruly collection of Boston boarders for his chorus, Holmes builds *pluribus* into his account even as he posits the political balancing act that was and is *unum* as a public goal worth pursuing. It is a doubly felicitous narrative strategy. Boarding proves potentially unifying from a literary point of view, since the author, through the figurative stroke of a moveable feast, achieves at least a tenuous formal coherence for a year's worth of moveable type—those varied and variable installments from a monthly magazine that were only later bound. Boarding proves democratically (if only tentatively) inclusive from a civic standpoint, in that it provides in the revolving-door reality of antebellum boarding an excuse for shared experience. No doubt the aptly named Autocrat sets limits to inclusiveness. He residually resists both boarders' mildly egalitarian rhetoric and boarding's being a de facto rhetorical venue for free expression. But with an anonymous, rootless group of boarders at his disposal, Holmes provisionally does propose political "common ground" in the shared conversation that was boarding. The author thereby provides a blueprint by which greater Boston, or his whole United States, might strengthen its institutional structures along boardinghouse lines. American multifariousness keeps proceedings playful here. Yet Holmes's brand of democratic inclusiveness demonstrates itself to be more than a weak tea.[16]

So central is boarding to the author's politico-literary project that his written message of mutuality finally resides in the very medium of metropolitan conversation, the substance and style of which were unique in this period to the antebellum boardinghouse. Urban boarding, in other words, is not just happenstance in the pages of "The Autocrat." It is a literary institution in its own right, metaphorically recommending the organizational apparatus of table talk as a necessary corollary to community, whether real or imagined. Community for Holmes specifically meant Boston proper, a city whose Massachusetts State House he once famously labeled the "hub" of the universe. True to form, the author accordingly has his Autocrat assume the self-appointed role of regional spokesperson—to "temper," in Van Wyck Brooks's phrase, the area's proverbial good sense and civilization "to the lambs who know not Boston."[17] Just as surely as community carries Bostonian overtones here, it also takes on the particular characteristics of antebellum boarding. "The Autocrat" is, after all, a work where the informal (in)civilities of serial boardinghouse breakfasts color the context of what Holmes's narrator, with much domestic suggestiveness, calls "this tenement of life" (4:462). It would seem fitting, then, that of the wide array of institutions featured in "The Autocrat," only the boardinghouse appears in bold type. Boarding is the institution that looms largest above all others; it provides a thematic point of reference for an otherwise inchoate collection of musings. Boarding is, in fact, the institution that collapses within itself the myriad institutional functions that appear over the course of this otherwise undigested assortment of texts.

Just as the author's fictional boarders gather to talk, Holmes gathers readers together under the aegis of a whole host of New England institutions—the boardinghouse chief among them—whose interlocking aims and memberships virtually made nineteenth-century Boston that estimable city upon a hill that its founders had intended it to be.[18] Courts and clubs, churches, charities, and newspapers all appear here as topics for discussion, as do lyceums, libraries, and legislative halls no less than schools, parks, and hospitals. These are the tangible signs of the "hub" that Holmes himself would locate on Boston's Beacon Hill. These are likewise the community-oriented support networks that his peripatetic contemporaries well might have sacrificed had they not learned to internalize, as historian Thomas Bender claims they had,[19] the principle of community when- and wherever they could not establish it in fact. Yet it is, for Holmes, Boston's boardinghouse that encompasses all other urban institutions. Boarding is the institution that brings the disenfranchised into the fold of an *Atlantic*-sanctioned community, where writer, characters, and readers have direct access to civilizing serial texts such as his own.

A few examples from these texts illustrate the author's public narrative practice, in which the figure of boarding is synonymous with civic belonging. The Autocrat, to begin, joins the academic classroom to the breakfast room when he provides free French lessons for his landlady's son. He thoughtfully shares one of the boy's written exercises with readers, the revision of which he proposes as "an economical mode of instruction" for children "in moderate circumstances" (3:316). Holmes's Autocrat also acts as benefactor for his widowed landlady (widows being boarding's most prominent, if not prosperous, entrepreneurs). The "narrative" of her great "disappointment" in life brings the Autocrat to tears, while his expenditures for board help to redistribute wealth from one who has it to one who does not (4:461). At intervals, the Autocrat even gives his morning's perorations a religious emphasis for the benefit of those boarders who might have skipped Sunday service. "The great theological question now . . . is this:—," he writes at one stage, only to cut himself short (4:465). Conceivably, the rewards of these household contributions—at once tutorial, financial, and spiritual—extend further than the boarder-narrator's immediate listeners. They reach readers as well. The Autocrat's morning pearls of wisdom, like his regular payments of rent, are so much freely bestowed boardinghouse coin for a broad American public who stand only to gain from such breakfast table largesse. Holmes would nourish his city and the surrounding precincts of his society with a charity that truly begins at home.

There is a danger, however, in the Autocrat's relying so heavily on orality, on making the written recordings of his spoken words the primary means for reaching his audience. That is to say, there are discursive risks involved in any program that connects with the public through speech when one tends toward tangents, as does the Autocrat. The very subject matter of his conversations, for example, spatially ranges as far afield in local landmark references as it does temporally, and by turns, contracts and expands the "real" time taken to visit these innumerable places of interest. Talk is proverbially cheap even for the city's elite. And so it is with little cost to his designated talker—with no outward show of vocal exertion—that Holmes can have his boarder-narrator shift readers swiftly and sharply about a Boston that seems as fractured as the Autocrat's speech is fleeting. We are in consequence invited on a most manic, if not impossible, walking tour of a metropolis that simply could not and should not be seen in a day, let alone in any given serial sitting. Faithful followers of "The Autocrat" series take in Boston's harbor, its tributary waterways, and Navy Yard before exploring a not-yet residential Back Bay and outlying towns like Cambridge. It is an erratic itinerary more easily spoken than performed.

Another of literary boarding's public benefits is that it should be so closely connected, as it is for Holmes, to the city that inspired it. Precisely by carrying readers outside parlor walls and into his urban milieu does the author insist on boarding's being more than a private, inside conversation. Because of his firm conservative standards, the Autocrat could hardly regard the big-city boardinghouse as a venerable institution, especially considering its relatively recent provenance. But he tacitly acknowledges that boarding was, by virtue of its ties to the metropolis, both socially relevant and institutionally central to his creator's civic agenda. For, despite his orthodox Boston worldview, the Autocrat's author was intellectually "a puller down of worm-eaten structures," as V. L. Parrington says,[20] rather than an advocate of anachronism. Holmes thus ensures that his domicile can accommodate as much urban diversity as his culture could contrive to have come knocking at his metaphorical door. Classes collide; genders contest; and geographical regions come to conflict at the author's establishment. A rational traditionalist on the one hand, yet domestically invested on the other, Holmes ultimately, if improbably, encourages conversation with the modern context that shaped boarding's very reasons for being.

The trope of the city accordingly lays the groundwork for many of the Autocrat's orations. His recurring urban conceit of modern mobility, in particular, converts literal breakfast table negotiations with housemates into imaginative figurations of city conditions. It is, for example, a metropolitan frame of mind that allows the Autocrat to metaphysically link his boarder companions on one conversational occasion to "a small community" of insects beneath an uplifted stone in a field. Here at the *grass roots,* as it were, members of the one colony are as much inclined to "scatter-ing," "crawling," and "compressed" cohabitation as they are at the other (5:620). The Autocrat similarly evinces a flaneur's enjoyment of urban *ebb and flow*. This latter metropolitan movement he alternately experi-ences while "ripping" up the waters of Boston Harbor in his rowboat, or else when pausing to "lie still over the Flats" as he ponders "what a city of idiots we must be not to have covered this glorious bay with gondolas and wherries," the better to taxi about town (7:880–81). No less sugges-tive of his urban environs is the allegory of *uprootedness* around which the Autocrat builds one memorable serial. Casting an unlikely admiring eye on the "leaking in of Nature through all the cracks in the walls and floors of the cities," he conjures in the uninspiring image of Boston's side-walk vegetation a parable of urban migration: country weeds together pull up rural stakes in his story for new boardinghouse beginnings in the city, to live amid the "streets" and "pavements" of their adopted "home" (11:505). Like the broad swath of his talk, the narrator's flights of verbal fancy reveal a mind (and mouth) in sympathy with modernity.

The Autocrat's virtuosic talk is in harmony with the dissonant dis-ruptions of an unsettled city. It is his facility with the flexible figure of boarding that makes Holmes's Autocrat the (not quite undisputed) lin-guistic master of his equally unsettled Boston household. Adept at his discourse, the narrator orally achieves what his fellow boarders instinc-tively recognize: first, that boarding as an institution would need to be at least as adaptable as the changeable set of city-dwellers who for the most part boarded out in antebellum America; and second, that the language of boarding would need to be similarly resilient, as receptive to swings in circumstance as it was hospitable to whatever chance metaphors the city should happen to produce. Boarder-speak was especially suited to Boston. Due to its small size and chronic residential instability in the 1850s, that city was exactly the type of environment that made boarding before the U.S. Civil War a necessary residential behavior for migratory people not unlike those who join the Autocrat at table.[21] The ringleader of Holmes's group of urban American transients thus talks the modern talk like boarders generally walk the metropolitan walk, with a restless energy that rattles walls.

Constitutionally sober, a man of some social standing, and guided in life by a reigning civic spirit, the Autocrat does not sport with words for the sake of linguistic play. His variable urban metaphors have a pur-pose that far exceeds strictly literary effect, and carry a higher design for the city's (and the country's) boardinghouse public. What the narrator calls "the infinite ocean of similitudes and analogies," and the resident divinity student explains as the capacity of "some minds [for] . . . coupling thoughts or objects that seem not in the least related to each other" (4:462–63), are not for the Autocrat an "odious trick of speech" (5:619). They are proof that "all things are possible" in metropolitan rhetoric, just as they are "in a republic" (5:619). The primary challenge before the Autocrat is to bring his high-minded imagination to bear on the workaday urban world around him. Holmes would not have his persona inhabit solely a city of the mind; he would see him create for Boston's boarders a habitable American metropolis, where the kind of harmonious community that perhaps had eluded them thus far in their personal urban experiences might become a reality. As the examples above illustrate, the Autocrat simultaneously accepts the city's not-quite-controllable linguistic slippage as cause for civic concern, even as he conceives of open boardinghouse discourse as an opportunity to secure a more civil society.

✦

Holmes had known satisfactory examples of functional urban community firsthand. As the son of a Calvinist minister, and with a mother of distinguished family lineage, the author was born into a stand-alone home just north of Harvard Yard. Boarding would assume a major part in the young Oliver Wendell Holmes's otherwise vaunted New England institutional heritage. His early years saw him graduate in stages from schoolhouse to meetinghouse to market house to college campus, only for him to leave the family's Cambridge residence for a Boston boardinghouse in the winter of 1830–31. Holmes entered Harvard's medical school in that year, and the common quarters that he kept in the city placed him within walking distance of lectures at Massachusetts General. If his new address at 2 Central Court was not exclusive, it was certainly not unseemly. Boarding in fact moved Holmes closer to the heart of his "hub." Paying what he described as a "reasonable rate" for his "attic," despite there being "a murderer of melody on the piano-forte in the next room who plays the deuce with my metaphysics," he was even then investing for the long term in a professional future that he felt would "give me a hold on the community in which I live." Holmes's boardinghouse base of operations additionally gave him direct access to a local store of cultural production. It was here that the aspiring physician initially dabbled in authorship, writing for the *New England Magazine* those occasional verse and sketches (an abortive try at boardinghouse miscellanies among them) that in time would turn Holmes, too, into an institution in his role as local literary celebrity.[22]

**Figure 3.1.** Holmes's Left Bank Paris boardinghouse, 1833–35. From the limited-run, Riverside Press illustrated edition of John T. Morse, Jr., *Life and Letters of Oliver Wendell Holmes* (Cambridge, Mass.: Houghton, Mifflin and Co., 1896): I, facing p. 86. Courtesy John Hay Library, Brown University.

But it was in Paris where Holmes most fully realized the boarding-house's importance as part of the tapestry of public life on offer in what his Autocrat calls "our Atlantic cities" (7:881). Beginning in March 1833, and continuing for some two years after, Holmes studied medicine in Paris while living at a Left Bank boardinghouse located at 55 rue Monsieur-le-Prince (figure 3.1). It would be fair to say that Holmes studied Paris as well during these years, again using his boardinghouse as a staging ground for immersion in the city. He was comparing Paris to Boston. The former afforded in his eyes a rich institutional life that surpassed New England's capital by comparison. As he wrote to his parents back in Cambridge, he found north of the Seine "the seat of most of the luxury and splendor of Paris," including the Louvre, Tuilleries, Palais Royal, "most of the public monuments, and all the brilliant streets of the metropolis." On the river's south side, meanwhile, closer to his own dwelling, was the bulk of the fabled French bureaucracy. Holmes singles out the "public buildings" for praise: Luxembourg Palace, the city hospitals, the French Institute, Sorbonne, École de Medecine, and law school. What with the novelty of it all, plus Holmes's eager endorsement of the equally accessible theaters and restaurants besides, he became yet another American swayed by the "far advanced" state of "society" that he came to identify with Europe. The City of Lights qualifies in his estimation as at once "enlightened," "civilized," and "improved."[23]

No less "civilized" is Holmes's boardinghouse headquarters, and it is in fact both the prime location and elevating tone of his not-so-humble home away from home that put institutional Paris within his reach. He sets the scene for his parents, commencing with the assurance that his monthly rent of forty francs, or about eight dollars, provides him with "a fair specimen of the common chambers of respectable people." It also has given him entrée into a rich communal life infused with a public-mindedness that, in a different time and place, might have passed under the watchwords "real republicanism," to borrow an apt phrase from the Autocrat (2:178). Remarking, for instance, on the weekday breakfasts with his landlord hosts, Holmes makes a virtue of sociability when he once more writes by letter that "I like the family where I dine very well indeed." Weekends spent out at the cafés find him no less engaged with his surroundings, since the ubiquitous journals left lying about make it "impossible to avoid French politics." Boarders even bring public life home with them: Holmes considers himself fortunate that, as he writes, "I do not happen to take a revolutionary turn, or I might have had the pleasure like a young man who boards at the same place with me of being kept under lock and key at St. Pelagies through all the fine doings [that is, the subversive opposition to France's contemporary leader, Louis Philippe] of July." Less perilous than "political association" was professional affiliation. Holmes and his circle of American medical students enjoyed an abundance of the latter with the "Englishmen we meet at the hospital every morning," whom the novice doctor reports to "have grown quite communicative and civil." No wonder Holmes could muse, "Well, I feel now as if I had known Paris from my childhood. I am as much at home, day and night, in the streets as in Boston, or almost so. . . . I can hardly conceive of any body's living in any other way so completely have I naturalized myself." Note that "natural" life for Holmes had come to include an alcove canopied bed, a "garcon" to clean his boots, linen napkins, silver forks, white sugar and water for breakfast, and an entire letter's worth of bric-a-brac that he lists among his possessions. Boarding before and during Europe had converted the New England provincial into a cosmopolitan citizen. With a community to include him, and a roof over his head, Holmes was prepared to be at home most anywhere in the world following his Paris education, provided the public life was right.[24]

If there were civic limits that Holmes would not cross—limits drawn largely by radical French conceptions of *egalité*—the young doctor-author-boarder nevertheless proceeded upon returning to the United States to re-create the institutional ideal that he had discovered while abroad. He reentered New England with participatory zeal. As early as 1836, Holmes had accepted a temporary position at the Boston Dispensary. This was also the year in which he helped found the city's Tremont Medical School (later incorporated into Harvard) and became a member of the Society for Medical Improvement. A two-year spell teaching at Dartmouth's Medical School found Holmes closing out the decade boarding in a Hanover, New Hampshire, hotel.[25] The Doctor (as he soon was known) married in 1840 and thereafter frequented as many Boston institutions, other than matrimony, as seems humanly possible: the Society for the Diffusion of Useful Knowledge, Harvard's Phi Beta Kappa Society, the Mercantile Library Association, the Athenaeum Library,[26] the Massachusetts Medical Society, and the American Academy of Arts and Sciences. Holmes was, furthermore, a fixture on the lecture circuit, a much-tapped commemorator, and a sought-after dinner-party guest. No longer boarding in fact—his growing family had moved to a home of their own at 8 Montgomery Place, where they remained until the year of "The Autocrat's" serial (in)completion—Holmes had so internalized boarding's communal principles as to locate therein his very sense of self. His proper home was all of Boston. Its people were his co-inhabitants. Holmes himself was the center of attention at the city's table.

With the launch of Boston's *Atlantic Monthly* magazine in November 1857, a by-now notable Holmes recognized more than a literary repository; he sensed an important discursive occasion for reaching and shaping an urban boardinghouse "(re)public" along civic lines that he envisioned. There was nothing new, we know, in the boardinghouse narrative strategy that he adopted for this purpose. Casually observing his life and times from the dining-room confines of a midrange Boston boardinghouse, the author's pedant-narrator represents but another installment of a familiar urban boardinghouse trope that had been circulating in American and European print since at least the 1830s. Holmes's deciding, however, to rework the boarder metaphor a quarter-century into its American life was no nostalgic gesture. Nor was it simple imitation. On the contrary, although he adopted the persona of an aging city-dweller, and selected a decades-old discursive formula, "The Autocrat's" author pointed boarding forward when he enlisted it into a project for an *Atlantic Monthly* periodical that was to date the nation's most ambitious venture at "high" periodical literature.[27]

Indeed, Holmes's politico-literary project with the "Autocrat" was to solidify the civil society and refined cultural standards to which the *Atlantic* aspired, while undercutting the claims of boarding's popular "lowbrow" subscribers to a prominent position within the model city that he imagined. Holmes's "Autocrat" is ultimately a rhetorical exercise in cultural politics. The author articulates a more reliably (and more responsible, he would have said) *middle*-class response to the metropolis than had his many "blue-collar" counterparts. Those writers labored within the same urban vein as he did; they employed a similar boardinghouse formula in countless residentially inflected pieces from the period. And, in doing so, they mythologized the city experiences of urban arrivistes like the aforementioned Harry Franco, journalist C. F. Briggs's eponymous, hapless, and high-profile antihero. It was not that members of Holmes's social station would have denied the mass of boardinghouse peoples a place in their public. As we will see, Holmes seats such peoples at his own discursive table. It was, rather, that the civil society entertained by Holmes and his peers demanded more from metropolitans than the average life-sustaining allowance expected by boarders—food, shelter, and upkeep. Quasi-domestic, and institutionally civic, boarding was for Holmes a politico-literary means to a socially engineered end. In ideological league with works like Donald Grant Mitchell's *The Lorgnette* (1855) and Thomas Butler Gunn's *The Physiology of New York Boarding-Houses* (1857), then, Holmes matched the message of his "Autocrat" with his *Atlantic* medium when he gave the respectable, literate, and literary middle classes who comprised his primary audience a genteelly conventional boardinghouse voice with which they could identify.[28] "This is the city," Holmes would have his self-patterned spokesperson say, and "these are its proper concerns" for a gentleman like me, or, with a nod toward the *Atlantic*'s general readers, for gentlefolk like us. That many of these same readers, who represented in their day a newly consolidated contemporary gentry, at some stage may have known boarding personally only would have enhanced the appeal of their like-minded author's "Autocrat."

What is striking and strange about this author-audience relationship is the strained residential context in which it occurs. The writer and his ideal reader might have agreed ideologically over the public fate of the urban nation, but they met with private conversational conflicts inside these texts. Absent from Holmes's serial is the shared civic-domestic purpose that originally framed the outside of his story. Boston by consequence becomes in "The Autocrat" a modern city built less on consensus than constant change and accommodation. Hence the Autocrat's ironic rhetorical fortunes: he who would manage table talk in the metropolis succeeds only in conciliating an unruly, and ultimately unmanageable, city of bumptious boarders. Holmes's primary shabby-genteel characters—including a landlady and her relations, a schoolmistress, a divinity student, an elderly gentleman, and one young working-class type, rough around the edges—double as the narrator's immediate listeners within doors. Their reactions as "readers" are mostly antagonistic. They indulge in unrestrained talk at table; often they ignore the Autocrat altogether; they invariably speak out of turn. Each reaction in its way disrupts the conversational coherence of these pieces. Taken together, such disruptions reveal a narrative design shaped around the same kinds of petty power struggles that boarders, literally living at arm's length, would have recognized as inherent to cohabitation. There was, and seemingly always would be, a tacit competition among crowds who engaged in close-quartered rituals of eating, sleeping, washing, grooming, and talking. What Holmes offers with his "Autocrat" is a serially fragmented profile of a fractious city, one whose fertile heterogeneity necessarily foiled such stable sociocultural hierarchies as the *Atlantic*'s adherents would have prescribed for their country. Boarding here is no perfunctory space. It formally and functionally approximates democracy in the unpredictable vocal variety of the Autocrat's fellow boarders. If the fictional peoples who populate these urban pages acknowledge any external authority, it is this: they collectively accept an unspoken rule that their supposed social betters would not dictate to them how to live their public or private lives.

Undeterred by modern urban democracy, the Autocrat proceeds all the same in his breakfast table campaign to promote the civil society that Holmes himself had experienced in Paris, and that both he and his fictional narrator would recommend to Americans as a city worth establishing. The author was well aware that Boston had its own institutions—boardinghouses among them—and the civic will thereby to build a better republic. What he tried to provide in "The Autocrat" were the discursive means, disguised in a disarmingly charming and ostensibly domestic boarding tableau, by which art might enact through imaged example the higher institutional life that he had in mind. To be is to board in this serial. To board is to belong: either to an aspiring boardinghouse society whose resident senior speaker would lift its members from the level of pedestrian existence; or else, and at the very least, to a fragile storyline in which disjointed morning talk is the literary tie that loosely binds the diverse peoples of a microcosmic city. As both a semi-autobiographical narrator-exemplar, and as a purveyor of narrative as such, Holmes makes available to his reading public what he believed to be a sounder, saner standard of community.

If the Autocrat encounters rhetorical resistance to his civic prescriptions from willful housemates, and if he himself to some extent has incorporated into his discourse the city's busiest metaphors, he nonetheless remains conservatively committed to the cause of cautious urban progress. Among the many challenges that he faces in building a better boardinghouse is populating his republic. Although he would be inclusive in his designs, the Autocrat locates somewhere in the vicinity of the boarder named John the kind of citizen whom his city would need to reform. John sits atop barrels outdoors. John smokes cigars on the residential premises. John, a presumed manual laborer, maintains a rather inflated opinion of himself, relating that "two or three other girls would drown themselves" should he marry (9:242). But above all, John takes pronounced changes in social standing for granted, something that the aristocratically mannered (and well-to-do, we later learn) Autocrat cannot abide. Says the vernacular John of the household schoolmistress, "Folks rich once,—smashed up. She went right ahead as smart as if she'd been born to work. That's the kind o' girl I go for" (9:242). The Autocrat demurs. He may retain a place in his urban institution for the Johns of the American 1850s. Yet John, from the narrator's perspective, ought not forget his private place indoors, or his public position without. The Autocrat's early comments on "self-made men" are worth quoting in this respect:

> The right of strict social discrimination of all things and persons, according to their merits, native or acquired, is one of the most precious republican privileges. I take the liberty to exercise it, when I say, that, *other things being equal,* in most relations in life I prefer a man of family. (1:56)

Of course "things" are not "equal" in the Autocrat's mixed-class residence. Nor would Holmes, a lifelong leader among Boston's ruling elite, necessarily want them to be.[29] The author as Autocrat was ready to recognize difference but simultaneously sought ways to contain it. Holmes did prescribe change for change's sake on occasion: the Autocrat's boon companion, the Professor, advocates "breaking up" a long-settled residence every now and then, and the Autocrat whole-heartedly agrees (10:366). This was not a call for America's moderns to abandon established verities, however. As Holmes's fictional twin explains, in what could be a pledge of priorities administered to applicants at his table, "To-day's dinner subtends a larger visual angle than yesterday's revolution" (12:619).

The Autocrat is as conscious of geographic place as he is of metropolitan people, and tries to strike the right regional balance at his household accordingly. As the serial's conversations continue, he devotes increasing attention to repairing the sectional (and figuratively structural) cracks that threaten his residence, and by symbolic extension the nation's edifice. In a subsequent "Breakfast-Table" series, featuring the same above-named friendly "Professor," Holmes explicitly brings sectional crisis to table in the persons of boarders "Little Boston" and "the Marylander." The latter personage instigates a resonant North-South debate with the New England caricature of a divinity student over "private property." Hidden behind their conversational façade is the more sensitive subject of slavery.[30] Meanwhile, back inside his own serial, the Autocrat broaches the civic conundrum of sectionalism through innuendo, anecdote, and indirection. Ever mindful of manners, he proceeds so as not to give unnecessary offense. Thus he says of "Southern gentry," "–fine fellows, no doubt, but not republicans exactly, as we understand the term" (2:179). The topic of "Caucasian" conflict in caste-conscious India also arises before the Autocrat makes brief mention of "West-Indian slaves" prior to reciting his interpolated poem, "The Two Armies" (3:319; 8:106; 11:245). With a sly invocation of traditional southern comfort, the Autocrat further holds forth on "Hospitality," which, he says, before precipitating a discussion of "our Northern cities," "is a good deal a matter of latitude, I suspect." Finally he speaks what is foremost in his mind when he wonders out loud what, in his day and age, is "provocative to the interchange of civilities." It is a question of some import for a nation divided between "two extremes" (12:628). As an ardent unionist, anti-abolitionist, and a man not immune from an inherited racial prejudice,[31] the author held deep convictions on these matters, although he keeps them in check here. The Autocrat, for his part, responds to his own rhetorical question by elaborating his boardinghouse metaphor with a martial figure of speech "not to be found," he assures us, "in Montesquieu or the journals of Congress":

> We are the Romans of the modern world—the great assimilating people. Conflicts and conquests are of course necessary accidents with us, as with our prototypes. And so we come to their style of weapon. Our army sword is the short, stiff, pointed *gladius* of the Romans; and the American bowie-knife is the same tool, modified to meet the daily wants of civil society . . . and come to close quarters. (2:55)

That "conflicts and conquests" are "necessary accidents" is a significant concession in 1857–58, with a civil war imminent. That "civil society" was still possible, however, even in the "close quarters" of a boarding-house occupied by the likes of a "Little Boston" and "Marylander," was an optimistic prediction that the United States as an institution would not be razed. Holmes's national home could and would stand.

Still there was work to be done. With his civic residence inhabited, and regional prejudices diplomatically poised, the Autocrat counsels re-creating in America the institutional sophistication that had so pleased Holmes in Paris.[32] Once again the Autocrat's Professor friend speaks in his stead when it comes to specifying what civic business he would have his countrymen perform. Worryingly, the Professor is "tipsy" at this critical moment after a night carousing with "the boys," and so raises a cloud of doubt over his own image of a revitalized city. He neverthe-less lectures in earnest. There are, to begin, no Boston boardinghouse Johns in the Professor's new order. Nor does he make mention of those forgotten working classes and immigrants whom historian Stephan Thernstrom labels in a later context "The Other Bostonians."[33] There are only people like the Professor. His list of worthy urban inhabitants is as follows:

> Judges, mayors, Congress-men, Mr. Speakers, leaders in science, clergymen better than famous, and famous too, poets by the half-dozen, singers with voices like angels, financiers, wits, three of the best laughers in the Commonwealth, engineers, agriculturalists, all forms of talent and knowledge. (5:624)

"Shipwrecked" with their wives and children "on a remote island"—the Autocrat, by contrast, requires a preexisting urban scene for his own exper-iment—the Professor would "splendidly" proceed to "reorganize society" with such men:

> They could build a city—they have done it; make constitutions and laws; establish churches and lyceums; teach and practice the heal-ing art; instruct in every department; found observatories; create commerce and manufacturers; write songs and hymns, and sing 'em, and make instruments to accompany the songs with. . . . There was nothing they were not up to, from a christening to a hanging; the last, to be sure, could never be called for, unless some stranger got in among them. (5:624)

The Professor's is a utopian undertaking at city-building. Or, to restate the case on Holmes's terms, his associate would rebuild the national boardinghouse from its foundations, substituting a methodical cultivation of culture for the comparative blind chaos by which the antebellum city selected boarders. The roster of inhabitants here includes only individuals of "talent." Excluded, presumably, is the chance "stranger," because of his strangeness. The Autocrat allows the Professor's alcohol-induced enthusiasm to pass without comment, save for the remark, "It didn't make much difference to me whether it was all truth" (5:624). All of which suggests that the Autocrat, notwithstanding his worldly wisdom, and despite his connoisseur's response to city living, was chiefly interested in preserving what a Boston man of breeding like himself might deem worth preserving should the nation begin again. In boardinghouse parlance, readers have arrived at a fashionable locale where the likes of everyman, American John, would reside at best down the block (figure 3.2). There was to be no raucous democracy in this institution. Urbanism would make way for urbanity. Only blue bloods need apply.

Conversationally "carnivalesqe,"[34] as Peter Gibian suggests, yet institutionally restrained, "The Autocrat" provisionally ends when the narrator's never-quite-completed monologues take an unequivocally conservative yet somewhat unexpected turn. Having devoted much of his disparate table talk to community, if not communion, the Autocrat one morning takes personal steps toward practicing what he preaches when he invites the attractive schoolmistress to join him on a ramble about town. One walk becomes two before walking itself emerges as another of the Autocrat's cherished institutions. That institution soon yields another, marriage. Before many more walks can occur, the Autocrat proposes a boardinghouse union of which the would-be warring North-South factions of the then United States might have taken notice. Offering to his female companion to "walk the *long path* with you," the Autocrat commits himself to a community of two, forged in a boardinghouse no less, both legally and spiritually binding (11:506). There is nothing subtle about the move on Holmes's part. First comes the wedding, which occurs in a house of worship. Then follows a reception back at the boardinghouse, from which the couple soon will depart to domesticate on a more intimate footing than was possible in a household of non-relations. Preceding these new beginnings will be a honeymoon to Europe. And the independently wealthy Autocrat (who, we learn, has been boarding because it humors him to do so) is prepared to pay for it all, just as he assures his wife that she never will have need to wage-labor again. The literal icing on the author's institutional cake comes courtesy of the

**Figure 3.2.** This *Scene in a Fashionable Boarding House,* No. 1, represents a considerably different social setting than that experienced by Holmes's Autocrat at his own Boston establishment. This high-toned "Scene" even might model the "better" boardinghouse that the Autocrat envisioned. New York: Bufford's Lithograph, ca. 1835–39. Courtesy American Antiquarian Society.

landlady's son, Benjamin Franklin. City-bred like his founding-father namesake, that thrifty young citizen has purchased with his own savings a wedding-cake decoration, which the groom describes as consisting of "two miniature flags with the stars and stripes." The "very pleasing effect" of the pastry, as the man of the occasion relates, is not simply sweet (12:632). It is both sacred and civic in that it recalls a national compact bigger than any boardinghouse, and far larger than urban New England.

The impending Civil War would test the strength of the United States' bond. Boarding, like other American institutions, registered with brutal honesty the breakdown of a national community at arms over slavery. To take but one example, southern legend holds that many a Confederate blockade runner, as well as a young rebel officer named Robert E. Lee, met his habitational needs early in the war by staying at landlady Kate Stuart's boardinghouse in North Carolina's Outer Banks. For their part, several New York boardinghouses quartered free blacks—who were

fleeing angry Irish mobs—during the city's Draft Riots of 1863. One such
house, the Bushnell boardinghouse, was home to no less a Union partisan
than the wife of Major General Solomon Meredith.[35]

But, as we have seen, it was perhaps the writers of Holmes's generation who were most attuned to boarding's political possibilities. Some
seven years before the author began his "Autocrat" series, one of his contemporaries sketched a "Singular Dream of Mr. Calhoun" that finds the
Dixieland senator deep in thought over the state of the nation while staying in his Washington, D.C., boardinghouse. The piece opens in January
1850, year of the failed Great Compromise, with the senator explaining
to his colleagues over the breakfast table the "singular dream" that he has
had the previous evening. Visited in his chambers, he relates, by another
founding father, George Washington, Calhoun finds himself rudely interrupted as he sat "writing a plan for the Dissolution of the American
Union." Washington chastises. The "Great Nullifier," Calhoun, relents.
And the nation survives, for but a short while longer.[36] If Holmes imagined the boardinghouse that might be, he did so alongside others who
feared for what it was to become.

✦

What boarding was, finally, was what it had been from the beginning—
modern. For all "The Autocrat's" ironies, the most ironic aspect of the
series is the cognitive dissonance created by the author's serial form.
A fundamental component of all literatures, according to the Russian
formalist critic Mikhail Bakhtin, is "the process of assimilating real
historical time and space." And it is precisely the serial nature of "The
Autocrat" that at once provides Holmes's unsatisfactory generic response
to Bakhtin's assimilative "process," and endlessly frustrates his protagonist, whose serial residential circumstances epitomize the time-space
ruptures of modernity. Bakhtin gives the name "chronotope" (literally,
"time space") "to the intrinsic connectedness of temporal and spatial
relationships expressed in literature." He further explains this "connectedness" as follows:

> In the literary artistic chronotope, spatial and temporal indicators
> are fused into one carefully thought-out, concrete whole. Time, as it
> were, thickens, takes on flesh, becomes artistically visible; likewise,
> space becomes charged and responsive to the movements of time,
> plot and history. This intersection of axes and fusion of indicators
> characterizes the artistic chronotope.[37]

Literary boarding ostensibly figures Bakhtin's "fusion," given its close creative involvement with (and historical boarding's "concrete" embodiment of) the modern metropolitan experience of time and space. Yet, the reiterative nature of rented residence, in tandem with the capitalist reification of commercial city space, likewise would seem to preclude the "thickening" by which Bakhtin's chronotope becomes "whole." Holmes's "Autocrat of the Breakfast-Table," in fact, cannot "assimilate" the problematic time-space relationship that Bakhtin's chronotope would afford him. He is serially situated in a repetitive periodical. He is provisionally bound by a coverless book. He is quasi-domestically leasing the ambivalent semi-privacy of boarding. The Autocrat might be at home with his conservative notions. He is dislodged from his settled ideas, however, by an ironic instance of Bakhtin's "intersection." That is to say, time and space may merge in Holmes's multiple (and multiplying) texts. But they do so on the basis of a modern residential practice, and a serially fragmented literary form, that together foreclose on the very concept of "fusion," of "concrete whole" closure of any kind.

His confident conservatism notwithstanding, the Autocrat thus expresses misgivings about the temporal-spatial predicament in which his serial-residential circumstances have situated him. Much of the Autocrat's table talk reaches readers as an acutely self-conscious metaconversation on the communicative limits of his rhetorical context. As we have seen, the Autocrat seldom speaks without interruption. Assertive tablemates and his own digressions often stop short his monologues, or else enforce on him the detour that is dialogue. There is, too, the disjointed nature of the Autocrat's conversation. In the very first paragraph, from the very first serial installment, with which he greets the *Atlantic*'s readers, Holmes's Bostonian ventures the (vaguely ridiculous) "philosophical proposition" that "all economical and practical wisdom is an extension or variation on the following formula: $2 + 2 = 4$," only to change course repeatedly in the succeeding paragraphs with inchoate rhetorical gestures signified typographically by what might be this serial's defining visual symbol, the long dash, "——" (1:48). The Autocrat subsequently makes all-too-brief mention of the German polymath Leibniz and mutual admiration societies before launching into the first of what will prove to be many long-winded speeches. There can be little conversational flow—and no Bakhtinian "fusion"—in a text(s) that formally internalizes the abruptness of table talk. Invariably to be continued, this serial cannot reach completion when there is always and forever another month to come.

Nor can the Autocrat avoid repeating himself, ad infinitum, within the cramped temporal-spatial confines of his limited monthly allotment of column space. There is a certain reassuring quality to the Autocrat's ideological consistency. Holmes's man knows what he thinks, and thinks much the same today as he did yesterday and will tomorrow. In conservative defense of constancy, and in explanation of his serial repetitions, he writes:

> —You don't suppose that my remarks made at this table are like so many postage-stamps, do you—each to be only once uttered? If you do, you are mistaken. He must be a poor creature that does not often repeat himself. . . . I shall never repeat a conversation, but an idea often (1:50).

Less reassuring is the necessitated nature of these repetitions. With a metaphorical nod to the period mechanization of print, the Autocrat suggests that his signature figurations are not the result of his fertile poetic process; they are the unavoidable offshoot of industrial plate-engraving technologies, which made possible the serial mass production on which the *Atlantic* depended for its mostly metropolitan circulation: "I shall use the same types when I like, but not commonly the same stereotypes," he says (1:50). Residing, moreover, in a location where variable houseguests and a rotating menu of meals were the unwritten rule, the Autocrat like the majority of boarders would have partaken of a peculiar modern process whereby the seeming variety of urban life incrementally became—in the form of his establishment's predictable daily patterns—the tedium of everyday sameness. Thus he can muster only muted appreciation for ersatz boardinghouse diversity. This the Autocrat accomplishes in a strategically bracketed narrative aside that recalls the congested, comparatively enclosed, and inherently repetitive residential setting in which he writes:[38]

> [I am so well pleased with my boarding-house that I intend to remain there, perhaps for years. Of course I shall have a great many conversations to report, and they will necessarily be of different tone and on different subjects. The talks are like the breakfasts, . . . . You must take them as they come. . . .] (4:457, brackets in original)

With so many housemates, one boarder must seem as stereotyped as one's favorite metaphors, or one's favored magazine. With so "many conversations to report," one morning's colloquy comes to resemble the one preceding it as well as the inevitable next boardinghouse breakfast to follow, despite the "different tone and different subjects" that inform each individual morning's conversational installment.

The Autocrat elaborates on his attitude toward seriality—as pertains to residence, reading, and writing—when he offers yet another of his favored literary forms, the Holmesian parable, to clarify his position on repetition. There was, he relates, "a certain lecturer" whose circuit found him "performing" away from his presumably coastal "home" "in an inland city." Invited to tea afterward by a small group of literary locals, the speaker is asked there about "his many wanderings in his new occupation." He responds as might the Autocrat (also a dilettante performer on the lecture circuit, we learn). Illustrating his answer is an analogy that figures the spatiotemporal dislocations of modernity: "I am like the Hume, the bird that never lights," he declares, "being always in the [railway] cars, as he is always on the wing." The Autocrat continues his parable, but with radical narrative collapsing: "—years elapsed," he says. "The lecturer visited the same place once more for the same purpose." Also the "same" is the question put to him at tea by his earlier interlocutor, who once more remarks on the speaker's "constantly going from place to place." The Autocrat punctuates his account with, "'Yes,' he answered. 'I am like the Hume,' and finished the sentence as before" (1:51).

No less than three modern morals emerge from this story. The first is spatial. Any urban-industrializing people—whether city-dwellers generally, boarders in particular, or self-improving participants of the lecture tour—must expect some "uprooting" in life. Indeed, they might expect the same in death, considering that "uprooting" is the term that the Autocrat uses in a later conversation on a grave-shifting act of "vandalism" that he reports having been committed against "three at least of our city-burial grounds" (10:365). The second lesson is temporal. City time, like railroad time, passes quickly enough that the temporal distance between "place to place" collapses, as does the distinction between now, later, and before. Such is the rapidity of time's passing that time itself would seem to stand still. Moral three is serial. Much like the lived experience of urban boarding, the discursive experience of the monthly magazine (or the lyceum lecture) must involve a certain sameness in the repetitive nature of the performance. Boarders no less than the producers and consumers of periodicals will find that the seeming difference of miscellany—involving (ir)regular rental on the one hand, and salable print on the other—tends to diminish under the standardizing pressures of modernization. When every urban day is different, when all periodical content evolves, then diversity as such bleeds into monotony.

Trapped inside this modern context, the Autocrat can only discourse in serial circles. If, as Thomas Bender writes, "modernity is a conversation with a past, and that past must be present,"[39] then the temporal/

spatial obsessions of Holmes's beleaguered boarder begin to reveal their psychic-dialogic source. Here are a man and a mind in "conversation" with the impersonal time-space forces that define the ambiguously public, un-"chronotoped" condition of the American metropolis midway through the nineteenth century. Modern time weighs especially heavily on an aging Autocrat, who betrays all the anxiety of a lifelong joiner whose own "time" for civic usefulness may well be passing. "Some time or other" he says in an early installment" (1:57). Phrases like "occasionally," "every morning," and "the other day" appear throughout the serial (1:57; 6:734). So cognizant is the Autocrat of time in the short term that he hears it literally ticking inside his own head: "Tic-tac! Tic-tac! Go the wheels of thought," he at one stage exclaims (8:105). Nor does he neglect the long span of historical time, and his own place and space therein. Ever the traditionalist, he waxes philosophical on the ripeness of age. "Certain things," he avers, "are good for nothing until they have been kept for a long while" (5:615). Among these he includes "our brains," which he compares to "seventy-year clocks" (8:105). He even treats the matter with uncharacteristic directness on one occasion, recalling, "I warned all young people off the premises when I began my notes referring to old age" (9:234). As for timepieces per se, he is ready to forego the frenetic immediacy of modernity for the steadier pace and leisurely gait of "The Flâneur,"[40] which figure Holmes featured late in life in an urban observer's poem set on Boston Common. For "the present," the Autocrat is far too flustered for flanerie. He might suggest the surface appearance of city equanimity, but he resists the impulse for true urban immersion, and warns against too much attentiveness to his here and now, declaring, "If a watch tells us the hour and the minute, we can be content to carry it about us for a life-time, though it has no second-hand. . . . The more wheels there are in a watch or a brain, the more trouble they are to take care of" (6:737; 7:871). However decorous he may be, Holmes's spokesman is finally defiant in his rhetorical resistance to the time-space collapse around him. He is not unlike the implied readers of the *Atlantic Monthly* in this respect. The very title of that magazine suggests an eternal, oceanic expansiveness. The very content of that journal—including as it did an inordinate proportion of early articles and tales treating classically timeless subjects, such as "The Ghost Redivivus" and "The Golden Milestone"—suggests a literary public that has grown tired of modern America's restlessness. The fear for Holmes and a fair share of his countrymen is this: that all American moments had become momentary, mere interludes of what the Autocrat calls "perpetual changes" (2:181).

Hence the final irony of "The Autocrat." The necessarily short-lived condition of serialization is hardly the medium for anyone who wishes to

endure. Nor is the close-quartered, short-term residence of Boston boarding a likely venue for literary longevity. It is precisely this friction between
medium and message that makes "The Autocrat of the Breakfast-Table"
so suitable a subject of study for anyone inquiring into the origins of
American modernity. However ideologically driven he is, then, and no
matter how eclipsed his self-styled "vision" of the domestic might be, the
author's Autocrat evinces the spirit of a citizen who is ready to meet the
modern on its own terms. His ties to tradition in fact steady him for the
"perpetual changes" that he must occupy, despite his desire to "not be
in unseemly haste" (12:628). "—I find," he decides, "the great thing in
this world is not so much where we stand, as in what direction we are
moving" (4:258). It is a sentiment with which any boarder would have
concurred. More reflective still, the Autocrat recognizes the subsuming
sprawl of the city, and concedes that soon he may lose easy access to
country. He nevertheless is prepared to "carry mountains" in his "brain"
and "have an ocean" in his urban "soul," if need be (9:501). Summarizing
this metropolitan perspective, he elevates his discourse from the merely
thoughtful to the epistemological: "The forms or conditions of Time and
Space, as Kant will tell you, are nothing in themselves—only our way of
looking at things" (9:502). Ever mindful of the grand scheme of "things,"
the Autocrat would seem to be pragmatic enough in the end.

A Boston boarder and serial author, the Autocrat adapts to the city
"Time and Space" that modern metropolitanism would have him inhabit.
Sensing the (irresolute) end of his serial, he resolves "to get as much as I
could into every conversation" (12:619), to "talk to you of many subjects
briefly" (3:319). Recognizing the periodical demands of the monthly magazine, he learns to simplify his "particular" composing process—"to see a
proof, a revise, a re-revise, and a double re-revise, or fourth proof rectified
impression of all my productions, especially verse" (2:184). Acknowledg-
ing the impermanence of urban residence, he concludes that "we die out
of houses, just as we die out of our bodies" (10:366). It might have been
as an American in Paris that Holmes himself had discovered and then
instituted upon his return to the United States the civic usefulness of the
transatlantic West's most modern, republican, urban institutions. But
Holmes's Autocrat did not need what Malcolm Cowley later would call
an "exile's return" from Europe to find a fittingly modern literary form
for his city condition.[41] This he found as an American in the antebellum
metropolis. He found this in Boston, boarding.

Chapter 4

# Concord Board: Democratic Domestic as Urban Organic

The organic form . . . is innate; it shapes as it develops itself from within, and the fullness of its development is one and the same with the perfection of its outward form.
—Samuel Taylor Coleridge, 1818

An explicit civic-aesthetic problem in Oliver Wendell Holmes's *The Autocrat of the Breakfast-Table,* boarding figures an implicit (and implicitly progressive) literary form in another of greater Boston's boardinghouse volumes from the period, Henry David Thoreau's *Walden* (1854).[1] The noted New England naturalist, essayist, and ethical agitator Thoreau might strike the casual observer as an unlikely boarder-author. Even less likely is the notion that *Walden* reads as a representative boardinghouse text, which it does. Thoreau's lyrical account of a purifying domestic experiment conducted in his native Concord woods is ostensibly sylvan, not urban, in contrast to much of the work from the city literary tradition to which *Walden* otherwise belongs. The author furthermore insists from the start of his narrative that the "*I,* or first person," must govern the by turns descriptive and ruminative pages of his prose (3), and thereby forestalls his entertaining the public and semi-private concerns that typically inform the substance and structure of so much of the corpus of boardinghouse letters. *Walden* nevertheless is a classic boardinghouse text. That is to say, *Walden,* like other examples of the boardinghouse genre examined in this study, is classically modern, and modern*ist,* in the determinedly versatile and fundamentally fractured literary forms that it adopts for the purposes of urban adaptation. It is the free and open play of communal dialogue,[2] for instance, and not what the writer calls the "narrowness" of monologue, that informs much of the "action" of a work whose defining rhetorical features situate it within the controlling context of the modern city (3). Inward-dwelling yet outward-tending, subjectively self-conscious yet acutely empirically aware, rurally situated yet city-sophisticated—*Walden* alongside so many boardinghouse texts is first and last an ambivalent metropolitan's meditation on the nature and necessity of rootedness in a rootless world.

Most pressing among this particular boardinghouse text's various paradoxes is the dilemma of literary form that necessarily met the antebellum boarder-author: how to construct a suitable discursive shape for a dynamic urban society that itself must have struck contemporaries as utterly shapeless. This chapter accordingly explores two related ideas that speak directly to the present study's interest in the rhetorical forms of the emergent urban literatures of the United States. First among these ideas is the formalist New Critical concept that scholar F. O. Matthiessen memorialized in his 1941 work *American Renaissance* as "the organic principle."[3] Building upon the romantic artistic tenets espoused by Thoreau's Concord mentor, the celebrity intellectual Ralph Waldo Emerson, Matthiessen explains organicism as an abiding literary belief among an elite group of mid-nineteenth-century American authors that "beauty in art springs from man's response to forms in nature" (*American Renaissance*, 135). Modern(ist) "Art," in other words, figures in Matthiessen's retrospective portrayal as a creative practice sensitively attuned to natural design. The "shapes of leaves, the wheat-ear, the pine-cone, the sea-shell, and the lion's claw" provide his since-canonized writers not merely with decorative patterns of embellishment to be imitated "endlessly" during the creatively auspicious days of the 1850s (135). Rather, "the organic principle" becomes for Matthiessen's authorial pantheon a literal species of natural literary structure—at once a base and elevating framework for surpassing through originating acts of creation what Emerson described by journal in 1832 as the "beautiful works" of "God's architecture" (138). That Matthiessen distinguishes Thoreau's *Walden* "as the firmest product in our literature" of "structural wholeness" testifies to his conviction in the "organic" underpinnings of that author's "craftsmanship" (173). It is a conviction that not a few of Matthiessen's postwar peers shared, and that certain revisionists in recent decades have perpetuated in studies that purportedly offer alternative readings of Thoreau's work.[4]

Here I propose an alternative reading of my own—one that seeks not to abandon or overturn formalist preoccupations with "organic" literary "form," but rather qualifies both of those critical categories with respect to an urban American discursive milieu that resides as far from Matthiessen's exquisite natural splendors as it did and does from Thoreau's much misconstrued "wilderness" retreat. This chapter proceeds from a chain of counterintuitive claims that would restore to Thoreau's opus the modern, metropolitan meanings of "wholeness" that constitute the book's very core: one, that *Walden* is not aloof from the city but obsessed with it; two, that this text is steeped in time-space disjuncture, and thus proficient in the antebellum print conversation on boarding that it epitomizes; and three, that temporal-spatial fracture is at once the pedestrian practice and artistic "principle" through which *Walden* achieves not inorganic incompletion, but the provisionally *urban* "organic" structure afforded by the unsettledness of city living. There is, in short, an apparent structural basis to the "craft" behind Thoreau's much-discussed book. Conventional interpretations of the text attribute its artistry to the author's seamless emulation of nature. In the analysis that follows, *Walden* instead derives the keystone to its construction from the well-documented domestic disruptions of urban New England boarding, modern problems with which the author, much to his dismay, was frustratingly familiar.

Closely allied to the question of *Walden*'s seemingly formless form is a concomitant paradox that draws this work into the same civic-literary conversation that governs Holmes's "Autocrat": structurally unstructured by conventional standards, and temporally-spatially compromised, *Walden*'s mock solitary shelter ironically figures a model "urban" example of communal inclusiveness. Home is but one of the many institutions scrutinized in the author's wide-ranging commentary on modern life, living, and letters. It is also, by metonymic suggestion, evocative of boarding's democratic potential as a habitat for the masses. Hierarchically organized, and conversationally contested, the Boston boardinghouse of Holmes's text resists the egalitarian ramifications of close urban quartering. Race-blind, and class eradicating, the "commonly" evoked domicile of Thoreau's creation is less a self-conscious exercise in what the radical individualist author styles mean "egotism" (31–32, 3), than it is a community-oriented experiment on the nation's republican potential conducted through formal literary experimentation. *Walden* thus sees its author "survey" two terrains simultaneously (285). One he affectionately calls "my neighborhood," wherein he would locate a domestic existence that satisfies the American political ideal of social unity achieved through diversity (331). The other, coextensive with the first, he encounters in his "imagination" while in search of a rhetorical form by which he might cohabit with *all* Americans—regardless of the prospects of their persons, and with the avowed intent to "settle" their displaced condition as they suffer through "this restless, nervous, bustling, trivial Nineteenth Century" (81, 329). In boarding Thoreau discovers a form that fits two functions, then. The final, if flexible, design of his work proves itself a civic sanctuary, and a serviceable aesthetic. "To act collectively is according to the spirit of our institutions," the author avers (110). And indeed it is the collective residential impulse of the modern metropolis by which he envisions bringing together all of the world's creation—animal and human, high and low, past and present, spoken and written—under one symbolic roof.

✦

It is worth recounting Thoreau's actual boardinghouse upbringing, the better to situate him in surroundings fit for a figurative conflation of the aesthetic, the confederal, and the domestic. The story of boarding begins early in the young writer's life and continues uninterrupted thereafter. His aunts Sarah and Betsey Thoreau kept the family homestead on the Concord, Massachusetts, village green as a genteel boardinghouse in the 1820s and 1830s. Heeding the example of her in-laws, Thoreau's own mother, having arrived back in Concord with her family following time spent in Boston, likewise generated additional household income by accepting boarders during this same period of her younger son's late childhood. The practice, like the boarders themselves, became a regular feature of Thoreauvian home life, so much so that the author's biographer, Walter Harding, writes of "a constant stream of people in the Thoreau household" creating a "constant hubbub." More boarding followed for Thoreau after he left home briefly for his formal education. He boarded in Harvard's dormitories during the mid- to late 1830s. Upon graduating he experienced still more boarding when he and his brother John accepted resident male pupils into the family establishment while they taught at Concord Academy's grammar school from 1839 to 1841. Newfound friend Ralph Waldo Emerson in turn offered his disciple Thoreau room and board at the Emerson home from 1841 to 1843. After relocating to New York to pursue authorship as a paid profession, Thoreau spent the next six months boarding, unhappily, with Emerson's brother William on Staten Island. He meanwhile wrote his first two pieces for publication, each perhaps not surprisingly a hasty reflection on habitat. The first, "The Landlord," is a playfully condescending sketch of a rustic country inn outside Manhattan. The second, "Paradise (to Be) Regained," is a dismissive book review of a utopian tract that, in its particulars, anticipates the communal living arrangements of the postbellum urban apartment building. Thoreau returned to Concord by year's end, and shortly thereafter assisted in the family's move to a new house on Texas (now Belknap) Street. He was for a brief while the only resident boarder, saving receipts for the money that he paid his father (a practice he continued throughout his life) for the privilege of shelter and upkeep. The subsequent two-year interval found Thoreau at Walden Pond, where the still young contrarian explored the limits of individualism while occupying a handcrafted cabin on property once more owned by Emerson; the latter's family mansion meanwhile had been converted temporarily into a commercial boardinghouse, albeit on a small scale. Thoreau left his wooded residence at Walden to rejoin his family at Texas Street, only to assist with another family move closer to town, at 259 Main Street, where Mrs. Thoreau recommenced the part of landlady to her regular renters, the by now permanent fixture that was her surviving son, and two Irish servants besides. Virtually born a boarder, Thoreau would die here in 1862, still boarding.⁵

It is tempting to read Thoreau's extended boardinghouse experience back into *Walden*. One well might interpret the author's seeming retreat to the woods—a self-administered residential inquest lasting from July 4, 1845, to September 6, 1847—as a declaration of secession from the frenetic boarder's world that he had known from his youth forward. Comments from the author's *Journal* in fact could support an anti-boarding reading of *Walden*, with Thoreau complaining as early as March 1841 that "I think I had rather keep a batchelor's [*sic*] hall in hell than go to board in heaven. . . . The boarder has no home. In Heaven I hope to bake my own bread and clean my own linen."⁶

Boarding figures as more than a negative presence in *Walden*, however; it is the positive premise on which the author constructs both his "whole" text, and the fragmented frame by which he resists conventional literary conceptions of "wholeness." In that resistance he converts modern, metropolitan anxiousness into a signature steadying gesture of artistry. *Walden* is of a piece with the author's entire oeuvre in this respect. Scholar Robert Milder describes Thoreau's lifelong "search," manifested in the body of his writings, "for an *imaginatively habitable* alternative" to his native town of Concord, with whose materially minded peoples and priorities the ardent idealist is said never to have felt at "home" (emphasis added). By conducting, says Milder, a symbolically residential "quest" "across space" and "through time,"⁷ Thoreau in effect transforms the very act of authorship into a quasi-domestic, peripatetic, and paradoxical art, one that we might characterize as *being-by-boarding*. Driven, on the one hand, by what Stanley Cavell calls the quintessentially "American" desires for "freedom," for "building new structures," and "forming new human beings and new human minds to inhabit them,"⁸ Thoreau gives voice in his work to historic forces that have made the New World a perpetual site for perennial (re)settlement. Hence the ground-breaking, foundation-laying, and home-building conceits that govern a text like *Walden,* the title of which work's second chapter, "Where I Lived, and What I Lived For," relates the wayfaring writer's more immediate reformist concerns with residence to the memorable principled Great Migration of his colonial New England Puritan forebears. Committed, on the other hand, to what Cavell names the "seasons" of "morning and moulting"—which is to say, to a renewable state of wakefulness and changefulness, as befits the inexhaustible cusp of the modern moment—the author sustains creative conditions under which he at best might "settle" restlessly (*Senses of Walden,* 43, 46). Thus, Thoreau can open what is arguably his masterwork in the forever fleeting "present" tense of the here and now, writing *Walden* as he does as "a sojourner in civilized life" who is "anxious to improve the nick of time" (3, 17). Yet, however concerned he may be with "the present condition of things," our "sojourner" author relies in this as in other works on an (ir)regular invocation of the there and then and the still to come, such that a constant inconstancy, or the spatiotemporal push and pull of a modernity caught between a resonant past, an unstable present, and an unpredictable future, finally sets his texts at the nexus of everywhere, nowhere, never, and always. It is a time and place that Cavell designates "the point of departure" (50). It is a "*sedes,* a seat," that the author himself situates in his "imagination" along what he calls in *Walden* the slipping "stream of time" (81, 85). It is the site at which any antebellum boarder such as Thoreau could have claimed brief sanctuary to *reside* in body and mind.

All of which is to underscore the irony of the writer's life, and art: a man who would have his readers "ma[k]e some progress toward settling in the world," to build some "substantial shelter" about their literal and figurative persons (85), relied personally and discursively upon so disruptive a literary form as boarding in the making and shaping of his work. *Walden,* in particular, might enjoin us to "settle ourselves" (97). But Thoreau so constructs the temporal-spatial contours of his text that its reader-occupants are left "forever fluctuating" in a "transient" moment that he otherwise compares unfavorably to a posited "permanent and absolute existence" (92, 102, 96). No American boarder—not even a self-mockingly described "sort of real-estate broker" like our author—reasonably could have claimed any purchase on "permanency" during the volatile years under which Thoreau conceived and created *Walden* (81). Nor does Thoreau pretend to what he terms an "unhurried" state in these pages (95–96). Rather, he openly acknowledges that his is a noisy nineteenth-century world in which "no dust has settled" (99), and where the constant din of distraction runs right "through Paris and London" just as it does "through New York and Boston and Concord" (97–98). It is only proper, then, that what he names "my residence," by which he means his book, paradoxically should *aspire* "downward through . . . mud and slush . . . to a hard bottom" of what "we can call [a] reality" that *Walden* never reaches (98–99). *Walden* instead rests "restlessly" on a formal foundation of boarding. It does so, moreover, both fittingly and functionally. A fractured form of residence for what the author calls "transitory" times, boarding endows Thoreau with a capacity to speak at once in, to, and through the timely "daily colloquies" of "modern man's speech" to an audience of fellow travelers as homeless as he (102). His boardinghouse medium accordingly *is* his message, even if that message lacks the conspicuous boardinghouse trappings of his Boston contemporary Oliver Wendell Holmes's serial musings in "The Autocrat."

*Walden* qualifies as an "unsettling" boardinghouse text to the extent that its author-narrator never settles. Like the consummate "peregrine" whom Cavell says he is (52), and like the fluently mobile boarder-flaneurs whom we have encountered before—Mortimer Thomson's "Doesticks," Fanny Fern's "Floy," Walt Whitman's newspaper persona, and Holmes's above-named "Autocrat," to cite but several—Thoreau's self-appointed spokesman expends the bulk of his energies in his book searching for a literary "structure" that suits his migratory means and needs. In that search he performs the narrative work of countless boarder-authors before and after him. That is to say, he redefines time and space in such a way that these paired components of storytelling assume the fractured form that we would expect from a text that aligns itself from its abrupt beginning to its diffusively philosophical end with the permanent impermanency of modernity. Having "travelled" [*sic*], in his own words, "a good deal in Concord" (4), having studied in depth the mysteries of "dwelling" (34), the steady but unseated narrative voice of *Walden* is ready from the first to declare life itself but a frustrated effort "to subdue and cultivate a few cubic feet of flesh" (5). So consumed is the author-narrator with "the gross necessaries of life"—boarding's basics, among which he includes "Food, Shelter, . . . and Fuel"—that he deems the "domestic" genetic, constituent of his very being, or "flesh" (11–12). Yet, because a final residence eludes Thoreau's speaker, he finally and naturally gravitates toward a rhetoric—boarding—that can accommodate his dis-accommodation. The narrator relates in this fractured form his iterative tale of the broken "home," which is to say, his unfulfilled search for a final habitat by which his "fingers" have never quite been "burned by actual possession" (82). *Walden* is less a successful "quest" for settled habitation, then, than a boarder-flaneur's account of an art form found through failure, at least as judged by domestic convention. Thoreau's book is not about home; it is about the formal literary consequences of having no home on which to base an unresolved relation of residence.

Those consequences crystallize in the modern, metropolitan conceptions of time and space that emerge in *Walden*'s telling. "Economy" is the title that Thoreau bestows upon the first chapter of his work. It is a resonant beginning, inasmuch as it signals the streamlined narrative practice by which the narrator "deliberately" (90), as he later says, distills an "art" (51) whose dimensions paradoxically achieve the look and feel of "superfluity" (77) by paring away all excess: that which is "omitted" (63), "contracted" (87), "crowded" (87), "confined" (87), and "subtracted" (111) enables him at once "to front only the essential facts of life" (90), even as it endows him with the capacity to forgo all "ornaments of style in literature" (48). Or, to restate the case residentially, he who has "dwelt, as it were," "a sojourner in nature," and so never "settled down" in the "modern drawing room," achieves in the speaker's estimation a surer "foundation" than he who relies on "houses built and paid for" (37–38). Thoreau as author might condemn the haste and waste of "outward civilization" (11). Yet, as an artist, he values that brand of boardinghouse modernity that presupposes mobility, and so denies accumulated "domestic comforts" to the era's most restless dwellers (27). "The best works of art," Thoreau writes in *Walden,* "are the expression of man's struggle to free himself" from a "condition" that he locates in the immovable "modern house with all its improvements" (37, 34). One might consider his own boardinghouse book from this liberating aesthetic perspective. Here, a "little distance, whether of space or time," not only frames and arranges the various interpolated tales that comprise his overall account; it describes his entire discourse (26). Making the most of what modernity withholds, he locates amplitude, infinitude, within a tightly fitted narrative structure where there is scant time and precious little room to maneuver. Worried by modern hurry, yet troubled by senseless rest, Thoreau inscribes the uncompromising pace and space of the metropolis into a text whose principled opposition to laxity, luxury, and self-indulgent leisure affords all the "Shelter" that readers have to "inhabit" (28, 34).

*Walden* reenacts the author's formal move toward a minimalist artistic mindset, fragmentally. It initiates this migration in the aptly titled "Economy" chapter by offering no unnecessary narration, and evincing but passing interest in constructing anything that could be said to resemble a well-rounded "plot," so-called. Indeed, Thoreau performs *as* literature the hard, clean lines that he prescribes in life when he recounts a quasi-domestic "quest" that recalls "Doesticks's" with its severe curtailment of context, its radical temporal truncation, and its studied spatial collapse. Here is the author's summary introduction, which, save for its bucolic trappings, well might serve as the housing history of some contemporary boarder:

> When I wrote the following pages, or rather the bulk of them, I lived alone, in the woods, a mile from any neighbor, in a house which I had built myself, on the shore of Walden Pond, in Concord, Massachusetts, and earned my living by the labor of my hands only. I lived there for two years and two months. At present I am a sojourner in civilized life again. (5)

An introductory "When" suggests a story already underway, with the author's decision to speak now, at this particular interval, thus arriving in medias res. Even in his absence, or silence, or both, the speaker tacitly acknowledges that the action of something or someone bigger than himself—say, the kind of "civilized life" that he might find in the city—has been ongoing in the interim. Also ongoing has been the rapid passage of time. Writing now in the "present," the narrator implies a past (at least) "two years and two months" prior when he references an earlier residence that seems by its casual topical retrieval and subsequent abandonment neither appreciably distant nor altogether significant. The temporal gap between yesterday, today, and tomorrow would appear to be easily bridged, in other words, much as any old "house" will suffice. Nor does the relation of space provide much narrative resistance. Spiraling outward from "I" to "house" to "neighbor," from "Pond" to Concord town to the greater state of Massachusetts, the lone first person of this passage overcomes all practical obstacles of physical distance; a single sweeping rhetorical gesture sets him within close proximity to his larger geographic region, New England. Even the speaker's syntax conspires to keep his own "sojourner" self fleet of foot, unencumbered by time, and otherwise in modern motion. A rapid succession of commas, qualifying phrases, and adverbial "in" clauses from the opening sentence keep the speaker in constant contact with a "there" that is not his current implied *here*. Likewise, the avoidance of end-stops in this same sentence provides the paragraph generally with a compulsive forward momentum, such as we have seen elsewhere among the era's boardinghouse writings. Thoreau, we know, was not one to rush, and canvassed comparatively little of his native country during his short lifetime. And yet he composes the very first sentence from *Walden* with all the flexible urban license of literatures written in an antebellum boarder's vein: time passes rapidly; space retreats improbably; pointed reflections on the makings and meanings of "house" predominate in the discussion and generate a debate over the domestic in which no one side prevails. This debate is not open-ended, however. It provisionally closes as it opens, with quick, unceremonious "Economy." There is forever another residence on the horizon.

Thoreau ostensibly records in *Walden* his "hunt" for a "home" that suits him (207), when in fact it is a serviceable storytelling form that eludes him—until, that is, he comes to recognize in boarding his preferred discourse. It is but another boardinghouse irony that the author should elect residential unrest as a means of narration, when in fact much of *Walden*'s pages otherwise comprise a paean to the rewards of planting and sustaining what passes here as an at least semi-permanent habitat. The author never announces outright his dawning narrative awareness; his is the gradual realization that the story of a residence unrealized is an optimal form for the tale to be told by masses of urbanizing Americans, himself included.

Thoreau's chosen persona in *Walden* both literally and figuratively walks his way into a functionally fractured literary form through his ritual residential migrations in and around Concord. Searching by foot for "shelter" (203–4), he at once discovers and performs a mode of narration that accommodates his modern, metropolitan boardinghouse conceptions of time and space. Scholar Robert Fanuzzi goes so far as to say that "Thoreau strolls through the woods as the flâneur," simultaneously seeking a "habitable" "sense of place" and "an aesthetic consciousness" by which to express "his experience" of the same. What with *Walden*'s repeated "references and allusions to city life"—especially, but not exclusively, including the eponymous pond as an urban-style port of call for local traders and sportsmen, and the often invoked Fitchburg Railroad line as a symbolic link from Concord to Boston, and by Boston to the world's bustling market economies beyond—Fanuzzi even can declare that the city "exists as metonymy" in *Walden,* thus making its resident talker the consummate city-walker as well.[9] Surveying the "farms, houses, barns" of his townsmen, Thoreau moves with free and unfettered ease about the quasi-domestic monuments that have been raised by his contemporaries (5). Not for him, he insists, the "crushed and smothered" "load" that must come with such "encumbrances" (5). Something habitationally different he envisions in the "provinces of fancy and imagination" (8): he passes with jaunty spatial license through Pleasant Meadow; he dallies but briefly at Baker Farm, where he once "thought of living" before he "went to Walden" (203); he flits through the ramshackle "home" of the immigrant Irishman John Field, whom he advises at "letting go 'bogging'" so as to join him "a-fishing" "far and wide" (203, 207–8). "Traveling" with but little "baggage," forgoing that "trumpery which has accumulated from long housekeeping" (66), Thoreau traipses his way "a rambler in the woods" to Walden Pond, where he exchanges walking for its residential equivalent, what he calls "squatting" (64). Much as he would "enjoy the land, but own it not," much as he would remain the perennial migrant and not sink into the "shallows and quicksands" of confined "settlement," he dismisses spatial distance as a determining factor of narration simply by proving no distance unbridgeable in his book (207). Thoreau's "city" is as walkable, and thus as knowable, as "Doesticks's" Manhattan. It is, that is to say, a space best inhabited by the boarder-flaneur, whose acquired narrative knowledge of urban space is, like Thoreau's, as much mandated by the exigencies of itinerant living as it is facilitated by the restless "quest" for a peripatetic aesthetic that captures in the eternal promise of "my next excursion" the unsettling spirit of the city (91).

Time proves as incapable of standing still in *Walden* as the spatially omnivorous narrator. Indeed, for a text so acutely conscious of the "natural" world's temporal rhythms—whether expressed in Thoreau's regular diurnal tributes to his "morning work" at "sunrise and dawn" (282, 17), or else manifested in his rapt appreciation for the sonorous seasonal signifiers of winter and the "vegetable" "hieroglyphic" of spring (308)—*Walden* runs riot in its narrative handling of temporality, so much so as to impart to the text a noticeable element of urban hurry. There was, in the author's words, a "transient character" to his short stay in Concord's woods (55). *Walden* time accordingly, organically, turns with much of the quick dispatch of the standard city storyline.

Efficient in its elision of space, the opening chapter "Economy" similarly establishes a conventionally unconventional urban narrative pattern through which time collapses as a discursive dimension that readers might actually inhabit. Thoreau speculates early that these same readers possibly "have come to this page," which is to say, to *Walden,* "to spend borrowed or stolen time" from the more mundane affairs of the workaday world. He even cautions, "As if you could kill time without injuring eternity" (8), before he later advises, "Take your time, and set about some free labor" (78). Yet, it is the author-narrator himself who evinces a ready willingness to flit back and forth across temporal intervals as if they did not exist. Within the syntactic space of a single sentence or paragraph, Thoreau is prone to switch rapidly between "tomorrow," "to-day," and "years past" in recalling his brief stay at Walden Pond—an experience which, he tells us, he has abridged still further for the "convenience" of

narrative purposes from "two years into one" (7, 16, 84). This last is a
telling temporal gesture, since it describes not only the overall arc of the
author's personal story, but also the discrete episodes of a wooded life
that seems in its recounting to have passed as fitfully as it does pasto-
rally. "To anticipate" is, in the author's mind, "to stand on the meeting
of two eternities, the past and future" (17). It is also, in *Walden*, "to telegraph" oneself, to tell one's own tale, in an "express" manner not unlike
that most modern of temporally-spatially confounding inventions (18).
Thoreau sorts, shuffles, and compresses time to suit his narrative needs,
with the result that time per se becomes less the product of empirical
observation than an almost incantatory mechanism divorced from any
objectively recorded correlative. "At other times," "For a long time," "For
many years" Thoreau impatiently reports at one stage in three staccato
consecutive paragraphs (17–18). "Sometimes," "at such times," "as quick
as thought" he elsewhere relates, before collapsing within the textual
space of a single page a hypertense reckoning of a fox-and-hound fable,
which breathlessly consists of a stray "moment," a "short-lived mood,"
a "morning," an "afternoon," an "evening," a "night," and a subsequent
"next day" (278–79). Nor does Thoreau restrict his temporal tinkering to
the short hand of the narrative clock. He is just as apt to bypass longer
interludes, as when he sweeps through entire life spans as follows: "The
laborer's day ends with the going down of the sun, . . . but his employer,
who speculates from month to month, has no respite from one end of the
year to another" (70). It is not simply the case that Thoreau deems the
"day . . . an epitome of the year," which philosophy (suggestively, because
seasonally, stated in the chapter "Spring") informs his personal beliefs and
basic behaviors (301). For this particular writer, it is ethically and artistically incumbent upon what Thoreau calls the "modern author" to write as
he lives (231). When he, like "every body," "is on the move," then the literary artist as Thoreau conceives him must create in the "outward" signs of
his work "the necessities and character" of the indwelling "inhabitant" of
modernity (151, 46), for whom the true "beauty" of "*belles-lettres*" must
reside in the interstices of fugitive time and space (47–48).

   Thoreau's not-so-quaint little Concord afforded precisely the temporal-
spatial conditions requisite for the correspondingly modern literature that
he duly produced. Historian Robert A. Gross argues persuasively for Concord's place within a Boston metropolitan community that bound coastal
city to inland suburb through increasing ties of commerce, population
exchange, and sheer spirit. An accompanying area press for housing, furthermore, made boarding out an unavoidable residential arrangement in
both locales, city center and suburb. Never, between the Revolution and

New England literary Renaissance, did Concord meet the U.S. Census Bureau's current minimal standard for an urban setting: a population of 2,500 or more. Yet that is not to say that Concord was what Gross calls "the timeless small town." Thoreau's Concord was instead a burgeoning center for transport, trade, and transients located a mere eighteen miles west of Boston proper, a place where boarding and boarders—as the author and his immediate family knew only too well—were (or were not) right at home.[10]

It was within this historical environment that Thoreau undertook the (in)complete (de)construction of theorist Michel de Certeau's "migrational, or metaphorical city." What the Frenchman calls "habitable spaces" do not in fact exist in the "mythic" metropolis. For de Certeau, the "exploding," "paroxysmal" modern urban milieu is inherently unstable, and affords the "pedestrian" merely compensatory "appropriation" of a "provisional" place "currently lacking in one's own vicinity." Promenading metropolitan Concord for a home to inhabit, *Walden*'s author might have trod solid ground as the motive force behind what de Certeau calls "a rhetoric of walking." But he simultaneously slips into a parallel "walking exile" perpetuated by city-dwellers' collective residential charade. De Certeau, no less than Thoreau, might believe in a "fine art of dwelling." When "every story is a travel story—a spatial practice," however, and when "stories about places" are themselves "makeshift things," then the attempted "enunciation" of "narrative structures" from inside a necessary "fiction" becomes an unstructured act of "improvisation." De Certeau concedes that readers of urban texts are at least capable of "insinuation," which he describes as a kind of temporary residence within the imaginary space-time conceived by someone other than ourselves. Thus, the reader of urban writing "makes the text habitable, like a rented apartment," while city-reading per se "transforms another person's property into space borrowed for a moment by a transient." Yet, such writings ultimately prove but "verbal relics." They are "anti-texts" whose imagined "presences" only mask the "diverse absences" left by those rare settled texts—or, in Thoreau's example, texts of would-be "settlement"—that "are no longer there," wherever "there" might be. It is both a practical and conceptual modern problem that de Certeau identifies. And it was one that Concord's best-known boarder-author could testify to in the "broken" discursive forms of *Walden*.[11]

If we have been slow to acknowledge the modern implications of those forms, then we would misread the very "craftsmanship" that F. O. Matthiessen and subsequent advocates of modernist formalism deem the best evidence of *Walden*'s completeness as a text. The conventional critical view on *Walden* since before the Second World War has judged Thoreau's work a coherent prose poem: its structure is said to derive from the natural symbols of the season-cycle; its dramatic form is attributed to the romantic self-growth of a protagonist whom Robert Milder names the work's "hero-narrator."[12] Lauriat Lane Jr. further articulated this view when he asserted apropos Matthiessen six complementary "sections" to *Walden*, the "various dialectical relations" of which are alleged to divide between three private/public "pairs." Among the former Lane includes the chapters "Reading," "Solitude," and "The Bean-Field." Each of these in its way captures the author-narrator alone in seeming solitude. Among the latter he includes the chapters "Sounds," "Visitors," and "The Village," wherein Thoreau's persona ostensibly mixes more freely with society, whether human or from among the animal creation. Pivotal to Lane's "pairs" is the "central" chapter "The Ponds." This he believes to be the unifying bond between the otherwise contrary public and private impulses that govern the work as a "whole."[13]

Antebellum boarding of course nullified the capacity of the twin conceptual categories public and private to act as a meaningful dichotomy, both in fact and formalist fancy; more than that, the residential unsettledness upon which *Walden* was built—and which the work as a "whole" is ultimately "about"—denies the author and readers alike the spurious aesthetic pleasures of balance, unity, or completion.

Yet perhaps the final proof of *Walden*'s *urban* organic "wholeness" resides in the unsettled phases and stages of its prepublication. Robert Sattelmeyer has observed the same competing impulses in Thoreau's work that formalists like Lane interpret as so many instances of neat "dialectical" interplay. Whereas his predecessors saw "wholeness," however, Sattelmeyer sees what he calls "gaps" in *Walden*'s construction. These "gaps" he attributes to *Walden*'s multiple drafts, no less than seven of which the author (never quite) completed between the midway point in his residence at Walden Pond and the work's official publication by the Boston firm Ticknor and Fields in 1854. Sattelmeyer himself provides a revisionist account of the many "revisions" that Thoreau made during this eight-year period, "revisions" which "were not directed toward filling out or realizing a design that he kept before him but toward incorporating stages of growth within a design that already existed."[14] As Robert Milder explains, "Because the 'design' was fixed and the 'growth' wayward and unforeseen," *Walden*'s creation "was a precarious effort liable to strange fractures and inconsistencies." Thus, with each successive draft, Milder continues, *Walden* came to "contain interpolations that strike new and discordant notes."[15]

I would venture that the "discord" detected by Milder is the discursive sound of modernity. That is to say, the "important discontinuities" that he highlights within and between consecutive drafts reveal an authorial "consciousness" that evolved as it "looked upon" its "subject and the cultural moment which enclosed it." Thoreau's, we know, was a metropolitan "moment," and there is sufficient reason to read his work as registering the deeply felt impact of city modernity on his artistic method, no less than on his monograph. Milder, for example, argues persuasively for *Walden*'s spatial expansion. He notes that individual chapters grow longer with each draft as the author revisits and refines attitudes already expressed on the page, or else signals altogether different directions in his thinking, themes, and tonal inflections. Time assumes added importance, too, as Thoreau gives increasing seasonal emphasis to separate drafts. The (almost) end result, says Milder, is a "temporally layered" work that seems as much a metatextual meditation on the process of composition as a final product. *Walden* as we know it today does retain traces of what Milder identifies as the author's "original design." But a recognition of the extent to which this work has been "focused, qualified, undercut, and superseded" reminds us just how much *Walden* is not only a work for *all* time;[16] it is a work that reflects the residential unrest of its modern urban American times during the convulsive middle decades of the nineteenth century. If *Walden* is "organic," its organicism is the peculiar byproduct of a prolonged and upsetting residence in and around the metropolitan margins of the new U.S. city.

Milder recommends "disconstructing" *Walden*'s fractured chapters one by one, as if the book were a "broken" boardinghouse narrative à la Holmes's "Autocrat." It is a fair recommendation, inasmuch as it proposes we read *Walden* in much the way that it was written—which is to say, non-holistically, or serially, from within the chronically (and, in this instance, chronologically) interrupted episodes of a not-quite-settled existence, and as the discarded part of a never-quite-realized domestic aesthetic. We nevertheless need not resort to Derridean strategies of reading to conclude what Thoreau's own contemporaries were able to surmise. Nearly a full century before the appearance of French theories of disambiguation, those who first encountered *Walden* during the years of its induction into the American canon reached a tentative general consensus on this work's distinguishing features. Their viewpoint speaks volumes on the author's modern(ist) craft. Writing in the *Atlantic Monthly* magazine toward the close of the nineteenth century, an anonymous commentator epitomized this emerging consensus in a review of a then-recent four-volume edition by the Boston publisher Houghton of Thoreau's major works. *Walden, Cape Cod, A Week on the Concord and Merrimack Rivers,* and *The Maine Woods* comprise the volumes in question. These are, in the reviewer's opinion, the obvious works to include in the collection, since they are "those which come nearest to finished books" among the author's lifetime of writings. It is worth noting that the reviewer here says "nearest to finished," which is tantamount within this context to saying "incomplete." Indeed, the *Atlantic*'s editorial spokesman on "New Books" goes on to issue a more sweeping statement that presupposes "finish" to be a defining trait of literary form, or the lack thereof. The reviewer writes as follows:

> From the nature of his studies and interests Thoreau was a journalizer rather than an artist. The artist faculty for *wholes* is strongest in *Walden,* for there again he is dealing with the one subject which possessed anything like *unity* in his mind, namely, Himself [emphasis added].[17]

Characteristic in this assessment is the familiar charge of egotism, which reviewers had made a staple of the cultural criticism that emerged from the late 1830s onward in response to Emersonian transcendentalism and its descendants. At least one reader by century's end continued to rank Thoreau among these last, whom a Harvard classics professor some fifty years earlier had described as proponents of a philosophy that "transcends time and space," before dismissing them as "mere dreamers, endeavoring to give to airy nothing, a local habitation and a name."[18] More germane to our discussion of an "organic" *Walden* is the *Atlantic* reviewer's final verdict on Thoreau's work. It consists largely of "fragments," he says.[19] Approaching "wholes" without realizing them, striving for "unity" without achieving it, Thoreau in this particular commentator's estimation did not even qualify as an "artist," at least not according to formalist terms that already were in the ascendant barely thirty years after Thoreau's premature passing in 1862.

What this and other commentators on *Walden* demand is a holistic response to an urban industrializing America that the fringe transcendentalist Moncure Conway in 1867 said constitutes "our modern world." Conway of course knew Thoreau the man, as opposed to the writer or the reputation. His Concord acquaintance embodied, or "made flesh," a Rousseauan "spirit" that "turned its back upon the world" and sought an "abode" to inhabit in "solitude." This was likewise the Thoreau that the writer's friend William Henry Channing remembered. Channing's Thoreau was the consummate "Poet-Naturalist," whose residence at "primitive" Walden Pond represented a withdrawal from our "modern societies." Similarly did a self-described "Hermit" recall *Walden*'s author several decades later. He praised that "attitude of mind" that once more sought "solitude" in the New England woods, and otherwise paid tribute to Thoreau for having "made Nature-writing the characteristic note of modern verse." This remark on "modern" literature notwithstanding, what was most "modern" about Thoreau in most recollections was the seeming *anti*-modern impetus behind both his life and art. Bemoaning the "industrial spirit" of a Gilded Age America that had risen from *Walden*'s antebellum nation, and otherwise excoriating the crass consumerism and commercialism that Charles Dudley Warner says shape our "modern sympathies," fond remembrance of Thoreau typically manages to patch over the apparent "fragments" of the writer's work so as to apotheosize the "whole" humanism of his "organic," earthly example. As Warner writes, "Thoreau on Walden Pond, reading the Greek poets and keeping an eye on the musk-rat and the squirrel and other like visitors, was [more] free of a much larger world than many who have been round the globe." It is a wishful vision, one far removed from the modern metropolitan boardinghouse frame within which Thoreau sought an entirely different version of "freedom," formally speaking. Thoreau the modern urban artist dwelled but briefly "on" Walden Pond, to borrow Warner's pointed preposition. He passed *through* Concord's woods just long enough to further an unfinished art form, which is not to say an art form that lacked "finish."[20]

✦

A polished rhetorical transcript of falling apart, *Walden* also figures a politico-literary discourse of communal coming together. It, like the vast majority of boardinghouse works from the period, transcends its separate aesthetic sphere to comment incisively on the ever-changing collective that is the American city. *Walden* alongside so much boardinghouse writing verbally renders modern metropolitan fracture as the most oxymoronic of "organic" metaphors. But however formally (un)refined *Walden* might be, it with the broad genre of boarders' letters is equally invested in the political and literary process by which a diverse urban people might organize themselves into "settlements"—and texts—that can cohere, despite a constant modern pressure to disperse. City modernity brought profound socio-aesthetic dislocations to the nineteenth-century United States, and seemingly kept its peoples, perspectives, and artistic strategies of representation in an antic state of unrest. Yet, Thoreau was not alone when he expressed a "common" contemporary interest in locating reliable mechanisms for sustaining the new nation's increasingly complex urban communities. The residential itinerancy inscribed by the author into the form of his work is one such mechanism, and accordingly performs a less than self-evident *civic* function. Thoreau's narrative freedom to roam in *Walden* structurally articulates his commitment to an ideally "open" community, wherein renters might exchange domestic time and space at will. His companion and seemingly contrary commitment to "neighborliness" meanwhile holds boarder-renters together, since it asks these mobile members of a variable national household to find stable reasons between them to continue in cohabitation. A text that insists on its right to drift thereby finds integrity in the "wholeness" of the collectivity.

Walden is the most democratic of boardinghouse texts in this respect. Just as the leveling tendencies of the American city found forceful expression in the nation's communal domiciles, whose individual occupants held equal hypothetical claim to the rights of their respective households, a comparable freedom characterizes the formal features of Thoreau's boardinghouse discourse. *Walden*'s "talk" anticipates the colloquial qualities of Oliver Wendell Holmes's "Autocrat" in that both are essentially, if not intentionally, demotic: every dweller therein will have his say, if not his sway, when and where the prevailing domestic rhetoric assumes the participatory parity of fluid conversation. The author here, however, situates readers and dwellers alike within a more-than-metaphorical boardinghouse frame where the practice of domestic sharing—of food, shelter, upkeep, ideas, small talk, long talk, and contested political-cultural identities—is elevated into principled resistance against any residual manifestations of self-aggrandizement. There can be no separate, selfish interests among residents when there is no willful imperative toward separate residence. *Walden*'s household prerogative to seek a single, suitable shelter for *all* thus relies at least in part on the creation of a popularly constituted American "cabin" that can withstand incipient "Autocratic" influences from within, as well as fractious modern forces from without. This text not only internalizes an urban inclination toward commotion, then, but counters its own dispersions with a unifying textual movement toward communion. Thoreau's boardinghouse art is in other words not unlike his boardinghouse life. Each is semi-privately conceived, yet ultimately communally concerned with creating and keeping the domestic paradox of an unsettled boardinghouse nation built both to stand fast and to last.

Much of the critical commentary devoted to reversing the assumption that Thoreau's "life in the woods" was, in his own words, a "lonesome" endeavor accordingly takes on added civic significance within this boardinghouse context (131). To read the author as an isolate, which is to say, in isolation, is to miss the strong communal commitments that he articulates in the pages of his narrative. Midway through the twentieth century, when the compelling claims of F. O. Matthiessen's "organicism" were at their influential peak, John Broderick argued that, notwithstanding Thoreau's evident interest in the individual, the author evinces an over-riding concern for the welfare of his community, be it local or national. Lawrence Buell and Leonard Neufeldt concur. Both more recently have situated Thoreau at the center of Concord life, despite the two-year term that he spent residing one mile distant from town center. Citing Thoreau's introductory remarks in *Walden,* with all their preoccupation with the thoughts and deeds of his "neighbors" (4), Buell describes the author as a kind of self-appointed "town" watchman, a central consciousness for those of his countrymen who were perhaps less equipped than he to cope with the complexities that attended "an age of rootlessness." Neufeldt similarly likens Thoreau's pond-side cabin to Concord's busy Middlesex Hotel, a modern institution signifying accelerated socioeconomic change; here, lounging locals and wayfaring strangers alike observed the vicis-situdes of an ever-more bustling "city" in the making. Lance Newman advances this line of reasoning even further. Abandoning the human world for the animal kingdom, he receives *Walden's* many metaphors of town life as suggestive not only of feelings of general "sociability," but as fulfilling as well a wished-for authorial "intimacy with wild nature itself." As Newman writes, "Thoreau weaves himself into a tightly knit community where nature occupies the far end of every social bond."[21] Such arguments imply this: whether nurtured in Concord or naturalized on the edge of "settled" society, Thoreau's sense of his self depended on his environs and so presupposed a self *in* society. The general consensus among a particular school of revisionists is that *Walden's* author declares not so much his independence as a civic-minded codependence on the people and places, the flora and fauna, of his surroundings.

Despite an entrenched belief among many readers in the author's "isola-tion," then, the "talk" inside the text of *Walden* is calculated to draw us into close participatory contact with contemporary public discourse and debate as they existed in Thoreau's New England. *Walden's* preoccupa-tions become our own, and chief among these is the author's abiding desire to recast what we now call domesticity in politico-literary terms. *Walden's* subtly understated premise is that, as Thoreau writes, "our lives are domes-tic in more senses than we think" (28). Assuming our acceptance of this premise, he additionally and syllogistically proposes, "We belong to the community," before he goes on to insist that we need not "forever resign the pleasure of construction to the carpenter" (46). Or, to restate the coefficients of this equation, Thoreau like the boarder he was advocates an expanded definition of the domestic, and reflexively relates the not-so-solitary dweller to society, or "the community," as would have been self-evidently necessary for one grown accustomed to housemates. Advancing forward from this "foundation" (45), Thoreau underscores the political applications of his habitational symbol when he urges his country's "architects so called" to construct a formal "frame" that meets the spatio-"temporal necessities" of "modern civilized society" (46, 30). No humble wooden edifice could carry so heavy a domestic load as this. Nor does Thoreau's rather glib recommendation, stated later, to "board them [that is, his countrymen] round the while" come close to satisfying his grand civic vision of a macrocosmic country's encapsulation as a microcosmic "community" that purposefully has learned to shoulder responsibility for sheltering itself (110). With one eye on his own private domicile, and the other on the metropolis of Boston, the sometime urban dweller who is *Walden*'s narrator-neighbor effectively delivers a domestically inflected address on the state of his nation's institutions. If boarding features figuratively in that address, it features centrally as well. For, upon the versatile flexibility of boarding as a politico-literary form does Thoreau base his discursive call for equal access to the varied institutions that comprise the American polity. No "ode to dejection" (84), *Walden* is from this residentially republican perspective an optimistic and democratic response-in-waiting to the restrictive institutional barriers that both surround and structure a comparatively conservative boardinghouse text like Holmes's "Autocrat."

Having designated house-building as *Walden*'s main metaphor, the author establishes the civic import of this, his favored figuration, by aligning it with a long and venerable tradition of his native region's public works. Thoreau records his signal Concord experience expecting that we as readers regard his residential venture as historically significant and consistent. Writing at one point that "the last significant scrap of news from that quarter [England] was the revolution of 1649" (95), he suggests toward the beginning of his account that his residence at Walden Pond is not only newsworthy; it is of epic proportions, in that it is coextensive in spirit with the seventeenth-century arrival on the continent of the first great wave of English settlers. The former domestic movement occurred in the early modern period. The latter transpires during the modern urban age. Both transact themes of "migration, settling, distance, neighborhood improvement, [and] departure" in their movements to and from Massachusetts, as Stanley Cavell explains, with what also could be a description of nineteenth-century boarders' behavior (*Senses of Walden*, 12). Thus does Thoreau pitch his "Solitude" (see the chapter title of that name) in terms that at once recall the Great Migration of an earlier era, and the metropolitan milieu in which he wrote. The Puritans had their "city on a hill"; the author has his home on the outskirts of town. Each location qualifies within his narrative as the foundational fruit of a shared labor, since each is undertaken by and for the people. All the world—Protestant Europe on the one hand, latter-day readers on the other—is invited to watch, moreover, so as to monitor the "progress" of these respective attention-grabbing residential spectacles.

The public work of *Walden* effectively extends the "public works" of nearby Boston (56). Our author-architect's Concord dwelling, that is to say, achieves at once the symbiotic status of a model antebellum home and a forward-looking Yankee enterprise built upon the example of cognate reformist institutions then emerging in the neighboring urban capital. Not only does Thoreau construct his civically signifying "shelter" so that the front door literally remains unlocked and so always "open"; he sets himself in like relation to his townsmen when he rhetorically asks with apparent disapproval, "What sort of space is that which separates a man from his fellows and makes him solitary?" (133). His personal domestic space accordingly occupies a place within a civic framework consolidated by kindred area establishments. A list of the communal institutions that complement Thoreau's New England cabin is as long as it is exhaustive. Home, church, and state receive mention in *Walden*'s pages. Schools, colleges, and universities also make their appearance. The author digs down to the bedrock basis of the institutional everyday in his search for the roots of a reality that might best be termed modernity: charity organizations, the library and lyceum, the press and post office, law, commerce, industry, agriculture, and manners all receive due discursive space. These are requisite building blocks in the author's modern commonweal. These are the (admittedly imperfect) public means by which an otherwise disparate people could and should come together in common purpose. Thoreau writes with ambivalent wonder at the blithe institutional indifference, or "contentment," of his French Canadian wood-chopping friend Alec Therien, for whom a solo walk in the woods affords as great a sense of civic belonging as "the house where he boarded" (145–46).[22] And yet, as *Walden*'s recurring references to colonial Concord's historic resistance to Great Britain remind both author and audience, there are certain public causes for which the author is prepared to make sacrifice. Home here is of a piece with "the people," and politically imbricated with a domestic "revolution" that continues forward for Thoreau from the English Commonwealth of Oliver Cromwell into a present post-*Walden*.

*Walden*'s larger cultural critique is this: institutionally, we have not as a nation fulfilled our original collective potential; residentially, we reenact that failure daily, despite our having "boarded" together for so long. Much, then, of what passes in the minds of Thoreau's contemporaries "as a necessary part of the machinery" of our "civilized" existence ranks low in the author's estimation (31, 168). Thoreau likens, for instance, "the modern house" to "the citizen's suburban box" (34, 47) and ridicules the flaccid institutionalism of his New England village as "a bell, a big gun, and a fire engine" (168). More pointedly, he complains, "Wherever a man goes, men will pursue and paw him with their dirty institutions, and, if they can, constrain him to belong to their desperate odd-fellow society" (171).[23] Such expressions of civic discontent amount to more than rhetorical posturing, in light of the genuine domestic strife that would climax in a U.S. Civil War that recalls Cromwell's in the ideological rancor that it bred, and that provided the political backdrop against which Thoreau composed *Walden* during the late 1840s and early 1850s. What our author bears witness to in *Walden* is a nation as close to institutional stalemate as was Holmes's some three years later when the latter conceived his "Autocrat" series for the *Atlantic Monthly* magazine. Already by the time of Thoreau's writing, his United States, no less than Holmes's, seemingly had lost sight of the informing ideals behind its social contract. Gone were the conspicuously public components of republicanism.

What makes possible the institutional renewal enacted in *Walden* is the author's staking the discursive basis of his narrative on *common* boardinghouse ground. Although Thoreau discouragingly inquires how we might "cooperate" and "*get our living together,*" when the "only cooperation which is commonly possible is exceedingly partial and superficial" (72, 71), he simultaneously calls for "the re-origination of many of the institutions of society" (150). Implicit in that call is the assumption that the populace *can* reassert control over its institutions, and so restore the body politic. Implicit, too, in the residential (re)arrangement of Thoreau's text is his conflating the civic aesthetic in which he abides with the chosen abode wherein he dwells. The form of his work *is* the equal access that characterizes boarding in the abstract, and that access ensures the active "household" involvement of the various "Visitors" who occupy *Walden* even in passing. Thus does the particular residential rhetoric that underwrites *Walden* sustain a functional alliance between self and society that would not have pertained outside of boarding's domestic context. For, despite his physical distance from town, the author throws open the doors to the collectivity that is his cabin, and so extends outward the institutionally rich communal life that is on offer there to any and all who are prepared to embrace it. His habitat is at once house, home, meeting place, and a site for useful instruction. Walden, too, is the locus that Thoreau elects for emphatically public acts of reading, writing, thinking, speaking, and doing that transact by the hour at his satellite address beside Concord's most monumental Pond. We as readers join in these activities by close association, benefiting as much by their edifying example as does their initiator. We likewise derive from the resulting shared experience of the text a sense of "wholeness" not to be found in more formally restrictive conceptions of "organicism," let alone in the social anomie that resulted, for Thoreau, from antebellum America's acquisitive, commercially driven cultural indebtedness to oneness. Heeding Thoreau's home, we might "humbly commune" and so "make the most rapid strides of any nation," he claims (108). It is a belief to which the author commits himself in word and deed when he has us inhabit a civic-literary paradigm of boardinghouse proportions.

The central tenet of this public place, Thoreau's broader Pond, is that the communities contained within classrooms and countries, or even among domestic company, arise not without effort; they are earned with much upkeep. To label Thoreau's communal compact with his people "visionary," then, as does Donald Pease in describing nineteenth-century American authors' general efforts to reconcile a self-interested present with the voluntary collectivism of their Revolutionary past,[24] is both to understate and obscure the depth of Thoreau's institutional commitments. The coming together that he "envisions" is as much a figurative national image by which he organizes his text as it is a "real" residential outcome that he would establish in fact. His politico-literary home is as much a metaphor for "hammering" a reconstituted community into his writings as it is a discursive structure (and a structural discourse) that he would see stand where other antebellum institutions have fallen or failed (57).

In building and inhabiting a showpiece civic-shelter, Thoreau imagines his increasingly fractured United States as comprising the kind of functional domicile for which he was hopeful, if not certain. Among the potential obstacles blocking national progress toward what we might call, in the residential vernacular, one big American boardinghouse were several practical, political, and philosophical impediments that trace to the temper of Thoreau's own life and times. In referencing, for example, his country's simmering sectional conflict over slavery—a conflict encoded in passages on "Webster's Fugitive-Slave Bill," as well as the narrator's justly famous windowsill inspection of battling black and rebel red ants—Walden's narrator deflates readers' belief that the "denizens" of his land might live in collective harmony, let alone avert a national institutional emergency (232). Thoreau further relates a host of seeming unholy alliances, each of which suggests a template for something other than group coherence. He partners the split personae and personalities of a Hermit ("And O, the housekeeping!" the latter cries) and Poet (223). He makes repeated mention of Christian and pagan (the philosopher Plato Thoreau names as "my next neighbor") (107). He cites throughout his volume the variant scriptures of East and West. Yet, rather than resolve the constituent differences of these "neighboring" pairs, the author allots equable discursive space (and time) to them all. *Walden* might house many an ostensible mismatch, but it also allows contraries to cohabitate conceptually, notwithstanding Thoreau's pronounced misgivings over social assembly. In his 1849 essay "Resistance to Civil Government," the author equates "the State" with his native Concord, and then symbolically withdraws from both when he asks if there is any civic establishment other than prison where "a free man can abide with honor."[25] He similarly expresses apparent communal despair in *Walden* when he declares, "Our life is like a German Confederacy, made up of petty states, with its boundary forever fluctuating" (92). Perhaps such authorial "Resistance" finally figures *Walden* an imperfect domestic setting: Thoreau cannot quite condone the "life" envisioned by many of his housemates; nor can he locate easily even one "free man" with whom he would be "knit together" in common cause and in emulation of regional New England ideals.[26] If his text is less than "whole," however, it does make metaphorically available through the residence that is Thoreau's rhetoric at least a tentative boardinghouse plan for forging the temporary togetherness of an otherwise disparate people.

A domestic imperative to associate, to cohabitate, thus structures narration in *Walden,* although Thoreau sets his text to temporal, spatial, and topical conceits that recall by suggestive association that most disruptive site of antebellum congregation, the city. It is the urban orientation of Thoreau's writing that ties his traditional community of Concord to a contemporary tale of metropolitan "progress"; it is the interpolation of his work by the city per se that makes compound accretion—of shelters, peoples, places, and spaces—both the theme that helps his individual chapters cohere and the formal tie that binds a book otherwise built from fragments. Throughout *Walden,* the centrifugal spread of the sprawling modern metropolis is offset only, if at all, by the centripetal stay-at-home lyricism of an author who would remain consistently fixed in his principles,[27] if not in his rotating choice of residences. The volatile local housing market, especially, situates *Walden* at an unstable interstice between manic migration and "holistic" (de)composition, in

which Thoreau "deliberately" depicts a ritual round of residential buying, renting, constructing, selling, and moving. In spite of its many avian
interludes, then, *Walden* is often on the wing, as it were, in figurative
flight from precisely the kind of ex-urban nesting arrangements that not
a few Bostonian railway commuters sought in the comparative peace of
"sleeper" communities located outside their bustling city.[28] Participating
as he did in an ascendant urban publishing world[29]—"boarding" beyond
the city, rather than right inside it—Thoreau himself was a culture industry commuter of sorts. As Lewis Mumford writes, "Walden was . . .
attached to Concord, and Concord in turn to Cambridge and Boston: so
even in isolation, Thoreau partook of the multidimensional social life of
the city."[30] Armed by extension with what Robert Gross calls a "suburban
vision,"[31] Thoreau came to occupy the proper frame of mind in which to
reflect on city residence. Indeed, he literally dwelt on a metropolitan edge
whose radial distance from city center increasingly seemed to be shrinking under the shadow of urban encroachment. From this critical position,
the accession of small Concord to the metropolis of Boston marked less a
revolution in consciousness on behalf of the author than a concession to
the inevitable evolution of habitation. *Walden* reenacts Thoreau's relocation out of town, but the text tends toward a discourse that coalesces and
communes.

In assembling resident readers inside his text, the author institutes typically urban terms that figure us as renters, not owners. We visit Walden
Pond on much the same footing as did Thoreau, who voluntarily migrated
onward after consecutive seasons there. *Walden* thereby presumes a
degree of domestic precariousness that many metropolitans would consider their birthright. Thoreau explains:

> In the savage state every family owns a shelter as good as the best,
> and sufficient for the coarser and simpler wants; but I think that I
> speak within bounds when I say that, though the birds of the air
> have their nests, and the foxes their holes, and the savages their
> wigwams, in modern civilized society not more than one half the
> families own a shelter. In the large towns and cities, where civiliza-
> tion especially prevails, the number of those who own a shelter is a
> very small fraction of the whole. The rest pay an annual tax for the
> outside garment of all. . . . (30)

A condensed chronicle of unsettledness, this passage writes the de
facto social bonding that is boarding across spatial, temporal, and cultural boundaries to suggest the comparatively recent corruption of our

collective "nesting" instinct. On the one hand, Thoreau's juxtaposing primitive "wigwams" with "modern civilized society" effectively extends Concord's current domestic restlessness backward into a mythic past, when the "family" *was* the collective, and the collective a "family" not strictly biologically defined. The suggestion here is that we are all, in our way, perennially in search of "shelter." Yet, "the coarser and simpler wants"—what "Doesticks" describes as "a fit habitation, wherein I might eat, sleep, change my shirt . . . , and attend to the other comforts of the external *homo*"—no longer today prove "sufficient" in an age given over to "outward riches" and "luxuries" (14). On the other hand, the author's "modern" city civilian suffers an additional residential disadvantage, one unknown even by the natural nomad to whom Thoreau pays tribute in these pages. To Thoreau's "savage" accrue the benefits of a life led in common with his tribe, whose implicitly uncivilized members prosper "whole," which is to say, "within" cohesive "bounds" that are denied the isolate "fraction" that is "civilized man" (30–31). Thoreau cites Massachusetts's colonial superintendent of Indians in rhetorical support of this point. He references seventeenth-century commentary to the effect that native dwellings, often "sixty or a hundred feet long and thirty feet broad," were "as warm as the best English houses" and thus fit to "lodge" anyone or everyone in surroundings that were intended to satisfy "necessaries of life" "no less physical than social" (12–13). As for the presumably independent homeowner, meanwhile, Thoreau reaffirms his initial assertion by insisting that the creature does not exist. In his reckoning, "the savage owns his shelter because it costs so little, while the civilized man hires his commonly because he cannot afford to own it" (30). Our author may acknowledge the economic necessity of renting in antebellum America. But his acknowledgment merely casts further domestic doubt on those in need of residential reassurance: he, the proud builder of a seemingly stand-alone cabin, favors the moveable roof of the "savage state" to the itinerant condition of "civilization" as the likelier structure to achieve bodily safety, social harmony, and communal longevity. By contrast, neither the book's "modern" dweller, nor with him the "civilized" nation, seems particularly equipped to "prevail" in the ongoing contest for a superior form of "shelter," "the outside garment of all."

Thoreau identifies a number of domestic alternatives to city civility and "savagery." Some of these border on the absurd, as does his deadpan proposal for residing in a small toolbox shed situated beside Concord's local railroad line: "You could sit up as late as you pleased," he writes, "and, whenever you got up, go abroad without any landlord or house-lord dogging you for rent" (29). Others among the author's residential notions exert less strain on the habitational imagination, but perhaps bear too close a resemblance to animal hibernation. His unforced endorsements of "caves," "dovecots," and "tents of thin cotton cloth" would fall under this latter category (28–29). It nevertheless is to Massachusetts's earliest boarding peoples that Thoreau returns in extolling the potential and paradoxical unifying virtues of the mobile household. His romantic championing of self notwithstanding, the author reserves his highest praise for the aforementioned tribe, "in making the life of a . . . people an *institution,* in which the life of the individual is to a great extent absorbed, in order to perfect that of the race" (31–32). It had become the custom of the author's countrymen to seek "comfort and independence" in the solitary "shelter" of the elusive proprietary home (33). Thoreau in part sustains that search for a proper domicile. He reverses the selfish associations that it had assumed in his day, however. What Thoreau proposes instead is a home that simultaneously satisfies the domestic "comforts," keeps formal, functional pace with its occupants' lifetime migrations, and figures *civil* "shelter" as a fundamentally tribal construct, in which "wigwams" radiate outward in widening spheres of inclusiveness. Home in *Walden* includes the "nests" of neighbors no less than it does the local community. Socially constructed, and philosophically conceived, the author's idealized household furthermore encompasses cities, "whole" countries, continents, hemispheres, and even stratospheres where "stars are the apexes of what wonderful triangles!" that "can be drawn as radii from one centre." Thoreau's home situates the planetary dweller among "the various mansions of the universe" (10–11). Home is where plural perspectives are compared and cosmic "shelter" shared.

If boarding out as a literary form accommodates authorial designs that are at once domestic, democratic, philosophic, and galactic, boarding proves equally adept at facilitating Thoreau's civic project. Much of *Walden* reprises the author's peopling his household vision with a suitable citizenry. The narrative result of that reprisal sees him making a nation by recounting the residents whom he assigns to occupy his master metaphor. We, his readers, meet the prerequisites of entry; our invitation into the author's home arrives in the companionable tone with which he addresses us from page one of *Walden*. Grain-feeding squirrels, a cheese-eating mouse, and a good many more additional "Visitors" besides, animal or otherwise, also implicitly pass the "thousand simple [domestic] tests" that the author administers to would-be housemates (10). "Spring" and "Winter" guests (from the corresponding chapter titles) likewise receive admittance into Thoreau's establishment.[32] He extends a warm welcome to any and all, in fact, who signal their willingness to subsist with a simple "shelter," scant provisions, and the mere three chairs that Thoreau keeps on hand to entertain "society" (140). There are few, if any, formalities at this household. Indeed, the owner-occupant narrator agrees by mutual consent with his residents to manage his corner of the aptly named *Concord* community on principles of plainness. It would be fair to say that the collective acceptance of plainness is the asking price for board, the author having determined beforehand to be as "sincerely" plain-speaking as he is plain-dealing with a people whom he would have "understand much that I have to say"—and demanding as much, or as little, in return (4, 65).

No less pedestrian are these people themselves. Throughout *Walden*, but particularly in the "Former Inhabitants" chapter, Thoreau assembles his account *as* a residential assembly by enlisting into his domestic enterprise those of Concord's forgotten citizens whom he would restore to their rightful positions within the polity. Adverse to exclusion, intent on an improved communal union, he is the most republican of boarders' keepers. Thoreau meanwhile so manages narrative time and space that they begin to collapse as he recasts his community in accordance with its metropolitan context. It is a felicitous instance of home maintenance, in that it locates his text within its proper modern moment, while permitting him to ameliorate, and then remove, those artificial barriers of race, class, ethnicity, and gender that historically have served to disenfranchise large segments of the American population from the national establishment. Bridging the past with a purposefully and politically reformed present, Thoreau leagues his speaker's first-person "I" in association with Concord's assorted area "others." As Lawrence Buell writes, Thoreau in this way expresses his resolve "to rebuild town society on his own terms." Or, as Peter Bellis explains, by this means does *Walden*'s author effect a "democratic" re-peopling of the woods that "recreates a varied and multiethnic, largely working-class community."[33]

Thoreau draws respectful portraits of his housemates, none of whom would have received entry at the residence headed by Holmes's Autocrat. There is "Zilpha, a colored woman," who spins linen for her neighbors. "Brister Freeman, 'a handy Negro,' slave of Squire Cummins once," resides with us, as does "Cato Ingraham, slave of Duncan Ingraham, Esquire, gentleman of Concord village" (257). The poor white potter Wyman also keeps house with Thoreau, adding the "art" of artisanship into the author's aesthetic "shelter"—itself no sheltered aesthetic (261). At home, too, is the hapless Irishman Hugh Quoil, our veteran of a foreign war. Of course Thoreau's roster is only a domestic reverie; it is an imagined reflection on local folk who once inhabited the woods around his cabin in "quiet desperation" but are now long since gone (8). By situating his civic commitment to the metropolitan moment in dialogue with his reverence for the human challenges of the residential past, however, the author erases spatial, temporal, and social distinctions with an inclusive embrace of Concord's downtrodden. These are the household neighbors whom Thoreau would have and hold. His domestic guests in turn abandon, respectively, the forlorn "little house," "dwelling," "tavern," and "tenement" that they inhabited in "tragic," forsaken circumstances prior to his arrival in order to enlist in Thoreau's communal coalition (257–58, 261–62). In doing so, they move from the margins of antebellum America to the hearth of a home where all are created equal, and keep house in common.

The boardinghouse as a literary form enables such forays into community construction. Here that form realizes minority voices that otherwise would remain silent. For, in civically reinstating a dispossessed people by bringing them home, Thoreau in effect returns to them the power of speech. Stated differently, as the habitationally challenged subjects of local lore, as the narrated members of a closed storytelling community that subjugates them with belittling phrases like "a handy Negro," the author's boarders previously have known none of the linguistic perquisites of citizenship. Indeed, having been denied a place at table for so long, they would not until now have been able to speak for themselves even if they had broken bread with their "betters." Thoreau's housing the hired help, as it were, interrupts the uncivil cycle by which they were kept passive in being talked *about,* and so it ends their silence as well. Now domestically protected, these "Former Inhabitants" emerge as current occupants, full-fledged members of Concord's boardinghouse discourse community, and as the rightful authors rather than objects of their own life stories. They remain lowly renters, but they have become narra*tors.* The necessary domestic plurality of boarding facilitates precisely this kind of poly-vocality. Thoreau goes one rhetorical step further, sanctioning as he does an egalitarian gathering of heads, hearts, skins, and tongues.

Boarding out might not represent in this literary instance the "knowable communities" that Raymond Williams identifies with the novel per se, a genre that enables authors to "show people and their relationships in essentially knowable and communicable ways."[34] Yet *Walden* is, if no novel, a discursive community inspired by cities which themselves know no bounds. In classic boardinghouse style, *Walden* teems with abbreviated incidents, none too small for relation, that unfold right before readers' eyes. We are witnesses to the minutiae of a strangely sylvan metropolitan everyday, whether we are present (in time and space) to watch each kernel of corn fed to hungry animals, to smile at the frolics of a laughing loon, or to monitor our author-landlord's dealings with woodchuck intrusions. Like the typical urban text, *Walden* offers varied characters, too, numbering into the dozens, all of whom we at some level grow to know through cohabitation. The above-named "Former Inhabitants" demonstrate as much. Indeed, by virtue of the pluralist conceptions of race, creed, and color that Thoreau inscribes into his account, *Walden* achieves a diversity that renders it more than merely "knowable" as a community. The expanded and expansive tenets of domestic acceptance that the author sets on flagrant display—what F. O. Matthiessen might call a truly "optative" instance of boarding out—suggest what Thoreau's "whole" boardinghouse nation, his American community writ large, would and should become in his habitational imagination.

*Walden* accomplishes its cultural work through the author's tireless discursive work, a significant portion of which involves his dialectically balancing seeming conceptual opposites at his poetic residence. Be they "northern" and "southern" "overseer," "slave-driver" and "fugitive slave," or "master" and "servant" (7, 71, 243), the unlikeliest of domestic partnerships come to constitute Thoreau's home. It is a politico-literary decision on the author's part, this wishfully fulfilled society of oddities. Communal controversy, conflicting opinion, and cultural difference are no cause here for maintaining separate residences; they invite cohabitation, rather, and highlight Thoreau's hope to rank that ideal private "shelter" of his mind among those "public buildings" on which the republic's welfare rests (140, 57). The author proves true, then, to his early word in *Walden* that he would "never paint 'No Admittance' on my gate" (17). His late chapter on "House-Warming" anticipates those "Former Inhabitants; and Winter Visitors" whom he soon thereafter incorporates into his residentially reformed union, and concurrently marks an important boardinghouse precedent on the non-discriminatory keeping of a habitable national establishment. His is a capacious cabin worth describing in full:

> I sometimes dream of a larger and more populous house, standing in a golden age, of enduring materials, ... which shall consist of only one room, a vast, rude, substantial, primitive hall, without ceiling or plastering, with bare rafters and purlins supporting a sort of lower heaven over one's head ... a cavernous house, wherein you must reach up a torch upon a pole to see the roof; where some may live in the fire-place, some at one end of the hall, some at another, and some aloft on rafters with the spiders, if they choose; a house

which you have got into when you have opened the outside door, and the ceremony is over; where the weary traveler may wash, and eat, and converse, and sleep, without further journey; such a shelter as you would be glad to reach in a tempestuous night, containing all the essentials of a house, and nothing for house-keeping; where you can see all the treasures of the house at one view, and every thing hangs upon its peg that a man should use; at once kitchen, pantry, parlor, chamber, store-house, and garret; where you can see so necessary a thing as a barrel or a ladder, so convenient a thing as a cupboard, and hear the pot boil, and pay your respects to the fire that cooks your dinner and the oven that bakes your bread, and the necessary furniture and utensils are the chief ornaments; where the washing is not put out, nor the fire, nor the mistress, and perhaps you are sometimes requested to move off from the trap-door, when the cook would descend into the cellar, and so learn whether the ground is solid or hollow beneath you without stamping. A house whose inside is as open and manifest as a bird's nest, and you cannot go in at the front door and out at the back without seeing some of its inhabitants. (243–44)

The "open and manifest" institution to which the author pledges his allegiance in this passage is but a rhetorically flourished version of the functional household that he in fact had established at Walden Pond. "All the attractions of a house were concentrated in one room" at that latter location, Thoreau relates. "It was kitchen, chamber, parlor, and keeping-room" (242). Not only is Thoreau's very real residential ideal multipurposeful, however. It is also purposefully nurturing—a "cavernous house," whose individual co-occupants could "choose" to secure some small modicum of personal space up in the "rafters" of a quasi-wigwam society. Thoreau's home is an "open" house, too, whose ingenuous residents neither would deign to disguise mundane domestic matters, nor disrespect any fellow dweller. Under properly aligned circumstances, one might say the realization of Thoreau's domestic dream resided in the antebellum boardinghouse itself: by default, that most "open and manifest" of contemporary residences, given contemporary metropolitan restrictions on time and space; by design, a mediation of the public and private, and thus the site of much cultural commingling; and so, in theory, if not always in fractured urban practice, the preeminent American setting for democratic dwelling prior to the U.S. Civil War.

As generous in populating his household as is Oliver Wendell Holmes's Autocrat exclusionary in recruiting for his, Thoreau yet would need to travel some discursive distance were he fully to succeed—whether locally, nationally, or globally—in "overcoming" an endemic metropolitan problem that urban planner Jane Jacobs names "residential discrimination."[35] *Walden*'s author democratically reworks the national domestic demographic so as to accept into his signifying "shelter" disadvantaged whites, Irish immigrants, and African Americans. His is in this respect a radically reimagined communal norm. With more than city livability at stake, however, with the institutional fate of his nation looming large over his literary labors, Thoreau necessarily would have to conjure more than figures of residential reform were he to achieve meaningful social change in his United States. He would need to institute his domestic vision at home. To a degree this would entail *self*-reform. For, despite the ideological distance at which he and "The Autocrat" reside, Thoreau in certain respects occupied a perspective of privilege that set him at a once-remove from the antebellum pedestrian. From innovative schools and area clubs, to Harvard Yard and learned assembly in Boston, Thoreau like Holmes's persona had enjoyed an intellectual elite's exposure to some of New England's most vaunted institutions. A classically constituted, scripturally sophisticated "Reading" as it is imagined in *Walden* thus represents an institution to which many a city boarder would not have had interpretive or linguistic access.[36]

Few boarders' establishments, moreover, would have conceived of the communities that they constructed as opportunities for inclusiveness, let alone as miniature societies that were somehow emblematically democratic. Yet, Thoreau *did* conceive of boarding in just this way before, during, and after Walden Pond. He thereby practiced the idealized notion of the domestic that he preaches in print. It was not your average household, for example, that held copies of abolitionist William Lloyd Garrison's newspaper *The Liberator* in its parlors. *Walden*'s author read this weekly sheet with much edification under his slave-sympathizing mother's roof,[37] where the boarders sometimes included runaway African Americans en route to Canada. In fact, boarding for the Thoreau family came to accommodate an advanced brand of racial reform, and with it a forward form of thinking: when landlady Thoreau added to her permanent roster of boarders Mrs. Joseph Ward and her daughter Prudence, both charter members of the Women's Anti-Slavery Society and later to become friends with Thoreau himself,[38] she signaled what seems in retrospect her household's enlightened determination to oppose one institution, northern boarding, against another, southern enslavement. Like the city, in short, boarding was for this mother and son the "crucible" for "public culture" that is Thomas Bender's Atlantic metropolis.[39] Yet if boarding in its Thoreauvian conception was a modern melting pot, it was also one that few among the more orthodox of "moderns generally" would have been willing to embrace as a national symbol of multicultural compact during the divisive middle decades of the nineteenth century (325).

Thoreau might have boarded at the metropolitan edge, but the "crucible" in which he practiced his domestic rhetoric does not relegate *Walden* to the fringes of polemical discourse. "We," an antebellum boarding people who "meet at meals three times a day," he writes, "and give each other a new taste of the old musty cheese that we are," "need not come to open war," either, and permit our differences to devolve into outright fighting. Rather than cause us to "live thick and [be] in each other's way," rather than see us "stumble over, and . . . thus lose respect for one another," the polarizing strains that can attend close household contact paradoxically register for Thoreau as an opportunity for social solidarity (136). Boarding is for him a field for neutralizing conflict through communal compromise. Doubly functioning as a literary medium and civic message, boarding for Thoreau converts temporal-spatial constraint into a mandate for mutual domestic tolerance. The author himself was prepared to board and let board on deep-seated egalitarian principles. For many of his contemporaries, communal association would have been less a principled pretext for coming together than a necessary corollary to crowded metropolitan proximity. No matter what the terms on which coherence occurred, however, boarding remained throughout the period a powerful institutional agent for a people who would not only be one, but live as one as well. The closely associative discourse of boarding in this way transforms a basic human instinct for domestic protection into a sanctioned residential venue for repairing political and interpersonal rupture.

No narrative work of fiction, the text and context of *Walden* suggest that rhetorical boarding might well reside far from the "airy" realms of romance that reputedly suited our transcendentalist author. The historical-habitational fact of boarding instead could provide the ontological ground of a true communal union, with the added fragile promise of countrywide reconciliation. An example from New England is suggestive in this respect. On July 4, 1849—exactly four years following Thoreau's migratory move to Walden Pond—boarding literally and politically rallied supporters at an Independence Day picnic held by the Massachusetts Anti-Slavery Society. Speakers for that afternoon's entertainment in Boston included the African American author William Wells Brown, the celebrated abolitionist orator Wendell Phillips, and yet another abolitionist, William Lloyd Garrison, whose newspaper writings Thoreau had read while boarding. Thoreau, in fact, attended these festivities, and most likely applauded Garrison's particular contribution to the proceedings. Much of the institutional interest that would work its way into *Walden*—including careful boardinghouse consideration of community, civility, and citizenship—framed the speech delivered by America's most prominent opponent of slavery. Indeed, the slave narrator turned editor Frederick Douglass reported months afterward in his own abolitionist *North Star* newspaper that Garrison had articulated that day a vision of U.S. cohabitation that Thoreau himself might have endorsed. A journalist for Douglass's paper summarized Garrison's remarks as follows:

> Mr. Garrison referred to the change of public opinion relative to colorophobia, citing in illustration, that a few years since a Haitian gentleman . . . could not succeed in obtaining accommodation in either a public or private boarding house in Boston; but that within the past few days a Haitian of equal standing with the former and whose complexion was not of an Anglo Saxon stamp, was admitted to first class fare at one of our most popular city Hotels.[40]

What the writer neglects to mention is that a few Boston boardinghouses *did* cater to blacks, as did separate but unequal establishments located in other major cities along the Atlantic seaboard. Another local paper, the *Colored American,* to that end ran racially specific advertisements soliciting African American houseguests.[41] Big-city boarders across the country adhered to additional prejudicial practices by further subdividing themselves along similarly culturally sensitive lines: of ethnicity—there were boardinghouses for widely reviled Irish immigrants, as there were for the less maligned Germans; of region—southern boarders often congregated in the same establishments when visiting cities in the North; and of profession—low-wage seamen, especially, kept domestic company in port cities throughout the nineteenth-century continental United States.[42]

Home for Thoreau was as much a subjective space of the artistic imagination as it was an objective place in the historical world of the emerging metropolis. What both he and Garrison imagined as an alternative to exclusionary shelter was a refuge where one and all could keep quarters in common. It was a timely residential suggestion whose time had not come.[43] Internally riven by formal frictions, divided by the contrary urges for mobility and stability, home as construed within the framework of civic boarding obeyed inherent "organic" limits that no "whole" nation could overcome during its prolonged modern(ist) period of crisis. Organicists, unionists, and abolitionists ideally would have instituted boarding to help us cohere in the face of modern fracture. America's urban moderns, by contrast, and with or without Douglass's "Anglo Saxon stamp" upon them, inhabited a troubled boarder's world where no wayfarer's rhetoric could stay the perennial threat posed by metropolitan residence, what we might call our collectively coming undone.

Chapter 5

✦

# Class Mapping the Literary Metropolis:
## A Residential Reading of *The Quaker City*

> Little I ask; my wants are few;
> I only wish a hut of stone,
> (A *very plain* brown stone will do,)
> That I may call my own;—
> And close at hand is such a one,
> In yonder street that fronts the sun.
> —Oliver Wendell Holmes, 1858

Behind the common modern(ist) aesthetic of boarding in the United States lies the mundane material fact of urbanization. Period American writers from the mid-nineteenth century faithfully confronted the ideologies of domesticity, civility, community, and democracy as they interrogated the antebellum household within the context of the new U.S. metropolis. The substantive shape of boarding as an art form nevertheless resides less in the rarefied air of abstract ideas than in the contemporary crucible of lived experience. Boarding's literary conceits, concepts, and everyday rhetorics finally signify little outside the frame of felt sociohistorical forces, without which there would be no urban American literature. Much as the nation's residents shaped the discourse of the city, the city shaped the pedestrian nature of residence at the boardinghouse dawn of modernity on these shores.

Subsuming the metaphors and matter of boarding is the determinative fact of social class. With the increasing density of urban settlement in the antebellum era came myriad instances of high-class, low-class, and middling city shelters either rising in close proximity within porously mixed neighborhoods or else adjoining one another on the same blocks, streets, and alleyways in highly congested semi-residential zones. Communal boarding of course had made close domestic contact the normative standard against which much of the West measured its experience of the modern. Yet, one of urban boarding's unforeseen consequences was to multiply the opportunities for interpersonal comparison among American co-occupants, and thereby awaken their latent tendency for domestic envy. City conditions invited residents to measure their apparent habitational worth against that of their housemates or the potential rivals from separate neighboring establishments. Any given individual conceivably had much to wonder and worry over: the state and stateliness (or lack thereof) of his private rooms; his dining-table treatment at the hands of landladies; and, above all, the type of domicile that he could afford to inhabit. Among boarders, the options with respect to these last ranged widely, from the communally shabby and shabby-genteel, to the plainly genteel and not-so-plainly sumptuous. A fortunate few owners, meanwhile, in principle might have shared city space with the aggregate masses of renters, but in practice they enjoyed (in several senses of the word) an altogether different urban America than did the rest of the domestically dispossessed. The commercially induced urge to attain distinction through consumption—in this case, involving the conspicuous possession of habitat—was not unique to the antebellum city; building, or at least inhabiting, a better home than one's neighbor long had been a custom of the country, too. But metropolitans across the continent came to occupy in these years a sliding scale of residential gradations that made group hierarchies manifest in domestic terms. That is to say, urban American class status at midcentury came to rest more and more upon a shifting modern threshold that reckoned the urban dweller's provisional place within an evolving domestic pecking order according to his capacity to acquire and maintain a sizeable store of limited residential capital.

For antebellum boarders, the chronic domestic comparisons attending modern residence multiplied the rhetorical occasions for registering, questioning, and even resisting an impersonal urban process that distributed the very real rewards and liabilities of social class status on the basis of a home that eluded so many in the city. Because boarders occupied a metropolitan housing market that traded in scarcity, their prospects for achieving domestic distinction in large part rested on their attaining to a level of habitat from which not a few Americans were excluded. Class mobility was a dream that they dared not inhabit, so long as scheduled rent payments constrained their savings, even while the area demand for (and price of) housing continued to climb and thus defer the sweet release of ownership.

Not every boarder's story features characters resigned or consigned to the downward class trajectory that often attended perennial rental.

Ik Marvel's recorded operatic observations in his *Lorgnette,* discussed earlier, represent but one example of a minority generic trend that saw the occasional boarder-narrator comfortably manage to preserve the greatest of domestic expectations, and the loftiest of social perspectives, despite co-residing without kin in a city of virtual strangers. Oliver Wendell Holmes's "Autocrat" well expresses this patrician boarder's worldview. With humorous feigned humility that sets him at some rhetorical distance from Marvel's outright condescension, Boston's senior boarder-statesman residentially conjures "Contentment" in verse as follows:

> "Little I ask; my wants are few;
> I only wish a hut of stone,
> (A *very plain* brown stone will do,)
> That I may call my own;—
> And close at hand is such a one,
> In yonder street that fronts the sun.

Like boarder-author Thomas Butler Gunn in his *Physiology,* Holmes's Autocrat looks beyond boarding for an ideal domestic situation. He at least implies as much by rhyming his "little" hope for a "hut of stone" to "call my own." That Holmes's persona must write these lines from current boardinghouse quarters suggests that said "hut" is not now available, however. Indeed, the speaker risks never realizing his mock-immodest "wants," since the residence he most desires is the proverbially not so "*very plain* brown stone" of metropolitan high society. Yet these, the rarest of residential prospects, are not for him unfounded in reality. Enveloping the ironic understatement of the poet's lines are a simple diction and casual phraseology that together betray an offhand familiarity with a residential upper crust that could count the proprietary urban town house, or "brown stone," among its actual possessions. So rare a residence would have been virtually unknown to the average boarder, but the Autocrat's highest domestic hopes are by contrast within easy reach. They are "close at hand," he says, in "yonder street" that "fronts" a "sun" that seldom shined so favorable a light upon the majority of metropolitans (11:502). Said "sun" does shine on the Autocrat, much as it illuminates similar narratives that figure boarding as less a function of city (mis)fortune than a fashion of and for urban privilege.

Complementing the boardinghouse writings of urban America's residential "betters" is a voluminous mass of literature that makes no pretense to domestic ascendancy. In fact, much of literary boarding runs in the rhetorical reverse of the "Autocrat" serials: the city-dwellers whom it depicts

often relinquish the prerogatives of a home they likely never knew only
to defer to the unwritten rules of tenancy. Rent itself served a constant
reminder of boarders' disempowered position within an emergent residential hierarchy. Paying occupants owed their subsistence, and thus their
obeisance, to owner-operators who controlled the cold cash and credit
transactions of modern habitation. Boardinghouse letters accordingly are
often meek, or mute, on the subject of tenants' collective subjugation to
the veritable "lords" of the urban land. Not all boardinghouse writers
and their protagonists subsisted quietly, however. Some among the genre's
authors and profiled characters greeted the city's growing residential
inequalities with a discourse of mild defiance that bespeaks the fledgling
formation of a proto-class-consciousness. The more self-aware members
of an informal boarders' brotherhood captured the class-inflected contours of antebellum habitat on the page, and in doing so gave candid
expression to what they believed to be the wrongs of metropolitan residence. If to write of hierarchical habitat is to *right* it, then presumably the
artists responsible for these latter protesting statements were engaged in
an earnest socio-literary effort at domestic reparation.

By revealing the widening rifts in mid-nineteenth-century residence, a
concerned cadre of America's boardinghouse authors composed a critical literature of class from the concrete conditions of city shelter. Scholar
Nicholas Bromell regrets the "relative invisibility" of manual labor in the
literature of the American Renaissance. Michael Denning declares the
class content of popular nineteenth-century narratives closed to latter-
day readers through inscrutable encoding. Amy Schrager Lang searches
in vain for an explicit "syntax" of class in antebellum fiction. Yet, the evidence of what Schrager Lang calls a "native" tradition of class-conscious
American literature resides precisely in the physical foreground of an
otherwise socially constructed contemporary home. On the strength of a
literal roof with walls—and, by extension, the gritty city streets surrounding them—does the body of boardinghouse writings figure a literary
tradition of incisive class commentary.[1]

✦

The conventionally unconventional boardinghouse author not only represents the material trappings of class in his writings; he (and, under special
gendered circumstances, she) portrays gross imbalances in urban residence
as a pernicious source of metropolitan class conflict. One such writer-
advocate is the antebellum sensationalist George Lippard. The topics and
tone of this Philadelphia writer's succession of best-selling city-mysteries

novels from the 1840s make plain the working-class commitments of their creator's entire oeuvre.[2] Indeed, Lippard's very upbringing prepared him for the literary activism that he undertook on behalf of the working-man's habitat in later life. He came of age amid the militant workers' protests of his adopted home city, where he received heady early exposure to a surge in labor union organizing during the decade between 1827 and 1837. Afterward, Lippard internalized the lessons of his adolescence as the country sank into the century's worst economic downturn. Orphaned, out of work, and reduced to occasional vagrancy by the impressionable age of fifteen, Lippard felt firsthand the laboring-class perils of poverty, unemployment, and homelessness that he would try to redress in subsequent years when he founded and oversaw a secret labor organization.

Lippard meanwhile transcribed his early class encounters into print publication by the tender age of nineteen. As a seasoned author he would explain his elected profession in retrospect as a type of "surveying" work, through which he could speak with reformist intent to what he identified as the "hideous disparities of Modern civilization." But as a young man he was already insisting in his radical fiction on the competing interests of American capital and labor. Anticipating by a few years the strident class critique of Karl Marx, and borrowing heavily from the French *roman-feuilleton* tradition of periodical prose sympathy for the working poor, Lippard spent much of the 1840s filling the pages of penny-press newspapers and cheap novels with a sharply class-edged message. The author reveals the high ideals of a serious utopian socialist in one of his many allegorical sketches from this period, wherein he converts Christ into a model "Mechanic" mouthpiece for his own class complaints. Lippard employs more straightforward tactics of advocacy as well, as instanced by his heralding at one stage in his career that day when "the Capitalist may no longer be the tyrant, nor the Laborer the victim." In all, this prolific inhabitant of the City of Brotherly Love spent the brief adult years of his life (he died in 1854, at the age of thirty-two) writing to help erase the inequitable distribution of wealth and well-being that he saw disfiguring his United States before the Civil War.[3] Inflecting his highly romantic imagination with a preliminary attempt at "proletarian" realism,[4] Lippard in league with like-minded writers of his literary generation *labored* on behalf of the urban worker even as he limned the outlines of a domestic discourse that, as we will see, aimed ultimately at residential betterment.

It is the urban domestic edifice that carries the burden of class inflection in this body of antebellum writing. So imposing a literal presence is city shelter in these works,[5] and so closely do authors key inhabitants' social status to the empirical weight of their respective residences, that the center of attention inside texts like Lippard's gravitates toward the physical foundations of signification. Such is the heft of the habitats portrayed here that the images they implant in readers' minds begin to belie their usual semiotic function. Domestic impressions circulate within these works as so many signified shadows, once removed from the actual objects they represent. And yet the discursive traces of inhabited places—the signifying description, say, of a multichambered rental on the "wrong" side of town—never fully sever their correlating connections to real-world residence. When artists impart so striking a materialist form to the writing of domicile, then readers must struggle to stray far from a home that looms disproportionately large within the most tangible of narrative frames. Or, to borrow Raymond Williams's formulation, when the denotative forces of modern industrial "Society"—manufactories, markets, and infrastructures—are dialectically understood to induce the connotative expressions of human "Culture," then a cultural index like literature "can be used as a special kind of map by which it is possible to look again at those wider changes in life and thought to which the changes in language evidently refer."[6] By the logic of this concept, when material things are seen to prompt written response—when household experience, for instance, is believed to structure super-structural reflection after the fact—then words themselves become a kind of directional register to "Society." Class-conscious American authors wrote so frequently of residence, and on such exaggerated materialist terms, as to make a scalable mountain of meaning from even the humblest of metropolitan homes. To read their inflated physical reminders of residence is to "map" a bewilderingly overbuilt urban milieu where city-dwellers were ranked on the basis of their presumed habitational worth. This rhetoric of domestic representation may be overdetermined,[7] but it conveys the shared social protest of its creators exactly because it protests too materially and too much, at once.

If modern urban writers following the flaneur worked their sidewalk observations into *physiologies,* then city discoursers like Lippard produced with their pens *physicalities* that "map" the material dimensions of the metropolis. Redirected toward the object world of urban residence, readers of these materialist texts encounter cityscapes whose signifying households represent a wealth of class-carrying data about home owners, occupants, and their surrounding environs. Here, the look and feel of the domestic—large and spacious, open and airy, closed and cramped— combined with the outward appearance of the neighborhoods they help sustain—sunny and smiling, dark and decayed, prim, proper, pretentious, or decidedly in the decline of disrepair—in part identify inhabitants according to their occupations, incomes, and relative social status. Shelter signifies, in short. And so, whether one looks closely for the shade and grade of brick, takes mental note of a broken pane of glass, or carefully counts the number of steps to an entranceway, he has entered into the discursive spirit of Lippard's rhetorical world. Class status is figured here through residence, and residence, in turn, is figured as the sum of tangible signs which structure domestic representation. Inside the imaginative space of this literary home, the cultural code of class literally has been written on the walls.

America's Renaissance writers conducted similar early object experiments in what Leon Chai calls the "subjective objectivity" of symbolism, but Lippard is unique among his contemporaries in that he exercised Chai's "practical poetics" within a modish city-mysteries milieu whose representational rhetoric he helped define.[8] The authors who subscribed to this popular genre represented a city of excitement and intrigue, shadow and light, bustling places and uncharted spaces. Their urban world is readable, but only as a "labyrinth" the generic forms of which Wyn Kelley associates with a kind of double semiotic trouble.[9] On the one hand, city-mysteries strained at literary representation, inasmuch as their practitioners suffered the epistemological struggle of trying to indite a modern metropolis whose sensory explosiveness their sensationalized writing only perpetuated. On the other hand, city-mysteries simultaneously entailed an implicit *social* struggle in their attempting to navigate an urban discursive space composed in (and conflicted by) class barriers.

This latter struggle may explain Lippard's attraction to city-mysteries, above and beyond their proving hospitable to his penchant for discursive hyperbole and spatial play. Not only did this exaggerating genre paradoxically provide a welcome central narrative consciousness to "guide" readers through the cognitively confusing new metropolis; it also afforded authors of a certain *framing* mindset an opportunity to expose the treacherous class terrain of urban social inequality in the bold relief of stark domestic contrast. In Lippard's much-read fiction, especially, the American boundary line between the stereotyped haves and have nots runs straight through the homes of an unequally inhabited city of "mysteries." Indeed, home counters chaos in Lippard's hands, since the dearth of domestic alternatives in his work effectively checks the mystery of the city with the interpretive bulwark of the residentially unmistakable. Lippard either couches wealthy oppressors in unearned urban comfort, or else literally, and far more frequently, buries the working classes in household oppression. Seldom does he accommodate two classes at once. Rarely do his narratives perform anything other than a predictable pantomime of

domestic unrest. In text after text, phenomenal residential surfaces testify to the habitational status of two-dimensional character types: to the
"upper ten" comes sheltered splendor; to the "lower millions" falls the lot
of the nondescript hovel. The parade of human faces might change inside
this formulaic housing hierarchy. Workers might resist their condition
and position within the residential spectrum. Yet, human habitat remains
for Lippard a socially directed means of charting what was for him the
unambiguous tale of contemporary class conflict.[10] Whether dignified in
their solidity, or weathered by neglect, Lippard's discursive domiciles are
seemingly impervious to the dynamic swings of antebellum urban society,
and thus constitute conspicuous reminders of the basic domestic facts of
class that confronted city-dwellers daily. If city-mysteries needed mapping, or what Lippard himself called "surveying," then the literary home
serves as the most reliable of reference points inside his urban imaginary.

✦

Lippard's most sustained effort at residential class mapping occurs in his
best-selling *The Quaker City; or, The Monks of Monk-Hall* (1844).[11] The
novel's sensational settings, sharp shifts in tone, and erratic pacing justify
its fabulous secondary subtitle, *A Romance of Philadelphia Life, Mystery
and Crime*. But if the author indulges a wild rhetoric of excess inside
his infrastructural frame, he conceptualizes socioeconomic disparity as a
literal domestic grid that must qualify the undeniable "Romance" of this
work. The book's main title (re)places Philadelphia on the linguistic map,
Lippard himself having coined the now-famous phrase "Quaker City"
for his adopted metropolis. His narrated storyline, moreover, concretizes
local gradations in social class through the physical signifying medium of
the city's housing hierarchy. Highlighting that hierarchy is the Gothically
impossible mansion Monk-hall. Its domestic doom and gloom darken the
various intrigues of Lippard's complex text, and yet *The Quaker City* is
finally less a house of patent fiction than a fiction of habitable houses.[12]
For Monk-hall itself is but one among many of the solid urban domiciles inside this sprawling volume by which the author is able to achieve
symbolic ideological commentary on his American region. The finest in
merchants' town houses, like the meanest of workers' retreats, here make
class conflict into something tangible to (be)hold, such that readers experience the author's subjective social geography as an objective lesson in
household topography. Calibrating Philadelphia with material consciousness, Lippard combines real city residence with romantic figuration to
make manifest the mid-Atlantic (mal)distribution of area wealth.

It is an unlikely rhetorical form for the book to take, considering its sordid basis in violent sexual scandal. Lippard's repeated denials to the contrary,[13] *The Quaker City* traces topically to the March 1843 murder trial of the avenging young Philadelphian Singleton Mercer, who in requital for his sister Sarah's seduction inside a local house of assignation openly tracked, attacked, and slew the perpetrator, Mahlon Heberton, before his own controversial arrest on charges of manslaughter. Lippard's novel relives the three eventful nights preceding the initial instigating episode from the December prior, in effect elaborating ad nauseam the titillating reportage of city newspapers. He himself a journalist of some note, *The Quaker City*'s author swiftly crafted a comprehensive, if embellished, account that appealed to the prying eyes of the reading public. Lippard made threatened female innocence his ostensible cause. Immoral male depravity he embodied as his requisite villain. And through repeated local color reference he enhanced his story's interest for Philadelphians. Whatever mercenary motives he might have had for writing, Lippard seems to have compiled his account as much from a vested interest in his source materials as from any desire for monetary gain or literary fame. A novel that began as a hastily assembled handful of serial pamphlets accordingly evolved over the course of its printed lifetime into one of the era's most sweeping discursive statements on social class formation in the antebellum nation.

*The Quaker City* opens residentially, within a world where domestic edifices comprise a cogent statement on class. "I say, gentlemen," is the complacent introductory remark of the genteel Gus Lorrimer, Lippard's handsome fictional stand-in for the slain seducer, Mahlon Heberton. Gesturing toward his three drinking companions late one evening in 1842, Lorrimer proceeds to ask, "Shall we make a night of it?" He continues, "Shall we elevate the devil along Chestnut street, or shall we subside quietly to our homes? Let's toss up for it—which shall have the night— brandy and oysters, or quilts and feather-beds?" (5). Issuing his question in the leisurely manner that he does, Lorrimer all but answers his own query; he is rhetorically self-assured, betrays no outward appearance of weariness, and so hardly seems ready to retire. Of greater importance for the corresponding concern of class, domestically defined, is the collective residential question to be settled—or not to be settled—by Lorrimer and his fellow pleasure-seekers. Once more the mere asking obviates the response, since Lippard already has oriented his story high atop the habitational class ladder through the content and context of Lorrimer's impromptu speech. The nocturnal setting of the scene in Chestnut Street, to begin, situates the novel at its outset in what long had been, by the

1840s, the acknowledged seat of the city's mercantile and banking elite. Thus does the author paint his opening pages in the figurative pink of prosperity. Lorrimer deepens this discursive shading when he suggests that he and the other men about town "toss" to decide how to spend the remainder of the "night." It is a telling suggestion: not only can they afford to lose the small currency of coinage in the occasional wager; any losses they sustain will have little impact on their outlays for the aristocratic fare of "brandy and oysters."[14]

The second half of Lorrimer's above proposal sets readers more squarely on an urban domestic footing, where class consists of so many residential signs. It is worth stating first the obvious: the individual members of Lorrimer's quartet hypothetically can return to "our homes" only because they indeed have "homes" to which to return. The possessive pronoun "our" implies ownership, and with it the sheltered distinction that accrued to the holder of an independent dwelling. Less obvious are the local ramifications of legally titled domestic possession. Despite being known regionally throughout the nineteenth century as the City of Homes,[15] Philadelphia nevertheless afforded the area's working classes something other than stereotypical house-holding privileges. As historian Stuart M. Blumin writes, the contemporary term "cottages," often used to describe the two-story row houses favored by Philadelphia's artisans and mechanics, could in fact amount to little more than a euphemistic mask for living conditions that were less than conventionally "respectable." Quarters were cramped, with but one room per floor. Families frequently resorted to double and triple occupancy, dividing the interiors of larger dwellings between them inside inner-city blind alleys and industrial zones. Few families could afford to own. And single males like Lorrimer generally lodged or boarded out.[16] Yet the words of this particular city-dweller indicate no such makeshift arrangements for him or his crew. His "quilts and feather-beds" impart the promise, rather, of a domestic autonomy and luxury that eluded the majority of urban laborers. Gus Lorrimer consequently steps forth from the woodwork of the text a type of exceptional (and independently wealthy, we later learn) "Chestnut street" householder. "Seated on the door-way of a four storied dwelling" nearby, "his right hand grasping a massive gold-headed cane," Lorrimer represents a demographic cross-section of the city for whom the "long shadows of the houses," as much or more as the fineries of personal appointments, signal the recherché nature of their class (6–7).

This pattern of residential mapping continues as the "mystery" of Lippard's fictional city evolves. Lorrimer's fateful boon companion, Byrnewood Arlington—for all intents and purposes the avenging

real-world brother, Singleton Mercer—like Gus carries with him throughout the novel material reminders of the domestic objectification of class.
As does Lorrimer, Byrnewood belongs to the city's most exclusive mon-
eyed circles. He admits as much when he casually states, "I'm the junior
partner in the importing house of Livingston[e], Harvey, & Co." (24). But
unlike Lorrimer, Byrnewood (unbeknownst to both men the sibling of
the woman whom our villain later violates) must earn his upkeep. Hence
his ability to finance his present three-day "spree," including the additional round of drinks that he and his newfound friend Gus finally prefer
to "quilts and feather-beds." There is no shame in Byrnewood's dirty-
ing his hands for dollars, however. Spared from stooping to the officious
level of peddler, like so many counter-jumping clerks, he can count upon
the genuine prospects of his profession to maintain his elevated social
status. His Philadelphia firm—what he calls his mercantile "house"—
conducts its business "along Front street," facing the Delaware River's
well-stocked warehouses and steady stream of ships (24). Here underneath this roof does Byrnewood spend the better part of his laboring
days, so that he practically and semantically works where he virtually
resides. His employment both figures and effects the residential advancement of the commercial classes. For Byrnewood and his mercantile peers
utilize the city's ports as but a non-manual means of converting the riches
of trade into tangible habitational capital. He and Gus may express an
immediate preference for "brandy and oysters." Upholding their taste
for edible, alienable property, however, are the feather-bedded retreats
without which men like Byrnewood would want the domestic pedi-
grees that set them at a socio-physical distance apart from the workaday
wharves.

Some 600 additional pages of city-"mystery" elaborate *The Quaker
City*'s domestic leitmotif, itself an object lesson in the urban American
culture of class. Coincidence plays a weighted role in this textual/social
mapping of residence. As it so happens, Byrnewood is revealed to be the
fraternal protector of the "fair maiden," in Lorrimer's words, whom the
latter had noticed weeks earlier "strolling down Chestnut street one evening" and so decided that he must possess sexually (13–14). From this
(un)fortunate premise does the narrative proceed, in due course spurring
the story into action through a related series of complications. In the
meantime, Lorrimer boasts to Byrnewood in a local oyster cellar (the
seat of their evening's entertainment) that he has lured the "flower of
one of the first families in the city" from her "home" with the spurious
promise of a marriage ceremony to be performed later that night (14).
Incredulous—with respect to the socioeconomic standing of the female

"flower," not her willing consent—Byrnewood asks, "How do you know she is respectable? Did you ever visit her at her father's house?" (15). His assumption is the novel's, the author's, and perhaps readers', too: that one can gauge class best by habitat, or "house." Byrnewood in fact rests so comfortably in this assumption that he wagers $100 that Lorrimer's "fair maiden" "has never been any better than a common lady of the sidewalk" (15). Or, in Lippardian terms, the woman must be disreputable enough that she resides outside the boundaries of a consensually recognized urban housing hierarchy; she must inhabit the lacunae of the streets, that is to say, and so occupy an unreadable realm beyond a proper "gentleman's" class map.

With the story thus poised to rush headlong toward Monk-hall, the residential den of thieves where Lorrimer plans to perpetrate his crime, Lippard momentarily suspends his narrative to *dwell* on the domestic class contrasts that comprise *The Quaker City*. Readers by this stage in the tale have observed how the "better" habitational half lives. A dashing Lorrimer and a prosperous Byrnewood loom as large in the novel as the imposing edifices that metonymically reflect their high stations in society. Lippard further literalizes residential wellness with the deliberate addition of characters who similarly inhabit their privileged positions within the upper echelons of social shelter. The author duly portrays the home of Mary Arlington, sister to Byrnewood and the human object of Gus's lust. Her domicile is just what readers would expect, Mary's father being a "respectable merchant" who has provided a lovely center-city mansion for his family (17). The professional gambler Colonel Mutchins, meanwhile, another well-heeled hypocrite in Lorrimer's entourage, occupies rooms at the top-tier United States Hotel on princely Chestnut Street. So, too, at least temporarily, does the peripatetic forger Algernon Fitz-Cowles, the seducer in a subplot all his own (figure 5.1). Then there is the cruelly cuckolded businessman, Livingstone, whose own "lofty" mercantile mansion is "situated," Lippard's narrator says, "in the aristocratic square . . . along Fourth street" (39). And so the novel unfolds: the separate domestic scenes may change, but any particular household episode might substitute for another. Such is the thrust of Lippard's metropolitan class critique. His "survey" of Philadelphia "high" society yields a monotonous capitalist sameness of spurious surfaces, the exterior attractiveness of which diminishes with each iteration. Teeming with diversity, the author's Quaker City shelters individual dwellers of an almost identical duplicity. Rife with fine residences, the upper end of Philadelphia's domestic spectrum presents a gaudily consistent façade of class-endowed self-indulgence.

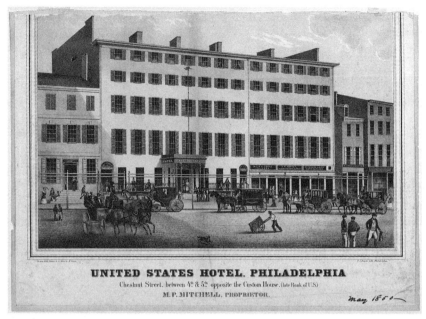

UNITED STATES HOTEL, PHILADELPHIA
Chestnut Street, between 4ᵗʰ & 5ᵗʰ opposite the Custom House.(late Bank of U.S.)
M. P. MITCHELL, PROPRIETOR.

**Figure 5.1.** After opening its doors in 1828, Philadelphia's grand United States Hotel welcomed both fashionable boarding locals and distinguished out-of-town guests, including U.S. President John Tyler. Located on Chestnut Street, opposite the Bank of the United States, this costly urban residence equally facilitated the making and spending of money. Philadelphia: P. S. Duval, Lithographer, 1850. Courtesy the Historical Society of Pennsylvania, Print Collection.

Lippard juxtaposes his indictment of leisured luxury at the higher altitudes of urban habitation with a purposeful depiction of working-class hardship, figured as so many underprivileged layers of domestic depth. There is some literary-historical justification for this recurring wholesale shift in the text's topoi from high to low inhabitance. For Lippard wrote in ideological sympathy with an antebellum discourse community for whom "the polarization of urban society," in Stuart Blumin's words, was a central tenet in their understanding of the modern city. In both its original European form, and its subsequent American circulation, the city-sketch genre that underwrote this worldview imagined the Atlantic metropolis as an imbalanced social composite of the fabulously rich and abysmally poor. The documentary utility of this discourse might have been limited, since authors who treated the city from a strict rich/poor dichotomous perspective generally omitted sizeable numbers of the actual urban middle classes from their formula. What writers like Lippard lacked in the way of social realism, however, they found compensation for in the engaging provocations of fictions that dared to represent class conflict domestically, which is to say, close to home. Whether they endorsed or rejected its claims, period readers responded to strong rhetorical/residential posturing that paired a de facto class of urban exploiters with the exploited classes beneath them. Readers' responses to such common generic touches in turn helped formalize discursive conventions through which class secured residential entry into the era's literatures.[17]

✦

With the publication of *The Quaker City*, author George Lippard not only literalizes and so stabilizes the class conventions of antebellum urban writing, figuring a physically domestic discourse in the measured materiality of his tale; he simultaneously renders the discursive city surreal, prefiguring the *de*stabilizing representational experiments of high literary modernism with a radical rhetoric of residence. Lippard in other words does not contrive his city "Mystery" merely for the sake of its own sensational spectacle. Nor does he separate the art of his "Romance" from the sincerity of his statement on laboring life. Rather, he makes the tangible, lived-in matter of modernity both his ostensible topic and artistic technique. Lippard crafts a class-conscious novel of urban American habitation so that its formal spatiotemporal distortions serve a higher functional purpose—at once to replicate and interrogate the unstable structural premises upon which he believed the new U.S. metropolis had been built.

The radicalism of Lippard's rhetoric is suitably architecturally sound. Believing the socioeconomic system of the present day to be patently punitive and hence unsustainable, the author makes the cognate hierarchies of residence and social scale the literal means of constructing a story as absurd in its wild conception as it is avant-garde in its stylistic execution. He meanwhile reserves as the end of his narration the *de*construction of the modern capitalist social structure, the seeming arbitrary distinctions of which he rejects on personal, political, and aesthetic grounds. Indeed, *The Quaker City* itself wants solid ground, and so rests restlessly within a quintessentially modern framework. The boldly nonsensical nature of Lippard's narrative manner, combined with the vertiginous vertical trajectory of his destabilizing storyline, conspire to create a work the action and arc of which enact the hallmarks of modernity, as soliloquized early, if unwittingly, in the novel by Gus: "Every thing fleeting and nothing stable, every thing shifting and changing, and nothing substantial!" (23). The novel's very form, moreover, *is* its function, given that the author's exaggerated urban discursive strategies enact as literature the leveling extremism that characterizes Lippard's attitude toward the ranked gradations of class. No matter the mimetic intent and effects of his household depictions—this work resides at the margins of non-representational artistry, some sixty years before the comparable visual time-space experiments on canvas conducted by cubists, futurists, and, later, the dadaists of high modernist Europe. *The Quaker City* accordingly makes a compelling case for revising the received understanding of literary modernism's twentieth-century emergence in America. Lippard's modern novel made its disruptive artistic mark not in the aftermath of a catastrophic First World War, but almost two decades prior to the start of an earlier and relatively domestic conflict, the U.S. Civil War of the mid-nineteenth century.

From a modern metropolitan perspective, the tangible materiality of Lippard's text dissolves into "nothing substantial," as Gus Lorrimer would say. And so it gives paradoxical expression to "the dissolution of perspective," a phenomenon that architectural historian Sigfried Giedion associates with a modern artistic "geometry" of movement, "simultaneity," and the multidimensional "interpenetration" of physical "planes," with their "equipoise and interrelations."[18] *The Quaker City* in fact dematerializes Gus's space-time precisely by verbalizing urban environs where "every thing [is] fleeting and nothing stable," where "every thing [is] shifting and changing." By thus capturing space-time at a cultural moment when both time and space seemingly had collapsed, the novel images forth an apparent representational impossibility. *The Quaker City* undermines its own signs, and with them the "substantial" residential structures on which Lippard's reigning social structure is based.

Giedion's "dissolution" begins at the outset of the novel and continues (ir)regularly from that point forward. Reprising the earlier scene in which a dissolute Gus Lorrimer and company establish their habitational worth, the author invites readers to watch as modernity's immateriality subverts the physical foundations of the city's built infrastructure. The city itself dissolves in distortion when viewed through the inebriating lens of urban industrial excess. That is the "dim perspective" afforded here (7), as three of the four "gentlemen" feebly venture their own respective attempts at what the narrator calls the "convivial" signification of the sidewalk (5). After delivering his precipitating utterance on "quilts and feather-beds," a blithely besotted Gus Lorrimer is seen "retiring" with "his vacant eyes" "to the shelter of an awning-post" (5). His "pursy" gambling companion Colonel Mutchins, meanwhile, pays apostrophic homage to "Brandy, . . . a per—perfect gentleman," before literally tripping himself up mid-sentence with, "how d——d irregular these bricks are" (5). The venial magazine editor Sylvester J. Petriken suffers most fully the force of modern transmogrification, with the flickering image of Philadelphia's famous Independence Hall prompting him to the following giddy insights:

> Look yonder at the statehouse——sing——singular phenomenon! There's the original steeple and a duplicate. Two steeples, by Jupiter! Remarkable effect of moonlight! Very——Doesn't its strike you, Byrnewood, that yonder watch-box is walking across the street, to black the lamp-post's eyes——for——for——making a face at him? (6)

Petriken encapsulates the absurdity of the "moonlight" scene when, after the assembled tipplers later reemerge from the "subterranean retreat" of an oyster cellar owned and operated by a "Virginia abstraction," he hypocritically channels the proverbial wisdom of the city's secular temperate saint, Benjamin Franklin (8–9). Echoing the annual almanac advice of Franklin's Poor Richard, Petriken declares, "Economy is wealth" (16). Yet, he never pauses to recognize the decidedly *un*economical devices of his own narration, let alone those of the larger text. Whether "tottering" with Lippard's characters in clouded "reverie" on city streets (6), or "wrapt in [the] comparative obscurity" of a "disreputable" "modern den" of iniquity (10–11), readers will "revel" "unsteadily," "helplessly," in the "drunken bout" that is the book's "initial letter to a long and dreary alphabet of crime, mystery, and bloodshed" (11). References detach from their referents. Surfaces deceive. And the tacit compact of storytelling—meaningful information offered, and meaningfully received—breaks down amid a series of false starts, unreliable observations, and severed narrative threads. "Gentle-men," Petriken says, "I don't know what is the matter with me— . . . There's somethin' queer a goin' on with my eyes" (11). It is an *im*material sentiment shared by the entire work, the rhetoric of which teeters on the brink of drunken (mis)representation.

Lippard literalizes genuine local disparities in urban wealth and want with his physical insistence on the tangibility of his tale; *The Quaker City*'s crystallization of class contrast nevertheless competes with the meltdown of meaning that occurs as the novel's plot (de)materializes.[19] Monk-hall is the text's domestic locus for this rupture in representation. With much ironic understatement, Gus Lorrimer innocently describes Lippard's most loaded sheltering sign as "a queer old house down town" (22). But to read this residence one first must find it, and then decipher the secrets lodged "within" its "impenetrable walls" (23). This proves no easy interpretive task, as evidenced by the circuitous route by which the story's inhabitants approach the novel's central urban structure. Accompanied by the unsuspecting Byrnewood, Gus and his soon-to-be adversary must grope their way toward Lorrimer's polluted rendezvous, notwithstanding the latter's intimate familiarity with an area where he has earned the tenure of a comparatively long tenancy. Lippard monitors the pair's slow progress as they advance "down Third street toward the southern districts of the Quaker City" (21). Their pace slowed further by the reduced rate of their leisured gait, they collectively step to "the corner of Eighth and Chestnut" (23), walk "up Walnut" and turn "left at Thirteenth" (25), before reaching an "ancient structure" on the "outskirts" of town (49, 46). The building itself is said to "occup[y] a space full as large as a modern square" (46). And yet the effect of this nocturnal migration on readers is dizzying and disorienting. As the narrator concedes, "It would take some knowledge of municipal geography to navigate" one's way through a "tangled labyrinth of avenues" toward this "old mansion" (48, 50, 63). Barring that "knowledge," the city is but a blur for readers who occupy an epistemological position similar to Byrnewood's. We stand with him as uncomprehending outsiders before the "fantastic shapes" of a signifying structure the likes of which we have never encountered before (50). His wonder is ours, as is his baffled cry, "This is rather a strange place—eh? Gus?" (53). We share Byrnewood's occluded point of view as well, such that the surrounding cityscape at best can be seen "looming in broken perspective" reminiscent of Giedion's (48). If Byrnewood's befuddlement is mutual, then his articulated response to the city's bewitchery is an urban people's plea against the madness of modernity: "I say, Gus, what a devil of a way you've led me! . . . —up one alley and down another, round this way and round that—damme if I can tell which way is north or south except by the moon!" (50).

However Lippard's core constituency of readers among the mechanic classes interpreted these confusing urban signs[20]—or, in Roger Chartier's formulation, whether and how laboring members of the expropriated achieved "appropriating" meaning of this text[21]—they would have derived much modern "knowledge" from the specific city residence of Monk-hall. The author interjects to comment on the importance of this literal/illogical home, prefacing its initial appearance with, "No reader who wishes to understand this story in all its details will fail to peruse this chapter" (46). Like the urban housing hierarchy on which it rests, Monk-hall itself comes into fractured focus with the novel's first full profile of its exterior features. Gus Lorrimer earlier had provided brief personal testimony on what he endearingly, if obliquely, calls this his "Club House" (23). Here the domestic details are by contrast more forthcoming, albeit third-person impersonal; their relation interrupts the story's development (or undoing) just long enough to disclose a spare omniscient history of the place and its surrounding peoples. Monk-hall, it seems, once stood proud in its pre-Revolution prime, during a day when the still-formidable edifice "stood in the centre of an extensive garden, surrounded by a brick wall, and encircled by a deep grove of horse-chestnut and beechen trees" (46). Urban encroachment has since overtaken this shelter, and left it a residential shadow of its former self "long after the city, in its southern march, had cut down the trees, overturned the wall, leveled the garden into building lots and divided it by streets and alleys into a dozen triangles and squares" (47). Standing firm amidst the city grid that is, and yet encircled by physical reminders of the residence it once was, Monk-hall figures a mark on the map of modernity, which condition Thomas Bender defines as "a conversation with a past . . . that must be present."[22] Commodified by capitalism, and reified as so many real estate "triangles and squares," Monk-hall likewise foretells the de-materializing dialectic of what Marxists call "historical materialism."[23]

Monk-hall is all solid "substance" in the author's main description, however. His would appear to be the stoniest of habitational masses located along the most slippery of modern slopes:

> The front of the mansion, one plain mass of black and red brick, disposed like the alternate colors of a chessboard, looked towards the south. A massive hall-door, defended by heavy pillars, and surmounted by an intricate cornice, all carved and sculptured into hideous satyr-faces; three ranges of deep square windows, with cumbrous sash frames and small panes of glass; a deep and sloping roof, elaborate with ornaments of painted wood along the eaves, and rising into a gabled peak directly over the hall-door, while its outlines were varied by rows of substantial chimneys, fashioned into strange and uncouth shapes—all combined, produced a general impression of ease and grandeur that was highly effective in awing the spirits of any of the simple citizens who might obtain a casual glance of the house through the long avenue of trees extending from the garden gate. (46)

Instantly recognizable in this passage are the literal domestic markers of class distinction that Lippard incorporates into his city discourse. Monk-hall's "massive" front door, its "heavy pillars," and its "cumbrous sash frames" gracing "deep" windows convey an adamant message of physical presence. Implicit in the combined weight of these "heavy" appendages is the narrative suggestion that both house and inhabitants *matter*. Readers will note further that the home's owner has spared no expense in its finish. An "intricate cornice," a roof with "ornaments," and a checkerboard brick façade of alternating red and black combine to create the novelistic image of something other than the utilitarian household. Indeed, a dominating diction of class-consciousness controls the passage, cowing the reader into a respect for the high and mighty edifice not unlike the "awing" of "the spirits" experienced by "the simple citizens who might obtain a casual glance" of the structure in passing (46). Words such as "surmounted," "ranges," "peak," "over," "rows," and "substantial" recapitulate within the very fiber of the house the graded social hierarchies that pertain in and *around* the house. Monk-hall's "general effect," then, might be "that of an ancient structure falling to decay," as the narrator maintains (50). But in light of "the tendency," of which historian William Cronon writes, for "human settlements to organize themselves into hierarchies,"[24] it would seem that Monk-hall literally, physically, and verbally aspires to rank residentially high among the "ease and grandeur" of the genteel classes on the back of the mansion's "one plain mass" of materiality.

It is yet another modern irony that Monk-hall should strive to rise above plainness on the freighted strength of its massiveness; it is the *vertical* orientation of that aspiration that induces a corresponding narrative paradox, by which this, the most material of texts, sits floating on its representational foundation. Much of what one would-be protagonist calls the novel's "planning and plotting" orients the text *horizontally*. Readers' "attention" is, he reminds us, "from first to last, riveted and enchained by one passage of breathless interest succeeding another, in transitions as rapid and thrilling as the changes of some well-contested battle" (260–61). Storyline action as such proceeds within the conventionally book-bound parameters of page-turning, notwithstanding its often following in the nonlinear footsteps of urban migrants like Gus, Byrnewood, and a host of supporting characters as they pad their wandering, if mostly level, way around the city (260–61). Monk-hall is no mere Gothic mansion, however. Nor does *The Quaker City* revolve around a single domestic "Mystery" the scope of which can be comprehended in a conventional narrative format. Rather, just as Lippard's novel anticipates modern literary form, the various physical buildings that structure its story image the perceptual, gravitational wrenching of modern architecture, as figured through that quintessence of the modern edifice, the skyscraper. Readers' interest in *The Quaker City* thus runs as well along a vertiginous *vertical* axis that makes a mockery of the traditional stability of home, even as it opens the novel's aesthetic boundaries to discursive dimensions heretofore unexplored and underrepresented in urban American fiction.

A raft of Lippard's residences reaches skyward, carrying the author's domestic rhetoric onto a metropolitan plane that rests, restlessly, high above pedestrian ground. Sylvester Petriken's Independence Hall, we recall, is memorable more for its redundant "steeple" than the constitutionally assembled "We," an earthbound American people that it metaphorically shelters. Readers furthermore later find "Fitz-Cowles at Home," in the words of one chapter title, in his fourth-story chamber at the Ton Hotel, an imposing "grand-edifice" that reportedly "*arises* along Chestnut street, a monster-building" (151, emphasis added). Yet it is the "strange" residential construct of Monk-hall that sets the text of *The Quaker City* at a vertical place apart from the body of contemporary urban writing. Not unlike the "stark, staring exclamation" that is architect Louis Sullivan's semantic description from 1896 for "The Tall Office Building Artistically Considered," Monk-hall functionally figures what Sullivan calls "the dizzy height" of the "weird, modern housetop."[25] At the hour of Lippard's writing in 1844, the advancements in steel-frame construction that eventually enabled the actual skyscraper were still several decades distant. The "new grouping of social conditions" that Sullivan says "found a habitation" in the "modern office building" nevertheless were extant already; urban congestion and the consequent spike in prices for city space thus had raised structures well before midcentury that reached to the provisional vertical threshold of five stories.[26] Writing in the early twentieth century, novelist Henry James would declare the skyscraper itself still more "expansively provisional," punning that these "monsters of the mere market" "never begin to speak to you, . . . with the authority of things of permanence or even of things of long duration. One *story* is good only till another is told, and sky-scrapers are the last word of economic ingenuity only till another word be written" (emphasis added).[27] Lippard would not have to wait to write verbal/vertical monstrosities of his own, and so express the rhetoric of a modern urban grotesque that defies the logical limits of the prevailing literary discourse in his day.

More than a mansion, then, Monk-hall like other urban structures from *The Quaker City* raises metropolitan "Mystery" to sub- and supra-textual levels, where written representation is most unreliable. The journalistic tradition from which Lippard emerged had made effective discursive use of the trope of depth to represent urban perfidy. Our author continues that tradition here, allotting Monk-hall three stories above ground, and three below, so as to grade the layers of despicable city behaviors available in one of Philadelphia's "vilest haunts" (155). The deeper the scene of dwelling, the more heinous the crimes committed: hence the collective decision by the self-styled inhabiting "Monks" of Monk-hall to "descend," as Monk Gus says, "one story under ground" to hold "incoherent" meetings of "confusion," "inebriety," and "intoxication" at their "bacchanalian" "board" (53, 55–56). Monk-hall's suitably "distorted" resident door-man, the human "deformity" Devil-Bug, meanwhile commits far worse deeds in the building's basement over the course of a depraved lifetime, and throughout the erratic course of the novel (53). It is, however, the (in)constant vertical movement between floors—and the (un)steady up-and downward narrative trekking of the text—that leaves *The Quaker City*'s readers reeling from the motions of modernity. Among the more localized instances of Lippard's discursive work at vertigo is what his narrator names Monk-hall's "western wing," from which "*arose* a square lantern-like structure, which the gossips called a tower" (46, emphasis added). Half-endorsing the urban "legends of the place," the author enti-tles the pivotal early chapter set in this, the mansion's loftiest "solitary chamber," "The Tower Room." Here is where Byrnewood, now captive to Gus and his conspiring Monks, awakens to the dangers to which he and his family unknowingly have been exposed. It is also here where Byrnewood endures a "heightened" impairment of his everyday senses, experiencing as he does a "mental struggle, that shook his soul to its foundations." Drugged senseless with opium by the devious Devil-Bug, and approaching asphyxiation from the smoke of a perversely "domestic" fire, which burns in a hearth with no chimney, Byrnewood experiences a mighty modern rush to the head that extinguishes his capacity for cogni-tion. "Now his brain seemed to swim in a wild delirium," we learn. And he can but flit in fitting urban fashion from his prone psychic condition through the "momentary intervals of consciousness." Shown "totter[ing] on the verge of the chasm" before one of the mansion's many literal pitfalls and trap-doors, he runs great vertical risk of dropping "far, far below," or "Down—down—*down*!" as Devil-Bug says, into the "gloomy void" of "the cellars of Monk-hall" (114–22, 180).

   Greater still is the risk posed to readers, for whom the novel's random "floor to floor" migrations figure what a former overnight guest at Monk-hall describes as a "queer" narrative "night-mare" that bodes no closure. To visit the "Tower" that is this visitor's text is to grow "entangled in the mazes of some hideous dream." The (un)"natural exaggeration" of city distortion makes much discursive headway there, producing "an impression of awe" in the "highly excited mind" of the occupant, whether resident metropolitan or reader of the vertical word. What results is an early antebellum instance of a modernist "urban aesthetic" that Thomas Bender distinguishes by its "preoccupation with unrestrained thrust for height."[28] Indeed, by alternately imaging skyscraping climbs "up from the depths" of the city, with ritual descents into the urban unknown "far, far, far below," *The Quaker City* even might be said to typify and anticipate the "expansion" in "vertical directions" of a discipline that scholars call "The New Modernist Studies" (63–68).[29] But in whatever "directions" it tends—whether massive immobility, or non-horizontal unrest—*The Quaker City* testifies to the signifying "mysteries" of literary modernism in mid-nineteenth-century America.

✦

For all its flirtations with "high" aestheticism, *The Quaker City* remains wed to working-class residence, the material source of Lippard's societal vision. Monk-hall, in particular, orients the novel toward a laboring location in the metropolis where not even the romantic pretense of prose can mask the reduced realities of habitat among the underprivileged occupants of the urban housing hierarchy. If Lippard initially sets his domestic agenda in a descriptive vacuum—the antebellum city abhors a vacuum—he finally objectifies his text in the buttressing literary figure of Monk-hall. Class accordingly continues to "matter" throughout the length, breadth, heights, and depths of the novel. *The Quaker City* holds close to its tangible roots not in spite of its modernist meanderings, vertical narrative practice, and relative time-space fractures, but *because* of them.

Readers will recall their first arrival at Monk-hall, which entails a direct urban encounter with what the narrator names "municipal geography." The text's syntactic compass leads us in our approach to the above edifice "up a narrow alley," "down a court," "up an avenue," and then "into a narrow street where four alleys crossed" (48). We stand at this juncture far from the prosperous promenades of Philadelphia's Chestnut Street. In due course, the narrator reveals that Monk-hall in fact is situated in the city's southern precinct of "Southwark" (49). This was the county's oldest district, by the 1830s the site of industrial rail and steel production, and home to a lively street culture bolstered by the area's active Working-men's Party and resident democrats and political Democrats. The stress and strain of intensive urbanization hit the city hard here, and Monk-hall registers the residential consequences. Flanked by a printing office on one side, and a stereotype foundry on the other, its once well-kept aspect now features broken shutters, bricked-over windows, and nailed-down doors. It is Giedion's "dissolution of perspective" from the entranceway, however, which best records the story of inner-city decline:

> On the opposite side of the way, a mass of miserable frame houses seemed about to commit suicide and fling themselves madly into the gutter, and in the distance a long line of dwellings, offices, and factories, looming in broken perspective, looked as if they wanted to shake hands across the narrow street (48).

Whatever domestic signs of gentility that once may have existed in this vicinity are gone. Monk-hall as an object-image has been lost amid a dense "mass of miserable frame houses." Sickly, obscuring "dwellings" appear "in the distance," "looming in broken perspective." The entire district has *descended* so low vertically, which is to say socially, that it has come to host a pawnbroker's shop where there are "rooms furnished for household use" (48). Gone, too, are the local gentlefolk. For, as the narrator relates, the "tenements adjoining Monk-hall" shelter "the mechanic and his wife, the printer or the factory man"—in a word, the urban working classes. Extending the socio-geographical reach of his tale beyond the promenading circuit of the flaneur, and writing well outside the scene of Philadelphia fashion, Lippard ensures that his story accommodates the city's laborers, whose cause he championed.

The text's material domestic surfaces are not its only accessible class markers; urban shelter signifies social hierarchy *inside* the novel's residential structures, too. A multitiered Monk-hall, especially, houses inhabitants from markedly different walks of metropolitan life, and thus represents in its vertically (dis)ordered interior a broad swath of the city's social divisions. As the observational "eye" behind the book's omniscient third-person narration, Lippard himself creates a mechanism of perspective to peer through the literal walls of Philadelphia's households, which he simultaneously takes so many pains to portray from the outside. His point of view is Asmodean in this regard, inasmuch as his penetrating gaze functionally lifts the city's rooftops to achieve the closest of close readings. Within the actual frame of Monk-hall, meanwhile, the author designates a surrogate Asmodeus in the character of Devil-Bug, the compound moniker of whose name aptly recalls the all-seeing demonic archetype of European legend. Here our Asmodeus figures the most watchful of household villains, and so facilitates the author's microscopic dissection of the local class microcosm. Whether standing narrative sentry at Monk-hall's foreboding front doors, or else diabolically supervising rented premises that he refers to as "my own home" (553), Devil-Bug assumes strategic vantage points within *The Quaker City* that help further Lippard's scrutinous review of the city's aggregate social classes. Through Devil-Bug's shifting physical/optical positions inside Monk-hall does the author transport readers from the deep "distant recesses" of the urban American "cellar" to comfortable heights several "stories above" common ground, where, the narrator reports, "the broadcloth gentry of the Quaker City guzzle their champaigne" (*sic*, 220). Inscribing class inside his discursive shelters, Lippard turns shelters inside out in service to his social survey.[30]

Boarding as a generic form enables this domestic project, in that it provides the narrative access necessary to expose those hidden facts of the urban working class otherwise withheld by the city's built exteriors. So prevalent are *The Quaker City*'s boardinghouse *interiors* that boarding itself becomes the most reliable window through which to view the obscured bases of local social standing within Lippard's novel. There are many such interiors from which to choose. Readers will recall, first, that Chestnut Street's elegant United States Hotel hosts several characters as long-term boarders. One of them, Fitz-Cowles, receives an exorbitant (and ultimately unpaid) bill for $652.12 ½, the price tag for the curtains he installed in his former rooms there (165). Events from the story also reveal that the wealthy widow Smolby, sole proprietor of the kind of rambling Southwark mansion that was subject to boardinghouse conversion in periods of economic decline, had entertained boarders at her own home during one such forgettable interval from her five prior marriages. Devil-Bug additionally relates that the nefariously flush Reverend F. A. T. Pyne and his now-deceased wife earlier "hired rooms in the house of the wider . . . in ---- street, near ---- street" back in the less remunerative year of 1825 (328). And Devil-Bug for his own part boasts of receiving "free" room and board "at public expense" alongside the "beauties for Cherry Hill!"—his "Hill" being a colloquial joke among area felons for their incarcerated stays at the Eastern Penitentiary in Philadelphia's Northern Liberties district (28, 272).[31] Not last but possibly least is the literal boardinghouse burial of the beleaguered carpenter John Davis,[32] who spends some six months boarding in the upper rooms of a house owned by a self-described "poor widow," the widow Smolby's less fortunate double, before committing suicide in a scene of sheltered despair (404).

It is an eclectic list, but one that demonstrates boarding's being not just incidental but central to the novel's sustained pattern of socioeconomic disclosure. Material markers of residence may frame class tangibly throughout *The Quaker City*. Yet, Lippard's is an "inside" story in the end, such that the insidious facts of class as they pertain to habitat find a fitting home *within* the permeable cultural space of boarding. In boarding no secrets of the city are secure; no privacy pertains when boarding will *out*. The author's class unmasking is thus abetted by the very structure of a domestic setting where the conventional narrative work of exposure requires comparatively little heavy lifting, as it were, by the writer. Close neighborly contact meant that historical boarders were to some extent defenseless before the eyes of onlookers. The thin partitions protecting their personhoods here translate into a text that reveals as much as it conceals about the class conditions of its inhabitants. A majority of these would hold a house in sole possession if they could; they cannot, and so board by necessity in the antebellum city. Lippard's narrator passes freely to and from their residential lives as a result. His writing invites readers to do the same, if they would deduce whom *not* to trust in a capitalist narrative economy overrun with imposture. The figurative lifting of damask curtains in Fitz-Cowles's darkened hotel room, for example, makes readers privy to the southern forger's being both a scoundrel and bounder. Similarly, after casting a furtive glance inside a former boarder's room at the widow Smolby's mansion, we receive the very key to the novel's tangled plot line: having fathered a child some fifteen years since, Devil-Bug retains domestic designs of inheritance (too complicated to explain) for a daughter whom he would see "roll in wealth, dress in silks an' satins, and be a lady all her life" (556). The relational tangle of co-occupancy, meanwhile, permits the mechanic Davis's landlady to perceive only too plainly the mounting troubles of a renter who subsists beside her. Through her we learn that Davis, having but recently shingled the Chestnut Street "Palace" of an insolvent bank president, has lost his savings in that same bank director's defunct financial institution (405). Lippard's boarder-carpenter responds to his loss with another act of rhetorical trespassing, asking apropos the author's thoughts on society's "superiors," "Then why have these people fine clothes and warm homes, when *I,* I, with honest hands, have no bread to eat, no fire to warm me?" (404–5). There is little in boarding to inhibit this inclination for domestic investigation, as these and like instances from *The Quaker City* make clear. In a work where the word "threshold" appears some thirty-two times,[33] and where characters, like readers, cross weak boardinghouse boundaries at will, narration as such gravitates naturally toward the generic form of urban exposé.[34]

Boarding's narrative intrusions are the novel's common denominator. Because the author writes from inside an "open" residential framework where the restrictions on household knowledge are few, even the pedestrian reader enjoys a modicum of omniscience. Lippard not only maps the urban working classes with his text in this respect. He produces a book to be consumed on the boardinghouse paradigm: an original "renter" of his city-mystery paid for the short stay of a serial encounter with the work; anyone allotting full purchase price for the tale's entirety was entitled to longer-term residence, and so bore witness to sights unseen by the average urban dweller.[35] The habitats here are glass houses, in effect, since paying readers—many of them quite likely boarders, among Lippard's core audience—are able to internalize privately those class matters which they typically might consider only in public, if at all. The story and structure of boarder-exposure in *The Quaker City* thereby achieve the democratic leveling effect that a writer for *Putnam's* magazine applauded a decade later: "I had always considered [a] . . . boarding-house a place of equal rights—where each inmate, paying his way, has as good a right to whatever his habits required as his neighbor."[36] Boarding is, in short, a people's prosodic device by which Lippard grants the "right" of communal access to most any home in his fictional city.

The epistemological privileges of boarding would not have been obvious to every one of Lippard's immediate readers, however. In admittedly qualified form, the City of Homes had made renting, if not owning, the individual domicile a realizable goal for many area citizens, even if only 10 percent of the local adult male population held outright claim to any real property at midcentury. Boarding historically was for this reason a residential last resort within Philadelphia's housing hierarchy. Mounting economic pressures in this period nevertheless brought more and more laborers of limited incomes to board. If, in 1840, only one percent of the municipality worked as boardinghouse keepers, supplying shelter, meals, and domestic services across class lines for sizeable groupings of guests, then by 1850 the rising cost of food, housing, and fuel combined—measured against the fixed wages of labor—meant that boarding had become not just another housing option for any and all classes, but a preferred cost-cutting response for a working class poised precariously on the brink of indigence.[37] Boarding may have retained a certain prestige in some quarters, among single center-city merchants, clerks, and professionals, especially,[38] but boarding by and large betrayed a lack of both social and financial currency. It also failed, or refused, to stem the cash transactions of the modern marketplace—weekly rent payments, in this case—notwithstanding calls by the day's domestic revolutionaries for a sacrosanct sheltering realm freed from the impurities of the market (figure 5.2). Indeed, much as boardinghouse walls could not disguise the lives of residents within, no amount of ideological posturing could abate the force of boarding without. As early as 1840, just as Philadelphians began to board in earnest, *O'Brien's Commercial Intelligencer* could list nineteen of the city's twenty-two "Principal Boarding Houses" as being run by widows, a perennially at-risk urban "class" that was often at pains to retain its middling social status without the assistance of a husband's salary.[39] Many among Philadelphia's more conspicuous class of manual

**Figure 5.2.** No. 168, at far left, was by the early 1840s one of several boarding establishments along Chestnut Street from which respectable Philadelphians might choose. Even here, a creeping commercialism set the residential tone: one could board, buy gas fixtures, and perhaps purchase *The Quaker City* at no. 178, "Hazard's Cheap Book Store," all on the same city block. From *Rae's Philadelphia Pictorial Directory & Panoramic Advertiser* (Philadelphia: Julio H. Rae, 1851): Folder 12. Courtesy The Library Company of Philadelphia, Print Collection.

laborers, meanwhile, were left to regret the individual homes they would never own, and so increasingly huddled together in downtown boarding-house districts, close to their place of employment. There was some small compensation in the camaraderie that came to men (unattached female boarders were comparatively rare, in Philadelphia as in other American cities) who inhabited shared houses, sat together at table, and conversed in common within a domestic setting that embraced what historian Richard Stott calls a "boardinghouse ethos" of mutual support, class solidarity, and sympathetic exchange.[40] But not even the comforts of ethical consensus would have compensated boarder-workers for their concomitant loss of autonomy, regardless of their gains in social perspective.

It is yet the storytelling advantages of microcosmic enclosure that allowed so many boarder-authors and readers from the period to revise their *residential* perspectives, and so re-conceive urban class consciousness itself on boardinghouse terms. In point of fact, collective housing harnessed the city's otherwise scattered inhabitants, overriding the physical distances between them. In point of form, the literary text and pretext of boarding combined to overcome the distance of social separation, and thus were a simple narrative convenience that assembled a particular people in a given place for a plausible purpose, on what must seem an (un)natural dramatic occasion. Boarding's scalable model of an (un)settled city thus became for some antebellum writers a favored discursive strategy for the domestic representation of social stratification. For others, it laid the discursive basis for a more advanced brand of class-conscious cultural analysis, one that reached its apotheosis with Lippard.

Colorful human examples of class contrast were a staple figuration among boardinghouse authors both before and after Lippard, and class *conflict* was the corollary figure that informed the domestic writing of those whose residential rhetoric was socially, hierarchically aware. The unabashed bourgeois Englishman Thomas Butler Gunn, for example, sampled the whole of U.S. society by way of boarding out in Manhattan during the mid-1850s. Or so he thought: Gunn disdainfully turns the blind eye of bias in his *Physiology of New York Boarding-Houses* (1857) toward "laboring men" whom he encounters cohabiting in ragged fashion at rental households along the city's working-class wharves; counterbalancing these impoverished reports are Gunn's more attentive renderings of "aristocratic" assemblage further uptown, where the inevitable boarding bank clerk or stockbroker was "very much alive to the inferiority of his social position" in the minds of housemates, if "inferior" he indeed were or was perceived to be (44). Decades earlier, Lippard's fellow Philadelphian Robert Montgomery Bird similarly converted urban occupancy into an occasion for social reflection. Bird has the hapless title character from his novel *Sheppard Lee* (1836) inhabit a wide assortment of different city shelters, a boardinghouse among them, as he climbs up and down the rungs of Philadelphia's social ladder through a succession of literal out-of-body experiences. The French novelist Balzac shares Bird's world-in-a-boardinghouse worldview, but from across the Atlantic. Continental Europe's most perceptive boarder-discourser claims with much conviction that the heterogeneously constituted Paris *pensión* from his book *Le Père Goriot* (1835) represents "the components of a complete social structure," "though in a small compass."[41]

Although their respective perspectives were mostly comprehensive, boarder-writers seldom addressed the peak of the residential pyramid, or what Gunn styles "tip-top" facilities (138). Few of the self-supporting professionals who purposefully engaged the question of class could afford such residences themselves; fewer still were inclined to devote close study to urban dwellers who knew so little of their own struggles for shelter. Contemporary coverage was wanting as a result on what one such writer, writing for *Harper's* magazine, called the "eminently respectable" communal establishments "frequented by a stagnant people, all well-to-do in the world." But if the high-end house generally was missing from boardinghouse discourse, then low-end houses appeared in the pages of print publication with frequency. So it was that the forgotten occupants of the urban-industrial social order dominated the literature of boarding by virtue of their disproportionate narrative presence. *Harper's* once more explored this, the nether side of the boardinghouse class divide, when it profiled a "poverty-stricken" "Cinderella" shop-girl boarder whose domestic situation, the title of the piece assures readers, was "Not a Fairy Tale." In one of the first American instances of literary boarding, meanwhile, novelist Catharine Sedgwick contrives for a hack-coach driver from her novel *Clarence* to name the occupants of yet another New York boardinghouse "the alms-house gentry," spitefully reminding a despised boarder population of residential pretenders of its place in the urban household hierarchy. One among Lippard's many imitators carried habitational representation to even greater working-class extremes. In *The Mysteries and Miseries of Philadelphia, as Exhibited and Illustrated by . . . a Sketch of the Condition of the Most Degraded Classes in the City* (1853), journalist J. L. Hammer portrays a neglected sector of the urban housing order—one still lower than boarding—when he writes of the grog shops, or "dens," that had arisen in the city's slums and were "in reality lodging houses . . . designed for the rest and entertainment of human beings." Boarding may have been no boon to one's social prospects in these writings. Yet it brought with it certain rhetorical benefits. To write here of home, first, was to test a prevailing domestic fiction, by which one's rank in the urban social order was calibrated solely on which grade of residence he should happen to inhabit. To write residence in a boardinghouse vein was additionally to take a generic perspective that enabled narrators to peer inside urban American society, even as they surveyed the external surfaces of city residence from a vertical perch on high in the metropolitan sky.[42]

✦

In the residential figure of Monk-hall, author George Lippard raises *The Quaker City*'s primary boardinghouse edifice; he adopts as well a penetrating domestic perspective on the inextricable connection between class and close quartering, as observed from the proximate vantage of co-occupancy. And indeed Monk-hall *is* a boardinghouse. It emerges over the course of the novel's early exposition that the building's anonymous proprietor has entered into a sublet agreement not uncommon in the antebellum period: Devil-Bug, as lead lessee, rents the property's rooms at his own discretion to various third-party renters, or boarders. Such has been Devil-Bug's success in this arrangement that, the narrator relates, not once has he neglected to "pay his rent with the regularity of clockwork!" during the period of his renewable lease (49).[43] Nor has Devil-Bug been remiss in his various duties as acting landlord. A busy housekeeper, he combines criminal deviltry with conventional domesticity. "Dinner time," for example, is the password that he requires from resident "Monks" on the first night of the novel's action before admitting them on to the premises (51). He later prepares "biled chicken and a bottle o' wine" for a visitor, merrily skipping up and down the mansion's stairs to obtain these kitchen items (107). And, in what proves to be a momentary suspension of gender roles, he tends the hearth of that same visitor's room, taking those pains practiced by "housewives . . . for domestic purposes" to keep a near-fatal fire burning brightly (109).

Monk-hall's occupants are a special breed of boarder, and Monk-hall itself a strange brand of shelter. Gus Lorrimer describes his "queer old house" and its inhabitants as follows:

> A queer old house, . . . where wine and women mingle their attractions, where at once you sip the honey from a red-lip, and a sparkling bubble from the champagne[.] Where luxuriantly-furnished chambers resound all night long with the rustling of cards, or the clink of glasses, or—it may be—the gentle ripple of voices, murmuring in a kiss[.] A queer old house, . . . where the very devil is played under a cloak, and sin grows fat within the shelter of quiet rooms and impenetrable walls. (23)

As a professional penny-newspaperman, Lippard would have been well-versed in popular print representations of Lorrimer's "red-lip" boardinghouse brothel, which is precisely Monk-hall's main "domestic" function inside the text. Urban prostitutes historically were not unknown to defy the prying eyes of suspecting landlords. The occasional "adventuress," wrote antebellum journalist James McCabe, was in fact well adept at maintaining the "guise of respectability" as she received paying clients inside boardinghouse rooms that were within easy reach of a household full of single males. Contemporaries, meanwhile, often mistook prostitutes and madams for regular boarders and keepers. Such misunderstandings were according to plan for certain enterprising women, who, reformer J. R. McDowell revealed, were operating brothels in Manhattan's genteel neighborhoods "under the mask of boardinghouses." Published directories for such houses began appearing in the 1840s, educating urban dwellers generally on an urban underworld that relied on boarding. There was even a local index for Philadelphia; its unnamed writer cataloged the city's "low pest house[s]" only a few years after *The Quaker City* first appeared.[44]

But for its imaginative trappings, Monk-hall might appear inside this compiled *List of the Gay Houses* of Philadelphia. Its chaperoning elder madam is one Mother Nancy, who, on cue, claims to be a "respectable widow" keeping a "respectable" house (504). The senior resident working girl is the long-since fallen Long-Haired Bess, who claims title "to the comforts of a home" for which she toils mightily and tragically (80). Monk-hall's bachelor boarders are its aforementioned Monks. They satiate their appetites for food and wine in dining-room commons downstairs; they "pay high," says Bess, for rented rooms upstairs, where they conduct sexual escapades before dawn's early light, after which hour they return to their duplicitous everyday lives in the city center (80). That Gus Lorrimer should resort to Monk-hall for the seduction of an unsuspecting Mary Arlington is no mere plot contrivance, then. It was at an assignation house-cum-boardinghouse on Philadelphia's Elizabeth Street where the real-world seducer Mahlon Heberton entrapped his victim, Sarah Mercer.[45] It is, accordingly, to a Southwark boardinghouse that Gus repairs for his violation of Mary, a crime that sets Lippard's boarders' story in motion.

The details of that crime become available to readers as a household "map" of urban class, imparted on the same narrative principles that paradoxically make boarding the thickest of material discourses, and an unmediated mode of representation. "Monk" Lorrimer might speak of the "impenetrable walls" that enfold his communal "home" (23). The narrator may describe Philadelphia itself as a veritable "wall of houses" (566–67). Yet the singular discursive structure of Monk-hall hides nothing behind its robust façade but the means of its own rhetoric of revelation. Boarding frames Lippard's book as the most transparent of residential figures, such that not even the insistent tangibility of the tale can impede our view of urban society inside the story's structure. Urban pretension is what this boardinghouse text represents. A city of social stations is what it sensationally reveals. Crowning Monk-hall's internalized urban hierarchy are the novel's highest-ranking (and highest-paying) boarders, who fittingly occupy rooms along the mansion's top floors. We as readers see past their outward deceptions courtesy of Devil-Bug's constant watchfulness. His excited exclamation, "There's a streak of light from the keyhole of his door!" (110), nicely describes the eavesdropping ease with which guests of the text look straight past the secrets of the story's most "respectable" citizens (figure 5.3).[46] Next in descending order upon the story's class ladder are Devil-Bug's two black henchmen. Stationed as silent guards on the mansion's main floor, they serve Lippard as emblems for the overlap of racial color and class within an urban world where whiteness no longer obtains symbolic purchase on innocence.

The Key to many a tale profound
Of strange intrigues and artful dodgings,
Is in the Keyhole to be found—
As all should know who live in lodgings.

**Figure 5.3.** Cheap lodging, and literary looking—antebellum boarding's residential perspective provides "The Key to many a tale profound." Courtesy The Library Company of Philadelphia, Comic Valentines Collection, ca. 1850.

But it is only upon their vertical arrival at basement level that readers reach the socioeconomic bottom of the author's signifying shelter. The "beams" from Devil-Bug's "lanthern" there expose to view Monk-hall's cellar (220), or Dead-Vault, one of the novel's few household chambers where occupants may abstain from the competitive residential posturing that is the crux of class for Lippard. Devil-Bug rejoices at such a city spectacle:

> Ha, ha, ha! While the broadcloth gentry of the Quaker City guzzle their champagne two stories above, here, in these cozy cellars of Monk-Hall, old Devil-Bug entertains the thieves and cut-throats of the town with scorchin' Jamakey spirits and raw Moneygehaley! Hark how the fellows laugh and shout in the next cellar! (220)

Having contracted with a neighboring pawnbroker to supply these, "The Outcasts of the Quaker City," with "vittels, lodgin' and viskey,"

Devil-Bug democratically admits the city's most degraded dwellers to free room and board, or what he calls "domestic fellicity" (*sic,* 221, 476). Spatial segregation keeps these "cut-throats," "thieves," and "Vagabonds" well-removed in squalid isolation from Monk-hall's paying housemates (476–77). The mere presence of the downtrodden (criminal or not) sets an important hierarchical precedent, however. Not only does the author's inclusive gesture pay tribute to the "migratory" and "floating" members of his audience—this in the words of *Holden's Dollar Magazine,* which, in caricaturing consumers of cheap print, employed terms often reserved for a shifting population of boarders[47]—but it extends the city's social structure to a degraded location the narrator describes as being "far beneath the earth, below the foundations of Monk-hall" (304). There is no "lordly structure" of affluence situated here (520). This is, rather, the scene of "Devil-Bug's Dream" being at least partially realized, in accordance with the apocalyptic, eponymous chapter of that title from *The Quaker City.* Lippard imagines through the sunken retreat of his basement-dwelling boarders a physical figure for an approaching epoch when the city's "towering mansions along the wide streets," his narrator predicts, "sink into the earth, slowly and almost imperceptibly, inch by inch" (385). In archaic Quaker dialect, the author here bids angry modern defiance to a "ye" who, "in the hours of infancy, have laid upon a mother's bosom, who have basked in a father's smile, who have had wealth to bring you comfort, luxury, and a home" (223). He sympathizes instead with "ye poor," whom he commands to "shout from your factories and work-benches, from your huts and dens of misery," in preparation for a prognosticated "Last Day" of "the guilty and blood-stained City" (384). Lippard, in short, would have us occupy at Monk-hall's deepest reaches the class condition of the city's unsheltered, if only in passing. Literally turning antebellum Philadelphia's class/glass house upside down, he inverts the conventional writing of residence by having the last and least of society's laborers rank a gratuitous first in the subversive, subaltern social order to which he exposes readers.

Having revealed the city's mysteries by way of boarding, the author abruptly abandons the serial effort at further reform by removing his protagonists from urban environs altogether. Mary, raped and chastened, returns briefly to the parental roof that she fled only days earlier in expectation of marriage. "My home!" "My home!" "My *home!*" she says, in a distressed cry of residential recognition that is tinged with the self-abnegating strains of renunciation: Mary no longer deems herself worthy of "home" (543). She in fact leaves Philadelphia forever for a snug cabin in the woods of Wyoming, in company with her newly married brother,

Byrnewood, and his wife and child. Theirs is an escapist nuclear family flight from city to country that abandons the metropolitan scene of
boarding; it recalls as well the vaguely erotic domestic dream for a rurally
sheltered hideaway once suggested to Mary by the seducer whom Byrnewood since has slain. If it is a quasi-boarder's pledge that Byrnewood
belatedly made in his sister's defense—"I will neither eat, nor drink, nor
sleep until I have washed out my sister's wrong, in this man's blood!"
(547)—then it is a recycled romantic (ir)resolution that the author offers
characters and readers at story's end. The wages, or rewards, for Byrnewood's having rectified city sin (his own included, for he, too, has practiced
the urban art of seduction) problematically amount to what the novel
so sorely lacks—a "real" residential retreat located somewhere between
metropolitan pomp and plenty on the one hand, and the depths of urban
sorrow and poverty on the other.[48] Lippard, in short, dismisses the very
question he poses in his novel with a response not logically allowed for
by the terms of that question: how can the city house *all* its inhabitants,
across class lines, at a most unaccommodating moment in urban American history? The working classes, Lippard suggests, could improve their
material lot in life by striving for an idyllic middling residence that simply
does not exist in his Quaker City. Middle is the gap on his boardinghouse
map, from which unmarked location the novel speaks volumes.

✦

Partial in its politics, if illogical in its claims, *The Quaker City* finally fits
the outsized form of its narration to the (dys)functional needs of readers,
for whom the novel's outrageous space-time figurations constitute literate
resistance to the equally impossible demands of the modern workplace.
On the one hand, the sheer bulk of Lippard's book argues against the
urban compromise of compression, whether rhetorical or historical, by
which boarding forever altered Americans' metropolitan imaginations.
Comprised of six discrete sections, without seamless transitions between
them, *The Quaker City* finds sufficient temporal-spatial breadth and depth
to outgrow the already generous limits of its own discursive shell. Lippard's novel sprawls: its several layered stories, and implicitly competing
protagonists, combine at great literal length to put the lie to abbrevia-
tion's being the uncontested tale of urban modernity. Readers as a result
wander where they want, when they want, and how they want within a
text whose overblown proportions are incongruously out of keeping with
its straitened urban-industrial context. On the other hand, *The Quaker
City* indeed does internalize the curtailing brevity of modernity, so much

so that the narrator's understated, tongue-in-cheek description of the story's first eventful evening of action—"a night somewhat crowded with incidents"—necessarily figures the full, if fractured, construction of the novel in its entirety (25). *The Quaker City*'s voluble narrator, ambulating characters, and seemingly random storyline together may ramble about antebellum Philadelphia with no apparent object in mind. Yet, there is (ironically, for a work otherwise opposed to the strict socioeconomic conditioning of capitalism) little inefficient waste to the author's words, since Lippard counters the prolixity of a city that genuinely never sleeps by streamlining all that is superfluous in his story. Close urban overlap—both of human capital and capitalist habitation—*is* the story inside his condensed urban frame, and Lippard stays formally, functionally true to that modern object in the end.

Such are the frantic pace and narrow space of *The Quaker City* that the novel reads as a template to time-space collapse. The text's modernist aesthetic may see it expand vertically, while its convoluted plot swells it to a size that belies its relative restriction to a single city domicile. But *The Quaker City*'s close confinement to boardinghouse *quarters* radically reduces the scope of the author's workaday world, such that the novel ultimately represents not urban excess, but the city deficiency of space-time. The proportions allotted the book's boarders recede so inexorably that metropolitan modernity in effect merges discursively here with disorientation. A blaspheming Byrnewood even pays homage to the text's intoxicating tendencies to and through the looking glass of distorted literary (mis)representation in terms normally reserved for tippling. His intemperate metaphor for fate not only suggests that something essential is missing from the author's metropolis; it likewise captures boarding's and the book's elegiac attitude toward spatiotemporal passing in an age of residential diminishment: "Damme—life's but a porcelain cup—today we have it, tomorrow we haven't" (12). This might be the text's domestically impoverished motto.

The novel opens and closes in a flurry of temporal hurry. A conscious narrative countdown begins from the start of action in the initial passage, with Christmas day but "three days off" (18), and a "terrible future" about "to break, in a few brief hours" (12). Nor can the would-be carefree Gus Lorrimer escape the slipstream of temporal acceleration. Echoing his sometime associate Byrnewood's alcoholic indiscretions, he reckons modern "life" as "brilliant and brief as a champagne bubble" when he conflates "today" and "to-morrow" in the confusion of self-induced delirium (23). Philadelphia's center-city State House meanwhile figures time in the fleeting tense architecturally; its chiming clock tower is a constant vertical reminder throughout the novel of a horrific metropolitan "moment" that Gus would just as soon forget (23). It is perhaps Byrnewood who takes city time's tumultuous passing hardest, however. As the story's climax approaches, he wears the "wrinkled visage" of a man "grown old" with the "agony of three days and nights" of city mystery. He in fact gives voice to the psychic effects of intense urban "suspense," as follows: "For three days and nights I have been the sport of one delusion after another! My brain hurts, my pulses are on fire! There is a mystery about this whole matter" (540). And yet Byrnewood does not bear the brunt of urban hypertime alone. Nearly all of Lippard's characters feel their minds reeling from city being, and so inhabit a fictional realm that his potential readers among the nation's urban working classes knew as no mere "Modern Romance," to borrow the title from one period literary offering. What a contemporary cabinetmaking apprentice called the "real scenes and actual occurrences" of laboring life possessed an unrelenting tempo of their own to match Lippard's or any other urban-oriented text. Indeed, for Ronald and Mary Zboray, not even "the seasonal and daily rhythms" of antebellum workers' leisure-time activities—chief among them "novel reading," according to our young apprentice—necessarily could stay the relentless pulsing movement of Gus Lorrimer's metropolitan "moment." Our cabinetmaker, for one, often found himself racing even on Sunday "rest" days to finish "a riveting thing" such as the English translation of Eugène Sue's seminal urban text *The Mysteries of Paris* (1842; trans. 1843), which, "if a person begins it he don't want to stop till he finishes it." *The Quaker City*'s quickened "rhythms" invite similar rapid reading, in keeping with its broken boardinghouse clock.[49]

Boarding also (de)regulates many of the novel's city spaces, at once upsetting and downsizing its domestic settings in particular. Not a few of these last literally rise to the occasion of metropolitanization as they physically overshadow the story's less substantial structures in a flagrant display of their comparative material advantage. Lippard's upper-class residences provide a tangible case in vertical point. Yet *The Quaker City* restrains even its grandest homes by curtailing the living space that it apportions urban dwellers generally, and rendering that, too, less the inalienable right of a privileged pursuit of happiness than the chance reward of peripatetic rental. The densely occupied neighborhood surrounding the great Monk-hall, for example, consists of stray "tenements and houses, gathered as thickly as the cells in a bee-hive" (50). Devil-Bug for his part enjoys the "cozy" confines of that same Monk-hall, taking refuge there in the building's abandoned cellar (220). The environing city, moreover, despite extending to "outskirts" that one socially climbing female character inhabits in early "penury," is matter-of-factly navigable by leaps and bounds that illustrate the city's uncanny compactness: the irrepressible merchant-provocateur Luke Harvey heroically motors "down" Philadelphia's Seventh Street, the narrator relates, "with as much speed as though he had a match against time, his hair and coat-flaps streaming in the wind" (198). Luke's foot-"race" against city-space ("There he goes like mad!" one witness observes) indeed replicates the unsettled state of those "restless spirits in the city" whom the narrator sets in the motion of "modern times" (198–99, 212). If it is the lot of even merchant millionaires like Luke's business partner Livingstone to be seen "hurrying along the crowded street" en route to "his stately mansion"—a crosstown feat that the blooded, landed aristocrat accomplishes in a mere "fifteen minutes"—then the great (but socially unrewarded) strides that the everyman Easy Larkspur takes in "perambulating the continent" represent the receding spatial condition that modernity has assigned the mansion-less masses (212–13). The country's very Manifest Destiny has become a walk around the block when its furthest reaches may be traipsed as a matter of course.

Because the majority of The Quaker City's inhabitants forever circulate inside a city, and a society, that would seem to be shrinking, no one save the evil incarnate Devil-Bug is at home in this novel. Gus Lorrimer's accomplice Buzby Poodle redundantly describes the "denizens" of a "magnificent Quaker City" bouncing between ostensibly disparate area shelters, many of which begin to overlap in his itemization. He includes "warehouses," "Churches," "Theatres," "Brothels," "Banks," "Insane Hospitals," "Companies," and "Alms Houses" in his indiscriminate list (164). But it is the forger Fitz-Cowles's repetitive domestic migrations that perhaps typify the dwindling art—or art of dwindling—that is boarding out in this book. Just one month prior to his temporary residence at Philadelphia's United States Hotel, Fitz-Cowles and his Creole manservant, Endymion, had kept rented house in the "corrupt" southern city of Charleston, South Carolina. One month prior to that, home had been New Orleans; again a month earlier, Boston was their floating base of criminal operations. It is a vagabond's life, this ceaseless running in (a)symmetrical circles from one impermanent (and disturbingly uniform) address to the next. It is as well a life that has confused the vagabond himself, with Fitz-Cowles asking unconcernedly, "How long since we first fixed our quarters in this city?" "Six months ago," is "Dim's" weary response from Philadelphia, before he proceeds to complain of the modern spatial travails that have seen him "been a travelin' about eber since. Led dis chile a debbil ob a life –" (155). When, because of boarding, home is forever to be found by "travelin' " onward, when the "crowded" city brings the next habitational horizon within commercially attainable reach, then home has become less the private emblem of worldly success than a residential deficit to be borne in public by a growing group of "debbils" not unlike "Dim."

Such is the paradoxical nature of its distortions, however, that *The Quaker City*'s domestic reductions salvage a quantum of space-time for readers. Temporally, the novel towers. Lippard requires some 400 pages to reach what he calls "The Second Day" of his account. Meanwhile, a mere "thirty-six hours" pass during the tedium of this prolonged interim, in which his appointed spokesman sees fit to "travel" at will "back some in our story" rather than adhere to a single straight line of narration (395, 404, 418). Those readers who are patient enough to endure this slow, disjointed unfolding of the author's fertile urban imaginary well might conclude that Lippard's storytelling strategy is to imitate his own description of a particularly suspenseful scene from the text: "It was but five steps forward, and yet . . . seemed an age in passing that trifling space" (463). Contradicting this conclusion is the emphatic spatial fact that the novel runs rampant over the possible physical limits of reported action. Like Luke Harvey, Lippard's story transcends conventional pedestrian bounds; it encompasses the entire city of Philadelphia and its Southwark suburb in one sustained rhetorical burst, and references as well the urban wilds of Manhattan before segueing into a parallel plot that carries us to and from the rural woods of New Jersey. Lippard's spatiotemporal frame is, accordingly, immodest in the extreme. It is not that the author, in attempting to articulate a mysterious metropolis for his audience, has "lost and forgotten" the dictates of "time and space" in "delirium," as the narrator says of a bewildered Byrnewood late in the tale (402). *The Quaker City*'s epic dimensions are instead the product of what scholar David Stewart calls "nonproductive" discourse. That is to say, precisely because the act of reading in the antebellum United States was construed as being *not* work, but leisure, sensational literature on the order of Lippard's afforded urban-industrial readers in particular both physical and psychological compensation for the day-to-day demands of their laboring lives. For many, the condensed conditions of city living, combined with the increasing regulation and oversight of the efficient modern work-place, made the urban work experience in Stewart's words "constraining, confining, mind-numbingly dull."[50] Its radical distortions of time, space, society, and domesticity, then, make *The Quaker City* seem from this critical perspective conducive to a kind of collective cessation of labor. An affordable passport tour inside the beguiling city, an exhaustive ride through the class contours of a boarders' metropolis, *The Quaker City* reads a welcome release from the cultural limitations of work and home in mid-nineteenth-century America.

✦

Whatever pleasures Lippard as author brought to city readers, he remained faithful throughout his career to the hard work of writing class through residence. This is not to deny the apparent destructive delight that he seems to have taken in his vocation. Indeed, *The Quaker City* closes with the author not only literally raising class consciousness by means of the careful final arrangement of his domestic edifices; he also playfully, if recklessly, tears down the fictional housing hierarchy of his creation. Perpetrating a material pun on the name of his character Livingstone, for example, Lippard permits Devil-Bug near story's end to torch what the narrator names the "doomed" ancestral mansion of the novel's wealthiest inhabitant (521). The resultant fire predictably "filled all space!" with flames, and destroys both owner and "home" as it rages out of control (524). There is no *stone* left *living* in the aftermath of this, the author's urban alternative for a conventional barn-burning. Nor does Devil-Bug himself escape the author's residential apportionment of poetic justice. Continuing with his literal mission to level the local cityscape, Lippard dispatches Monk-hall's errant keeper through suicide. Devil-Bug dies after arranging for a "massive piece of rock"—what he presumes to "a-been a piece o' th' foundation o' Monk-hall"—to come tumbling upon his head after plummeting from several stories above the lowly Pit where he resides (554, 556). He thus *vertically* leaves a life of crime while only narrowly escaping the clutches of Philadelphia's police, who arrive near the novel's conclusion to apprehend their man for his most recent round of misdeeds. It should be noted that Lippard does not have Devil-Bug suffer through protracted death throes. "It was but for an instant!" the narrator writes, before our boarder-no-more expires after precipitating his own foundational stoning. But if Devil-Bug's departure is decidedly unsentimental, it is also unmistakably domestic. As the narrator explains in his terminal description of the scene, "Then a sound like a *mighty building,* falling to the ground, shook the cavern" (556, emphasis added).

To judge from the tangible domestic tropes that inform his life's work, Lippard well recognized the extent to which his frequent recourse to the "sound" of class shelters come crashing down resonated with his readers. The year 1849 stands out as perhaps the high-water mark of the author's surveying work in this respect. Writing in the *Quaker City* weekly newspaper, edited and co-published by Lippard following *The Quaker City*'s extraordinary sales success, he spent some several months monitoring area class conflict through a collection of articles on Philadelphia's homes. In his sketch of "An Every-day Dream," for instance, he brings a Quaker landlord to confront a working woman tenant as the latter asks for an extension on her January rent payment, an amount totaling $7.33. Capital's response to labor is cold and clear. The landlord states, "How does thee expect to live in my house without paying rent? If thee can't pay for the house-shelter thee should not live in a house." Lippard pursued the theme further in another series called "Legends of Every Day," most of which once more revolved around material depictions of domestic edifices. Legend 1 finds a forlorn seamstress, the seventeen-year-old Sally, dying in a "narrow court" where she and her family share a "humble home." Sally's "day-worker" father, washerwoman mother, and factory-hand younger brother gather around her as she breathes her last. Quoting Christ, she says, "In my father's house there are many mansions." She goes on to explain that the words "were not said by one who lived in a large house, . . . [but] by one who was of the Poor, who wore the dress of the poor workman." Legend 2 returns to the top of the housing hierarchy, portraying a wealthy businessman dying in his "splendid mansion" after an aborted rent-collecting trip to the "hovels" that he owns in a distant part of the city. Legend 3 considers the causes and consequences of urbanization; legend 4 proposes a utopian dream of adequate worker housing; legend 5 weighs the competing claims of nature and nurture in a Philadelphia slum. And so the "legends" continue, culminating after the appearance of some dozen like parables on residential inequality.[51]

Lippard brought down his discursive house at year's end. By December 1849, he had begun work on a novella that once more made the material mapping of class both his overt subject and preferred literary method. The work in question accordingly sets fictional fire to its central shelter, thus providing incendiary commentary on the structural sources of social friction in his city. With *Life and Adventures of Charles Anderson Chester,* Lippard employs a direct narrative approach in conveying his obvious message.[52] We need not read between the lines of his class map; he literally illustrates his meaning with a graphic domestic rhetoric that leaves little to the urban imagination in this fictional representation of what Samuel Otter describes as Philadelphia's "foundational instability" (figure 5.4).[53] Lippard's story loosely follows Philadelphia's election night race riots from October 1849. More important, *Chester* offers yet another residential tour of the city's socioeconomic mysteries and miseries, both of which the author complicates with the introduction of racial coloring

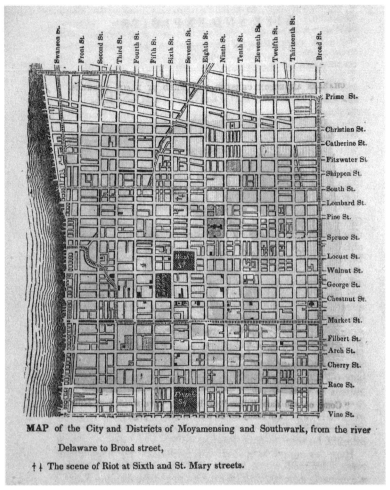

MAP of the City and Districts of Moyamensing and Southwark, from the river Delaware to Broad street,

† ‡ The scene of Riot at Sixth and St. Mary streets.

**Figure 5.4.** Philadelphia's famous grid, class mapped by author George Lippard. In its pamphlet printing from 1849, this literal figure appears opposite the title page to Lippard's short novel *Life and Adventures of Charles Anderson Chester.* Courtesy The Library Company of Philadelphia.

into his discussion of class. As with so many of Lippard's characters, the white scion of privilege Chester is for lack of a better phrase injured by architecture,[54] enacting as he does a downward spiral of antebellum residence—from New England college-town hotel, to Walnut Street mansion, to inner-city flophouse/lodging house, and on down the domestic ladder—that lands him at last in the city's racially mixed Moyamensing district. The prodigal son Chester eventually turns gang leader, and is on hand in this depressed southern Philadelphia precinct when it erupts in one of the area's many race riots from the 1840s. It is in fact Chester's stabbing by an African American barkeep-landlord that sparks this particular riot. Local whites rally to the murdered man's defense. Houses reputed to be black havens burn. Low-income black and white workers, who otherwise might find common material and ideological cause in the residential rights of labor, turn on each other in violence. *Chester* in this way records a contemporary cohabitational conflict with vengeance. If, in his remaining years, Lippard primarily labored on behalf of workers in his capacity as an active union organizer, his body of work as a class-conscious boarder-author continues to test the boundaries of an incipient literature of class in a manner that still matters.

Chapter 6

✦

# Boarders, Brothers, Lovers:
# *The Blithedale Romance*'s Theater of Feeling

My heart was a habitation large enough for many guests, but
lonely and chill, and without a household fire.
—Roger Chillingworth, from Nathaniel Hawthorne's
*The Scarlet Letter*, 1850

Antebellum literature occupied uncommonly melodramatic ground in
popular works by the likes of best-selling author George Lippard, and
yet the genre of boardinghouse letters was not inclined solely toward
the rhetorical excesses of works such as *The Quaker City*. Boarding was
similarly hospitable to the more tempered discourse of sentiment. Literary boarding brought to an already emotionally implicated art form
the straitening conditions of urban housing. It thereby further intensified
contemporary American culture's receptiveness to socio-personal states
of heightened feeling. The more boarders who resided at any one address,
after all, the greater was the collective store of sentiment on offer there;
the greater, too, was the likelihood, within boarding's radically collapsed
spatiotemporal context of close contact, that pent-up sentiment would
find expression. Boarding, in short, redoubled the potential discursive
force of affect simply by creating causal conditions that were likely to
sustain strong manifestations of sentiment in the short term. It ironically
did so, however, by residing outside the sanctified space-time of the antebellum home. That private zone of domesticity was the very coordinate
of culture denied by boarding. But if boardinghouse letters nullified the
sympathetic base on which so many period sentimental texts depended,
they did not necessarily obviate affect per se. Boarding, rather, gradually
shifted the modern focal point for feeling out from under the figurative
stage lights of domestic-sentimentalism, into comparatively sterile urban

environs where affect was held at a high premium, and would therefore have to be found before it could be flaunted.

In boarding, the distinctive melodramatic *effects* of affect transformed the discursive conventions of urban American sentiment. It is, appropriately, the oft-noted dramatic quality of U.S. author Nathaniel Hawthorne's body of writing that perhaps best demonstrates the complex quality of this city literary transformation, by which boarding "on the boards" emerged as a favored more-than-metaphor for emotional depth (or lack thereof) and display among the era's readers and writers. Theatrical motifs are conspicuous in Hawthorne's short fiction from the 1830s and 1840s. Repeated staging of his acclaimed novel *The Scarlet Letter* (1850) confirms a wish among not a few contemporaries to rank the author alongside the nation's playwrights, given his fictional gift for compelling mise-en-scène. But it is the dramatic trappings of Hawthorne's fourth novel, *The Blithedale Romance*[1] (1852)—with its emotionally charged plot twists and love triangles, in boardinghouse environs—that have led any number of scholars to apply the theater as the most fitting figure for that book as well as the author's evolving views on art and life.[2]

If writers since Shakespeare have deemed all the world a stage, and all its inhabitants players, then modern literary men and women in the antebellum United States increasingly came to extend the long-standing theater analogy for life's vicissitudes to a more immediate dramatic arena that they were able to locate in everyday boarding. Among the American writers to explore (and exploit) most fully these dramatic possibilities was Hawthorne. This chapter proposes not only that the boardinghouse is the central motif of *Blithedale;* it suggests as well that Hawthorne's primary concern as he brought his project to completion was to relay to his readers the impact that close-quartered urban habitation was having on our collective affective lives. Hawthorne himself knew boarding personally. The antebellum reform culture of which he writes resorted to the boardinghouse as a national platform of operations, as we will see. Boarding, we also know, was very much in vogue with authors on both sides of the Atlantic throughout the nineteenth century. Appearing additionally on several levels in the novel in question, the boardinghouse provides a conceptual framework for interpreting the ambivalent intricacies of *Blithedale*. The novel does address reform, as is evident from the text. It anatomizes human relations, too, as do most of Hawthorne's writings. One need only witness this particular work's romantic storyline for evidence of its interpersonal themes. *Blithedale* even exposes the sexual tensions that emerge between its characters—hence we can account for so much of the novel's drama. Yet, a more encompassing view of the book indicates that social reorganization, group psychology, and narrative explorations of intimacy are all something other than incidental to *Blithedale*'s overriding dramatic interest; they are direct byproducts of a real-world boarding ritual that the author pointedly inscribed into his text.

With *Blithedale*, Hawthorne has produced a book-length testament to the *emotional* implications of improvised living on an entire generation of boarding Americans. The author himself inhabited both a sentimental age and a largely (if not exclusively) feminine literary tradition that Jane P. Tompkins describes as "awash with emotion." What Tompkins calls the "other" American Renaissance of female feeling in fact applies as much to Hawthorne as it does to the popular women writers who were his professional peers.[3] Tompkins's sentimental flood-tide in other words touches *Blithedale,* where the word "heart" appears some 100 times.[4] As for the boarding component of the boarding-feeling formula that governs this chapter, it indeed seems significant, inextricably so, that hundreds of thousands of Hawthorne's contemporaries had been huddled together under boardinghouse circumstances in the wake of urban industrialization. They shared close quarters in or near the nation's sizeable cities, where private and public spaces increasingly overlapped, and they often experienced as a result the kinds of feelings for fellow boarders that were exaggerated in exact proportion to the proximity of their house-mates. One easily could find friends, or enemies, in boardinghouse surroundings, where both were to be found right under residents' noses. Human tempers accordingly rose and fell with so many close-dwellers within literal touching distance, although such strained feelings often were offset by the natural affections that arose among people who ate, laughed, wept, and slept under the same roof from week to week, and month to month. No less likely was love in the boardinghouse, the occurrence of which was to be expected since the young and unattached who formed boarding's main constituency not infrequently were thrown upon their own resources—and upon each other—in tight-knit surroundings that facilitated male-female or even same-sex bonding. In short, just as the cultural importance of feeling reached new heights in an acknowledged age of sentiment, the contemporaneous age of boarding elevated the frequency and poignancy of modern human contact and all the emotional trials that went with it. Hawthorne studies the meanings of boardinghouse feeling in his novel. There, a complex boardinghouse figure contributes a markedly dramatic dimension to the troubled social transactions that plague a quasi-fictional community of would-be boarders.

Not only is *Blithedale* dramatic; the novel proves equally tragic in the heatedly intensifying exchanges that it contrives between boarding house-mates. If Hawthorne is a sentimentalist by expression, if not profession, then he is one who cautions against the consequences of a modernity conducted indoors by counting the costs of itinerant living on the aforementioned *heart* at the heart of his narrative. His worries were familiar: that boardinghouse society, a society of extremes in the eyes of many, was poised to replace conventions of family, fidelity, and *feeling* with some freewheeling boarder-alternative. That alternative might redefine conventional sentiment on unfamiliar, which is to say, unacceptable, terms. Or else sentiment as such might lose meaning altogether in hardened boardinghouse hearts. Wounded egos and hurt feelings litter the domestic spaces shared by boarders in *Blithedale*. The *felt* impact of the novel's interpersonal relations is great, this at a moment when the metropolitan West had institutionalized boarding. Making a watchword of restraint, finally, Hawthorne voices the fears of reluctant antebellum moderns for whom the enforced society of boarding undermined the sympathetic foundations of society itself. The rhetorical "play" of *Blithedale* is anything but playful. Hawthorne's novel is at last a moral drama, in which the wayward search for an emotional home is unhappily circumscribed by the narrow sentimental dimensions of this "boarder" *Romance*.

✦

How does *Blithedale,* a work ostensibly concerned with communal reform, qualify as a book "about" boardinghouses? The obvious response to that question derives from chapter 18 of the novel proper, "The Boarding-House." Yet, this particular episode is but one among many boarding fragments in a story filled with such figures from beginning to end. There is also, for example, the matter of the author's dramatis personae. Each of Hawthorne's main characters directs the reader toward a real or approximate urban boardinghouse, inasmuch as they all four have been either lodgers (boarding, minus the meals) back in Boston, or else remain occasional boarders in that city at different points in the plot. Narrator Miles Coverdale sets the novel in suitably disjointed residential motion when he leaves what he calls his "bachelor-apartments" for an experimental agrarian colony in the nearby countryside (5). The ardent prison reformer Hollingsworth also abandons Boston "lodgings" to join community members like Coverdale outside town (30). Meanwhile, the women's rights advocate Zenobia makes a repeated practice of shuttling back and forth in dramatic strophe/antistrophe fashion between "Blithedale"—the community so named by our reformers, who for a spell share its simple farmhouse in common—and a high-toned boardinghouse in the city. Her half-sister Priscilla arrives at Blithedale from the "cheerless" room of an urban tenement house occupied in tandem with her ne'er-do-well father, Old Moodie (185). Thus does boarding and its affiliated living arrangements feature in the lives of Hawthorne's central characters. More of the same awaits one of them, Coverdale, decades after Blithedale's members disband. The discursive result of such to-and-fro motion is what one commentator residentially names an "engaging vacancy" of boardinghouse-style "abstractions of movements and spaces" at the center of the author's text.[5]

A related "vacancy" awaits all of Hawthorne's main fictional players at the radical reform commune where they assemble as the novel opens. Communal living forms but another permutation on a boarding experience that they would seem to embody. Or, to restate the claim, scenes shift in Hawthorne's novel, but boarding as a simple function of setting remains unchanged. Although subsequent chapters such as "The Boarding-House" and "The Hotel" make explicit Hawthorne's interest in boarding—as do the habitational backgrounds of his protagonists—the bulk of the novel's action at Blithedale keeps the boarding phenomenon a constant. Boarding is in effect cyclical and inescapable in Blithedale.

There is a certain historical logic to Hawthorne's employing this specific narrative structure. Preceding Blithedale's publication in 1852 was a decade that saw enough Americans agitated by recent economic instability, and captivated by the lingering religious revivals of the Second Great Awakening, to turn a fad for experimental communes into a serious movement to remake the United States. Boardinghouse-style accommodations were the key to the commune. On the one hand, the communal optimism of a few thousand adherents meant joint agricultural and manufacturing enterprises on sites purchased for the purpose. On the other hand, the communal aspirations of many proponents of reform translated into voluntary shared quarters consisting of a room, food, fuel, and washing for those "associates" who were hoping to live together in a new kind of harmony—an arrangement not unlike big-city boarding, but with a critical difference. Dollars and cents drove boarding as a business; cooperation and not market competition created the commune. Private boarding was in other words all take and no give, with residents leaving the chores of domestic maintenance to their paid hosts. By contrast, communitarians got what they gave, "free" board coming to those who labored a full day for each day's stay on shared premises. A rejoinder to both the selfish stand-alone home and the cash transactions of metropolitan boarding, communal boarding at places such as the much-publicized Brook Farm, in West Roxbury, Massachusetts, was thus familiar enough to fit within existing domestic paradigms, and foreign enough to generate national interest. Hawthorne of course cites Brook Farm as the model for Blithedale in his volume's preface. In doing so, he establishes his commune as part of a larger reformer-boarder pattern within and without his book.

As was the case with antebellum boarding practices generally, the varieties of boarding represented in *Blithedale* merely repeat a boardinghouse experience that seemed to wax more and more uniform regardless of the house or inhabitants. Because communal boarding rarely if ever satisfied subscribers' highest ideals, that critical difference separating a Brook Farm or Blithedale from the boardinghouse down the block was often more apparent than real. In the city or out, and whatever its ideological underpinnings, a house full of boarders, even sympathizers (a loaded term here), was typically less utopian than pedestrian. Communal boarding *felt* like a boarding experience long since available elsewhere in America. Workers' dormitories resembling those of industrial Lowell, Massachusetts, reappeared at the Northampton Community, for example, where members resided in rooms situated on a restored silk mill's upper floors— dubbed "the factory boardinghouse" by local residents.[6] Moreover, the line separating big-city boarding from its communal counterpart was a fine one at best. Reformers had forsworn the capitalist marketplace, but they often located their communes within hailing distance of big cities, whose trade they relied on for their survival. The results of such a positioning were predictable. At Brook Farm, the short distance from city to country commune made for a separate class of mostly urban, non-laboring "boarders" (the title used by residents and others for paying wayfarers); these latter inhabitants welcomed the affordable $4.00 fee for a week's boarding package, and quickly came to outnumber working members.[7] Many of these same visitor-dwellers no doubt retraced the eight miles home to private boardinghouses back in Boston, where 10 percent of the population already boarded or lodged by the end of the antebellum period.[8] Others rotated into the revolving slots left by their peripatetic predecessors. Between 1844 and 1847, the final stretch of Brook Farm's eight-year existence, the community expanded its activities beyond agriculture to include manufacturing. It received in return hundreds of artisans and tradesmen from the city's downtown business districts, where boarding was the residential rule. These newcomers needed no second baptism to West Roxbury boarding. Like the weekenders who had arrived before them, they adapted to a way of life that effectively had them traveling in one big boardinghouse circle.[9]

The author himself was implicated with the rest. Scouting out a home for his wife-to-be, Sophia Peabody, he had stayed at "the Farm" for half a year after it opened in 1841—at first earning his keep as an associate by shoveling manure in the fields, then fleeing to Salem for three weeks, and finally, before deciding that Farm life was incompatible with his author's calling, returning merely to board with his comrades. His case illustrates the fact that a "new" communal view of domestic living was not so new after all: before he boarded at Brook Farm, Hawthorne had boarded in Boston when he was working in the city in 1839; he would do so again, with regret, a decade or so later before he began work on *Blithedale*. The boarding-on, boarding-off again pattern was typical of the times.[10] And it only gained strength under the unwritten rules of association. Hawthorne's sometime Concord neighbor, Ralph Waldo Emerson, sensed the Brook Farm contradiction when he dismissed the venture in his journal as "only a room in the Astor House hired for the Transcendentalists," recalling an elite Manhattan hotel that accepted long-term boarders.[11] Implicit in Emerson's objection are three distinctions without a difference that frame Hawthorne's narrative: boarding to better society, boarding to facilitate industry, and boarding as a consumer commodity. The contrary, yet intertwining, tendencies of these disparate boarders' forces escape the dilettante reformers of *The Blithedale Romance*. They did not escape Hawthorne, whose book inheres in this very boardinghouse dilemma.

Chief among boarding's attendant complications at Blithedale are the overly dramatized feelings, or scarcity thereof, to which Hawthorne's boarders subject each other in scene after scene of bad behavior. The Blithedalers evince a penchant for deception, for disguise, when they are not busy remaking America in microcosm at their agricultural retreat, and mutual betrayal is the outcome of the novel's endemic disingenuousness.[12] Zenobia's moniker is not her own. Old Moodie alternates his eye patch on separate appearances. Coverdale proves less than forthcoming in his account. And the mesmerist Westervelt holds some secret power over the two leading female characters. Such interested play-acting gives the lie to honest reform and takes on disturbing overtones as the novel unfolds. Nor is hypocrisy offset here by what Karen Halttunen calls a Victorian "cult of sincerity."[13] The virtual theater of affective misdirection by and large supersedes mutual confidence at Blithedale.

It also creates a narrative climate of distrust, one which brings out the worst in Blithedale as a group and makes a mockery of genuine emotion. Coverdale early on issues Blithedale's hypocritical mission statement after he leaves off lodging to board with other self-styled progressives. The two-facedness that he demonstrates in making his insincere decree is an omen of more troubling developments to come. Aglow with what he terms "good companionship," he mentions a communal desire to have "shouted" out, like the "bluster" and "shrill . . . blast" of a winter's wind, "blithe tones of brotherhood." He further hopes with his fellows thereby to make "cordial sympathy" the basis of "the reformation of the world." Coverdale's means, however, if not his stated end, underscore how and why the similarly inclined, would-be brothers and sisters of Blithedale must violate their own credo. To begin, Coverdale promptly abandons any pretense of "good companionship" and brands as "The churl!" a passing traveler who ignores his salutation (12). His embrace of "brotherhood" would appear to be little more than rhetorical. Group "sympathy," moreover, tends to break down in *Blithedale* at precisely those episodes like this when characters dramatize their feelings rather than share them in quiet, concealed scenes without witnesses. There are many of the former moments here, precious few of the latter. For, as our narrator's "shrill . . . blast" of an utterance indicates, and as close board-inghouse quarters dictate in subsequent chapters, personal privacy and the candid expressions of feelings that one would expect to accompany it are boarder-casualties in Hawthorne's book.

Stated simply, boardinghouse feeling becomes boardinghouse "bluster" in a cramped, exposed habitational space where residents figuratively find themselves on stage. It is upon this same platform that Hawthorne's spot-lighted performers withhold their truest expressions of mutual affection, and thus achieve the emotional stalemate that is *Blithedale*. Leon Chai writes that for Hawthorne, "affection" per se comprises "the whole sen-tient life of the individual subjective nature, in its relation to others." "The essence of the affections," in other words, the very force by which emotive modern beings achieve "transcendence of the limits of time and space" between them, "inheres in the subjective *relation* between one individual and another." Because "the life of feeling exists," then, for Hawthorne, "only in the consciousness of the indissoluble ties that bind us to each other," the text of *Blithedale* reaches readers virtually life*less*. The domes-tic collectivity that is our characters' commune ironically inhibits what Chai further describes as "the formation of a collective whole," so that the book's emotional locus—what Chai calls its "nexus of affection"—all but necessitates the affective grandstanding of a Coverdale instead of sup-porting sentiment drawn from the heart without fanfare.[14] Outside the farmhouse, Hawthorne's Hollingsworth accordingly delivers insensitive diatribes against the weaker sex—to the two women who adore him. He is as a fictional construct in some respects nothing but unscripted delivery, since he possesses little if any redeeming sentiment for anyone but him-self. Priscilla, by contrast, half-conceals herself from her house-mates out of what passes within the text for shyness. By novel's end, no one, readers included, knows the secrets of this Veiled Lady, the show-name given her by Westervelt in her capacity as a celebrity spiritual medium. Zenobia also role-plays without intermission, leading Westervelt once more to remark, "What an actress Zenobia might have been!" (240). His words apply to all of Blithedale's inhabitants. Individual guests in this boarder's forum have so successfully separated the normally constitutive acts of feeling and speaking and doing that the one no longer proceeds from the other. They stand before us as actors, more consumed by the effect of the household self they project than the cause that they supposedly hold in common.

As the built-in boardinghouse theatricalization of *Blithedale* continues to unfold, none of Hawthorne's subjects, least of all Coverdale, pauses to ponder the consequences of conspicuously revealing, or concealing, true feelings. Perched undetected in his treetop lookout, what he names his "hermitage," or else surveying the property's expansive grounds with prying eyes, Coverdale spends much of his Blithedale sojourn as an unsuspected audience of one for boardinghouse performances that otherwise might pass undetected. He neither trusts nor is trusted. He is all take and no give, like the stereotype of a big-city boarder whose household demands rise with the rate of the rent that he pays. He furthermore deflates his own stated desire for "brotherhood" with Blithedale's boarders (let alone "the world" beyond Blithedale) by interfering in their emotional lives.[15] Coverdale alone (a tautology, given that he is constitutionally incapable of being anything but) personifies an authorial warning against boardinghouse feelings, which in Hawthorne's mind would seem to be subject to being seen, seized upon, and so distorted. There is little in the novel that bodes well for harmonious cohabitation, either: as a group, Blithedale's domestic dwellers expend constant thought on others, but their "common" thoughts as such proceed from a selfishly calculating predisposition for self-management, which impulse precludes the pretext of communal altruism on which they have assembled. The historical Brook Farm ultimately went bankrupt. The fictional Blithedale begins emotionally impoverished.

✦

It is understandable that Hawthorne should insist on the vacuous *drama* of boarding-feeling, an insistence that resonates well beyond the discursive confines of his text. Both historical and imaginary instances of boarding often occurred in, around, or between literal dramatic acts that cast doubt on boarders' capacity for straightforward feeling. Residents at Brook Farm and Blithedale, for instance, spent evenings, holidays, and winter months honing their dramatic skills in light theatricals, *tableaux vivants,* readings, and recitations. Feigned feeling constituted a sort of sport at the commune, and Hawthorne's Zenobia was hardly alone in her advanced skills at this art.[16] *Blithedale*'s author, moreover, had sensed as early as 1838 the performative nature of public lodgings, lodgers in his estimation having been made players by default of their non-domestic condition. During a short stay at Boston's Tremont House hotel—an establishment located right in the midst of the city's theater district—he worried in his journal over "what sort of domesticity" might be in store for those permanent tenants who had grown accustomed to "eating in public, with no board of their own," and so acted out family life under the glare of gas lights suspended from a chandelier.[17] Some boarders manipulated the unspoken emotional rules binding such situations. One, a former "tragedian" strapped for cash, surpasses Blithedale's histrion-ics when he appears in the *Atlantic Monthly* "strid[ing] up and down his room with much gnashing of teeth and other stage indications of distress," so as to induce his landlady to forget his arrears in rent.[18] Cul-tural conservatives additionally long have likened the reform commune itself, with or without chandelier stage-lighting, to a socially irrespon-sible brand of theatrics. Richard Francis explains that the Brook Farmers whom Hawthorne knew personally were accused (even by the author) of *playing* at reform in boardinghouse surroundings once-removed from reality, much as they indulged in the kinds of theatrical entertainments featured in Hawthorne's novel.[19] Boarders' reform feelings are from this vantage a charade. Their communal way is staged.

Hawthorne himself instances a related strain of cultural conservatism in resisting communal reform *through* the boardinghouse. At issue in his resistance to the motives and meanings of collective endeavor were an entire culture's feelings for feeling at a historical crossroads that point-edly coincides with the rise of the American city. At precisely that moment when the mounting pressures of urban society in the aggregate seemed to threaten the safety of sentiment itself, at a time when the basic human building blocks of like, love, and even eros deferred more and more to the impersonal mechanisms of a metropolitan market revolution,[20] reformers and boarders alike proposed survival strategies to modernity, which in their traditionalist opponents' view had made meaningful emotion a prac-tical impossibility. These latter offered to curb what they deemed modern excess as it appeared in cities and industry; progressives proposed instead to adapt *to* cities and industry as a sensible response to a society that was even then reorganizing under boarders' feet. Both proposals worked well—perhaps too well—inasmuch as they did as much to make the modern permanent in America as they did to resist its inevitable spread. Hawthorne among many sensed that conventional national sentiment might never recover as a result.

The author provides some indication of his own opinions early on in the novel when he contrives for Coverdale to illustrate two communal contradictions, both of which promise to sacrifice fellow feeling in a congeries of dramatic complications. The first of these contradictions involves Blithedale's stake in what farmer Silas Foster calls "market-gardening." That endeavor has residents raising produce for Silas's "city-folks" at a profit, and Coverdale notes the inconsistency when he calls communitarians to task for joining the "greedy, struggling, self-seeking world" rather than uphold their own non-competitive tenets. He writes "that, as regarded society at large, we stood in a position of new hostility, not new brotherhood," reminding readers that pure sentiment was not a legitimate option in that kind of capitalist environment (20).[21] The second contradiction arrives with Blithedale's mass of new recruits, who do not so much corrupt sentiment as dilute it, at least in Coverdale's view. He relates that Blithedale (like Brook Farm) received in its first few months of operation an influx of "boarders, from town and elsewhere, who lived with us in a familiar way, sympathized more or less in our theories, and sometimes shared our labors" (62). The equivocal "more or less" and "sometimes" suggest a rather weak sympathy. Coverdale confirms as much when he says, "Our bond . . . was not affirmative, but negative." That is to say, "We had individually found one thing or another to quarrel with, in our past life" but "did not greatly care" what replaced it. The "union" formed by these brother-boarders in turn lacks strength and could not, the narrator continues, "reasonably be expected to hold together long" (63). Modern commerce and noncommittal boarders have crept through Blithedale's back door and jeopardized the community's affections.

According to many of Hawthorne's contemporaries, boarding presumed such unstable emotional foundations, an outlook that *Blithedale* would seem to endorse. Writer Fannie Benedict tried and failed to look at boarding's bright side: she found through personal experience that "sympathy naturally attracts kindred souls," and so even at boardinghouses, "lasting and valuable friendships are founded by those thus thrown together." As a boardinghouse, however, could "never" in her eyes "be more than a stopping place," she at last concedes the dim prospects of sentiment for roving residents. New York playwright William Northall dispensed with Benedict's search for a silver lining in the shared domestic edifice. He spoke on behalf of boarding's many detractors when he explained why, in 1851, Manhattan's boarders spent so much time at the theater. Boarding, he said, had sacrificed fellow feeling at the altar of the itinerant living that it facilitated. Northall in fact answers Hawthorne's 1838 query over "what sort of domesticity" boarders enjoyed when he avers that "boarders will be polite to each other, and strictly observe the courtesies of life; but the *heart* has little to do with this. It is but the *cold* observance of rules necessary to a selfish comfort and respect." Anticipating Coverdale, down to the same diction, he goes on to lament that "there is no *bond* of *union* among the lodgers of a boardinghouse; and scarcely anything short of a murder or suicide has sufficient interest to cause one boarder to *feel* an interest in what may be occurring to the gentlemen in the next rooms" (my emphasis).[22] That dearth of feeling, Northall concludes, carried residents of the boardinghouse to the playhouse. Boarders there would meet with staged courtships, rote soliloquies, ersatz adventures, and the orchestrated pratfalls of paid players—all of which, in Northall's estimation, would have to satisfy more personal boarder-longings otherwise unmet. To feel something, *anything,* was better than the urban alternative of feeling nothing in the modern residential scheme of things.

Boarding in *Blithedale* bears an uncanny correspondence to Northall's formulations. Coverdale, like our contemporary commentator, likewise regrets the comparatively weak boardinghouse "bond" or "union" that pertains at his commune. The novel in which Coverdale plays so large a part in fact affords the very murder or suicide that Northall conjectures. With the Blithedale domicile, finally, hosting so many theatrical performances, and with the novel itself being narrated by a confessed theatergoer in Coverdale (40), the community of Hawthorne's creation begins to provide a patterned textbook example of why and how, in Northall's view, boarders sought playhouse recompense for the sentiment denied them at home.

With what Northall calls the "unsympathizing materials" of boarding at his disposal, Hawthorne makes much ado in *Blithedale* from the meaningful emotion that the book lacks. For, despite the occasional attention-grabbing spectacles of this boardinghouse "Romance,"[23] the text primarily achieves its impact with readers not through the easy inducements of cheap plot surprises, but by means of the affective absences that here are thought to inhere in communal living. Hawthorne's novel is thus not so much "unsympathizing" as *non*-sympathizing; it pretends at the sentiment that it never secures. Blithedale's boarders may strain after impulses that *seem* like genuine feelings, but their separate pursuits yield scant emotional satisfaction in the end. Hawthorne's characters, in other words, simulate sentiment because, in the conventional paradigm to which the author subscribes, boarding and feeling remain mutually exclusive. Emotions are not just exaggerated in *Blithedale*, then. Feeling within this fiction is something other than characters' bluff and bluster. Affect inside this novel instead amounts to a spurious stage-effect, in accordance with the antebellum belief that little but performative feeling was forthcoming at the boardinghouse. From this skeptical vantage point, communal utopianism is not the only illusion sustained by the narrative. Boarder-feeling itself is sham, simulacra, a prop for appearance's sake.

✦

Consensual, if not communal, sex is the predominant form of performance that boarder dis-sentiment takes in *Blithedale*. In lieu of what Walt Whitman later would call "adhesive" feeling, by which he meant the brotherly (or sisterly) tie that binds men or women together, Blithedale's inhabitants have settled for a mere *physical* manifestation of the same, or what the poet termed "amativeness."[24] These two forms of affective expression are complementary for Whitman. They cannot and do not coexist in Hawthorne's novel. As reformer-*boarders*, his characters have opted out of the conventional mindset and domestic setting in which genuine affection was thought to reside within the realm of "real" residential possibility. Trapped as they are inside boardinghouse confines where love finds no admittance, forsaken as they have been without an outlet for the most private palpitations of their hearts, they defer to sexual stirrings which, like the melodramatic motions of the stage, set something that just barely resembles a sound emotional sensibility within their reach. The fear for those like Hawthorne is that the internal workings of boarding have turned too much of a good thing—which is to say, human contact—into a ready excuse for the next best thing, the casual sexual encounters that were reputed to prevail at America's boardinghouses. Boarding, in short, perverts what otherwise might pass as pure sentiment in Hawthorne's novel. Society and intimacy bleed together inside the boardinghouse coordinates of this book, replacing more chastened nineteenth-century notions of male-female relations.

One could even argue that the author concerns himself less with the reform urge than with the sexual urges attendant upon close human habitation, a reading legitimized by the boardinghouse context of this text.[25] There are by any count too many boarders' bodies within convenient reach here, too many personal yearnings, too many human egos set at cohabitational touching distance. The resultant heavy sexual suggestiveness that is evident in much of the narrative thus should come as no surprise, since the characters themselves have ample communal opportunities for something besides brotherly love. Coverdale initiates a recurring narrative pattern of striptease when he mentally undresses Zenobia at their first meeting. His lascivious wishes are later fulfilled after he discovers her partially clad corpse being pulled from its watery grave—a disturbing scene with necrophiliac overtones, and the inevitable boarder-onlookers. Zenobia throughout the novel conceals what potentially could be a revealing sexual skeleton inside the figurative closet she once shared with her former companion, Westervelt. She and Priscilla now love Hollingsworth, as Coverdale comes to do during a convalescent spell spent under his friend's managing care. Hollingsworth in turn would seem to have feelings for only himself, before he unconvincingly redirects his affections toward Priscilla. Or, to summarize, everybody loves somebody; nobody loves the narrator, Coverdale. It is the very high density of these mixed emotions that lends *Blithedale* the overabundance of drama that it possesses. And it is the narrow boardinghouse parameters within which such sentiments occur that substitutes the fleeting modern pleasures of recreational sexual encounter for more durable affection.

From this boardinghouse perspective, *Blithedale* is a markedly different book. Its boarders turn lovers so consistently as to collapse the two categories. One need only consider the example supplied by the ironic sexual foreplay of that opening encounter between Coverdale and Zenobia to realize the extent to which the strategically arranged tête-à-tête among co-tenants comes to supersede "serious" sentiment inside this text. Offered her hand upon meeting, the narrator reports its being "very soft and warm" (14). He releases his hold to obtain a better view of his sister-reformer. The personal prospect—or prospect of her person—that in turn greets Coverdale meets with his approval. "She was, indeed," he reports, "an admirable figure of a woman . . . with a combination of features which it is safe to call remarkably beautiful" (15). Zenobia all but begs for these lingering looks with her behavior, claims Coverdale. He depicts her smiling wide, complimenting him on the occasional verse that he has circulated in print, even teasing that she will sing his poems when the mood suits her. It is a rather risqué first impression, and Coverdale excuses his behavior with a she-asked-for-it defense, declaring that Zenobia's "free, careless, generous modes of expression" one "hardly felt to be decorous, when born of a thought that passes between man and woman" (17). The meeting comes to an abrupt end when an unnamed Blithedaler interrupts their improvisational love-pairing, only for similar cat-and-mouse exchanges between boarders to occur the length and width of Hawthorne's novel. Zenobia and Coverdale instigate this game, but others follow their immodestly acted lead.

So completely is sexual interplay built into Hawthorne's boardinghouse book that each of the parties implicated in this, the narrative's preferred manner of human exchange, begins to perform the oxymoronic part of independent, uninhibited communitarian as a matter of course. Home to men and women alike, the boardinghouse of this text provides a habitational occasion for bridging the gender gap that the feminist Zenobia so often invokes. There can be no separate spheres here, practically speaking. There are for the most part only single boarding men and boarder maidens like our Blithedale crew. Both were within bodily reach of the objects of their respective sexual desires. Both were liberated by residential circumstance that found them free from the conventional combined constraints of kin and chaperon. Residing however and with whomever they pleased, they were prepared to board and let board, so long as personal ties did not grow too tangled, as they do at Blithedale.

Steeped as he was in the popular press of his day,[26] Hawthorne would not have been innocent of a discursive tradition that made frequent reference to the unfettered sexual activities that were believed to be an intrinsic feature of period boarding. The physical flirtations that he only hints at with respect to Coverdale and Zenobia were widely suspected among boarders elsewhere and made for good copy in what historians refer to as the "flash" press. Of special interest to the study of boardinghouse letters is a quartet of New York periodicals from the early American 1840s that both documented and propagated what their most recent students call an "urban male sporting culture." It would be no exaggeration to say that the "sporting weekly" reveled in the ribald lore of the nation's cities, especially that revolving around its boardinghouses. Indeed, this freely circulating, semi-pornographic "new genre of American publication" buttressed what scholars have identified as an emergent sexual subculture which, in many respects, derived from the socio-personal situations engendered by boarding.[27] The sheer numbers of boarders who give, receive, and/or seek some form of "love" inside this city discourse would indicate that contemporaries were hungry for the sexual content that was latent, if not explicit, in boardinghouse print. A March 1842 letter to the editor of a sexually suggestive newspaper, the *Whip Satirist of New-York and Brooklyn,* is firm on this point. Stripped of what the writer calls the "false modesty" of the mainstream press, the *Whips* of the antebellum periodical world "converse freely," the writer says, "on any subject that may be brought on the carpet without thinking of every word before we dare speak it." Provocative sexual narrative, in short, was welcome inside such broadsheets. And with "boarders being sensible young men," our "Satirist" continues, they "generally" were resourceful enough "to find a Whip" to read, and so "devour with great eagerness" those artfully rendered accounts of what transpired behind the scenes at urban boardinghouses in the mid-nineteenth-century United States. To gainsay such a claim would be to deny the material evidence afforded by a "Monday morning ransack" of any city "boarder's rooms." Lady boarders, too, were thought to be wise to boarding's sexual non-secrets, and so qualify as well in our writer's mind as devoted readers of serials like the *Whip*. He himself testifies to having witnessed "immediately after breakfast" one morning a certain female boarder with a familiar-looking "newspaper sticking out of her reticule." "*Vive la Whip*," he concludes, "and the girls that partronise it."[28]

Hawthorne was joined by scores of the era's writers who handled the sexual subject matter of boarding with full frankness. There was, for example, titillating commentary on boardinghouse women not unlike Zenobia. "Fast boardinghouse women," a writer from the *Atlantic Monthly* called them, before rehearsing the conventional notion that boarding was for such brazen females simply an entrée into "the old man-trap line." Hawthorne himself, boarding in Boston in May 1850, reported one such specimen in his journal when he wrote of a household banking-clerk spending "the greater part of the night" in the "private" chamber of the resident brunette, "Miss—." It was generally believed that male boarders also had to beware of landladies, often widows, who were reputed to be on the prowl for husbands. Journalist Thomas Butler Gunn describes a whole class of boardinghouses where "you're expected to make love to the landlady." There were widely reported cases as well in which solicitous landladies even sought to pawn off their own daughters, as the essayist N. P. Willis observed of the "matrimonial speculation" that he found at a budget "twenty-shilling" boardinghouse in New York. Such suppositions as Willis's were endemic to the genre. For if, as the keeper of Dickens's fictional London boardinghouse says, boarder-love was "very natural. When two young people get together, you know . . . ," then Oliver Wendell Holmes's "Professor" persona assessed the situation rightly when he sensed "boarding-house romance" in the air at his Boston establishment, where a fetching female boarder at table's end unfailingly attracted the attention of resident boarder-bucks.[29]

And yet the moral majority's view on boarder-relations was Hawthorne's—that they were not only less than "natural," but prohibitive of the sentimental idealization of feeling. Performer Tony Pastor devised a pre-vaudevillian tune by way of illustration: he sang of a man whose wife bore "two thumping little codgers"; one was his, while "the other was the lodger's!" But a projected increase in population was not the real source of worry. Boarding, rather, threatened to debase transatlantic emotional standards with a collective affective norm that was at once troublingly unsympathetic and dangerously unorthodox. Englishman John Neal demonstrates the root cause of the concern with unwitting deadpan when he speaks of male boarders bundling three to a bed, "spoon fashion." While there was nothing unusual, least of all sexual, about innocuous male bunkmates, or even a full-blooded man like Hollingsworth nursing Coverdale back to health, Walt Whitman spoke privately of bringing men back to his boardinghouse room for something more than late-night literary talk. What occurred there emerged in 1846, when New York police charged two young wage earners with sodomy transacted while they were cohabitating in the same boardinghouse chamber. French novelist Balzac reminds readers of the direction in which love in the boardinghouse was tending. Outside the Maison Vauquer, the capital boardinghouse of his 1835 work *Le Père Goriot,* he situates a marble Cupid. For one "fond of symbols," declares Balzac's narrator, it stands "as an allegorical representation of Parisian love," boarder-style, "which can be cured at the nearby hospital for Venereal Disease."[30]

✦

Mounting fears—not entirely unfounded—of a budding "free love" movement accompanied the conservative cultural criticism of boarding, and further colored an emerging alarmist discourse of the nineteenth-century metropolis. Hawthorne's novel contributes to this discourse by directly addressing the curious reform vision of Frenchman Charles Fourier, whose teachings ignited an antebellum attempt to restore human "passions" and so save the industrial West with an elaborate boarding-house plan. Fourier enters Hawthorne's book through Brook Farm, which had reconstituted itself on a Fourierist basis some two and a half years after the author abandoned the communal venture. Fourier*ism* as a collective cause did not peak until the final years of the decade. Those were important years for our purposes. On the one hand, it was during this interval that a number of Fourierists turned actual free lovers in principle or practice, inviting accusations of anarchy, blasphemy, and antisocial sentiment. On the other hand, these were years that saw Hawthorne produce a novel depicting four vaguely Fourierist reformers at an emotional impasse. Deep feeling has escaped all of them, and the desire for some elusive physical substitute begins in turn to overtake the platonic basis of their communal relations. The author in effect has relinquished sentiment to boarder-sex in *Blithedale,* contributing a Fourierist dimension to the discussion of the depletion of emotion in modern civilization.

Hawthorne read from Fourier's works in preparation for *Blithedale.* What he encountered in the process was an elaborate plan to reorganize existing social relations in accordance with the Frenchman's theory of "passional attraction." Fourier begins his critical analysis of modernity by identifying a twofold problem. Society, he believes, unnecessarily facilitates a pernicious antagonism among its members. It also has made man a shadow of his uninhibited self by denying the free expression of "passions" like friendship, love, and a craving for variety, the so-called "butterfly" passion. Universal harmony would result once society allowed these passions to develop unhindered. And the society that best enabled that development was what Fourier termed the Association, where a communal "phalanx" of 1,600 diverse persons would function as a collective economic unit by dividing productive labor into those endeavors which individual members deemed most "attractive." Housing this passionate panacea would be an Olympian boardinghouse, or "phalanstery" (figure 6.1), where the isolating influences of kinship would yield to an associative family bound by ties of work and affection, not by blood. Fourier thus quantifies by a nascent social science human feelings that sentimentalists, for one, would never have dared to disturb.

Nor did Fourier cease his social tinkering there. His phalanstery would defy sexual convention on a number of fronts, as, in the minds of many, communal living itself was wont to do. Women, to begin, were to be as *passionate* as men. That is to say, they were to have fertile opportunities for self-development outside the home. Such a plan would have been anathema to Hawthorne, whose domesticated spouse Sophia he referred to by letter as "mine ownest dove." Fourier, too, in his unadulterated form dispensed with marriage outright. He instead sanctioned what a writer in Brook Farm's Associationist periodical *The Harbinger* described as nonconjugal relations based on "entire bodily freedom." Or, as Henry James, Sr., explained in the introduction to his 1849 translation of *Love in the Phalanstery,*[31] written by one of Fourier's French disciples, Fourierists had renounced the hoarding of flesh endemic to single-spouse relationships, just as communalists had rejected those free-market practices by which avaricious capitalists stockpiled their ill-gotten wealth. There was an added benefit to redistributing sexual wealth in this way, says the French author of *Love:* phalansteries promoted "hygienic measures" to avoid the sexually transmitted diseases acquired by Balzac's Parisian boarders. If this was modernity, then many Americans, boarders included, wanted no part of it.

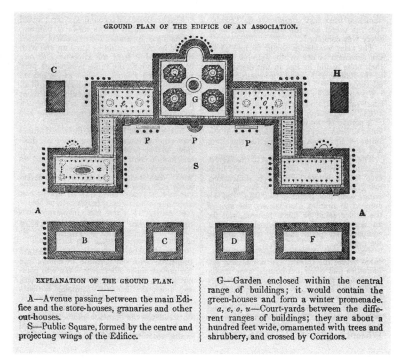

GROUND PLAN OF THE EDIFICE OF AN ASSOCIATION.

EXPLANATION OF THE GROUND PLAN.

A—Avenue passing between the main Edifice and the store-houses, granaries and other out-houses.

S—Public Square, formed by the centre and projecting wings of the Edifice.

G—Garden enclosed within the central range of buildings; it would contain the green-houses and form a winter promenade.

a, e, o, u—Court-yards between the different ranges of buildings; they are about a hundred feet wide, ornamented with trees and shrubbery, and crossed by Corridors.

**Figure 6.1.** The grand plan of boarding at Fourier's proposed phalanstery. From the American Fourierist disciple Albert Brisbane's *Association; or, A Concise Exposition of the Practical Part of Fourier's Social Science* (1843), p. 21.

Like his middle-class audience, Hawthorne balked at Fourier's proposals and writes an unsettling account of a Fourier-friendly experiment in the throes of affective dysfunction. The novel, indeed, takes pains to express the author's various misgivings. It affords, first, satirical free-love moments, as when Coverdale suggests Virgil's "*Ara nudus; sere nudus*"— "Strip to plow, strip to sow"—as an impractical answer to a colony-wide dress code, before he defers to Silas Foster's plea not "to astonish the women-folks" (64). Also on offer in *Blithedale* are angry denunciations, like Hollingsworth's, of the "abominable corruptions" that Fourier presumably would permit at his "consummated paradise" (53). In between these moments of unquestioned laughter and projected disaster appears the ambivalent commentary of Coverdale. He remarks reservedly at one stage that "the footing, on which we all associated at Blithedale, was widely different from that of conventional society." He explains his observation by adding that the boardinghouse at Blithedale—we learn later of an abortive plan "to erect a Phalanstery"—"seemed to authorize any individual, of either sex, to fall in love with any other, regardless of what would elsewhere be judged suitable and prudent" (72, 128). All of which suggests that Hawthorne's story directs enough negative remarks toward Fourier as to place it in agreement with one period religious newspaper, which editorialized against the Frenchman's system for being hostile to "conservative influences" and upholding a doctrine of "promiscuous" relations between the sexes.[32]

This "promiscuous" is essential to combining boarding and Fourierist readings of *Blithedale*. It was the same word used by a writer in 1843 when he conceptually—and disapprovingly—linked boardinghouses, theaters, taverns, and other places of "promiscuous resort." It was the label employed by one of Dickens's London boarders, who, upon learning that another's room adjoined the household parlor, responded with an astonished, "How very promiscuous!" Promiscuity was also the order of the day at Brook Farm. Even before the community's planned phalanstery burned to the ground months prior to completion, the overwhelming majority of young and unattached inhabitants invited accusations of sexual misconduct at communes generally by virtue of being just what they were—young and unattached. At least fourteen marriages stemmed from love connections formed on the grounds. A certain female resident bragged about the number of her "flirtations" there. Another Brook Farm male proposed an on-site "rejected lover's sympathizing group." He may or may not have been joking, considering what one divorcée (not an anomaly at the Farm) identified as the ambiguous area that Association created between "intimate communion" and "genial trustful friendship." But above all else, the fact that one of Brook Farm's former occupants—an on-again, off-again New York boarder, as well as a card-carrying Fourierist—emerged as the leading U.S. spokesman for literal free love did nothing to rebuff charges that promiscuity was rampant in American reform circles. That his pushing of behavioral boundaries occurred at a Long Island location called Modern Times must have struck a vocal group of anti-moderns as some sort of vindication.[33] That American Free Love as a legitimate social movement emerged the same year as Hawthorne's novel is a coincidence perhaps best appreciated by the boarder-readers of 1852.

✦

Back inside Hawthorne's novel, the complicated love affairs at the Blithedale farmhouse, in conjunction with the considerable narrative space the author allots to sexual innuendo, combine to warn against a radically democratic sentiment shorn of sacrosanct feeling that might prevail should Fourierism take hold in America. Many sensed that this imported ideology already had infiltrated Brook Farm, and would proceed to do the same at some model phalanstery of the future unless it was fended off with stiff resistance. Informing these fears was the belief that Fourierism would, or could, spread throughout America's cities as its pseudoscientific rendition of "love" passed from the phalanstery to what one writer called "these great Phalanstery-like hotels," or urban boardinghouses, where the sexual exploits of inhabitants were already a source of concern.[34]

The novel concentrates these fears in chapter 13, "Zenobia's Legend," a dramatic set piece that encapsulates the sexual tensions that pertain between boarding and Blithedale. At a glance, little about "Zenobia's Legend" suggests boarding, and yet cohabitation is both its formal and functional subtext. The chapter draws attention to itself as an evening's ensemble that situates all of Blithedale's boarders in the same room. Once gathered, they do what not a few boarders would in fact do on a quiet night; they entertain themselves with theatricals. On stage is Zenobia. On hand is her sister-boarder Priscilla—the inspiration of the "legendary" story that Zenobia performs and, as the lecture-circuit phenomenon known as the Veiled Lady, the attraction that draws the lodger-bachelor Coverdale out of his rooms at the beginning of the novel and later from his boarders' hotel near novel's end. Boarding thus frames Hawthorne's staging of the scene.

The "Legend" that both readers and Blithedale's boarders actually receive maintains the cohabitational context of this important interlude. We will recall first Coverdale's earlier visit to witness the Veiled Lady. That outing occurred the night before his departure for Blithedale, and ended with him wondering if the beatific vision that he beheld on stage was, as rumored, a "beautiful young lady" (6). After a nightcap of sherry, repeated the next "forenoon" with a friend, he turns his attention to matters seemingly more momentous than stage women, leaves off bachelor-boarding, and prepares himself for a loose form of boarding by Association (8). The parallel to Zenobia's "Legend" is striking. What she titles "The Silvery Veil" in her own performed story opens with a roomful of Coverdales:

> A party of young gentlemen . . . were enjoying themselves, one afternoon, as young gentlemen are sometimes fond of doing, over a bottle of champagne; and—among other ladies less mysterious— the subject of the Veiled Lady, as was very natural, happened to come up before them for discussion. (108)

Like the narrator, these "gentlemen" are bachelors. The odd hours they keep, the midday cheer of which they partake, and the "ladies" they bandy

about in small talk reveal them as such. They are also, again like Coverdale, pleasure-seeking theatergoers.[35] What's left unsaid is that Zenobia's
"gentlemen" are likely boarders as well. Most antebellum boarders were
single young men, historically,[36] and were known to frequent evening
entertainments like the theater. The "Legend" in this reading leans on
boarding for its full meaning.

Boarder-sexuality, rather, is the covert theme of Zenobia's "Legend."
Among the party of young admirers who offer toast to her fabled Lady is
our male lead, Theodore, who like Coverdale burns to learn the identity
of a mysterious stage performer. Theodore accordingly leaves his fellow
tipplers—at an undisclosed locale—to steal surreptitiously into the Veiled
Lady's dressing room at the local assembly hall. With "sparkling wine"
in his head, mischief on his mind, and the hour at or near midnight,
he soon greets a "maiden" who, upon discovering his trespass, presents
him with two choices: as the Lady decrees, he either can "lift my veil!"
that "hides my face" and forfeit future contact for present satisfaction,
or else kiss the "virgin lips" behind that same veil—sight unseen—and
so plight himself in love and marriage to her forever (112–13). Theodore
must choose between sex and sentiment, a choice that many a seasoned
boarder-bachelor before him had made. Yet, inasmuch as he is already
possessed—he rents, we might say—of a boardinghouse heart without a
permanent home, Theodore like much of the rest of his boardinghouse
fraternity already has sacrificed the commitments associated with socio-
personal obligation for the anticipated physical pleasures of chance
confrontation. He is thus unfazed by the Veiled Lady's proposal; he in
fact implies that he is no stranger to such proposals when he flippantly
decides against sentiment, stating that "the odds were ten to one that her
teeth were defective; a terrible drawback on the delectableness of a kiss!"
(113). The Veiled Lady's otherworldliness in other words represents a
world of affect that a boarding Theodore cannot access, let alone compre-
hend. Each party in the exchange speaks a different language of "love,"
the one articulating lofty thoughts of heart and home, the other colloquially voicing a caddish craving for meaningless amorous encounter. The
"heart" of this miscommunication is not necessarily a modern problem,
but it becomes one by virtue of its boarding orientation.

Theodore makes his choice and chooses wrong. He lifts the veil only to
discover a "pale, lovely face, beneath" (114). Tellingly, Theodore forgoes
more than just a kiss in this instance. As Zenobia moralizes, his punishment
is a lifetime of bachelor-boarding among his associates in that unnamed
place: "His retribution was, to pine, forever and ever, for another sight of
that dim, mournful face—which might have been his life-long, household,

fireside joy" (114). It is a grim message for Zenobia to have delivered to Blithedale's roomful of boarders, who likewise as tenant-inhabitants enjoy no "household," no "fireside," no domestic source of sentiment to call their own. Grimmer still, at least from Theodore's standpoint, is that the "Legend" concludes without the sexual consummation for which he thought he had bargained. But, as Lauren Berlant notes, because an unremitting relational anxiety shapes the household experience of Blithedale's boarders—with so many singles ever on the cusp of becoming couples— sexual penetration per se nevertheless remains one of the larger novel's (the tale outside the tale) operative metaphors.[37] Indeed, the Veiled Lady's "impenetrability" proving incomplete preserves a boardinghouse reading of Blithedale precisely by omitting the story's expected outcome (111). The assumption among Hawthorne's prurient-minded contemporaries was that all boarders' stories would eventuate in much the same way: back at the boardinghouse, over in the commune, or out at the phalanstery, it was not a question of if sexual contact would come, but when, and on whose terms—the Theodores of this boarders' world, or else that rare principled sentimentalist.

There is a lower level to which boarding without feeling might descend. Chapters 17 and 18, "The Hotel" and "The Boarding-House," to that end mark the ironic modern apotheosis of boarding in the book. The narrator by now has left Blithedale for more hotel-boarding in Boston. With the death-knell of his own communal idealism still ringing in his ears, he somehow is not—or perhaps somehow is—disheartened enough to continue to board. He in fact is rejuvenated by his hotel visit. Declaring himself an "epicure," Coverdale speaks as follows from his room in appreciation of the flavor of promiscuous urban boarding:

> Whatever had been my taste for solitude and natural scenery, yet the thick, foggy, stifled element of cities, the entangled life of many men together, sordid as it was, and empty of the beautiful, took quite as strenuous hold upon my mind. I felt as if there could never be enough of it. (146)

A connoisseur of boarding, Coverdale delights in the "stir of the hotel." The "entangled life of many men together" it affords, "sordid as it was," he states, and troublesome as it had been at Blithedale, generates enough sensory stimuli to keep this "epicure" content. There are "the loud voices of guests, landlord, or barkeeper" to sample. There are the "arrivals or departures" of an endless supply of new neighbors. Even "chamber-maids scudding along the passages" make for a "whole house" of "bustling," boarding enjoyment. His inviolate self thus violated—*penetrated* might be the proper term[38]—Coverdale partakes of a "sordid" pleasure more indebted to flesh than feeling (146).

Hawthorne expresses his objection to such pleasures indirectly, through symbolic association. Both boarding and boarders emerge in his portrayal as being in league with another form of "sordid" commercial urban behavior, one to which women without sufficient domestic resources sometimes turned as a means of city survival. The author duly hands his bachelor Coverdale a cigar. He seats him in a rocking chair by his hotel window, the narrator's "legs and slippered feet horizontally disposed." Into his lap he drops the "dullest" of books. And thus Hawthorne brings his character into character: boarded, recumbent, and prepared for something more engrossing than the "narrative" he holds between his knees, Coverdale reminds readers of a place—not far from the metropolitan boardinghouse—where a city-slick single man of his background might find a different (or not) kind of pleasure than that which he enjoys at his temporary shelter (147). Peering out his hotel window, sipping sherry, Coverdale becomes absorbed by an actual boardinghouse situated across the way, and in that absorption—taken, again, "horizontally"—*Blithedale*'s latest boardinghouse recalls a real-world boardinghouse bordello. It was at just such an establishment that Coverdale could have secured affection without emotional entanglement, if that is what he desires. Hawthorne, well-versed in scarlet women, watches on at a once remove with the rest of us.

There were at least three contemporary responses to the kind of urban boarder-sex on display here. Sensation-mongers Ned Buntline, George Foster, and George Thompson gleefully peopled the city boardinghouses of their writings with *seeming* naïfs. It was the duplicitous shock value of boardinghouse sex, not its transparency (it seldom was transparent), that caught their antebellum imaginations. Even Hawthorne indulged in this discursive device when he remarked in 1850 on a young Frenchman who, by all appearances "orderly and decorous," used their Boston boardinghouse as a staging ground for what the author called "gross Saxon orgies."[39] Laughter was another response to the sexual subtext of boarding. The running gag of Peter Pendergrass's *The Magdalen Report: A Farce in Three Acts* (1831), for example, is that all America has given in to boarding-whoring. Housemaids leave off dishwashing en masse to become call girls. Boardinghouse-keepers turn brothel-operators not half as fast as runaway demand, with landlady Mrs. Loosely complaining, "Oh that I had a larger house!"[40] Englishman James Burn supplies a third rhetorical response to boarding's under-the-cover misdoings. He excoriates American boardinghouses for corrupting "the notions of personal liberty . . . entertained by young people of both sexes" in residence. Having condemned the cause, he sermonizes over the effect:

> I have no hesitation in saying that many of these houses are hotbeds of vice and every species of immorality. In fact, the immoral tendency of the system is freely admitted by all intelligent and well-meaning men, and is acknowledged to be a serious blot on the national character.[41]

This last rhetorical posture most closely corresponds with Hawthorne's, as indicated by the aimless direction that his narrative takes after it has been set sentimentally adrift. When feelings fail at *Blithedale*'s multiple boardinghouses—and they do fail—its resident boarders proceed to make a despairing contest out of contact. Their bodies rout non-bodily affection. Mindless touching, and not soulful feeling, becomes the dominant form of expression between them. The author does not wallow, however, in what he and others deemed the problematic divorce of boarding from feeling; nor does he sport with the subject, as do so many sensational writers of the day. But nor is Hawthorne's response—dejected as it is—an unequivocally self-righteous condemnation of what he would seem to perceive as a social evil. There is, rather, a marked note of sadness in *Blithedale*, which note begins to make the work read as something like a boardinghouse farce in reverse: instead of heartfelt laughter at home's expense, the text insists that there is no levity in the tendency of boardinghouses toward communal physicality.

Coverdale crystallizes the author's critique back at his hotel window, where, reclined and comfortable, he reduces boarding to a deplorable social-developmental stage that renders it indistinguishable from licentiousness. *Blithedale*'s inveterate bachelor-boarder now dispenses with all pretense at feeling, after he discovers that Zenobia and Priscilla have taken up residence in a well-appointed boardinghouse that faces his own establishment. Aroused at the unexplained circumstances of their being so close at hand, he successfully awaits a "glimpse" of the "graceful" Zenobia, before "making out" the "girlish shape" of Priscilla (154–55). It is an almost masturbatory moment between boarders—consensual on one side, blissfully ignorant on the other, and contingent upon the exposed female form of open-door boarding.[42] The theatrical effect created by drawing-room curtains, which frame Coverdale's view, ostentatiously sets a dramatic boardinghouse stage: the evident pleasure that the narrator receives in this scene places him in absentia at one of the many brothels, peep shows, model-artist performances, or cheap theaters that had appeared in the metropolitan West during the middle years of the nineteenth century. Part of what one historian calls the "promiscuous paradigm" of these decades, the sometimes real, sometimes simulated, sex of these entertainments was the mainstay of a burgeoning sporting scene that depended for its business on *promiscuous* boarder-bachelors like Coverdale. With disposable income in their pockets, and urban ennui in what the narrator calls their "cold" collective "heart," boarding's many men about town increasingly cured "home-sickness," as Coverdale styles it, not just by looking but touching the urban attractions within and without their rented rooms (154).[43] Hawthorne allows modern boarder-promiscuity to run what he would have readers believe is its alienating course.

✦

The novel's climax arrives in the wake of Coverdale's bitterness at securing no emotional ties by which, at last, to define himself. For weeks he has resented being denied even a peripheral place in the exclusive boarders' bond shared by Zenobia and Priscilla in Boston. Nor has he been able to salvage his friendship with Hollingsworth, so that he can write with regret of a recent past, "These three had absorbed my life into themselves" (194). Having once, in other words, been able to harness his sense of self to his housemates, achieving a limited boarders' version of what Caleb Crain calls "sympathetic ecstasy" in the process, Coverdale now finds himself alone, unloved, outside the affective bounds of even the makeshift community that he has inhabited for upward of a year.[44] As a bachelor, he might have expected as much. But as a boarder-bachelor, his emphatic one-ness at this point in the novel represents the antithesis of his very being as a boarder. Somewhere between sentiment and sex should have rested a compensatory boarders' form of feeling. For Coverdale, compensation has not been forthcoming.

Hence his return to Blithedale, where he is eager to retrieve what appears in hindsight to have been a more affectively rewarding brand of boarding than is available to him elsewhere. The text suggests that Coverdale has arrived too late to find true feeling, however. Despite his optimistic expectations, he cannot overcome what he terms his "solitude," and so returns to the country only to experience more of the anomie of city anonymity. He speaks of a "somber mood" afflicting him in his journey, "befitting one who found himself tending towards home, . . . conscious that nobody would be quite joyed to greet him there" (204–5). Meeting him instead are the fraying relations of Blithedale's rural society, which reveal to him the extent of his own displaced personhood. The farmhouse is empty, the barn door swinging on its hinges, the community dog nowhere to be found. "So cold a reception" does Coverdale receive that he achieves a major, if belated, realization: the residual vacancy that he feels—or does not feel—is as much personal-internal as it is communal-residential (209). Where once was his heart now stands a boarder's house without hope. Whether emptied or occupied, home for him no longer can be a retreat of feeling.

*Blithedale*'s extravagant finish belies such sobering sentiments. In keeping with his work's counterintuitive tendencies, Hawthorne employs chapter 24, "The Masqueraders," to reveal rather than disguise the carnal frame that has shaped his story from its beginning. A novel's worth of sexual innuendo ends in the "revels" that Coverdale, in search of Blithedale's boarders, stumbles upon in canvassing the surrounding woods, where residents have assembled for a final foray at the gratuitous play of role-play. The occasion—there is none. Hawthorne proceeds seamlessly from evoking an unremarkable autumn afternoon to detailing a veritable boarder's orgy, as if boarder-orgies were themselves unremarkable. The scene as Coverdale pictures it is promiscuity incarnate. There are "allegoric figures from the Faerie Queen" flitting about him. Incongruous couples of "grim Puritans" and "gay Cavaliers" pass "arm in arm, or otherwise huddled together." An "Indian chief" with "uplifted tomahawk" puts in an appearance, and "near him, looking fit to be his woodland-bride," is the huntress Diana. All are outdone at conviviality, at feigning fun, by a "vivacious little gipsy" who moves indiscriminately—boarder-like, one might say— from one group to another. Coverdale's first impression is readers' last: "Voices, male and female; laughter, . . . of fresh young throats" (209–10). It is a fitting image for the book's failure, sentimentally speaking. Seeking lasting feeling, the text settles (or not) for "fresh young" inconstancy.

As his story assumes its final shape, Hawthorne seems increasingly committed to a dystopian vision of the commune. Boarders' bodies quite literally drop while the novel reaches its denouement, their affective aspirations sinking like so many stones. Hollingsworth pledges his life and love to Priscilla, not Zenobia. Zenobia scorns love and takes her own life, a collective suicide. Coverdale ends where he began, lodging in some loveless location in Boston. Free love among these boarders has become a zero-sum game in which the final score reads no love at all, rather than love won but lost. Like so many historical Brook Farmers, Priscilla and Hollingsworth do marry and establish a stand-alone home of their own. Yet, theirs is a romantic mismatch, since their future proves barren and careworn—even when compared to the cold boarders' condition that came before. Indeed, Coverdale reports years after the fact that their marriage has been monotonous and monogamous, whereas the utopian boarding they had prophesied would have been, hypothetically, polymorphously perverse. Hawthorne does not brook the apparent perversities of Blithedale. He punishes glib passions masked as emotion. He closes a self-involved cooperative. And he completes his novel, so *like* a dramatic theatrical, with an unreliable narrator's last gasp at feeling—with Coverdale confessing to a "love" for Priscilla which, one suspects, he never felt. If *Blithedale* is a tragedy, it is one enacted by a former boarder-author for whom the sweetest substitute for sentiment would seem to be revenge. In the end, *Blithedale* believes antebellum boarding to be a mere masquerade; it proposes communal quartering as a pantomime performance of sexual desire, devoid of all feeling. If Hawthorne's discursive position seems untenable, then one would do well to remember that sentimental culture was already, by the 1850s, suffering from dislocations of urban industrialism that decidedly placed sentiment on the defensive.[45] The laissez-faire behavioral license that pertains in Hawthorne's novel is thus but a fictionalization of contemporary fears that a whole nation—and not just an ad hoc population of boarders, who were coping with a societal shift toward cities and industry—had been sympathetically stranded by the rationalizing requirements of the modern. To see housemates turning bunkmates is no joke within this rhetorical-historical context, even if such sophomoric examples of bedroom humor sustained the popular genre of boardinghouse drama with theatergoers for years. *Blithedale* is no generic drama, and yet its author figures a domestic chorus in pronouncing his misgivings about a culture that had distanced itself from traditional sources of feeling. Meaningful emotion here is noticeably scarce. Family is nothing short of missing. And neither home nor heart achieves the emotional space-time necessary to reside in this book. Such is boarding's legacy to sentimental letters.

# Epilogue

> The house was a good house—not very old.
>
> —Edgar Allan Poe, "The Murders
> in the Rue Morgue," 1841

In the end, antebellum boarding tended more toward death than the love that Hawthorne's *Blithedale* denies, inasmuch as the dead and dying co-occupy the pages of boardinghouse letters with great frequency. Boarders were of course mortal, and like the narratives that contained them terminated in time, no less than in corporeal/storyline space. Perhaps more important, boarding as both a literary form and as a form of human behavior marked a fitting, final transition for the many American moderns who passed from the hurried world of the mid-nineteenth century to an un-harried next as paying guests. In death, the restlessness of boarding yielded at last to a more permanent place of rest.

Boarding itself was mortal. Having reached its peak capacity in the 1850s, the metropolitan boardinghouse thereafter entered a long period of decline. The lodging house, tenement house, apartment house, and suburban home combined by the turn of the century to render the boardinghouse ever more a residence of the past. Boarders in a sense kept company at the close of life with their dwindling domiciles in this respect. That is to say, boardinghouses themselves went the way of boarders, the gradual decease of the former prefiguring the latter's inevitable passage from youthful promise to aged obsolescence.

Yet, despite their downward trajectory, boarders and boardinghouses together have undergone a revival of sorts in our own day. Boarding first achieved a regional afterlife following the Civil War. As boarding along the nation's northeastern seaboard slowed into the Gilded Age and after, it simultaneously was expanding into the still-developing U.S. South and West. Long-delayed market and industrial revolutions led the way, finally penetrating these pockets of premodern resistance.[1] Urban-style living—namely, boarding—arrived shortly after, the necessary corollary of nationwide modernization. Boarding traveled in other directions as well. Crossing the Rockies, bypassing Mason-Dixon, the boardinghouse also entered new avenues of popular cultural expression at the dawn of the twentieth century. Music no less than literature and film wrote the boardinghouse into ragtime, wartime, hard times, blues, and old-time string-band classics. In addition, and looking ahead a few decades, baby-boom authors, in league with millions of television viewers, since then have managed to retain a prime place for boarding at this, the start of another century. Having died, boarding lives on in the Western urban imaginary, providing the source for much of what passes to this day as mainstream life and living-room art.

Long before that revival, the grand boardinghouse finale seems to have struck a responsive chord with boarder-authors throughout the transatlantic world. To end one's lease on life—or better yet, to read of some other renter's contract expiring, literally and permanently—caught the public imagination at a historical moment when boarding was in fact the setting within which many metropolitans breathed their last. A short stroll through antebellum letters accordingly reveals the strong scent of boardinghouse death. The French novelist Balzac releases his aged boarding protagonist, Père Goriot, in the upstairs chamber of a Paris boardinghouse. One suspects it is the paradoxical isolation of city living that kills the old man, as an unmoved housemate begs his fellow residents when the occasion comes to "leave Père Goriot alone" so they can continue with the evening's meal. The widely read Catharine Sedgwick developed an American version of the same conceit. Her miser "Smith" dies penniless and friendless in a New York boardinghouse garret at the opening of Sedgwick's novel *Clarence*. Fanny Fern repeats the morbid motif with her sketch of a "sick bachelor," alone in a "gloomy" boardinghouse room, awaiting a doctor's visit. Meanwhile, author and editor Sarah Josepha Hale extends boardinghouse death to its nineteenth-century rhetorical limits by turning a fictional hotel dining-room into the unlikely place of one boarder's wake. There is nothing sentimental about death at Hale's house. Nor is there elsewhere: inquiring how a just-deceased boarder "cut up"—which is to say, how much money he left behind—one diamond-studded resident in the Boston boardinghouse of Oliver Wendell Holmes's "Professor at the Breakfast-Table" series from 1859 reduces boardinghouse death to its base essentials. All of which is to say that there was once an acknowledged figure for checking out from this world; antebellum boarding provided the form of that figure, in less than sacred ways.[2]

Maybe more than any other writer from the period, American author Edgar Allan Poe elected death in the boardinghouse as a standard feature of his work. Few would deny death's presence in the author's oeuvre. But Poe, like so many of his contemporaries, did not simply contemplate death in his poetry and prose; he did so in company with his own and his characters' confining boardinghouse surroundings. Poe famously—and, perhaps, residentially—composed his poem "Dreamland" from the quintessential position of modernity, "Out of Space—Out of Time."[3] Yet it was fittingly with what one scholar calls the "condensed" quality of his *short* story form that Poe was able at once to approximate the circumscribed scope of the modern metropolis, even as he demonstrates an "inmost structure" of "syntactical control" that William Carlos Williams lauds on the highest modernist "prosodic grounds."[4] Poe's biographer, Kenneth Silverman, detects an "urban note" already beginning to appear in his subject's fiction in the late 1830s and early 1840s. This was, not coincidentally, the period of Poe's residence in Philadelphia and New York. It was also the most boarding-intensive span of his life. The author, his wife Virginia, and his mother-in-law, Mrs. Clemm, left Manhattan in early 1838 for the metropolis due south, landing in the Philadelphia boardinghouse of Mrs. C. Jones at 202 Arch (now Mulberry) Street. No Poe was dying at the time, although Virginia's tuberculosis was never more than in remission. If anything, Philadelphia boarding was itself associated in the author's mind with starvation, the family reduced at this stage to accepting handouts from a friend to make their board payments. By the middle of the next decade, the Poes were back in Manhattan and staying in a boardinghouse on Greenwich Street. Food this time was plentiful, and the rent cheap, but the residence itself was decrepit: "The house is old and looks buggy," Poe wrote to Maria Clemm. So the couple moved to an establishment off Broadway, near Clinton Street, where an aspiring writer reports having visited Poe in his boardinghouse rooms on the second or third floor of a nondescript dwelling. Poe appears at this time in poet Richard Henry Stoddard's description as the Vincent Price of boarders. Says Stoddard, "He [Poe] was slight and pale, . . . with large, luminous eyes, and was dressed in black."[5] Poe in due course would begin to compose boardinghouse fiction to match the tenor of his mind, the author having made no secret of his disdain for cities and his preference for the stand-alone home when- and wherever he could afford it.

    When read with antebellum boarding as a reference point, Poe's work from this period—like that of significant numbers of his peers—conjures boardinghouse death in subtle ways. Poe's short stories thus reflect not only a certain urban intolerance, but also, and more important, a death-in-the-boardinghouse pattern that recurs throughout the literary record of the day. Many of the author's perennially read works feature both

boarding and death in equal measure, should we condition ourselves as
readers to make that disturbing residential connection. "The Fall of the
House of Usher" (1839) unfolds through the consciousness of a bachelor-
narrator who is "boarding" in the dysfunctional ancestral hall of friend
Roderick Usher. "The Man of the Crowd" (1840) comes to us through
another bachelor-narrator, this one boarding while convalescing at a London hotel. The eponymous "William Wilson" (1839) flees the shadow of
his former self on a tour through metropolitan Europe after boarding
through his school days at Eton and Oxford. He tours Paris, Vienna,
Berlin, and Moscow—no doubt boarding along the way—before slay-
ing his doppelgänger in Rome. "The Masque of the Red Death" (1842),
too, continues the trend. Poe's protagonist in this work, one Prince Pros-
pero, accepts 1,000 courtier "boarders" into his palace to escape a pesky
plague, only for death figuratively to come knocking at the door. Boarding out is downright dangerous in Poe's fiction.

      Another of his tales, "The Murders in the Rue Morgue" (1841), offers
some clues as to why the author arranges for the deaths of so many boarders. The story indeed does serve witness to the virtuoso aesthetic effects of
which Poe was capable, as any reader can testify. It likewise remains for
many a blueprint for the carefully wrought detective fiction of a later age.
Yet there is an additional trait by which we might remember this short
narrative—its skillful handling of death in the antebellum boardinghouse.
"Murders" opens with an unnamed narrator accepting his faded gentleman friend, Auguste Dupin, into the shuttered mansion that he is renting
in a retired neighborhood of Paris. The clairvoyant Dupin "boards" for
free, and the two men quickly establish a comfortable platonic bond that
Kenneth Silverman invokes as a fitting figure for a hard-luck author like
Poe, considering the latter's alleged "lifelong yearning for domesticity."[6]

      Outright residential ownership is not at issue here; autonomous urban
space-time is instead at stake. And, by the speaker's standards—proxy
for Poe's—the two men have reached an elusive metropolitan domestic
ideal. "We existed within ourselves alone," boasts the narrator (166). Or,
in other words, they might be renters, but they have not been reduced to
boarding, lodging, or some makeshift communal equivalent pressed upon
them by the exigencies of city living. Moving forward, this decidedly
urban story predictably increases the tempo of its leisurely beginning,
and so foregrounds its metropolitan spatiotemporal orientation after
somewhat abruptly switching scenes to the Rue Morgue. At that fictional
city block, the mother-daughter pairing of Madame and Mademoiselle
L'Espanaye for some six years running have been in the "sole occupancy"
of a four-story townhouse otherwise surrounded by Parisian apartment

buildings (166). Like the narrator and Dupin, the widowed woman and her child "lived an exceedingly retired life," writes Poe (171). They also lived an enviable one, given the rarity in that time and place of so privileged a form of residential independence. Such had not always been the case, however. Having formerly accepted tenants in the past, the women soon grew "dissatisfied" with that arrangement (171). They thus evicted the jeweler who once lived with them—a man who himself had "under-let the upper rooms to various persons"—and claimed the house as their own, "refusing to let any portion" (166).

Lest we conclude that Poe wrote "Murders" as an ode to *not* boarding, we need only turn a few pages more to arrive at a graphic rendition of death in the boardinghouse. Poe challenges the rules of a preexisting rhetoric by further sensationalizing a boarding-dying motif that was already a proven discursive device among contemporary authors. And yet for Poe, death in the boardinghouse was no mere contest at communicating shock. It was a highly personalized written gesture penned by a man for whom boarding was the humiliating byproduct of a low-wage writer's life, and for whom death was a constant companion in that life no less than in his art.

When death comes, then, for the L'Espanaye women, it arrives with a vengeance. Moreover, it imposes boarding upon the bodies of two city women who had dared to defy a modern housing trend that the author himself had been forced to endure. That imposition is as violent as it is swift. An escaped orangutan—belonging to a French sailor who rents rooms in another part of town—duly ends the L'Espanayes' metropolitan idyll after it scales the four stories to their upper chamber and enters without invitation. The enraged animal dispatches the mother by tossing her out the window down to "a small paved yard in the rear of the building" (170). No less grisly is the fate of the daughter, whom the beast beats senseless before cramming her remains up the household chimney. The detective's mind, a mind like Dupin's—mixed with a boarder's worldview, a sensibility not unlike Poe's—will note the final resting spots of the two victims. Madame's "paved yard" is an oxymoron of sorts, a stubbornly fatal pastoral anachronism for the would-be homesteader living amidst Paris's millions. Mademoiselle's chimney is no less brutal a reminder of the costs of city living. Straining after middle-class domestic bliss—a condition more often than not built around a symbolically central hearth—this child of a seemingly *real* urban estate figuratively is lain to her final rest in Poe's well-placed fireplace, where she might under different circumstances have been converted to ashes. With her and Madame both rests that supposed urban autonomy they had coveted. For, in the aftermath of their death, a continuous stream of police investigators and nosy neighbors passes through their front door (not the fourth-story window), converting their supposed domestic fortress into a decidedly *open* house. The structure that the women had inhabited most likely will revert to taking tenants. In that sense, the murders of "Murders" mark not so much death *in* a boardinghouse as they spell the end of the stand-alone urban home. Dupin's departing rejoinder for the Prefect of Police, whom he outsmarts in solving the "crime," is as follows: "I am satisfied with having defeated him in his own castle" (192). These words suggest that even Poe's knowing protagonist has overlooked the author's primary point, however. In the bitter logic of Poe's urban tales, there are no "castles," since the characters of these stories are something other than domestically invulnerable. Poe's city people in fact more often *die* than thrive—sometimes while boarding, or, like the L'Espanayes, while taking pains *not* to board.[7]

Boardinghouse mortality was less and less a worry for later generations of Americans and Europeans. That is not to say the Western world learned to cheat death in the waning days of the nineteenth century. Rather, the boardinghouse itself was in rapid decline. The period from 1860 to about 1900 witnessed a number of socio-cultural changes that made boarding seem at once undesirable, unnecessary, and even passé.

Leading the decline were a new set of economic constraints that undercut the supply-side appeal of boarding as a business decision. With the influx of immigrants to America after the Civil War, not only was the demographic face of the nation's cities changing, but so, too, was the complexion and "mainstream" status of boardinghouses and keepers alike. Rising urban land prices and the spread of tenement slums were forcing much of the U.S. middle classes to the suburbs. With them went the often widowed landladies who formerly had monopolized the boardinghouse trade of America's city centers, but who now felt the above-named double bind: rising operational costs, combined with the fear of ethnic mixing. Taking the place of native landladies were immigrant women. These latter were less fastidious with (to them) foreign notions of gentility, and they soon learned that they could make rented residences profitable by eliminating the once-sacred meals from the traditional boardinghouse package. The boardinghouse thus became the lodging house by way of individual acts of self-interest made by recent arrivals on U.S. shores. Multiplied hundreds, thousands, of times, the meal *not* served ended boarding's decades-long dominance.

Lodging additionally had the great weight of demand in its favor. Smaller lodging houses by century's end had appeared in dense clusters of immigrant neighborhoods, where available housing was limited.

Accommodating six or seven tenants, these residences became a popular residential destination for unskilled workers from southern and eastern Europe who aspired to something other than the miseries of tenement life. The larger lodging houses, meanwhile, capable of holding ten to twelve renters, became home to a swelling middling class whose boardinghouse exodus eventually would direct them to the modern apartment building. Lower white-collar workers were in the meantime leading the charge to the lodging place. Their sheer numbers tilted the urban housing balance forever away from boarding to lodging. This habitational shift also reflects a strong preference among renters for the depersonalized—some might say sterilized—settings of the lodging house. Skilled and semiskilled natives joined the likes of clerks in lodging. British and Canadian immigrants appeared in the larger houses, too, as did second- and third-generation Europeans along with a sizeable pool of working women. In short, boarders across the board followed the drift of urban housing and lodged with ever-increasing frequency. The day might come when they would "settle down" and relocate to the suburbs with others of an emerging middle class, a move made easier in those days with improvements in commuter rail transportation. Until then, and despite the complaints of Progressive reformers like Jacob Riis—for whom the alleged "lodger evil" remained a source of much concern[8]—the lodging house would usurp that critical position in American life once occupied by the boardinghouse.

But the death of the boardinghouse involved more than basic economics. As suggested, city-dwellers as a whole came with time to prefer the independent lifestyle afforded them by lodging. A developing urban infrastructure of cafes, bars, and restaurants meant that many room-renters, single young males in particular, would never miss the shared meals and family-like obligations of boarding. Moreover, and again through practice, the consumer choices gained by this impersonal urban support network came to represent for many not only the liberation of the pocketbook but the very license to cultivate a signature sense of self through an infinite variety of purchase decisions. Lodging possessed a *style* of its own that the implied communal uniformity of boarding could not rival. High-income white-collar workers still might board in finer houses and hotels as a matter of course. Yet, boarding with luxurious benefits was itself a consumer decision in a marketplace of proliferating housing options now dominated by lodging. City supply and demand, then, to some extent helped shift the residential balance of the metropolitan West. But so, too, was the emerging modern urban personality implicated in this transition, as the comparative independence of lodging occluded the enforced, groupthink togetherness of boarding.[9]

The boardinghouse nevertheless has enjoyed a robust literary afterlife. Lodging itself had begun to win a larger and larger share of the American imagination with its ascendancy as a social phenomenon. As a result of its higher profile, that is, the lodging house now shared precisely that urban imaginative space which the antebellum boardinghouse of old had enjoyed alone.[10] But this is not to say that boardinghouse letters simply disappeared overnight. On the contrary, and in a seeming instance of art defying (rather than merely imitating) life, boardinghouse letters entered a renaissance of sorts, even as the real-world boardinghouse died its long and drawn-out death.

A transatlantic world reared both on boarding and its literary discourse to this day has shown no signs of abandoning the boardinghouse; that world instead has managed to preserve for boarding a position of importance in the wider culture. Examples of this persistence are many. The late Victorian writer "Juloc" compiled the older-style rental arrangements then still available in Europe with his memoir *Boarding-House Reminiscences* (1896). The American playwright Leonard Grover wrote four full acts of metropolitan boarding for the stage in *Our Boarding House* (1900), which work reads as a primer of modern preoccupations: street cars, newsboys, elevators, flying machines, commerce, finance, real estate, Italian immigrants, and divorce all receive close boardinghouse scrutiny. Appearing some twenty years later, the comic-strip curmudgeon Major Hoople occupied the serial columns of another "Our Boarding House," as boarding came to inhabit a parallel newspaper universe from the 1920s until 1981. Various works set just before and during the Second World War further treated readers to British seaside boarding, as in Dorothy Whipple's quaint tale "Boarding-House," and to full-blooded boarding American servicemen, from whom Robert Antoni draws a batch of *Erotic Folktales* (2000) incident to an island army base off the coast of Venezuela. Nostalgic for the fin de siècle Paris boarding that she never knew, finally, children's writer Emily Arnold McCully even has opened the boardinghouse from her *Mirette on the High Wire* (1992) to future apartment-dwellers and homeowners.[11] Indeed, boarding well may appear in works that the youths of today read to their own sons and daughters tomorrow.

Boarding was also capable of keeping elite artistic company in its second coming. Louisa May Alcott contrives for her much-beloved Jo March, from *Little Women* (1869), to take her most significant steps toward adulthood through seven months of big-city boarding. In his novel *The Portrait of a Lady* (1881), Henry James's expatriate American Mrs. Touchett indirectly rebuts boarding's liberating tendencies, associating as she does her country's predilection for communal housing with what she perceives to be its bumptious national insistence on politico-cultural independence. The imperial Englishman Rudyard Kipling meanwhile brought boarding to the South Seas when he sang of wandering sailors' loves in "The Ballad of Fisher's Boarding-House" (1888), while heroine Lily Bart's death in a workers' New York boardinghouse ironically breathes some twentieth-century life into belletristic boarding at the close of Edith Wharton's *The House of Mirth* (1905). James Joyce immortalized boarding with his Hibernian tale "The Boardinghouse," found among the collected tales of *Dubliners* (1914) and anticipating by a few years the Italian realist Federigo Tozzi's 1917 piece of the same name. Back across the Atlantic, Sherwood Anderson not only boarded among his fellow bohemian artists in Chicago, but drew on that experience when he wrote a contrastingly somber portrait of small-town boardinghouse disillusionment in *Winesburg, Ohio* (1919). Nineteen-sixties' suburban London boarding is the subject of Irish author William Trevor's novel *The Boarding House* (1965), while peripheral boarding on the distressed socioeconomic edge of America more recently has been the investigative focus of journalist Barbara Ehrenreich in her controversial exposé *Nickel and Dimed* (2001). In Western letters, at least, and despite the societal shift toward lodging, the boardinghouse has kept a room of its own.[12]

It would be fair to say that boarding matured with and in the West, even as it disappeared as a strictly defined residential practice. For not only did the boardinghouse continue to appear in print throughout the twentieth century and on into the twenty-first, but it has reached as well the public's eyes and ears through a variety of alternative media. During his professional training in Germany, for instance, Australian composer Percy Grainger was so inspired by Kipling's boardinghouse verse that he set it to music in the orchestral work *Fisher's Boarding-House* (1899), performed in F sharp major. Boarding also has entered the realm of mass visual communications. American film legend Frank Capra, likewise keen on Kipling, managed in only his second turn in the director's chair to shoot the twelve-minute silent short *Fultah Fisher's Boarding House* (1922). Hollywood has never since tired of boarding. The 1928 film *The Last Command* revolves around the tinsel-town boardinghouse of an exiled czarist general, who now earns a living as a movie extra. *The Ladykillers,* from 1955, stars acclaimed actor Alec Guinness as the London ringleader of a motley group of boarding thieves. The boardinghouse boasts at least one Oscar in the 1977 foreign film *Madame Rosa,* whose title character operates a makeshift boardinghouse for the illegitimate children of post-imperial France. Nor has prime time been able to resist boarding. With some boardinghouse imagination, one might easily see the concept of boarding out behind the modern sitcom. Whether it be *The Honeymooners, All in the Family,* and *Upstairs, Downstairs,* or *Happy Days, Laverne and Shirley, Three's Company,* or *Seinfeld,* boarding-based situations long have been a risible remedy for that ever-elusive, idyllic middle-class home. MTV's *The Real World* and the Hawaiian hotel of Fox Television's *The North Shore* have gone one step further. The "real" TV promised by such programs has turned the internal interpersonal workings of the boardinghouse inside out, converting communal domestic life into a spectator sport for adolescents and young adults—those viewers, that is to say, who are perhaps not quite prepared to purchase a home of their own.[13] The result of boarding's long life is plain enough for anyone to see or hear: on the big and small screens, or even in the orchestra pit, the boardinghouse remains front row and center in the popular mind.

One possible explanation for this residential resilience lies in the quiet counteroffensive that boarding and boarders together have conducted over the last 150 years. It would seem that boarding out, to begin with, has been built into the very same domestic arrangements that were designed to replace a form of antebellum behavior which many metropolitans of the late nineteenth and early twentieth centuries were ready to forget. Much as the modernizing Americans of 1840 to 1860 often finessed the categorical and practical differences between boarding and lodging, or between the boarding*house* and paying for room and board with some small nuclear family, their city-living descendants have found that boarding out is in fact the foundation on which any number of subsequent housing compromises have been built. More than semantics was at stake in the turn-of-the-century lodging house, for example, where tenants shared an occasional meal "at home" with landlord or neighbor. Principled commune dwellers and today's urban co-op apartment owners are also at best one step away from boarding, whether they realize it or not. Catskills hotels trace a direct line of descent to the Jewish boardinghouses that appeared in this region of the United States during the early twentieth century. Thus, it is hardly surprising that many of the aforementioned boardinghouse films and sitcoms were produced by American Jews—a historically floating population not unlike boarders—who came of age in America's northeastern cities and learned early to locate laughter in their shared experience of the mountain getaway.[14] Any recent guest of a bed-and-breakfast, moreover, might ask how, if at all, antebellum boarding was different from what we now consider to be a form of rest and relaxation. There were and are important distinctions to be made between boarding out by necessity and boarding by choice. Yet, however we today decide to designate renters, urban space-savers, and diners-out who eat in common with others, we might remind ourselves that boarding by some other name still remains a close approximation of a once-universal boardinghouse experience. There is no longer a boardinghouse on every city corner, and suburbs everywhere are often interpreted as a rebuke to what was formerly a familiar boardinghouse lifestyle. But boarding as a culturally expressive form continues to inform a wide range of human activities, and so maintains its place in the modern imagination.

Another potential source of boarding's durability traces to related developments in the modern world. With the close of the Civil War, urban industrialization spread rapidly across the U.S. South and West, as it already had done (and continues to do) throughout Europe. America's newest regional cities, like the cities, industries, and markets of the northeastern seaboard earlier, comprised a still-expanding—and newly reunifying—nation, thereby re-creating the conditions under which boarding had thrived in antebellum times. There were magnet metropolises like San Francisco and Denver, which even before the Civil War had utilized boarding to meet their respective pressing housing needs. Or there were southern cities like Atlanta, where the rise of rail, the arrival of northern migrants, and the consequent spread of commerce found locals relying on the postbellum boardinghouse to accommodate a swelling population of transplants and tourists.[15] Boarding at the end of the nineteenth century and beyond had much of an entire continent left to conquer. It might have fallen out of favor elsewhere in the United States, but the boardinghouse was no lost cause.

On the contrary, the American urban imagination of the country's comparative provinces was quick to register the boardinghouse as one of many modern changes in its midst. The literary boardinghouse in fact remained an important artistic vehicle for fathoming urbanization in the nation's regions. And so, while Laura Ingalls Wilder, in her "Prairie Books" series of the 1930s and 1940s, omitted mention of her personal contact with boarders at her father's family-run hotel in Burr Oak, Iowa, during the 1870s—an experience presumably registering with the author as decidedly *un*-prairie-like—her literary peers were prepared to incorporate boarding into their works precisely *because* boarding out remained a sustaining modern rite. Mark Twain, for example, conceived the rough-and-tumble boardinghouse as a metaphor for the rapidly settled Carson City, Nevada, that he captures in his early work *Roughing It* (1872). With his *Mamma's Boarding House* (1958), decades later, author John D. Fitzgerald similarly describes boarding among Native Americans, cattle barons, Mormons, and an emerging middle class in the Utah Territories

during the Taft administration. The South had its own growing urban
middle class; it had its former slaves as well, the two groups not always
being mutually exclusive. Perhaps it was an anxious racial urge to set
these residential worlds apart that compelled Oliver Wenlandt to write
*The Nigger Boarding-House* (1898), a post–*Plessy v. Ferguson* dramatic
send-up of African American boarding. Wenlandt keeps his races separate—there are no white characters in his work; his black boarders are,
in addition, unequivocally unequal, inasmuch as the author depicts them
with full childlike simplicity for a farce that would (dis)grace the minstrel
stage. Aside from such anomalous illustrations of regional boardinghouse
writing, however, boarding-based studies of modernization at the supposed margins of America could achieve moments of the sublime as well.
No less a literary figure than Thomas Wolfe spent the formative years of
his childhood at a boardinghouse in Asheville, North Carolina.[16] Wolfe's
*Look Homeward, Angel* (1929) defines its protagonist's southern experience through the boardinghouse—"Dixieland" is the name of the novel's
central edifice—just as our reception of countless more boardinghouse
books depends on a willingness to accept boarding as the means by which
more than one modern author—be it in the North, South, East, or West—
has inhabited his ever-more urban environment.

Much as big-city boarding survived through far-reaching mass media
such as television and film, the regional boardinghouse has retained its
place in modern life via avenues other than the printed word. Boarding's entrenchment beyond the text began at least as early as the 1930s.
Both boarding and lodging were on the wane during that decade, but the
boardinghouse in particular entered the repertoires of homegrown musi-
cians in those same years. Maybe it was nostalgia for a seemingly simpler
boardinghouse time. Or perhaps it was simply a tongue-in-cheek strategy for forgetting the fallout from the Great Depression. Whatever the
case, a sharp historical reduction in migration and immigration rates, the
resultant shift in the balance of supply and demand for urban American
housing, and the appearance of a welfare state promoting home ownership for low-income families were not, combined, sufficient countervailing
forces to silence boarding. The boardinghouse remained on the national
airwaves, much as it remained on stage in front of American music audiences reeling from a national crisis. In 1934, for instance, the Skillet
Lickers, then America's best-known string band, rolled into San Anto-
nio for their last recording session at the Texas Hotel, group leader Gid
Tanner playing fiddle on the playful number "Tanner's Boarding House."
The song did not concern a literal boardinghouse; the American habitational imagination seldom restricted itself to the facts of boardinghouse

life as such. Rather, Tanner imagined all America—blessed with a benevolent president, Franklin Delano Roosevelt—in effect boarding out at the expense of the federal government. Tanner sings: "Eat corn bread and taters, too, and drink out of a gourd,/My boarding house, my boarding house, where folks don't pay no board." Rhythm Willie and His Gang struck a less upbeat note with the number "Boarding House Blues," while West Virginia's old-time traditionalists The Kessinger Brothers restored some semblance of boardinghouse optimism with their rendering of the classic "Boarding House Bells Are Ringing Waltz." It would be a few years yet before U.S. males mobilized in and around Washington, D.C., to prepare for war, with many of them housed in the boardinghouses that appeared just after December 7, 1941.[17] Until then, and even after, Americans remained as ambivalent toward boarding as the modernizing West had been with respect to its cities from the very beginning.

To claim that the antebellum boardinghouse died, then, is to miss its residual meaning for the American urban imagination before, during, and long after the Civil War, a period spanning some two centuries of metropolitan development. The boardinghouse hardly has been the sole component of a nimble urban imaginary during that time, and yet it has proved both its importance and endurance by weathering a host of social and cultural changes that otherwise would have argued against the persistence of boarding as a national habit. If we can no longer board out just as antebellum Americans did, then we nevertheless can reconnect the chain of boardinghouse thoughts, images, and conceits by which they formally and functionally adapted to the cities rising around them. Those cities are rising still, and so all signs indicate that boardinghouse life, letters, and mixed media will continue to enable the more-than-metaphorical mind to inhabit a modern world.

NOTES

Introduction

The epigraph for this chapter is from Honoré de Balzac, *Le Père Goriot* (1835), trans. Burton Raffel (New York: W. W. Norton, 1994), 15. The French author Balzac found inspiration for this passage in Paris.

1. Q. K. Philander Doesticks [Mortimer Thomson], *Doesticks; What He Says* (New York: E. Livermore, 1855).

2. Janis P. Stout's definition of cities will serve in this study: simply, "large agglomerations of dense population, structures, and ready commodities." From Stout's *Sodoms in Eden: The City in American Fiction Before 1860* (Westport, Conn.: Greenwood, 1976), 4.

3. Marshall Berman, *All That Is Solid Melts into Air: The Experience of Modernity* (New York: Simon and Schuster, 1982), 13–36. See also Michel de Certeau, *The Practice of Everyday Life*, trans. Steven F. Rendall (Berkeley: University of California Press, 1984), 91–114; and David Frisby, *Fragments of Modernity: Theories of Modernity in the Work of Simmel, Kracauer, and Benjamin* (Cambridge, Mass.: MIT Press, 1986), 1–37.

For commentary on the modern in America, see Lewis Perry's *Boats Against the Current: American Culture Between Revolution and Modernity, 1820–1860* (New York: Oxford University Press, 1993), which argues for the rise of the American modern in the decades before the Civil War. In *No Place of Grace: Antimodernism and the Transformation of American Culture, 1880–1920* (Chicago: University of Chicago Press, 1981), T. J. Jackson Lears by contrast conventionally marks the United States's emergence into the modern at the end of the Civil War, after which date he additionally posits the national rise of *anti*-modernism.

4. For more on nineteenth-century Europe's urban residential patterns—and the literary forms that both accompanied and informed them—see Sharon Marcus, *Apartment Stories: City and Home in Nineteenth-Century Paris and London* (Berkeley: University of California Press, 1999).

5. Georg Simmel, "The Metropolis and Mental Life," in *The Sociology of Georg Simmel*, trans. and ed. Kurt Wolf (New York: Free, 1950), 409.

6. Betsy Klimasmith, *At Home in the City: Urban Domesticity in American Literature and Culture, 1850–1930* (Lebanon, N.H.: University Press of New England, 2005), 39.

7. R. W. Emerson, March 20, 1842, from *The Journals and Miscellaneous Notebooks of Ralph Waldo Emerson*, ed. William H. Gilman et al., 16 vols. (Cambridge, Mass.: Belknap Press of Harvard University Press, 1960–82), 8:204.

8. Fuller, in a letter to friend James Freeman Clarke, August 14, 1845, from *The Letters of Margaret Fuller*, ed. Robert N. Hudspeth, 6 vols. (Ithaca, N.Y.: Cornell University Press, 1983–94), 4:136.

9. Robert Alter, *Imagined Cities: Urban Experience and the Language of the Novel* (New Haven, Conn.: Yale University Press, 2005).

10. As Theo Davis explains, the very concept of "experience" carried a precise meaning for authors in the nineteenth-century United States. Davis states that American writers from the period understood "experience" to possess "form . . . as a necessary condition upon which it [literature] can come into being." Literary Americans, that is to say, "did not think of experience, particularly of the experience relevant to texts, as [an] undistinguishable subjective category." "Experience," rather, was understood to be "a discrete integrity apart from the particularity of individual subjects," while literature itself was considered "a form of being governed entirely by the typical"—with Davis describing "the experience" of a contemporary text "as a composition made from the analytic narration of emblematic images." See Theo Davis, *Formalism, Experience, and the Making of American Literature in the Nineteenth Century* (New York: Cambridge University Press, 2007), 27–28.

11. Postmodern theorists highlight a distinction between personal "place" and impersonal "space." According to this logic, which I employ here, "place" is a known, non-abstract quantity, capable of inspiring emotional attachment. By contrast, "space" is comparatively abstract, unknown, and uninspiring; it fills the hypothetical void between "places." See Yi-Fu Tuan, *Space and Place: The Perspective of Experience* (Minneapolis: University of Minnesota Press, 1977); and Edward W. Soja, *Postmodern Geographies: Reassertion of Space in Critical Social Theory* (London: Verso, 1998), 43–75.

12. Lloyd Pratt, *Archives of American Time: Literature and Modernity in the Nineteenth Century* (Philadelphia: University of Pennsylvania Press, 2010).

13. Alter, *Imagined Cities*, ix, 145; and Robert Alter, *The Pleasures of Reading in an Ideological Age* (New York: Norton, 1996), 176; Klimasmith, *At Home in the City*, 1–10; Deborah Epstein Nord, *Walking the Victorian Streets: Women, Representation, and the City* (Ithaca, N.Y.: Cornell University Press, 1995), 49–115; and Raymond Williams, *The Country and the City* (New York: Oxford University Press, 1973), 163–65.

In *The Image of the American City in Popular Literature, 1820–1870* (Port Washington, N.Y.: Kennikat, 1981), 5–6, Adrienne Siegel implicitly extends this generic argument to American literature by documenting early national, antebellum, and postbellum novelistic interest in the city. For the years between 1774 and 1839, she finds just thirty-eight urban novels published in the United States. Between 1840 and 1860, the number of U.S.-published urban novels climbs, in Siegel's estimation, to 340.

14. See, respectively, Patricia Okker, *Social Stories: The Magazine Novel in Nineteenth-Century America* (Charlottesville: University of Virginia Press, 2003), 1–28; Walt Whitman, as cited in "Song of Myself," from *Leaves of Grass* (Brooklyn: Fowler and Wells, 1855), first edition reprint from J. R. LeMaster and Donald D. Kummings, eds., *Walt Whitman: An Encyclopedia* (New York:

Garland, 1998), 55; Margaret Beetham, "Towards a Theory of the Periodical as a Publishing Genre," in *Investigating Victorian Journalism*, ed. Laurel Brake et al. (New York: Macmillan, 1990), 19–32; David Henkin, *City Reading: Written Words and Public Spaces in Antebellum New York* (New York: Columbia University Press, 1998), 101–36; and Linda K. Hughes, "Turbulence in the 'Golden Stream': Chaos Theory and the Study of Periodicals," *Victorian Periodicals Review* 22 (1989): 117–25. For the quotation from Poe, refer to his collected *Essays and Reviews* (New York: Library of America, 1984), 1415. On lyric, see Ivy Schweitzer, *The Work of Self-Representation: Lyric Poetry in Colonial New England* (Chapel Hill: University of North Carolina Press, 1991), 73; and Northrop Frye, "Approaching the Lyric," in *Lyric Poetry: Beyond New Criticism*, ed. Chavisa Hošek and Patricia Parker (Ithaca, N.Y.: Cornell University Press, 1985), 31–37.

15. James V. Werner, *American Flaneur: The Cosmic Physiognomy of Edgar Allan Poe* (New York: Routledge, 2004), 1. On female flanerie, see Janet Wolff, "The Invisible *Flâneuse*: Women and the Literature of Modernity," in *The Problems of Modernity: Adorno and Benjamin*, ed. Andrew Benjamin (London: Routledge: 1989), 141–56.

16. Charles Baudelaire, "The Painter of Modern Life" (1859), from *The Painter of Modern Life and Other Essays*, ed. Jonathan Mayne (London: Phaidon, 1995), 9–10.

17. The flaneur's twentieth-century philosopher, Walter Benjamin, argues that the flaneur saw the city as *continuous* with self rather than *external* to self. The flaneur to which Benjamin refers in making this assertion is that of Baudelaire, in whose work the urban masses lurk as shadowy absence instead of overt presence. Walter Benjamin, "On Some Motifs in Baudelaire" (1939), in *Illuminations*, ed. Hannah Arendt, trans. Harry Zorn (London: Pimlico, 1999), 163.

18. Dana Brand, *The Spectator and the City in Nineteenth-Century American Literature* (New York: Cambridge University Press, 1991). Brand's thinking on the flaneur is revisionist. He argues, first, that the flaneur has a seventeenth-century English origin, and not, as is commonly thought, a nineteenth-century French one. Second, Brand's flaneur arrived in America via the popular periodical essays of Addison and Steele and then through the sketches and novels of Charles Dickens. This latter claim is essential: the flaneur was available to America's Renaissance writers, says Brand, at that exact moment when the city became a central subject in their works. Brand cites Poe's short story "The Man of the Crowd" (1840), Hawthorne's novel *The Blithedale Romance* (1852), and Walt Whitman's poetic persona in *Leaves of Grass* (1855) as three prime instances of the flaneur's importation into American literature.

19. Brand, *Spectator and the City*, 40.

20. Charles Dickens, "The Boarding House," from *Sketches by Boz* (1836; tale originally appeared in the *Monthly Magazine* in two installments, May and August 1834), in *Dickens' Journalism: Sketches by Boz and Other Early Papers, 1833–39*, ed. Michael Slater (London: Phoenix Giants, 1994), 304. Dickens had English imitators, not just American ones. See Joseph C. Neal's short piece

on a London boardinghouse, "The Crooked Disciple; or, The Pride of Muscle," from *Charcoal Sketches, or, Scenes in a Metropolis*, with illustrations by David Claypoole Johnston (Philadelphia: E. L. Carey and A. Hart, 1838), 194–206.

21. For an overview of Balzac's ambivalence toward cities, and his country-man Baudelaire's oblique poetic treatment of them, see Peter Brooks, "The Text of the City," *Oppositions: A Journal for Ideas and Criticism in Architecture* 8 (1977): 7–11.

22. Fuller reviewed the English translation of Balzac's novel on its release in the United States. Refer to her *Tribune* piece, "French Novelists of the Day," for Feb. 1, 1845, as cited in *Margaret Fuller, Critic: Writings from the New-York Tribune, 1844–1846*, ed. Judith Mattson Bean and Joel Myerson (New York: Columbia University Press, 2000), 54. Burton Raffel, the most recent translator of Balzac's novel, cites James at length in his introductory remarks. See Balzac, *Le Père Goriot*, vii.

23. James L. Machor, *Pastoral Cities: Urban Ideals and the Symbolic Land-scape of America* (Madison: University of Wisconsin Press, 1987), xi.

24. Brand, *Spectator and the City*, 8 (for a summary). Brand describes Amer-ica's nineteenth-century infatuation with the flaneur at length in his volume on the subject.

25. Wolff, "Invisible *Flâneuse*," 142.

26. Susan Buck-Morss, "The Flaneur, the Sandwichman and the Whore: The Politics of Loitering," *New German Critique* 39, second special issue on Walter Benjamin (Autumn 1986): 103.

27. Ihab Hassan, "Cities of Mind, Urban Words: The Dematerialization of Metropolis in Contemporary American Fiction," from *Literature and the Urban Experience*, ed. Michael C. Jaye and Ann Chalmers Watts (New Bruns-wick, N.J.: Rutgers University Press, 1981), 97–99.

28. Benjamin, "Motifs," 165.

29. David S. Reynolds's is perhaps the most noteworthy example of this trend. See his *Beneath the American Renaissance: The Subversive Imagination in the Age of Emerson and Melville* (Cambridge, Mass.: Harvard University Press, 1988). See also Michael Denning, *Mechanic Accents: Dime Novels and Working-Class Culture in America* (London: Verso, 1987); Hans Bergmann, *God in the Street: New York Writing from the Penny Press to Melville* (Phila-delphia: Temple University Press, 1995); Wyn Kelley, *Melville's City: Literary and Urban Form in Nineteenth-Century New York* (New York: Cambridge University Press, 1996); Paul Lewis, "'Lectures or a Little Charity': Poor Visits in Antebellum Literature and Culture," *New England Quarterly* 73, no. 2 (June 2000): 246–73; and Mary Esteve, *The Aesthetics and Politics of the Crowd in American Literature* (New York: Cambridge University Press, 2003), 1–58.

30. Refer to Stuart M. Blumin's work on New York *Tribune* staff writer George G. Foster. Blumin regards Foster's city-column newspaper serial from the 1850s as an advance in nonfictional portrayals of the city. From Blumin's "Explaining the New Metropolis: Perception, Depiction, and Analysis in Mid-Nineteenth-Century New York City," *Journal of Urban History* 11, no. 1 (November 1984): 9–38.

31. Siegel, *Image of the American City,* 5; and Stout, *Sodoms in Eden,* 3–4, 15.

32. Lawrence Buell remarks explicitly on "the comparative exclusion of the city and the marks of industrialization from New England literature of place through the Civil War, especially since New England was the first region to industrialize" (300). Yet, he also explains that New England writers were aware of metropolitan developments in the United States, not least because many of them had made personal urban migrations in order to pursue authorship as a paid profession. This latter point here receives further treatment in chapter 1. For more on "minimization," see Buell's *New England Literary Culture: From Revolution Through Renaissance* (New York: Cambridge University Press, 1986), 301.

33. Jennifer Rae Greeson reinterprets not just the content of city literature, but also its context—that is to say, the tacit belief that city literature need be written by urban-based authors, or that this literature need confine itself to one particular U.S. region (namely, the northeastern urban-industrial seaboard) in its appeal. See Greeson's "The 'Mysteries and Miseries' of North Carolina: New York City, Urban Gothic Fiction, and *Incidents in the Life of a Slave Girl,*" *American Literature* 73, no. 2 (June 2001): 277–309.

34. Amy Kaplan, "Manifest Domesticity," *American Literature* 70, no. 3 (September 1998): 581–606.

35. Sarah Josepha Hale, *Keeping House and House Keeping: A Story of Domestic Life* (New York: Harper and Brothers, 1845).

36. Two important exceptions are Betsy Klimasmith's work on the discourses of nineteenth-century American urban domesticity, cited above, and Sharon Marcus's scholarship, also cited above, on corresponding discursive practices in Paris and London. In keeping with her European focus, Marcus centers her discussion on the literatures of communal city living generally, and more or less bypasses boarding, which, as she rightly notes, carried American associations among contemporaries. Klimasmith's study, although it addresses both literary boarding and *Ruth Hall* directly, restricts her inquiries to the urban novel form. As I explain in this and subsequent chapters, I interpret boarding to be a discrete literary form, informed by but distinct from the novel, short story, sketch, and other like forms.

37. The comment comes from Fern's fellow boardinghouse author and sometime friend, Thomas Butler Gunn, whose published writings receive further attention in chapter 1. Refer to Gunn's Manuscript Diaries, vol. 7, Dec. 6, 1855.

38. Fern and Doesticks's creator, Mortimer Thomson, shared more than misleading naming practices for their work. In addition to their common bond in writing about boarding, they also were close personal friends. Thomson was a regular attendee at Fern's informal literary salons, conducted from her Brooklyn home in the late 1850s. He also, following the death of his first wife in childbirth, married Fern's younger daughter, Grace, in the spring of 1861, despite the rumored objections of Fern herself. For more on Thomson's involvement with Fern, refer to Gunn's Diaries: vol. 10, Dec. 22 and 24, 1858, and March 16, 1859; vol. 11, Nov. 13, 1859; and Vol. 16, May 12, 1861.

39. Thomas Butler Gunn, *The Physiology of New York Boarding-Houses* (New York: Mason Brothers, 1857), 31.

40. Wolff, "Invisible *Flâneuse*," 154.

41. For a universalist reading of Thoreau's writings, see Wai-chee Dimock, "Planetary Time and Global Translation: 'Context' in Literary Studies," *Common Knowledge* 9, no. 3 (2003): 488–507.

42. Richard F. Teichgraeber III, *Sublime Thoughts/Penny Wisdom: Situating Emerson and Thoreau in the American Market* (Baltimore: Johns Hopkins University Press, 1995).

43. Robert A. Gross, "'The Most Estimable Place in All the World': A Debate on Progress in Nineteenth-Century Concord," *Studies in the American Renaissance* (1978): 1–15; and Robert A. Gross, "Transcendentalism and Urbanism: Concord, Boston, and the Wider World," *Journal of American Studies* 18, no. 3 (1984): 361–81.

44. Not all recent commentators write with regret of the theatrical qualities of cities. Jonathan Raban, in his influential statement on the performative aspects of postmodernity, celebrates precisely this feature of metropolitan London in *Soft City* (New York: E. P. Dutton, 1974).

45. Roosevelt made his remarks to a meeting of the American Defense Society held in New York City on January 3, 1919. In this his final public message, the former president spoke as follows in the aftermath of the First World War: "We have room for but one language in this country, and that is the English language, for we intend to see that the crucible turns our people out as Americans, of American nationality, and not as dwellers in a polyglot boarding house." See Joseph Bucklin Bishop, *Theodore Roosevelt and His Time, Shown in His Letters*, 2 vols. (New York: Charles Scribner's Sons, 1920), 2:474.

46. For perhaps the clearest indication of this renewed interest in literary urbanism, refer to the special issue on "Cities" from *PMLA* 122, no. 1 (January 2007).

47. As of 1950, there were eighty-six world cities with populations greater than one million. There were 400 such cities as of 2006. And there will be an estimated 550 by 2015. By contrast, what scholar Mike Davis calls the "global countryside" has reached its peak population and should begin to shrink hereafter, heralding what he calls a "new urban order." For additional world urban data, consult Davis's *Planet of Slums* (London: Verso, 2006), 1–2; for the above quotation, see p. 7.

## Chapter 1

1. Whitman made these remarks as the newly hired editor of the New York penny newspaper the *Aurora*. See his "New York Boardinghouses" (March 18, 1842), from *Walt Whitman of the New York Aurora*, ed. Joseph Jay Rubin and Charles H. Brown (State College, Penn.: Bald Eagle, 1950), 22–23.

2. Whitman's remarks on "Wicked Architecture" ran as a series in the New York newspaper *Life Illustrated*. Here he writes that seven out of ten New York homes either had served as commercial boardinghouses, or else casually accepted an occasional boarder. See Whitman's column for July 19, 1856, from

*New York Dissected: A Sheaf of Recently Discovered Newspaper Articles by the Author of Leaves of Grass*, ed. Emory Holloway and Ralph Adimari (New York: Rufus Rockwell Wilson, 1936), 95.

3. Historian Edgar W. Martin writes that in 1860, four-fifths of the American population remained rural—this after the most intensive period of urbanization in the nation's history. Rural Americans, says Martin, continued to opt when- and wherever possible for the single-family home. See Martin's *The Standard of Living in 1860: American Consumption Levels on the Eve of the Civil War* (Chicago: University of Chicago Press, 1942), 148.

4. Nina Baym explains that "nineteenth-century parlance" made the word "apartment" synonymous with "room," both being defined as "any living space with its own outdoor entrance or with a door leading to an outside hallway." A rented room in a boardinghouse fit this definition. Thus, long before there were apartments in the current sense, there were boardinghouse *apartments*. See the explanatory notes to Maria Cummins's novel, *The Lamplighter* (1854), ed. Nina Baym (New Brunswick, N.J.: Rutgers University Press, 1995), 435. An English visitor to America captured the linguistic difficulties peculiar to U.S. boarding: "'Going a-boarding' in America," he wrote, "means lodging and boarding both. Lodgers are invariably called 'boarders,' and 'Where do you board?' is the only way of asking a person where he lives, if he has not a house of his own." Thomas Colley Grattan, *Civilized America*, vol. 1 (1859) (New York: Johnson Reprint, 1969), 111–12.

Even the early national lexicographer Noah Webster searched for a more reliable definition of "boarding" in vain. The 1859 edition (Webster passed away in 1843) of Webster's steady-selling unabridged *Dictionary* (Springfield, Massachusetts: G. and C. Merriam) also blurs the distinction between *boarding* and *lodging*. To begin, Webster variously gives "board" as noun—as in "entertainment, food, diet"—and verb. In the latter case, "board" can be either transitive—as in "to furnish food, or food and lodging"—or intransitive, such that one receives rather than furnishes "food, or food and lodging." Webster's entry for "boarder," meanwhile, tautologically compounds the boarder-lodger problem by defining "boarding" *through* "lodging": "One who has food or diet and lodging in another's family for a reward" (133). Although Webster's definitions for both "lodger" and "lodging" are less than definitive, at least in their relation to "boarder" and "boarding," they do reveal a distinction that seemed widely recognized in practice, if not in speech. Both "lodger" and "lodging" carry for Webster decidedly short-term connotations, more so even than boarding. He gives "lodger" as "one who lives at board, or in a hired room, or who has a bed in another's house *for a night*." "Lodging," in its noun form, appears in turn as "a place of rest *for a night*, or of residence *for a time*; *temporary* habitation; apartment" (673, my emphasis).

5. From Kenneth A. Scherzer, *The Unbounded Community: Neighborhood Life and Social Structure in New York City, 1830–1875* (Durham, N.C.: Duke University Press, 1992), 264–65. For a comprehensive account of boarding, see Wendy Gamber, *The Boardinghouse in Nineteenth-Century America* (Baltimore: Johns Hopkins University Press, 2007).

6. Scherzer, *Unbounded Community,* 99, 264–65, 262–63. See John Modell and Tamara K. Hareven, "Urbanization and the Malleable Household: An
Examination of Boarding and Lodging in American Families," in *The American Family in Social-Historical Perspective,* 2nd ed., ed. Michael Gordon (New
York: St. Martin's, 1978), 57.

7. On boarders versus lodgers, see Michael Gordon, *The American Family:
Past, Present, and Future* (New York: Random House, 1978), 59. For the antebellum perspective, refer to "White Mice," *Atlantic Monthly 5,* no. 29 (March
1860): 333.

8. Elizabeth Blackmar, *Manhattan for Rent, 1785–1850* (Ithaca, N.Y.: Cornell University Press, 1989), 64. For a parallel discussion of boarding as a
form of women's labor, see Wendy Gamber, "Tarnished Labor: The Home, the
Market, and the Boardinghouse in Antebellum America," *Journal of the Early
Republic* 22, no. 2 (Summer 2002): 177–204.

9. Blackmar, *Manhattan for Rent,* 63.

10. Boarding did not abate immediately after the Civil War; nor did boardinghouses simply disappear. On the contrary, American boarding fought a long
but losing battle against alternate housing options throughout the remainder
of the nineteenth century up until the Great Depression of the 1930s. Historian
Michael Gordon argues that it was the postbellum period, which saw America's
urban industrial infrastructure (and thus its need for close-quartered housing)
begin to match that of England's, that marked boarding's American prime. And
yet two factors worked against boarding after the close of domestic combat in
the nineteenth-century United States. The first was the combined alternative of
the lodging house and its closely related successor, the newfangled apartment
building. By the late 1860s, America's middle classes, a sizeable constituency
that earlier had elected to board, were demonstrating an increased readiness for
living arrangements that were less structured than those afforded by boarding.
The lodging house fit this description, as did the imported model of Parisian-
style urban apartment buildings. The one in effect promised a more flexible
form of boarding, while the other replicated the single-family dwelling but on
a reduced scale. The second postwar factor working against boarding was the
Progressive social reform of the 1880s and 1890s. In many reformers' eyes,
"the lodger evil" (Modell and Hareven, "Urbanization," 52), as many activists
called crowded urban living of whatever stamp—whether in tenements, lodging
houses, or even boardinghouses—was the antithesis of the private middle-class
home that they espoused for all Americans, immigrants and working-class "others" included. Such prescriptions worked against boardinghouses, since even
those on the lowest rungs of the housing ladder often internalized Progressive
notions of urban order and cleanliness and began to favor apartment buildings.
Gordon, *American Family,* 59; Modell and Hareven, "Urbanization," 51–52;
and Scherzer, *Unbounded Community,* 97.

11. An overview of nineteenth-century census-recording practices indicates
the problems inherent in interpreting census data. One finds, for example, in
the 1850 federal census (as in previous and subsequent surveys) a column heading for "Profession, Occupation, or Trade of such Male Person over fifteen

years of age." A listing for "Boarding" here would indicate the male household head as a boardinghouse keeper and his residence, in turn, as a boardinghouse. As most boardinghouse keepers were women, the census therefore doomed large numbers of boardinghouses and their keepers to obscurity. It is no less difficult to determine an individual's boarder status, as opposed to occupation. The left-most column for period census returns features a heading for "Dwelling-houses numbered in the order of visitation." One listing here translates as one separate residence. The next column over records "Families numbered in the order of visitation." When multiple surnames appear for a single household—and, more important, when those names are not the same as the household head's and thus indicate the presence of non-kin—one might read the names of these "strangers" as boarders. Any exhaustive count of nineteenth-century American boarders would need to perform this kind of check for each and every city and state, from every completed census, for the entire antebellum period. No one has yet undertaken this herculean task.

12. Modell and Hareven, "Urbanization," 52.

13. Blackmar (67), Gordon (59), Modell and Hareven (54–60), and Scherzer (101) all insist on the urban orientation of antebellum American boarding, without denying the continued existence of nineteenth-century rural and suburban boarders.

14. From Stephen A. Mrozowski, *Living on the Boott: Historical Archaeology at the Boott Mills Boardinghouses, Lowell, Massachusetts* (Amherst: University of Massachusetts Press, 1996), 83.

15. Sean Wilentz describes (and names) New York's "metropolitan industrialization" during the formative years of American workers' class consciousness. See his *Chants Democratic: New York City & the Rise of the American Working Class, 1788–1850* (New York: Oxford University Press, 1984).

16. From Siegel, *Image of the American City*, 3–5.

17. Blackmar, *Manhattan for Rent*, 299; Martin, *Standard of Living*, 148.

18. Fannie Benedict, "Boarding-House Experience in New York," *Packard's Monthly Magazine* 1, no. 1 (1869): 101.

19. Although rare, "steady" boarders paid slightly lower rates than their "transient" counterparts—this according to Isaac Holmes, an Englishman exploring the American eastern seaboard in the 1820s. Refer to his *An Account of the United States of America, Derived from Actual Observation, During a Residence of Four Years in That Republic* (London: Henry Fisher, 1823), 268.

20. Martin, *Standard of Living*, 167; Modell and Hareven, "Urbanization," 57; Stuart M. Blumin, *The Emergence of the Middle Class: Social Experience in the American City, 1760–1900* (New York: Cambridge University Press, 1989), 148, 168, 188; Gunther Barth, *City People: The Rise of Modern City Culture in Nineteenth-Century America* (New York: Oxford University Press, 1980), 43; and Scherzer, *Unbounded Community*, 98–99.

21. Michel de Certeau, *The Practice of Everyday Life*, trans. Steven F. Rendall (Berkeley: University of California Press, 1984), 93.

22. Modell and Hareven, "Urbanization," 54.

23. Neil Harris, *Humbug: The Art of P. T. Barnum* (Boston: Little, Brown, 1973), 20; James Sterling Young, *The Washington Community, 1800–1828* (New York: Columbia University Press, 1966), 97–109; and Paul E. Johnson and Sean Wilentz, *The Kingdom of Matthias* (New York: Oxford University Press, 1994), 88.

24. Modell and Hareven, "Urbanization," 57.

25. Amy Bridges includes boardinghouse keepers with clothiers and grocers in a lower-middle-class grouping that ranks just one socioeconomic rung above manual laborers. At 10 percent of New York's gainfully employed men in 1855, this group consisted of a number of former members of the ostensible working classes (immigrants especially) who had climbed their way into the ranks of small capitalists. It also included women, whom Bridges does not mention in this respect, and whose status as boardinghouse keepers prevented them from having to enter the non-domestic labor force at all. See Bridge's *A City in the Republic: Antebellum New York and the Origins of Machine Politics* (New York: Cambridge University Press, 1984), 48.

26. Boarding did produce a few rare casualties. One was the 25-year-old apothecary L. A. C. Jules, who died from some lead-tainted wine that he drank at his New York boardinghouse. From "Lead Colic Produced by Claret," *Scientific American* 1, no. 26 (December 24, 1859): 414.

27. Philip Hone, as cited in Edwin Burrows and Mike Wallace, *Gotham: A History of New York City to 1898* (New York: Oxford University Press, 1999), 694–95.

28. For the quotation, see Benedict, "Boarding-House Experience," 100. On postmodernity, refer to David Harvey, *The Condition of Postmodernity: An Enquiry into the Origins of Cultural Change* (Cambridge, Eng.: Blackwell, 1990): 302–4.

29. On contemporary Europe's move to the modern domestic, see Sharon Marcus, *Apartment Stories,* 17–50, 83–116. Refer to the "Epilogue" of this present study for further discussion of the U.S. transition to lodging houses, and, later, apartment houses.

30. Historian George Pierson reports on Tocqueville's initial boarding-house encounters in *Tocqueville in America* (1938; rept. Gloucester, Mass.: Peter Smith, 1969), 40–42. Tocqueville records in his journal the difficulties that he encountered in locating a "*pension,*" drawing a specific contrast between that form of domicile, "an inn," and a "private" house. See also Alexis de Tocqueville, *Democracy in America,* vol. 2 (1840), ed. J. P. Mayer, trans. George Lawrence (New York: Harper and Row, 1966), 537; Mary G. L. Duncan, *America as I Found It* (New York: Robert Carter and Brothers, 1852), 203; Charles Mackay, *Life and Liberty in America; or, Sketches of a Tour in the United States and Canada, in 1857-8,* vol. 1 (London: Smith, Elder, 1859), 44; H. F. Fleischmann, "Herr Fleischmann on the Industrial and Social Life of the Americans," *International Magazine of Literature, Art, and Science* 4, no. 2 (September 1851): 160; and Alfred Bunn, *Old England and New England, in a Series of Views Taken on the Spot* (London: Richard Bentley, 1853), 37.

31. Thomas Butler Gunn, *The Physiology of New York Boarding-Houses* (New York: Mason Brothers, 1857), 20. An English émigré, Gunn worked as both a journalist and caricaturist for New York's newspaper world from the late 1840s through the Civil War, after which he returned to his native England.

32. Kenneth A. Silverman, *Edgar A. Poe: Mournful and Never-Ending Remembrance* (New York: HarperPerennial, 1992), 220; Alfred Habegger, *My Wars Are Laid Away in Books: The Life of Emily Dickinson* (New York: Random House, 2001), 191–96; Martha Ackmann, "The Matrilineage of Emily Dickinson" (Ph.D. dissertation, University of Massachusetts at Amherst, 1988), 178–93; and Hershel Parker, *Herman Melville: A Biography, vol. 2, 1852–1891* (Baltimore: Johns Hopkins University Press, 2002), 465, 795.

33. Caleb Crain, *American Sympathy: Men, Friendship, and Literature in the New Nation* (New Haven, Conn.: Yale University Press, 2001), 68; and William Dunlap, *The Life of Charles Brockden Brown*, vol. 1 (Philadelphia: James R. Parke, 1815), 64–67. Brown boarded briefly in Philadelphia during the early 1790s with boon companion William Wilkins. A few years later, on his frequent trips to New York before moving there on a permanent footing, Brown normally stayed in a private home occupied by two close associates. He chose boardinghouse accommodations on occasion, as he did on a trip to Long Island's Rockaway beach, a popular rest and recreation site for New Yorkers. Also refer to Charles H. Brown, *William Cullen Bryant* (New York: Charles Scribner's Sons, 1971), 132; Henry A. Beers, *Nathaniel Parker Willis* (Boston: Houghton Mifflin, 1885), 220–23; and Harriet Jacobs, *Incidents in the Life of a Slave Girl* (1861), from *The Classic Slave Narratives*, ed. Henry Louis Gates, Jr. (New York: Penguin Books, 1987), 481.

34. Martin Duberman, *James Russell Lowell* (Cambridge, Mass.: Riverside Press, 1966), 37; and "Editor's Easy Chair," *Harper's Monthly* 6, no. 35 (April 1853): 704.

35. The radical democrat Buntline perhaps discovered in hotel boarding an ideal life. Unless one paid for the privilege—and few did—eating, drinking, reading, smoking, and lounging were conducted in decidedly public settings at the antebellum American hotel. Overnight guests usually did sleep in private rooms, however. The English traveler Charles Mackay explains the precise nature of boardinghouse accommodations further in his *Life and Liberty in America*, 1:42. On Buntline, refer to Jay Monaghan, *The Great Rascal: The Life and Adventure of Ned Buntline* (Boston: Little, Brown, 1952), 114–68.

36. William Charvat, *Literary Publishing in America, 1790-1850* (1959; rept. Amherst: University of Massachusetts Press, 1993), 1–37. In *A Fictive People: Antebellum Economic Development and the American Reading Public* (New York: Oxford University Press, 1993), Ronald J. Zboray updates the urban implications of Charvat's argument as he explores the nationwide consequences of a city-based print revolution in antebellum America.

37. Charles Frederick Briggs, "The Homes of American Authors," *Putnam's* 1, no. 1 (January 1853): 23–30. On "double insignificance," see Bayard Taylor's partly autobiographical retrospective novel *John Godfrey's Fortunes; Related by Himself: A Story of American Life* (New York: G. P. Putnam, 1865), 200.

38. For more on this urban economic imperative, see Michael Gilmore, *American Romanticism and the Marketplace* (Chicago: University of Chicago Press, 1985).

39. Nicholas K. Bromell, *By the Sweat of the Brow: Literature and Labor in Antebellum America* (Chicago: University of Chicago Press, 1993), 2–38; and Denning, *Mechanic Accents,* 2–61.

40. *New York Tribune* editor Horace Greeley supplies a real-life instance of this narrative in his personal memoir, *Recollections of a Busy Life* (New York: J. B. Ford, 1868), 80–90. James Parton, Greeley's biographer, earlier rehearsed the basic plot line in *The Life of Horace Greeley, Editor of the New York Tribune* (New York: Mason Brothers, 1855), 122–32.

41. N. P. Willis, "Cheap Boarding and True Love," *New Mirror* (October 21, 1843): 38; "A Screw Loose," *Harper's Monthly* 15, no. 89 (October 1857): 629; "Meredith Demaistre, the Pet of the Parvenus," *American Whig Review* 13, no. 74 (February 1851): 132; "Bored to Death," *Harper's Monthly* 18, no. 107 (April 1859): 658–59; and Hershel Parker, *Herman Melville: A Biography, vol. 2, 1852–1891* (Baltimore: Johns Hopkins University Press, 2002): 132. The review of *Pierre* comes from a writer for the New York *Herald* (September 18, 1852). Melville never explains the exact status of the Church of the Apostles, where his protagonist spends the bulk of his miserable urban experience. En route to the Apostles, however, Pierre does encounter two instances of boarding: one at the hotel (most likely a stand-in for New York's Astor House) of his estranged cousin, Glen Stanly; the other at the hotel/boardinghouse (Melville keeps things vague) where Pierre and his female companions reside before settling in, again, at the Apostles. See Melville's *Pierre; or, the Ambiguities* (1852), ed. Harrison Hayford, Hershel Parker, and G. Thomas Tanselle (Evanston, Ill.: Northwestern University Press, 1995), 220, 237, 242, 269. The residentially precarious position of the title character in Melville's short story "Bartleby, the Scrivener" (1853) lends itself to interesting boardinghouse readings as well.

42. Sheila Post-Lauria, *Correspondent Colorings: Melville in the Marketplace* (Amherst: University of Massachusetts Press, 1996). Like scholars Nina Baym, Cathy Davidson, David S. Reynolds, and Ronald Zboray, Post-Lauria emphasizes the diversity of readers in antebellum America, as well as a "correspondent" heterogeneity in terms of available literary forms and reading habits for the period as a whole. Post-Lauria departs from these scholars' shared insights in at least one respect, however. She rightly points out that certain periodicals in antebellum America knowingly identified themselves with particular ideological, political, and literary values. *Harper's,* for instance, took a nonpartisan stance and aimed its family-oriented reading material at a largely middle-class audience, while a magazine like *Putnam's* targeted similar readers but defied the Harper brothers' comparative political conservatism and literary sentimentalism. For a typical boardinghouse advertisement, finally, refer to "Wanted—a Boarding-House," *Harper's Weekly* (October 10, 1857): 652.

43. John Kasson, *Rudeness and Civility: Manners in Nineteenth-Century Urban America* (New York: Hill and Wang, 1990), 28.

44. Kasson, *Rudeness and Civility,* 115.

45. Michel Foucault, "What Is an Author?" (1979), trans. Jasúe V. Harari, in *The Foucault Reader*, ed. Paul Rabinov (New York: Pantheon Books, 1984), 108–9.

46. Young, *The Washington Community*, 99.

47. Karen Halttunen, *Confidence Men and Painted Women: A Study of Middle-Class Culture in America* (New Haven, Conn.: Yale University Press, 1982).

48. Donald Grant Mitchell [Ik Marvel], *The Lorgnette, or, Studies of the Town by an Opera-Goer* (New York: H. Kernot, 1855), 17.

49. Gunn's two co-illustrators were Alfred Waud and Frank Bellew. By all accounts, Waud was the most gifted graphic artist of the three. He would go on to earn fame as an illustrator of the Civil War. Bellew had high literary aspirations and kept company accordingly. His later credits include *The Recollections of Ralph Waldo Emerson* (1884).

50. Charles Mathews, *The London Mathews* (Philadelphia: M'Carty and Davis, 1824), 24–26; Fritz A. H. Leuchs, *The Early German Theatre in New York* (1928; rept. New York: AMS, 1966), 72–73; Benjamin A. Baker, *A Glance at New York: A Local Drama in Two Acts* (1848; rept. New York: S. French, 189–?); Axis Theater Company revival, June–July 2003 (July 19, 2003, at the Axis Theater Co., Greenwich Village, New York; Randy Sharp, director); and Samuel Beazley, *The Boarding-House; or, Five Hours at Brighton; A Musical Farce in Two Acts,* music by Charles Edward Horn (London: C. Chapple, 1811). On the American performance schedule of Beazley's play, see George C. D. O'Dell, *Annals of the New York Stage 2* (New York: Columbia University Press, 1927), 389, and 3 (1928): 350, 366; Reese D. James, *Old Drury of Philadelphia: A History of the Philadelphia Stage* (Philadelphia: University of Pennsylvania Press, 1932), 639, 651, 677; and Nell Smither, *A History of English Theatre in New Orleans* (New York: Benjamin Bloom, 1944), 328. For a later version of dramatic boarding, see Helen Green, *At the Actors' Boarding House and Other Stories* (New York: Nevada, 1906).

51. Halttunen, *Confidence Men and Painted Women*, 172–74; Kasson, *Rudeness and Civility*, 216–56; James W. Cook, *The Arts of Deception: Playing with Fraud in the Age of Barnum* (Cambridge, Mass.: Harvard University Press, 2001), 23–29; and *Godey's Lady's Book* 67 (October 1863): fold-out after p. 288.

52. Lawrence Levine, *Highbrow/Lowbrow: The Emergence of Cultural Hierarchy in America* (Cambridge, Mass.: Harvard University Press, 1988).

53. William Knight Northall, *Before and Behind the Curtain; or, Fifteen Years' Observations Among the Theatres of New York* (New York: W. F. Burgess, 1851), 6–7.

54. *The Banbury Guardian* (England), "Death of Mr. Thomas Butler Gunn, A Veteran Journalist" (April 14, 1904).

55. Random titles from Beazley's catalogue of more than 100 plays suggest boardinghouses in various ways. Selections include *The Boarding-House* (1811); *Jealous on All Sides; or, The Landlord in Jeopardy* (1818); and *Where Shall I Dine?* (1819).

56. From "A Tale of a Fashionable Boarding-House on Greenwich between C. and D. Streets," *The Sporting Whip* (Feb. 11, 1843) [AAS Newspapers].

57. Anna Cora Ogden Mowatt Ritchie, *Evelyn; or A Heart Unmasked: A Tale of Domestic Life* (Philadelphia: G. B. Zieber, 1845), 3.

58. Peter Gibian, *Oliver Wendell Holmes and the Culture of Conversation* (New York: Cambridge University Press, 2001), 50–66.

59. Kasson, *Rudeness and Civility*, 72–77.

60. See note 13, from the "Introduction."

61. Baker, *Glance*. Baker's b'hoy naturally resides at a Bowery boarding-house. See also Leuchs, 72–73; William Dean Howells, *A Hazard of New Fortunes* (1890; New York: Penguin Books, 2001); and Tennessee Williams, *This Property Is Condemned* (1952). See, too, the 1966 film version of Williams's one-act play; director: Sydney Pollack; screenwriter: Frances Ford Coppola (with others); starring: Natalie Wood (as Alva Starr) and Robert Redford (as Owen Legate). Refer as well to Toni Morrison, *Sula* (New York: Knopf, 1973) and, for another haunted boardinghouse, Gene Wolfe's short story of the same name, "The Haunted Boarding House" (1990), from *Strange Travelers* (New York: Tom Doherty, 2000), 209–38.

## Chapter 2

The epigraph for this chapter is the epigraph to Sarah Josepha Hale, *"Boarding Out": A Tale of Domestic Life* (New York: Harper and Brothers, 1846).

1. See Richard Brodhead, "Sparing the Rod: Discipline and Fiction in Antebellum America," from *Cultures of Letters: Scenes of Reading and Writing in Nineteenth-Century America* (Chicago: University of Chicago Press, 1993), 22. Brodhead says that the home on offer in contemporary domestic literature was no fait accompli. It was a process, not a completed end product. Begun during or even before the antebellum period proper, it was still "emerging" with the middle class at century's end. On the socioeconomic obstacles to a completed market revolution and its attendant middle-class lifestyle, see Stephen Conway, ed., *The Market Revolution in America: Social, Political, and Religious Expressions, 1800–1880* (Charlottesville: University of Virginia Press, 1996).

It should be noted that nineteenth-century domesticity did not restrict itself to the territorial United States, or even the urban-industrial West. The "imperial domesticity" of expansionist American foreign policy at the turn of the twentieth century broadcast U.S. notions of home abroad, even as a concurrent cultural embrace of corporate rationalization transformed domesticity both as an idea and social practice inside the geopolitical boundaries of the United States. See Amy Kaplan, "Manifest Domesticity," *American Literature* 70, no. 3 (Sept. 1998): 581–606; and Martha Banta, *Taylored Lives: Narrative Productions in the Age of Taylor, Veblen, and Ford* (Chicago: University of Chicago Press, 1993).

For a historical overview of the urban implications of domesticity, see the following: Blumin, *Emergence of the Middle Class*; John Kasson, *Rudeness and Civility*; Christine Stansell, *City of Women: Sex and Class in New York City, 1789–1860* (Urbana: University of Illinois Press, 1986); and Halttunen, *Confidence Men and Painted Women*.

2. Nina Baym, *Woman's Fiction: A Guide to Novels by and About Women in America, 1820–1870* (1978; Urbana: University of Illinois Press, 1993), 13–15, 17–18. The singular "*Woman's*" from the title of Baym's work carries implications for any boardinghouse analysis. Much as Baym will not generalize for all women in her readings of individual female texts, this present study maintains that no single domestic paradigm is conceptually adequate for all of antebellum America, and that the people and places of that period warrant consideration on something other than conventionally domestic terms.

3. Commentators have downplayed the generic distinctions between romance and the "real" in early American literature. Nina Baym maintains that the "detailed descriptions" encountered in domestic fiction "are sometimes idealized but more often 'realistic.'" Lawrence Buell emphasizes the iconic quality of those households he locates in period New England literature, even as he credits regional author Harriet Beecher Stowe with a sturdy Victorian realist imagination. Philip Fisher devotes an entire monograph to searching for domestic-mimetic "hard facts" in the pages of the historical, sentimental, and naturalist novels that appeared throughout the American nineteenth century. For more on realism and romance in domestic fiction, see Baym, *Woman's Fiction*, 26; Buell, *New England Literary Culture*, 266–68, 304–18; and Philip Fisher, *Hard Facts: Setting and Form in the American Novel* (New York: Oxford University Press, 1985).

4. According to the 1850 U.S. census definition of "city," any settlement the size of 2,500 inhabitants and above received that special designation. Thus, we truly can say that boarder populations in locations such as New York, Boston, and Philadelphia qualified as legitimate cities, both on an absolute and per capita basis.

5. Strictly defined, "separate spheres" refers to the antebellum attempt to *separate* home from a commercial marketplace often identified with the nearest big city. As part-residence, part-business, part-urban landmark, the boardinghouse renders such a separation impossible, and so severely compromises a favored antebellum conception of home. See Baym, *Woman's Fiction*, 28.

6. Richard P. Horwitz, "Architecture and Culture: The Meaning of the Lowell Boarding House," *American Quarterly* 25, no. 1 (March 1973): 64–82.

7. For a historical overview of nineteenth-century domesticity, see Charles Sellers, *The Market Revolution: Jacksonian America, 1815–1846* (New York: Oxford University Press, 1991), 237–68. Barbara Welter explores related domestic questions in her essay "The Cult of True Womanhood: 1820–1860" (1966), from *Locating American Studies: The Evolution of a Discipline*, ed. Lucy Maddox (Baltimore: Johns Hopkins University Press, 1999), 43–66. Historian Mary Kelley, meanwhile, provides a specific literary context for domestic questions in *Private Woman, Public Stage: Literary Domesticity in Nineteenth-Century America* (New York: Oxford University Press, 1984), 220–21, while Stuart Blumin crucially ties domesticity to the American middle class in *Emergence of the Middle Class*, 190–91.

The competing scholarly views on the culture of sentiment, or sympathy, are well-known and do not need restating here. See Ann Douglas, *The Feminization of American Culture* (New York: Noonday, 1977); and Jane P. Tompkins, *Sensational Designs: The Cultural Work of American Fiction, 1790–1860* (New York: Oxford University Press, 1985).

8. The editors of this special issue of *American Literature* promised to "complicate" the topic of literary domesticity with "regard to issues of race, sexuality, class, region, religion, occupation, and other variables." See guest editor Cathy N. Davidson's comments in her opening "Preface: No More Separate Spheres!" *American Literature* 70, no. 3 (special issue, *No More Separate Spheres!*, September 1998): 443.

9. The most recent example of boarding's deferral to the domestic appears in scholar Betsy Klimasmith's work *At Home in the City* (discussed later in this chapter, and in the notes for the "Introduction" to this volume). For all its critical insights, *At Home in the City* misinterprets boarding in several respects. To begin, Klimasmith opens her study of modern urban epistemologies in the 1850s, and so ignores a long and formative foreground in which boarding evolved not only as a residential practice but, more important, as a modern literary form. Furthermore, as I explain in my "Epilogue," although the boardinghouse in literature continued well past its antebellum prime, boarding itself began a decades-long decline after the Civil War as an increasing preference for lodging houses, tenement houses, and apartments ended its former prominence. Klimasmith glosses such distinctions in communal urban living—and their literary corollaries—when it is precisely such distinctions that distinguish the different stages of urban habitat and urban writing alike. Klimasmith similarly diminishes boarding's importance on the basis of genre. The main thrust of her study is to harness urban architecture with the specific literary form of the novel for the latter half of the nineteenth century. This interpretation overlooks a diverse body of writing that I have styled "boardinghouse letters," among which the novel is but one of many forms. Third and finally is the question of scope. As the remaining chapters of this study indicate, boarding's import extends well beyond "urban domesticity." Boarding also informed contemporary attitudes toward love, death, community, class formation, and even institution-building in America. Indeed, boarding arguably bypassed the conventionally "domestic" altogether.

10. Refer to Nina Baym's introduction to Maria Cummins's *The Lamplighter* (1854). See also Baym's *Woman's Fiction*, 26, 45–46.

11. Douglas, *Feminization*, 168; Tompkins, in her afterword to nineteenth-century novelist Susan Warner's *The Wide, Wide World* (1850; New York: Feminist Press at CUNY, 1987), 584–608.

12. On the fate of America's big-city boardinghouses, in and out of print, see the "Epilogue" to this study.

13. Walt Whitman, "Wicked Architecture," *Life Illustrated* (July 19, 1856), from *New York Dissected*, ed. Holloway and Adimari, 92, 96.

14. Hale was not the first American author to relate boarding to the barroom. Several years earlier, Walt Whitman wrote a temperance tract called *Franklin Evans*, in which the title character—a former boarder and reformed drunk—blames the boardinghouse for his fall from the wagon. Says Evans,

"Boarding-houses are no more patronized by me. . . . The comforts of a home are to be had in very few of these places; and I have often thought that the cheerless method of the accommodations drives many a young man to the bar-room, . . . where the road to intoxication is but too easy." Evans also offers what he believes to be an ideal domestic solution to the boarding/drinking problem: "I would advise every young man to marry as soon as possible, and have a home of his own." From Walt Whitman, *Franklin Evans; or, The Inebriate; A Tale of the Times* (1842), ed. Jean Downey (New Haven, Conn.: Yale College and University Press, 1967), 183.

15. The family does make partial recovery. Hale concludes her novel by having Mr. Barclay, a former cotton broker, secure the position of overseer at a large cotton mill outside Boston, specifically in "L – ." Hale of course means Lowell, Massachusetts, the heart of the antebellum American textile industry and the site of large boardinghouse-style dormitories for mill hands. As an overseer, Mr. Barclay avoids more cohabitation. Hale assigns the Barclays a home of their own—provided by the mill, as in fact would have been the case for a managerial-level worker—and thus restores to the family "'domestic peace'" (128).

16. Fanny Fern, *Ruth Hall: A Domestic Tale of the Present Time* (1854; New York: Penguin Books, 1997).

17. "Editorial Notes—American Literature: Fanny Fern's *Ruth Hall*," *Putnam's* 5, no. 26 (February 1855): 216.

18. George William Curtis, "Editor's Easy Chair," *Harper's Monthly* 10, no. 58 (March 1855): 551.

19. *Ruth Hall*'s original publisher, Mason Brothers, reported this sales figure.

20. Hayden White, *Tropics of Discourse* (Baltimore: Johns Hopkins University Press, 1978), 3–4.

21. Klimasmith, *At Home in the City*. For an explanatory statement on "openness and connectedness," see p. 14. For direct application of the latter principle to *Ruth Hall*, refer to pp. 46–50. And, finally, for the direct citation on urban "possibilities for growth, change, and progress," see p. 15.

22. Fern's recent biographer, Joyce W. Warren, reports that Fern and her second husband, Samuel P. Farrington, settled into their own home at 68 Belknap Street, Boston, in 1849. By the next year, the marriage had soured, and the couple moved with their growing family to a boardinghouse at 14 Kneeland Street. Fern records this experience in her 1856 novel *Rose Clark* (New York: Mason Brothers, 1856). See Warren's *Fanny Fern: An Independent Woman* (New Brunswick, N.J.: Rutgers University Press, 1992): 85.

23. Warren (78) gives 7 Columbia Street, Boston, as the author's residential address for this period. The boardinghouse at that location was run by Mr. and Mrs. J. B. Hill. Mrs. Hill formerly had been a housekeeper at the experimental Brook Farm commune in West Roxbury, Massachusetts; her husband and several other of the Hills' Boston boarders actually had been Brook Farmers who were committed to the cause. For more on Brook Farm and boarding, see chapter 6 of this study. One of Fern's housemates reports the weekly rent at their address to have been $3, a standard rate at low-end boardinghouses during this

period. This same former housemate claims that the resident boarders overall had little money at their disposal.

24. Fern's third husband, James Parton, was a journalist-biographer and his wife's literary executor. He was also an ex-boarder who collaborated with the English writer and illustrator Thomas Butler Gunn—author of *The Physiology of New York Boarding-Houses* (1857) and the American authority on boarding—on a book the two men wrote together. A friend of Parton's and later Fern's (whose *Ruth Hall* the conventional Gunn labeled "a bad-hearted book"), Gunn in fact visited J. Parton on and off at the latter's boardinghouse on Waverley Place before Parton and Fern married in January 1856. Thereafter, Gunn renewed his visits to the newlyweds, who were boarding in spells at the stylish Delancy House and then the Waverley House hotels. To gain an idea of how the Partons fared domestically, one might consult the "Hotels" heading under the "City Lodging" section from *Sheldon & Co.'s New York Directory* (New York: Sheldon, Lamport, and Blakeman) for 1845, which displays an advertisement for the Partons' preferred Waverley House, nos. 54 and 56 Broadway. The proprietor, one Willard Whitcomb, "pledges himself to those Ladies and Gentlemen who may select the 'Waverley House' for the purpose of permanent board or transient accommodations, that every attention necessary to secure their comfort will be at their command" (8). From the Waverley, the couple repaired to a starter-home in Brooklyn before settling permanently in a townhouse at 303 East Eighteenth Street, Manhattan.

Upon Fern's death in 1872, James Parton published a memorial volume on the life and writings of his late wife. That volume contains extracts of Fern's work spanning her twenty-year career. See *Fanny Fern: A Memorial Volume Containing Her Select Writings and a Memoir*, ed. James Parton (New York: G. W. Carleton, 1873), 43, 54–59, 197, 202–3. The specific piece cited, "My Old Ink-Stand and I; or, the First Article in the New House," comes from the first batch of contributions that Fern made as part of her own regular column, begun in January 1856, in Robert Bonner's *New York Ledger* newspaper. Note that Fern's first recorded contribution to boardinghouse letters came earlier. On January 21, 1854, the Philadelphia *Saturday Evening Post* ran an article from the then still Boston-based Fern, titled "Boarding-House Experience"; the piece offers opinions on the problem of boarding under sharp landlords. Warren contextualizes these writings in *Fanny Fern*, 119, 150–55.

25. Ronald J. Zboray complicates the stereotypical portrait of who those readers were. According to Zboray, records from the New York Society Library, 1854–56, indicate that one "Leonard" Wyeth charged Fern's *Ruth Hall* during this interval. Similarly "sentimental" works in fact dominate his charge record, casting doubt on the familiar gendered assumption that the antebellum literature of affect was intended only for, or read exclusively by, women. However sizeable was her male reading public, Fern's readers did include at least one 21-year-old male whom the federal census for 1850 reveals was then living with his merchant-father at 776 Broadway. See Zboray's *A Fictive People: Antebellum Economic Development and the American Reading Public* (New York: Oxford University Press, 1993), 170–71.

26. Sandra M. Gilbert and Susan Gubar, *The Madwoman in the Attic: The Woman Writer and the Nineteenth-Century Literary Imagination* (New Haven, Conn.: Yale University Press, 1979).

27. Fanny Fern, *Rose Clark*, 245–46.

28. Lydia Maria Child to Charles Loring Brace (Dec. 5, 1838), LMC Personal and Miscellaneous Correspondence; and Lydia Maria Child, *Letters from New-York* (first series, 1843), ed. Bruce Mills (Athens: University of Georgia Press, 1998), letters 14 (Feb. 17, 1842, p. 62), 21 (June 16, 1842, p. 231, for an editor's note on the Child-edited abolitionist newspaper containing her *Letters*, *The National Anti-Slavery Standard*), and 29 (Oct. 6, 1842, pp. 125–32).

29. Catharine Maria Sedgwick, *The Power of Her Sympathy: The Autobiography and Journal of Catharine Maria Sedgwick*, ed. Mary Kelley (Boston: Massachusetts Historical Society, 1993), 73–105, and editor's introduction, p. 3 (for Sedgwick's "boarded round" quote, made by letter Oct. 5, 1851) and p. 20 (on Sedgwick's boarding school education). See also Sedgwick's "The City Clerk," from *Tales of City Life* (Philadelphia: Hazard and Mitchell, 1850), and *Clarence: A Tale of Our Own Times* (London: Henry Colburn and Richard Bentley, 1830), 1:20–21. Patricia Larson Kalayjian calls Sedgwick's *Clarence* no domestic fiction. Given the novel's interests outside the home, *Clarence* is instead, claims Kalayjian, "one of the first novels of the modern American city" and "a powerful critique of contemporary society." From Kalayjian's "Disinterest as Moral Corrective in *Clarence*'s Cultural Critique," in *Catharine Maria Sedgwick: Critical Perspectives*, ed. Lucinda L. Damon-Bach and Victoria Clements (Boston: Northeastern University Press, 2003), 104–5.

30. Sensational author George Thompson recounts a life spent writing and boarding in *My Life; or the Adventures of George Thompson* (1854), in *Venus in Boston and Other Tales of Nineteenth-Century City Life,* ed. David S. Reynolds and Kimberley R. Gladman (Amherst: University of Massachusetts Press, 2002), 326. Refer as well to Thompson's *City Crimes; or Life in New York and Boston* (1849), ibid.

31. Harriet Beecher Stowe, *Uncle Tom's Cabin; or, Life Among the Lowly* (1852; New York: Oxford University Press, 2002), 25–27.

32. Lydia Maria Child to Charles Loring Brace (Sept. 27, 1842); and Child, *Letters from New-York*, letter 30 (Nov. 13, 1842), 132.

33. Gillian Brown, *Domestic Individualism: Imagining Self in Nineteenth-Century America* (Berkeley: University of California Press, 1990), 1.

34. Nord, *Walking the Victorian Street*, 11.

35. Fern, *Rose Clark*, 263.

36. Fern's biographer, Joyce W. Warren, prefers the term *kunstleroman*, so as to stress the portrayal in *Ruth Hall* of the protagonist's development as an artist. See Warren, *Fanny Fern*, 122.

37. Lauren Berlant, "The Female Woman: Fanny Fern and the Form of Sentiment," in *The Culture of Sentiment: Race, Gender, and Sentimentality in Nineteenth-Century America,* ed. Shirley Samuels (New York: Oxford University Press, 1993), 267.

38. William Cronon, *Nature's Metropolis: Chicago and the Great West* (New York: W. W. Norton, 1991).

39. Betsy Klimasmith, *At Home in the City*, 48.

40. Duncan, *America as I Found It*, 194–208. Duncan and others confine their comments on boardinghouse life in America to the nation's "busy cities," as Duncan states (197). In the view of Charles Mackay, another English observer who visited North America, U.S. boarding as a "rule does not apply to the rural districts." It exists as a phenomenon worth talking about only "in the cities of America." See Mackay, *Life and Liberty in America*, 1:43.

41. Historian Kenneth A. Scherzer explains that, while married boarders were not uncommon in New York's nineteenth-century boardinghouses, families with children under the age of ten were. Boarding in fact began in Manhattan as a way for "semiautonomous" males in their twenties—who were too old to languish at home, and too young (read: too poor) to marry—to establish themselves in the city, where more and more of America's youth came in search of work. Not having children, young male boarders preferred not to board with children. Keen to the needs of their chief clients, boardinghouse keepers in turn discouraged families with children from boarding, at least in the neighborhoods of lower Manhattan where boarding secured its largest antebellum constituency. The result was a child-patterned checkerboard for New York's neighborhoods. Boardinghouse-heavy areas downtown had far fewer children within their precincts. Locations further uptown, meanwhile, saw fertility rates that far exceeded those in downtown areas, and so saw a proportionately larger child population as well. Not by coincidence, these same uptown areas offered private accommodations, like single-family dwellings, in greater (if not great) numbers for those who could afford them. For the most part, boarders could not afford them. See Scherzer, *Unbounded Community*, 110, 267–68.

42. Mackay, *Life and Liberty in America*, 1:44; and Harriet Martineau, *Society in America*, vol. 3 (London: Saunders and Otley, 1837): 132. Note that Martineau was not the first to draw a connection between boarding and race-slavery. There was a widespread perception (popular among the English) that Americans boarded at all because of a shortage of reliable domestic help in the United States. English visitor Charles Mackay blamed that supposed shortage on two New World factors: first, Americans' republican principles, which led native whites to regard menial household service as beneath the dignity of citizenship; and second, the perception that those who did work as domestic servants—"negroes and the newly imported Irish," in Mackay's formulation—"too commonly . . . know nothing whatever of any household duties" (42).

Indeed, African Americans and Irish did provide the primary basis for domestic help in antebellum boardinghouses. This was or was not problematic, depending on one's perspective. Englishwoman Sarah Mytton Maury denied there was a shortage of domestic help in America. There were, she avers, some two years before the Fugitive Slave Law of 1850, enough good slave servants in the South to make northern boarding unnecessary. See Sarah Mytton Maury, *An Englishwoman in America* (London: Thomas Richardson and Son, 1848),

193, 196–97; and Gunn, *Physiology of New York Boarding-Houses,* chapter 24, "The Boarding-House Whose Landlady Is a Southerner," 214–25.

43. William Henry Milburn, *The Pioneer Preacher; or, Rifle, Axe, and Saddle-Bags, and Other Lectures* (New York: Derby and Jackson, 1859), 195; Duncan, *America as I Found It,* 197–98.

44. Milburn, *Pioneer Preacher,* 195–96; James Dawson Burn, on "sensational literature," in *Three Years Among the Working-Classes in the United States During the War* (London: Smith, Elder, 1865), 6.

45. Martineau, *Society in America,* 134.

46. De Certeau, *Practice,* 91–114.

47. It was not uncommon for domestic writers from the antebellum period to impose their personal household visions on boarding. The boardinghouse story of the "humble" Bags, an urban dry-goods bookkeeper, is emblematic in this respect. Bags resides "up town" at a Broadway boardinghouse run by a Mr. and Mrs. Squab, and counts himself fortunate to occupy his current quarters. He describes his boardinghouse as "small, neat, clean, and well furnished," much like the idealized period home. Moreover, the bread and coffee are excellent. Mr. Squab is genial. Mrs. Squab is attentive. Bags can only conclude, "It seems to be the aim of the establishment to attain, though on a small scale, the highest perfection to which boarding-house keeping, as a system, can be raised." This "visionary" scheme he calls a "flattering success." From "How I Live, and with Whom," *Putnam's* 3, no. 15 (March 1854): 320–21.
*Ruth Hall* records a lesser boardinghouse success in Ruth's cousin, John Millet, who like her has migrated to the city for better employment prospects. On cue, his parents worry about the "hard" lot awaiting their "sensitive son." Mrs. Millet in particular worries about John's domestic prospects, stating, "I hope he has a nice boarding-house among refined people, and a pleasant room with everything comfortable and convenient about it; he is so fastidious, so easily disgusted with disagreeable surroundings" (257). That the Millets could harbor such hopes at all suggests a residual place for boardinghouses within the contemporary ideology of domesticity.

48. Elizabeth Hewitt, *Correspondence and American Literature, 1770–1865* (New York: Cambridge University Press, 2004), 2.

49. This oft-repeated phrase appeared frequently in contemporary print advertisements for boardinghouse rooms to let. For an example of Fern's appropriating this phrase for ironic purposes, refer to her short sketch, "Boarding-House Experience," from *Fanny Fern: A Memorial Volume,* ed. Parton, 292.

50. "Our Sons," *Harper's Monthly* 17, no. 97 (June 1858): 61; Fanny Fern, "Glances at Philadelphia," in *Fanny Fern: A Memorial Volume,* ed. Parton, 502; Gunn, *Physiology of New York Boarding-Houses,* 299; and "Andrew Cranberry—Attorney at Law," *Putnam's* 1, no. 1 (January 1853): 19.

51. Susan K. Harris, "Inscribing and Defining: The Many Voices of Fanny Fern's *Ruth Hall*," *Style* 22 (1988): 613; Berlant, "The Female Woman," 270; and Jaime Harker, "'Pious Cant' and Blasphemy: Fanny Fern's Radicalized Sentiment," *Legacy* 18, no. 1 (2001): 52.

288        Notes to Pages 116–120

## Chapter 3

1. Oliver Wendell Holmes, *The Autocrat of the Breakfast-Table* (Boston: Phillips, Sampson, 1858). Two members of Holmes's initial audience deserve special mention. The first was the authority on New York boarding, journalist Thomas Butler Gunn, who admired the sometime boarder Holmes. Upon hearing from an acquaintance that Holmes had "created a disagreeable impression" at Boston's Sketch Club, Gunn wrote in his diary that "the fault may have lain with the club—one is loath to believe unpleasant things of the brilliant 'Autocrat.' " Note Gunn's conflating author and narrator. Another of the *Autocrat*'s admirers was the New York lawyer and diarist George Templeton Strong, who delighted in reading early installments of Holmes's work. Strong also admired Gunn's *The Physiology of New York Boarding-Houses* (1857), suggesting an interesting parallel between two of the age's better-known boardinghouse pieces. See Strong's *The Diary of George Templeton Strong, 1820–1875*, 2 vols., ed. Allan Nevins and Milton Halsey Thomas (New York: Macmillan, 1952), 2:393 (Sunday, March 28, 1858), 349 (Tuesday, July 14, 1857); and the Thomas Butler Gunn Diaries, vol. 12, Tues., Nov. 23, 1858 [MOHS].

2. Holmes's "Autocrat" material first appeared in Boston's new *Atlantic Monthly* magazine beginning in November 1857. Holmes thereafter collected the resulting twelve monthly installments in book form one year after that date, in November 1858.

3. Oliver Wendell Holmes, "The Autocrat of the Breakfast-Table: Every Man His Own Boswell," *Atlantic Monthly* (Nov. 1857): 48. All further references to Holmes's text are to the original serial edition, not the bound book of the same title.

4. Jürgen Habermas, *The Structural Transformation of the Public Sphere: An Inquiry into a Category of Bourgeois Society* (1962), trans. Thomas Burger (Cambridge, Mass.: MIT Press, 1989).

5. Although Habermas considers print to be a conduit of open communication, he discounts the commercial press for producing private commodities that benefit individual owners rather than general members of the public. Like boarding, his print world "blurred" the "clear line separating the public sphere from the private." From Habermas, *Structural Transformation*, 181.

6. Stanley M. Elkins, *Slavery: A Problem in American Institutional and Intellectual Life* (1959; rept. Chicago: University of Chicago Press, 1976), 27–37. For a related institutional view of the Civil War, see David Donald, "An Excess of Democracy: The American Civil War and the Social Process," in *Lincoln Reconsidered: Essays on the Civil War Era* (1960; New York: Random House, 1984), 209–35. For the contemporary Englishman's comment, see Thomas Grattan, *Civilized America*, vol. 1 (1859; rept. New York: Johnson Reprint, 1969), 109–15.

7. On June 16, 1858, delegates at the Republican State Convention in Illinois nominated Abraham Lincoln as their candidate for the United States Senate, pitting him against Democrat Stephen A. Douglas. In accepting the nomination, Lincoln addressed his colleagues with a speech containing the line,

"A house divided against itself cannot stand." The now famous remark paraphrases a statement from the New Testament.

8. In *A Little Commonwealth: Family Life in Plymouth Colony* (New York: Oxford University Press, 1970), historian John Demos examines the private household of early Plymouth as a representative text by which to read the public assumptions and motives informing seventeenth-century English settlement in the New World. One might consider the antebellum boardinghouse, particularly its New England metropolitan variant, in a similar spirit—that is, as a microcosm for the contemporary public sphere of greater Boston.

9. "Community" refers here both to the quantitative and qualitative aspects of social organization. On the one hand, any and all societies depend on the accretion of certain sustaining institutions: families and households; businesses providing goods and services; schools, churches, and hospitals. A "community" might be said to exist when a sufficient number of these institutions cohere. On the other hand, the social organization of a community depends not just on numbers but on the interplay of its constituent parts. Not only must the component structures of a given social organization cohere; the peoples and groups assembled in a society must see themselves as a "community" if that entity is to exist in a strict sociological sense. See *Sociology: An Introduction*, 2nd ed., ed. Neil J. Smelser (New York: John Wiley and Sons, 1973), 89.

10. John Kasson, *Civilizing the Machine: Technology and Republican Values in America* (New York: Penguin Books, 1976), 63; Blumin, *Emergence of the Middle Class*, 192; and Martin Green, *The Problem of Boston*, (New York: W. W. Norton, 1966), 41.

11. Charles Frederick Briggs, *The Adventures of Harry Franco: A Tale of the Great Panic*, 2 vols. (New York: F. Saunders, 1839).

12. For most of the early national period, and continuing through the antebellum era, the nation's elected representatives boarded by regional bloc in Washington, D.C. Historian James Sterling Young writes that individual local boardinghouses, which usually held about thirty residents each, consisted within themselves of southerners, westerners, New Englanders, mid-Atlantic men, and so on, without any attempt made at achieving domestic sectional heterogeneity. Perhaps not surprisingly, these boardinghouse blocs voted unanimously on the floor of Congress some 75 percent of the time. Young is clear on the outcome of this arrangement. The institution of Washington boarding, he states, transformed another "national institution," Congress, "into a series of sectional conclaves" (99). From James Sterling Young, *The Washington Community*, 97–109.

13. Gibian, *Oliver Wendell Holmes and the Culture of Conversation*.

14. David S. Shields, *Civil Tongues & Polite Letters in British America* (Chapel Hill: University of North Carolina Press, 1997).

15. *The Atlantic*'s original masthead underscored the politico-literary nature of its content by advertising itself as a "Magazine of Literature, Art, and Politics."

16. Tea is indeed central to Habermas's historical understanding of the European public sphere. By Habermas's reckoning, early eighteenth-century London hosted some 3,000 coffee houses, where the brewed beverages of tea,

followed in later decades by coffee and chocolate, encouraged open discussion by an emerging middle class of literary, socioeconomic, and political topics. The common meals served in America's nineteenth-century metropolitan boarding-houses arguably continued this democratic trend. See Habermas, *Structural Transformation*, 27–33.

17. Van Wyck Brooks, *The Flowering of New England, 1815–1865* (New York: E. P. Dutton, 1936), 349.

18. Ronald Story, *The Forging of an Aristocracy: Harvard & the Boston Upper Class, 1800–1870* (Middletown, Conn.: Wesleyan University Press, 1980), 3–23. As the title of Story's study suggests, Harvard is in his analysis the citadel of Boston's institutional life. It is, too, a class-restricted training ground for institutional leadership, with the founders and members of organizations like Massachusetts General Hospital and Boston's Athenaeum deriving in large part from prestigious Harvard Yard. Holmes himself was a Harvard alumnus, and his Autocrat makes repeated mention of the college at Cambridge in his talks.

19. Thomas Bender, *Community and Social Change in America* (New Brunswick, N.J.: Rutgers University Press, 1978), 86. The great irony for Bender in this alleged internalization of communal norms, seen especially in the replication of family and friendship alliances among migrants, is that community itself became a "common denominator" in scattered locales throughout the antebellum United States.

20. Vernon Louis Parrington, *Main Currents in American Thought: An Interpretation of American Literature from the Beginnings to 1920*, 3 vols. (1927, 1930; New York: Harcourt, Brace & World, 1958), 2:455.

21. Boston was no exception to the general antebellum rule of explosive urban growth. Metropolitan Boston accordingly met the primary preconditions for mass boarding. What made the city exceptional was its small geographic area. Confined to a narrow peninsula, Boston was severely restricted in its outward growth, and so saw much of its population increases occur internally. One result was a high population density within the city proper. Another was the creation of social conditions that enhanced the appeal of boarding. Contributing, too, to the rise of boarding in contemporary Boston was the lack of low-cost public transportation at midcentury, which slowed the growth of suburbs where an emerging middle class otherwise might have chosen to relocate. As in other U.S. cities, moreover, the desire by Boston's manual laborers to reside near their place of work, often near the city's central business district, further made the boardinghouse a favored form of area residence. With 145,000 inhabitants in 1851, then, and with a third of that number entering and leaving the city each day, Boston was by most any standard a city in flux. It was also by all accounts a city in desperate need of additional housing. The Englishman Thomas Colley Grattan was not alone when he bemoaned Boston's "extreme" housing shortage upon his arrival in the city from England in the late 1850s. By housing, Grattan meant the stand-alone home, not the boardinghouse, finding as he did the "general vulgarity" of boarding to place it beyond serious consideration as a residential option. From Peter R. Knights, *The Plain People of Boston, 1830–1860: A Study in City Growth* (New York:

Oxford University Press, 1971), 19, 66; Susan L. Porter, "Making 'A Home for Some of the Finest People': The Politics of the Genteel Boarding House in Nineteenth-Century Boston," p. 5, a paper delivered at the annual meeting of the Organization of American Historians (March 27, 2004), Boston, Massachusetts; and Grattan, *Civilized America,* 111–12.

22. Medical students and doctors accounted for the majority of boarders at Holmes's first Boston boardinghouse. There were occasional writers as well. Among the latter was Sarah Josepha Hale, who would go on to edit the Philadelphia periodical *Godey's Lady's Book* and write her own boardinghouse account, the novel *"Boarding Out": A Tale of Domestic Life* (1846). For more on Hale and her novel, see chapter 2 of this study. On Holmes and Boston boarding, see Eleanor M. Tilton's *Amiable Autocrat; A Biography of Dr. Oliver Wendell Holmes* (New York: Henry Schuman, 1947), 70–79. Holmes's professional and residential commentary comes from his correspondence: Holmes to childhood friends Phinehas Barnes (March 1831 and Feb. 22, 1832) and James Freeman Clarke (May 11, 1836). From John T. Morse, Jr., *Life and Letters of Oliver Wendell Holmes,* 2 vols. (Boston: Houghton, Mifflin, 1896), 1:69–72, 73–75; 2:269–72.

23. Oliver Wendell Holmes by letter to parents, May 21 and Oct. 30, 1833. From Holmes's Miscellaneous and Additional Papers, 1825–94 [Houghton].

24. Ibid. See the following dates, all from 1833: May 21 and 31, June 21, August 30, and October 30. On Holmes's cosmopolitanism, as evinced through his "Autocrat," see Lawrence Buell, *New England Literary Culture,* 301, 316.

25. Holmes's Cambridge contemporary, the poet Henry Wadsworth Longfellow, had boarded earlier at the same hotel during his own term teaching at Dartmouth.

26. Holmes was to make frequent use of this particular institution while writing his "Autocrat." The wide-ranging reading habits of his narrator meant that the author himself often needed to consult reference books from his local lending library.

27. Richard Brodhead explains that the *Atlantic,* while occupying a place in the same contemporary literary culture that fostered high-circulation story-paper fiction and best-selling domestic novels, nevertheless "helped institutionalize the nonpopular 'high' culture that came to exist 'above' the domestic or middlebrow world of letters" in America. From Brodhead's "Starting Out in the 1860s: Alcott, Authorship, and the Postbellum Literary Field," in *Cultures of Letters,* 79.

28. Edited in its early years by a succession of Boston's literary luminaries— in order, Francis Henry Underwood, James Russell Lowell, James T. Fields, and William Dean Howells—the *Atlantic Monthly,* writes Richard Brodhead, made "high-class family entertainment" its organizing principle. Although the *Atlantic's* board members would have had few commercial objections to a broad audience, their explicitly high-toned editorial designs provide a fair indication of the middle- and upper-middle-class readers whom they targeted. Refer to Brodhead's *The School of Hawthorne* (New York: Oxford University Press, 1986), 100.

29. Peter Dobkin Hall writes of Holmes's "mixed origins"—his father's backcountry beginnings, and his mother's being a proper Bostonian. For Hall, however, Holmes nevertheless shared the anxieties of other members of Boston's ruling class in the 1850s over whether and why they deserved their high stations in life. See Hall's *The Organization of American Culture, 1700–1900: Private Institutions, Elites, and the Origins of American Nationality* (New York: New York University Press, 1982), 198–219.

30. Oliver Wendell Holmes, "The Professor at the Breakfast-Table," *Atlantic Monthly* 3, no. 16 (February 1859): 232–41; and *Atlantic Monthly*, 4, no. 26 (December 1859): 751–70.

31. Holmes's father, Abiel, had lived for a time early in life in Georgia, where he claims to have met with unobjectionable slaveholders. He passed along his observations to his son. An adult Oliver Wendell Holmes lent his not inconsiderable political support to the "Great Compromiser" of 1850, statesman Daniel Webster (another purveyor, with Lincoln later, of the "house divided" biblical allusion), and in 1855 delivered an anti-abolitionist lecture in Manhattan that expounded on the supposed superiority of the white race. For more on Holmes's views on slavery and the Civil War, see Louis Menand, *The Metaphysical Club: A Story of Ideas in America* (New York: Farrar, Straus and Giroux, 2001), 16.

32. The Francophile Autocrat speaks often of his own Paris experience. What he was doing there he never explains. But at one point he digresses, in a momentary merging with the doctor-author, ". . . when coming home from my morning's work at one of the public institutions of Paris . . ." (12:620). Not by coincidence do long sections from the serial appear in French.

33. Stephan Thernstrom, *The Other Bostonians: Poverty and Progress in the American Metropolis, 1880–1970* (Cambridge, Mass.: Harvard University Press, 1973), 4–6.

34. In *Oliver Wendell Holmes and the Culture of Conversation*, Peter Gibian insists that the Autocrat refrains from imposing some central, genteel Boston Brahmin's conversational authority at his breakfast-table. Gibian instead sees the continual outbursts from the Autocrat's supporting cast of characters as indicative of "democratic decentralization" and "carnivalesque vocal diversity" (72–73).

35. Refer to *Southport Secrets*, compiled by Donald Knute Johnson. Also see "Kate Stuart Boarding House" (Southport, N.C.: Southport Historical Society, 1998): 72–75 [NCC]; and the United States flag (with thirty-six stars) flown by the Bushnell boardinghouse during the war and donated by Mrs. Meredith to the Henry Luce III Center for the Study of American Culture [NYHS].

36. The author of the piece was the Philadelphia writer George Lippard. From "Legend VIII: Singular Dream of Mr. Calhoun," *The White Banner* (1851): 118–20. For more on Lippard's racial and political views, see chapter 5.

37. Mikhail Bakhtin, "Forms of Time and of the Chronotope in the Novel: Notes Toward a Historical Poetics," in *The Dialogic Imagination*, ed. Michael Holquist, trans. Caryl Emerson and Michael Holquist (1981; rept. Austin: University of Texas Press, 1994), 84.

38. The Autocrat is worth quoting in full on this point: "May I beg of you who have begun this paper . . . to pay particular attention to the *brackets* which enclose certain paragraphs? I want my 'asides,' you see, to whisper loud to you who read my notes, and sometimes I talk a page or two to you without pretending that I said a word of it to our boarders" (9:235).

39. Thomas Bender, *The Unfinished City: New York and the Metropolitan Idea* (New York: New York University Press, 2002), xv.

40. Oliver Wendell Holmes, "The Flâneur," from *The Complete Poetical Works of Oliver Wendell Holmes*, ed. H. E. S. (Boston: Houghton, Mifflin, 1895), 284–86.

41. Malcolm Cowley, *Exile's Return: A Literary Odyssey of the 1920s* (1934; rept. New York: Penguin Classics, 1994).

## Chapter 4

1. Henry David Thoreau, *Walden* (1854; rept. Princeton, N.J.: Princeton University Press, 1971).

2. Gibian, *Oliver Wendell Holmes and the Culture of Conversation*, 7–8.

3. F. O. Matthiessen, *The American Renaissance: Art and Expression in the Age of Emerson and Whitman* (New York: Oxford University Press, 1941), 133–75.

4. For a representative New Critical reflection on *Walden*'s literary form, see Lauriat Lane Jr., "On the Organic Structure of *Walden*," *College English* 21, no. 4 (1960): 195–202. Among New Historicist readings that retain the formalists' earlier interest in compositional "fusion," the leading example remains David S. Reynolds's *Beneath the American Renaissance*.

5. The details of Thoreau's boarding experiences presented here come from Walter Harding, *The Days of Henry Thoreau: A Biography* (1962; rept. Princeton, N.J.: Princeton University Press, 1982), 21–22, 86, 127, 177. The cited passage appears on page 22. For the particulars of Thoreau's short 1843 stay in New York, see pp. 140–41. Thoreau's two "New York" pieces appeared that same year, respectively, in the *Democratic Review* for October and November. Note, too, that Thoreau boarded in various New England locations while working as a surveyor, as he did in Haverhill in the spring of 1850 (274).

Few besides Emerson scholars realize the depth of the Concord sage's commitment to domestic reform. It was in fact a reform impulse, combined with the flagging health of his second wife, Lidian, that led Emerson to agree to a minor household revolution beginning in 1846. Starting that year, and continuing for sixteen months afterward, Emerson's family simultaneously elected to confine itself to a restricted portion of its Concord home, and to let out the remaining rooms to one Mrs. Marston Goodwin. Goodwin in turn brought in additional boarders—five or six at a time, plus her four children—so that the Emerson household during these years functioned as something of an "ordinary" suburban Boston boardinghouse. With upward of sixteen to eighteen bodies in his house on average, a harried Emerson, after inspecting his protégé's civic-domestic project at Walden, contemplated his own such experiment across the pond from Thoreau during this same interval. See two of Emerson's biographers for further details on this period in his life: Ralph L. Rusk, *The Life of Ralph Waldo Emerson* (New York: Charles Scribner's Sons, 1949), 311; and Robert D. Richardson, Jr., *Emerson: The Mind on Fire* (Berkeley: University of California Press, 1995), 175, 429–30.

6. Henry David Thoreau, *Journal*, vol. 1: 1837–1844, ed. John C. Broderick et al. (Princeton, N.J.: Princeton University Press, 1981), 1:277–78 (March 3, 1841).

7. Robert Milder, *Reimagining Thoreau* (New York: Cambridge University Press, 1995), 29.

8. Stanley Cavell, *The Senses of Walden* (1972; rept. Chicago: University of Chicago Press, 1992), 9.

9. Robert Fanuzzi, "Thoreau's Urban Imagination," *American Literature* 68, no. 2 (June 1996): 321.

10. Sociologist Neil J. Smelser resists the notion that metropolitan status resides merely in vast agglomerations of people. He defines "metropolis" as "a great city together with its immediately surrounding territory, including many rural and urban communities that may have been self-sufficient at some time in the past." The key to this greater metropolitan community's interdependence is, for Smelser, the commercial network formed between the city itself and hinterland. See Smelser, ed., *Sociology: An Introduction*, 85. In his studies of nineteenth-century Concord, Robert Gross employs a similar understanding of metropolis. Of particular interest for purposes here are his "Transcendentalism and Urbanism: Concord, Boston, and the Wider World," *Journal of American Studies* 18, no. 3 (1984): 361–81 (the quotation above comes from p. 361); and "'The Most Estimable Place in All the World': A Debate on Progress in Nineteenth-Century Concord," *Studies in the American Renaissance* (1978): 1–15.

Thoreau, too, understood the rise of the American metropolis as an important social phenomenon. While living on Staten Island in 1843, he wrote home of what since has become an accepted tenet of urban studies—the proverbial power imbalance between city center (Manhattan, in this instance) and satellite community. He states, "But it is rather derogatory that your dwelling-place should be only a neighborhood to a great city—to live in an inclined plane." Refer to Thoreau's Staten Island letter to his mother, written May 11, 1843, from *The Correspondence of Henry David Thoreau*, ed. Walter Harding and Carl Bode (New York: New York University Press, 1958), 100.

11. Michel de Certeau, *The Practice of Everyday Life*, xi–xii, 91–114.

12. Milder, *Reimagining Thoreau*, 53.

13. Lane, "On the Organic Structure of *Walden*," 200.

14. Robert Sattelmeyer, "The Remaking of *Walden*," in *Writing the American Classics*, ed. James Barbour and Tom Quirk (Chapel Hill: University of North Carolina Press, 1990), 61, 75.

15. Milder, *Reimagining Thoreau*, 53–54.

16. Ibid., 53–55.

17. "Comment on New Books," *Atlantic Monthly* 73, no. 435 (January 1894): 138.

18. C. C. Felton, "Emerson's Essays," *Christian Examiner* 30 (May 1841): 253–62, in *Emerson and Thoreau: The Contemporary Reviews*, ed. Joel Myerson (New York: Cambridge University Press, 1994), 89.

19. "Comment on New Books," 138.

20. Moncure D. Conway, "The Great Show at Paris," *Harper's* 35, no. 206 (July 1867): 251; William Henry Channing, "Henry Thoreau, the Poet-Naturalist," *The Living Age* 120, no. 1553 (March 14, 1874): 645 (rept. from the *British Quarterly Review*); Paul E. More, "A Hermit's Notes on Thoreau," *Atlantic Monthly* 87, no. 524 (June 1901): 858; and Charles Dudley Warner, "The Demand of the Industrial Spirit," *North American Review* 139, no. 334 (September 1884): 218–20.

21. John C. Broderick, "Thoreau's Principle of Simplicity as Shown in His Attitudes Toward Cities, Government, and Industrialism" (Ph.D. dissertation, University of North Carolina-Chapel Hill, 1953), 115–27; Lawrence Buell, *New England Literary Culture*, 300; Leonard N. Neufeldt, *The Economist: Henry Thoreau and Enterprise* (New York: Oxford University Press, 1989), 3–4, 10; and Lance Newman, "Thoreau's Natural Community and Utopian Socialism," *American Literature* 75, no. 3 (September 2003): 515–16.

22. Comments from Thoreau's journal suggest that Therien was "content" residing not only outside the reach of most civic institutions; he was happy boarding out as well. Thoreau recounts one of their conversational exchanges over residence as follows: "I said to Therien, 'You didn't live at Smith's last summer. Where did you live? At Baker's?' 'Yes,' said he. 'Well, is that a good place?' 'Oh, yes.' 'Is that a better place than Smith's?' 'Oh, a change of pasture makes a fatter calf.' " From the entry for Feb. 14, 1855, as cited in *Men of Concord and Some Others as Portrayed in the Journal of Henry David Thoreau*, ed. Francis H. Allen (Boston: Houghton Mifflin, 1936), 121.

23. Stanley Cavell residentially restates Thoreau's Lockean formula when he writes "that power over us is held on trust from us, that institutions have no authority other than the authority we lend them, that we are their architects" (*Senses of Walden*, 82). Cavell's rephrasing similarly echoes words from Thoreau's Walden journal: "I have found that the outward obstacles which stand in my way were not living men—but dead institutions. . . . I love mankind I hate the institutions of their forefathers." From *Journal*, vol. 2, 262 (coming after June 20, 1846).

24. Donald E. Pease, *Visionary Compacts: American Renaissance Writings in Cultural Context* (Madison: University of Wisconsin Press, 1987).

25. Imprisoned in Concord (for one night) during the Mexican War over his refusal to pay a poll tax, Thoreau—a would-be institution builder—had as his cellmate a destroyer of institutions in the person of a convicted barn-burner. See Thoreau's "Resistance to Civil Government" (1849), from *The Writings of Henry D. Thoreau: Reform Papers*, ed. Wendell Glick (Princeton, N.J.: Princeton University Press, 1973), 63–90. The quotation comes from p. 76.

26. It has become a critical commonplace to identify Thoreau's two-year term at Walden Pond as a kind of self-induced conversion experience, a pivotal moment during which he turned from intellectual to activist. As John Broderick

explains, the years 1845 to 1847 saw the author advancing "from philosophic aloofness to practical social action, from Emersonian idealism to the championing of John Brown, from individual isolation to collective identification" (115).

27. In *New England Literary Culture*, 300–323, Buell proposes a mid-nineteenth-century New England literature of "antiemigration propaganda" (323), in which genre he includes *Walden*.

28. As many Concordians rearranged their local domestic lives, many more were moving to nearby towns or else the magnet cities of alternate regions altogether. The influx of Irish immigrants into Boston, and thus Concord, after 1845 further complicated New England's settlement patterns. For more on the housing market of Thoreau's Concord, see Neufeldt, *The Economist*, 45–46.

29. Urban print's antebellum ascendancy was not attributable solely to the city's sophisticated publishing and distribution infrastructures. Hans Bergmann explains that period cultural production was a phenomenon both *in* and *of* the city, inasmuch as the runaway success of New York's penny press in the 1830s and 1840s precipitated marked metropolitan changes in the style, tone, and substance of the nation's literature, even among New England's transcendentalists. From Bergmann's *God in the Street: New York Writing from the Penny Press to Melville* (Philadelphia: Temple University Press, 1995), 19–40.

30. Lewis Mumford, *The Urban Prospect* (New York: Harcourt, Brace and World, 1956), 131.

31. Gross in fact applies this phrase not to Thoreau but to another Concordian, Ralph Waldo Emerson. See "Transcendentalism and Urbanism," 363.

32. It should be noted that winter business thrived at urban boardinghouses during the American nineteenth century. Those so inclined, and with adequate financial resources, often sought the snug confines of the city during the year's colder months. Thoreau appropriately welcomes enough "Winter Visitors" in *Walden* to warrant a separate compound chapter title of that name. The season of spring was similarly significant in the annual boardinghouse calendar. It was during this three-month period that many of the nation's residential leases terminated, prompting occupants to pack and seek shelter elsewhere—often, but not always, on the specific day of May 1. *Walden*'s "Spring" chapter is thus its most animated, as all Concord seemingly comes to life in accordance with metropolitan America's May Day moving rituals.

33. Buell, *New England Literary Culture*, 333; and Peter J. Bellis, *Writing Revolution: Aesthetics and Politics in Hawthorne, Whitman, and Thoreau* (Athens: University of Georgia Press, 2003), 134. Bellis applies his communally conscious reading of *Walden* to other texts and authors from the American Renaissance. In his own words, "Hawthorne, Walt Whitman, and Thoreau had [all] sought to fashion a new version of community in response to the nation's economic and racial divisions" (153).

Thoreau's heeding the housing needs of area indigents coincides with a regional service tradition. In his study of U.S. public housing, *From the Puritans to the Projects: Public Housing and Public Neighbors* (Cambridge, Mass.: Harvard University Press, 2000), Lawrence J. Vale credits New England's Puritans with establishing a 350-year American tradition "of public obligation to socially and economically marginal people" (1–2). Vale cites a history of Massachusetts institutions—private charities, almshouses, work- and settlement houses, model tenements, and working-class suburbs, to name a few—that together reflect a continuing, if now secular, seventeenth-century Puritan imperative to sustain the community by supporting one's neighbors. A less charitable view of New England charity informs a literary work contemporary with *Walden*. The anonymous author of *New England's Chattels; or, Life in the Northern Poor-House* (New York: H. Dayton, 1858) argues that the regional impetus for residential benevolence derives not from Christian love, but the venial desire for economic profit. In Thoreau's day, it was not uncommon for New England villages to sell at annual auction to the lowest bidder the legal right to maintain the local poor. Whoever purchased New England's paupers agreed by this arrangement to feed, shelter, and work area "chattels" on the poorest of terms (35).

34. Raymond Williams, *The Country and the City* (New York: Oxford University Press, 1973), 165.

35. Jane Jacobs, *The Death and Life of Great American Cities* (1961; rept. New York: Vintage Books, 1992), 72.

36. Female mill hands in Lowell, Massachusetts, fared better than most boarders in this respect. Boarding in company-constructed boardinghouse dormitories during the 1820s and 1830s, women operatives had the ample institutional life of Lowell proper at their disposal outside of work. Lowell's civic infrastructure included reading rooms, circulating libraries, lecture halls in its Institute and Lyceum, as well as churches in abundance and a Society for the Diffusion of Useful Knowledge. The literary-minded among the women also founded their own journal, the *Lowell Offering*, wherein operatives' sketches, poems, stories, and essays occasionally depicted the public culture associated with the Lowell experience itself. One graduate of Lowell boarding and textile spinning in fact could reflect with fondness on her factory as an "*Alma Mater*." In *Walden*, by contrast, Thoreau figures the factory girl not as a member of the institutionally advantaged, but as a type of the oppressed: "Consider the girls in a factory," he says (136). For more on Lowell boarding, see the introduction to *The Lowell Offering: Writings by New England Mill Women, 1840–1845*, ed. Benita Eisler (Philadelphia: J. B. Lippincott, 1977), 13–41. For additional firsthand testimony on civic-industrial boarding, consult Harriet H. Robinson's *Loom and Spindle; or, Life Among the Early Mill Girls* (1898; rept. Kailua, Hawaii: Press Pacifica, 1976), 25.

Female factory workers were not alone in attempting to achieve personal enrichment through the institution of boarding. Young urban clerks and other aspiring middle-class bachelors—the core constituency of a nineteenth-century U.S. boarder population—also sought self-improvement within the kinds of voluntary associations that abounded in a place like Boston. The boardinghouse itself was an improving community of sorts. One contemporary male reports having listened and learned enough from his better-educated housemates to be able to "astonish my less fortunate friends, by advancing an opinion and displaying a wisdom they can neither understand nor appreciate." Other big-city boarders benefited from easy access to music societies, fraternal clubs, libraries, and service groups, all often located but a few blocks from their boarding-house doors. Refer to the remarks of the self-styled boarder "Bags" in "How I Live, and with Whom," *Putnam's* 3, no. 15 (March 1854): 325. See also Howard P. Chudacoff, *The Age of the Bachelor: Creating an American Subculture* (Princeton, N.J.: Princeton University Press, 1999), 34; and Thomas Augst, "The Business of Reading in Nineteenth-Century America: The New York Mercantile Library," *American Quarterly* 50, no. 2 (June 1998): 267–305.

37. Robert Sattelmeyer, *Thoreau's Reading: A Study in Intellectual History, with Bibliographical Catalogue* (Princeton, N.J.: Princeton University Press, 1988), 51.

38. Harding, *Days of Henry Thoreau*, 22.

39. Thomas Bender, *New York Intellect: A History of Intellectual Life in New York City, from 1750 to the Beginnings of Our Own Time* (Baltimore: Johns Hopkins University Press, 1987), 167.

40. "Boston, July 15, 1849," *North Star* (August 24, 1849).

41. On August 15, 1840, the *Colored American* newspaper ran an advertisement for a "Boarding House in Boston." The proprietor of said house was one "Brother" Joel M. Lewis—presumably black, and reputedly "an intelligent, a very respectable and worthy man, all of which, with his experience, renders him an agreeable host." Lewis's residence at No. 4 Southack Street offered the additional advantage of being in "a very pleasant and healthy part of the city, and but a few minutes' walk from the celebrated Common."

42. As antebellum New York's premier boarder-journalist, Thomas Butler Gunn recorded in his *Physiology* that civic Manhattan officially facilitated immigrants' internal domestic exile by selling city licenses (at ten dollars a year) to the landlords of boardinghouses that specifically hosted new U.S. arrivals (264). Boston, for its part, and by virtue of its large Irish population in the period, maintained many such houses. Gunn also writes of Bostonians separating themselves into New England habitats when visiting Manhattan (210), replicating a trend begun earlier by transitory southerners. The New York boardinghouse boasting a southern landlady was in fact for Gunn a familiar site in the city. He found at one representative establishment "a kitchen full of darkeys" and a wait staff comprised solely of "free niggers" (217). Implicit in Gunn's taxonomy of metropolitan boardinghouses generally is his sense that domestic diversity was something to be avoided rather than encouraged. Speaking of the hazards of boardinghouse community, he remarks, "We have often thought that the most appropriate simile we could hit upon for a Boarding-House is afforded by what showmen denominate 'a Happy Family'; where a number of animals of incongruous, antagonistic, and conflicting natures, are confined in a single cage" (298). For more on the contemporary sailor's boardinghouse, finally, refer for one example to the *Sixth Annual Report of the Managers of the Seaman's Aid Society of the City of Boston: Written by Mrs. S. J. Hale, and Read at the Annual Meeting, Jan. 9, 1839* (Boston: James B. Dow, 1839), 17–18 [AAS Printed Materials]. Note that the "Mrs. Hale" mentioned here is the American boarder-author and *Godey's Lady's Book* editor Sarah Josepha Hale.

Note, too, that the aforementioned Seaman's Aid Society later would advertise on the back page of its *Thirteenth Annual Report* (Boston: Eastburn's, 1846) a "Mariner's House" at 221 Ann Street, Boston, where boarder-sailors were sure to find a "wholesome" residence (33).

43. Its civic limitations notwithstanding, Boston-area boarding did serve various political functions during the U.S. Civil War. The residential case of Mrs. Susan Forbes provides one suggestive example. Throughout the 1850s and 1860s, Forbes operated a Boston boardinghouse where abolitionism and unionism formally constituted the household ideologies. Forbes regularly attended local abolitionist lectures before the war. Whatever lessons she might have learned there from lecturers Theodore Parker and Wendell Phillips well might have reappeared at the table over which she presided. With war imminent, and with hostilities having commenced, both Mrs. Forbes and her boarders continued to attend torchlight processions held on the city Commons in support of the northern cause. See Susan E. Parsons Brown Forbes, Mrs. Alexander Barclay, Diaries, 1841–1908 (box 1, octavo vols. 14–23, 1856–65) [AAS Manuscripts]. In Worcester, Massachusetts, meanwhile, the Worcester Soldiers' Relief Society provided boardinghouse-style room and board to New England's returning combatants after fighting ended in 1865. Drunkenness was rampant among the homecoming men, but heated quarrels between them were rare. From the Worcester Soldiers' Relief Society, Records, 1861–1865 (folder 11 and octavo vol. 5) [AAS Manuscripts].

## Chapter 5

1. Nicholas K. Bromell, *By the Sweat of the Brow: Literature and Labor in Antebellum America* (Chicago: University of Chicago Press, 1993), 3; Amy Schrager Lang, *The Syntax of Class: Writing Inequality in Nineteenth-Century America* (Princeton, N.J.: Princeton University Press, 2003), 4–8; and Denning, *Mechanic Accents.*

2. Scholars contest the working-class content of George Lippard's work. One of Lippard's earliest commentators (also an architectural historian) adopted the extreme populist position when he wrote of his hero as a "Poet of the Proletariat." See Joseph Jackson, "George Lippard: Poet of the Proletariat," unpublished manuscript biography of Lippard, ca. 1930 [HSP Manuscripts, Joseph Jackson Collection, box 1, folder 12]. Among active scholars, David S. Reynolds is the most vocal spokesperson both for Lippard's "proletarian" politics and the *laboring* qualities of his writings. For an overview, refer to three of Reynolds's studies: *George Lippard* (Boston: Twayne, 1982); *George Lippard: Prophet of Protest: Writings of an American Radical, 1822–1854,* ed. David S. Reynolds (New York: Peter Lang, 1986); and *Beneath the American Renaissance.* Heyward Ehrlich provides a complementary view in "The 'Mysteries' of Philadelphia: Lippard's *Quaker City* and 'Urban' Gothic Fiction," *ESQ* 18, no. 1 (1972): 50–65. And a contemporary reviewer of Lippard's work further maintains that the author's writing "appeals, in structure, plot, incident, and very often language, to the very lowest sympathies and tastes." In a word, Lippard was bound in this commentator's estimation to be "read by the mass," a

code word then as now for the working classes. From "New American Writers," *Holden's Dollar Magazine* (July 1848): 423.

Others deny the author's working-class radicalism. Larzer Ziff has called Lippard a "traditionalist" for his apparent personal investment in "eternal social verities" (97). Christopher Looby characterizes Lippard as less an egalitarian democrat than a proponent of those conservative values espoused by the producers (and readers) of domestic-sentimental literature. Leslie Fiedler, finally, concedes Lippard's having contributed to a new nineteenth-century literature of a "working class," even as he more broadly describes Lippard's fiction as "subpornography" (81), given the author's heavy stylistic reliance on sex and violence. See the following: Ziff's *Literary Democracy: The Declaration of Cultural Independence in America* (New York: Penguin Books, 1982), 87–107; Looby's "George Thompson's 'Romance of the Real,'" *American Literature 65*, no. 4 (December 1993): 651–72; and Fiedler's "The Male Novel," *Partisan Review* 37, no. 1 (May 1970): 74–89.

3. For additional personal testimony on Lippard's working-class commitments, refer to his periodical writings: "The Utility of Novel Writing," *Quaker City Weekly* (May 19, 1849): 3 [HSP Newspapers]; "The Carpenter's Son," *Nineteenth Century*, vol. 2 (January 1848): 72–99 [HSP Periodicals]; and "Editorial Department," *White Banner* (1851): 141 [Library Company Periodicals].

4. Denning, *Mechanic Accents*, 65–84.

5. Cultural studies scholars subscribe to a "semiotics of city living," in which the urban built environment is a text to be interpreted. Historian David Henkin reworks this concept literally. Henkin contends that antebellum urban dwellers had before them a variety of actual readable materials—street signs, advertisements, billboards, handbills, and newspaper columns, among others—that made "reading" the city a less-than-figurative enterprise. For a conventionally semiotic view of the city, see John F. Kasson, *Rudeness and Civility*, 70–111. For Henkin's revisionist reading, consult his *City Reading: Written Words and Public Spaces in Antebellum New York* (New York: Columbia University Press, 1998).

6. Raymond Williams, *Culture and Society, 1790–1950* (1958; rept. New York: Columbia University Press: 1983), xiii.

7. For an explicitly "Marxist geography" of modernity, see Edward W. Soja, *Postmodern Geographies: Reassertion of Space in Critical Social Theory* (London: Verso, 1998), 43–75. By ideological contrast, Philip Fisher examines the modern American "space" of free-market capitalism in "Democratic Social Space: Whitman, Melville, and the Promise of American Transparency," *Representations* 24 (Autumn 1988): 60–101.

8. Leon Chai, *The Romantic Foundations of the American Renaissance* (Ithaca, N.Y.: Cornell University Press, 1987), 23, 48.

9. Kelley, *Melville's City*, 10.

10. Lippard is not the only commentator on antebellum America to rank residence as a constituent element of class. In his study of national class formation, Stuart M. Blumin names five facets of nineteenth-century life—work and consumption patterns, formal and involuntary association, family organization,

and residential location—the comparative, qualitative differences in which contributed to the creation of a hierarchical society in the United States. See Blumin's *Emergence of the Middle Class*, 11.

11. George Lippard, *The Quaker City; or, The Monks of Monk-Hall: A Romance of Philadelphia Life, Mystery and Crime* (Philadelphia: G. B. Zieber, 1844). Lippard began writing his novel in September 1844, after which date serial installments appeared every two weeks in pamphlet form until calendar year's end. The completed novel appeared between boards in 1845 under Lippard's own imprint. Citations here are from the 1845 text, reissued recently by editor David S. Reynolds (Amherst: University of Massachusetts Press, 1995).

12. In Larzer Ziff's aforementioned reading, *The Quaker City*'s serial episodes cohere on the single fictional setting of Monk-hall (*Literary Democracy*, 96). Ziff furthermore contends that setting and not plot structures the novel, an interpretation with which my own domestic reading more or less agrees.

13. See Lippard's preface for *The Quaker City*'s completed 1845 edition, where he defends his own orphaned sister while insisting that his story does not derive from local current events.

14. Philadelphia's historical oystermen conducted brisk business, the shellfish in which they specialized being an abundant local favorite. The Philadelphia oyster opener was likewise a stock figure in literature, often invoked as a representative of the city wage-laborer. The oyster eater, meanwhile, generally was considered a member of at least the middle classes. See Andie Tucher, *Froth & Scum: Truth, Beauty, Goodness, and the Ax Murder in America's First Mass Medium* (Chapel Hill: University of North Carolina Press, 1994), 16.

15. According to William Howard Russell, journalist for the *Times* of London and a visitor to the region at midcentury, "Philadelphia must contain in comfort the largest number of small householders of any city in the world." From Russell's *My Diary North and South*, ed. Fletcher Pratt (New York: Harper, 1954), 16–17.

16. Notwithstanding the many hardships they faced, Philadelphia's antebellum laborers compare favorably to New York's. Far fewer workers from the former city inhabited the kinds of crowded, infested tenements that scourged lower Manhattan during the second half of the nineteenth century. In addition, while by 1870 Philadelphia averaged as a whole six persons per home, or 1.24 families per dwelling, New York saw averages of 14.72 and 2.90, respectively, reflecting a much greater housing crisis for Philadelphia's northern metropolitan neighbor. See Blumin, *Emergence of the Middle Class*, 144–49. For more on Philadelphia's period housing history, refer to Sam Bass Warner Jr., *The Private City: Philadelphia in Three Periods of Its Growth* (Philadelphia: University of Pennsylvania Press, 1968), 52.

17. Blumin, "Explaining the New Metropolis," 15. Whereas Blumin emphasizes Lippard's making "little alteration" to the rich/poor binary terms of the urban sketch genre, David S. Reynolds, in *George Lippard: Prophet of Protest*, 2, reminds readers of the author's work that its informing rhetoric lacks rigorous historical accuracy. Some statistical information from the era therefore better illustrates the "polarization of urban society" of which Blumin writes. By

the end of the 1790s, the top 10 percent of Philadelphia's citizens, according to fortunes measured in real property, owned about half of the city's wealth, with a substantial middling set of professionals and master craftsmen holding the rest. By 1860, Philadelphia's top 10 percent owned 90 percent of the wealth; a privileged one percent owned 50 percent. From Bruce Laurie, *Working People of Philadelphia* (Philadelphia: Temple University Press, 1980), 11–12.

18. Sigfried Giedion, *Space, Time and Architecture: The Growth of a New Tradition* (1941; rept. Cambridge, Mass.: Harvard University Press: 1965), 431–41.

19. In *Emergence of the Middle Class*, 232–37, Stuart Blumin contends that antebellum Philadelphia saw less conflict between its classes than consolidation. Consolidation per se was an ongoing process, however. On the one hand, a vital local tradition of labor militancy persisted well into the period, as workers contested their becoming permanent wage laborers. On the other hand, well-to-do Philadelphians were similarly subject to changes in station. The city could count more millionaires than New York in 1845—the year in which Lippard completed *The Quaker City*'s serial run—but the personal fortunes of these and many more modestly wealthy inhabitants often depended precariously on risky mercantile ventures and real-estate speculation. With, finally, the influx of Irish and German immigrants in the late 1840s and after, class formation continued an incomplete process as the area slowly absorbed a staggering demographic mass of both manual and non-manual laborers. For a brief historical overview, see Gary Nash, *First City: Philadelphia and the Forging of Historical Memory* (Philadelphia: University of Pennsylvania Press, 2002), 163–64; and *Philadelphia: A 300-Year History*, ed. Russell F. Weigley (New York: W. W. Norton, 1982), 327.

20. Debate continues over the composition of an antebellum audience for cheap fiction like Lippard's. The author's contemporary biographer, John Bell Bouton, who was most likely assisted in his hagiography by his human subject, established what long has been the standard view on the readership for *The Quaker City*. Bouton says that Philadelphia's "laborers, the mechanics, the great body of the people" received with much enthusiasm the novel's first two serial installments, which sold at 12½ cents apiece. Literary historians at the dawn of the twentieth century were inclined to agree. Ellis Paxson Oberholtzer, for one, writes that Lippard's readers consisted of "mechanics, laborers, shopgirls, farmers and farmers' wives," "the great body of the population to which the printing-press was now making its appeal." Recalling Bouton, Oberholtzer extends Lippard's audience from city to country and from male to female, but preserves a larger working-class orientation that seems by this later stage to have become de rigueur. Witness Leslie Fiedler. Writing in 1970, Fiedler could assess Lippard's readers—not the "poor" or "lower orders," he says, but the "working class"—without finding it necessary to explain the sociological bases of his terms. Refer to Bouton's (and Lippard's) *The Life and Choice Writings of George Lippard* (New York: H. H. Randall, 1855), 19 [Library Company Printed Materials]; Ellis Paxson Oberholtzer, *The Literary History of Philadelphia* (Philadelphia: George W. Jacobs, 1906), 252–53; and Fiedler, "The Male Novel," 79.

In assessing the readership for dime novels, others have challenged the popular "proletarian" view. Andie Tucher explains that readers of the penny press—the venue in which Lippard serialized most of his fiction—did not derive exclusively from the working classes. Rather, her studies of contemporary newspaper advertisements suggest that prosperous urban businessmen also constituted at least a target audience for cheap dailies, if not a fully realized one. In his examination of the New York Mercantile Library, meanwhile, Thomas Augst finds that young urban clerks, for the most part on the socioeconomic ascendant, demonstrated just as strong an appetite for antebellum fiction, cheap or not, as their working-class peers. From Tucher's *Froth & Scum*, 14–18; and Augst's "The Business of Reading in Nineteenth-Century America: The New York Mercantile Library," *American Quarterly* 50, no. 2 (June 1998): 267–305.

Michael Denning, finally, questions the very attempt to reconstruct an image of antebellum readers. In his *Mechanic Accents*, Denning avers that the identification of once-living, breathing readers is "historically unimportant." Moreover, the "desire to discover 'how such readers read' is unrealistic," he says, and symptomatic of "antiquarian empiricism" (263).

21. Roger Chartier, *The Order of Books: Readers, Authors, and Libraries in Europe Between the Fourteenth and Eighteenth Centuries*, ed. Lydia G. Cochrane (Stanford, Calif.: Stanford University Press, 1994): 1–23.

22. Bender, *Unfinished City*, 15.

23. Soja, *Postmodern Geographies*, 44.

24. Cronon, *Nature's Metropolis*, 279.

25. Louis H. Sullivan, "The Tall Office Building Artistically Considered," *Lippincott's Monthly Magazine* 339, no. 3 (March 1896): 403.

26. Ibid.

27. Henry James, *The American Scene* (1907; rept. New York: Penguin Books, 1994), 60–61, 63.

28. Bender, *Unfinished City*, 34.

29. Douglas Mao and Rebecca Walkowitz, "The New Modernist Studies," *PMLA* 123, no. 3 (May 2008): 737–38.

30. On the Asmodean figure in nineteenth-century American literature, see Dana Brand, *Spectator and the City*, 20.

31. Lippard's varied literary experimentations with domesticity include his handling of the contemporary house-breaking narrative, which quasi-genre he utilizes for the purposes of a subplot in *The Quaker City*. Not only has Devil-Bug served a prison term in the "big house"; he joins with two other accomplices to rob (and kill) the widowed homeowner Smolby. See the sensational novelist George Thompson's full-length example of the house-breaking genre in his *The House Breaker; or, The Mysteries of Crime* (Boston: W. L. Bradbury, 1848).

32. A mystical Christian with working-class sympathies, Lippard revered the biblical Christ as a manual laborer. He even associated in his own mind the twin Christian messages of brotherhood and redemption with the figure of Jesus the Carpenter, a savior who would build a "home," or church, to house all men. Lippard elaborates these symbolic associations in his story "The Carpenter's Son." See note 3, above.

33. The number does not include multiple instances of "threshold" on the same page, of which there are several.

34. There is a long tradition in American fiction of unveiling the urban underworld. Among the writers of the early republic to reveal the concealed misdoings of city-dwellers was the influential Philadelphian, Charles Brockden Brown. Although Lippard read, admired, and emulated Brown's locally set 1799 novel, *Arthur Mervyn*, he made a unique contribution to the urban exposé by bringing to it what David S. Reynolds describes as a fresh "penny-press liveliness," as well as a determined "egalitarianism" that had not existed previously within the genre. From Reynolds, *George Lippard*, 54–55, 112.

35. Lippard's novel originally was to have appeared in ten serial installments, each costing 12½ cents, with an estimated cost for the whole work of $1.25. Lippard and his publisher abandoned that plan after the first seven episodes had appeared, however, thereafter publishing the book in its entirety in two large volumes. Volume 2 alone cost $1.00 upon its appearance in April 1845. From "Literature Notices," *Philadelphia Home Journal* (April 2, 1845): 3 [HSP Newspapers].

36. "Watering-Place Worries," *Putnam's* 4, no. 23 (November 1854): 555.

37. Bruce Laurie (*Working People of Philadelphia*, 12–13, 46) writes that as of 1850, the "typical" Philadelphia wage earner incurred annual expenses of about $500. Most workers earned from $275 to $375 per year. Domestic survival thus often depended on one's willingness to improvise—for example, to forsake the consumption of meat, substitute wood for high-cost coal as fuel, and purchase secondhand clothes. Another strategy for survival was to accept boarders into one's home, provided that one had a home to keep and let for that purpose. Warner, *The Private City*, 135, provides a rough profile of central Philadelphia's boarder population for the year 1840, while Blumin, *Emergence of the Middle Class*, 165–73, 232–33, helpfully describes the heterogeneous socio-spatial patterning of the city's nineteenth-century neighborhoods.

38. The city's single boarders were not alone in their domestic exclusiveness. Joining them were couples of high fashion, high income, or both. In visiting the United States, Englishwoman Francis Trollope wrote that Philadelphia's "first class" of "young married persons board by the year, instead of 'going to house-keeping,' as they [the Americans] call having an establishment of their own." From Trollope's *Domestic Manners of the Americans* (London: Whittaker, Treacher, 1832), 227.

39. On Philadelphia's widowed boardinghouse keepers, see *O'Brien's Commercial Intelligencer* (Philadelphia: John G. O'Brien, 1840): 57 [HSP].

40. For more on a reputed "boardinghouse ethos," refer to Richard Stott, "Workers in the Metropolis: New York City, 1820–1860" (Ph.D. dissertation, Cornell University, 1983), 273. It is also worth recording a contemporary worker's report on urban American boarding. According to the author of *The British Mechanic's and Labourer's Hand Book, and True Guide to the United States* (London: Charles Knight, 1840), "In any of the principal eastern cities he [the "working man"] may meet with very good boarding [by the week] for two dollars and a half . . . , but for three dollars and a half, he can get first-rate

fare at all mechanics' houses, which will suit him much better than those which have the reputation of being a step higher, and for which he would have to pay four or five dollars" (48).

41. Robert Montgomery Bird, *Sheppard Lee* (New York: Harper and Brothers, 1836) [Library Company]; and Balzac, *Le Père Goriot*, 20.

42. "Board for a Lady," *Harper's Monthly* 13, no. 75 (August 1856): 358; "Cinderella—Not a Fairy Tale," *Harper's Monthly* 12, no. 70 (March 1856): 503; Sedgwick, *Clarence*, 1:39; and J. L. Hammer, *The Mysteries and Miseries of Philadelphia, as Exhibited and Illustrated by . . . a Sketch of the Condition of the Most Degraded Classes in the City* (Philadelphia: n.p., 1853), 14 [Library Company Printed Materials].

43. Journalist J. L. Hammer reports that the "capitalist" of Philadelphia's Moyamensing district, a neighborhood adjacent to the Southwark of Lippard's Monk-hall, could rent the room of a lodging house from an absentee owner for 12½ cents per day—the very same price as an original serial installment for *The Quaker City*. Said "capitalist" in turn might lease sleeping space on the floor of that room for two cents per person, continuing in like manner until bodies covered the entire floor. See Hammer, *Mysteries and Miseries*, 15.

44. On boardinghouse bordellos, see Scherzer, *Unbounded Community*, 105–9; Marilyn Wood Hill, *Their Sisters' Keepers: Prostitution in New York City, 1830-1870* (Berkeley: University of California Press, 1993), 196–197; and Timothy J. Gilfoyle, *City of Eros: New York City, Prostitution, and the Commercialization of Sex, 1820–1920* (New York: Norton, 1992), 166–68, 374–75. Like boarders elsewhere, boarder-prostitutes normally shared meals with housemates and kept their own bedrooms.

The boardinghouse bordello was a mainstay of cheap antebellum print. So-called "sporting weeklies," in particular, catered to young male city-dwellers by reveling in prurient tales of forbidden boardinghouse activities. Refer to *The Sporting Whip* (Feb. 11 and 25, 1843) [AAS Newspapers] for a sampling. See also James D. McCabe, *Lights and Shadows of New York Life* (Philadelphia: National Publishing, 1872), 506–7; J. R. McDowell, cited in Hill, *Their Sisters' Keepers*, 93; *Fast Man's Directory to the Seraglios of New York, Philadelphia, Boston, and All the Principal Cities in the Union by a Free Loveyer* (New York, 1859) [Yale, Beinecke]; *The Bachelor's Guide, and Widow's Manual* (New York: A. G. Powell, 1842) [AAS Printed Materials]; and *A Guide to the Stranger, or Pocket Companion for the Fancy, Containing a List of the Gay Houses and Ladies of Pleasure in the City of Brotherly Love and Sisterly Affection* (Philadelphia: n.p., 1849) [Library Company].

In accordance with the Catholic convent theme of "Monk" hall, it is worth noting that New York's Magdalen Society anticipated boardinghouse bordellos with its boarding-style house of refuge for reformed prostitutes, many of whom relapsed. Consult the *First Annual Report of the Magdalen Society of New-York* (New York: J. Seymour, 1813). Note, too, that the character Luke Harvey from *The Quaker City* uses the term "pest-house" to describe Southwark's Monk-hall (45). The character Paul Western, in a retrospective cameo appearance, calls it a "brothel" outright (60).

45. From "Mercer Trial," Philadelphia *Public Ledger* (March 30, 1843): 1–2 [HSP Newspapers]. The house on Elizabeth Street allegedly was kept by a "mulatress" named Mettore (2). For an earlier, New York version of a comparable case—again with fatal consequences for one of the parties involved—see Patricia Cline Cohen, *The Murder of Helen Jewett: The Life and Death of a Prostitute in Nineteenth-Century New York* (New York: Alfred A. Knopf, 1998), 90–110.

46. Legend records that the author, penniless in the early 1840s, squatted for a spell in an abandoned Philadelphia mansion near Franklin Square, which structure would reappear in *The Quaker City* as Monk-hall. Lippard's first biographer, John Bell Bouton, suggests further that the building in question at once fired Lippard's literary imagination, and inspired his inquisitive boarding-house perspective: "Lippard, alone, 'sole monarch' of all he surveyed in that empty house, enjoyed a fine field for the exercise of his imagination," "peering through the keyholes of the hundred rooms, and wondering what awful mysteries were locked within them." From Bouton, *Life and Choice Writings*, 14.

47. *Holden's Dollar Magazine* (July 1848): 423. The novel's episodic structure, encouraged by *The Quaker City*'s serial publication, also provides a parallel with the short-term abruptness of boarding.

48. Not until the 1850s, near the time of the author's death, did light passenger rail service between central Philadelphia and the city's western suburbs permit what today would be considered a comfortable middle-class existence based on independent home-ownership. Even then, the city's suburbs were often the exclusive preserves of the well-to-do. See Laurie, *Working People of Philadelphia*, 10.

49. Christopher Clark, ed., "The Diary of an Apprentice Cabinetmaker: Edward Jenner Carpenter's 'Journal,' 1844–45," *Proceedings of the American Antiquarian Society* 98, pt. 2 (October 1988): 303–94. Clark's cabinetmaker is the aptly named Edward Jenner Carpenter (1825–1900), who boarded with his employer in the western Massachusetts town of Greenfield during the mid-1840s. As Clark writes, "Greenfield was not Boston, by any means," and yet the literary materials and venues (including a local literary club) that Carpenter had available to him suggest the extent to which the town fell within the New England metropolis's sphere of cultural influence. Among but some of the works that Carpenter eagerly read were Sue's aforementioned *The Mysteries of Paris*, Justin Jones's *The Burglars, or the Mysteries of the League of Honor: An American Tale* (1844), the sensational temperance tale *Easy Nat, or Boston Bars and Boston Boys* (1844), and the above-named *The Omnibus of Modern Romance (Six Inside!!)* (1844). For the quotations from Carpenter, see his diary entries for Monday, August 19, 1844, and Friday, October 18, 1844, pp. 353, 363. Ronald J. and Mary Saracino Zboray discuss antebellum reading practices at length in "Reading and Everyday Life in Antebellum Boston: The Diary of Daniel F. and Mary D. Child," *Libraries & Culture* 32, no. 3 (Summer 1997): 285–323. See page 288 for their discussion of the "rhythms of reading." For more on the content and context of antebellum reading, see also Kevin J. Hayes, "Railway Reading," *Proceedings of the American Antiquarian Society*

106, pt. 2 (October 1996): 301–26; and Tom Glynn, "Books for a Reformed Republic: The Apprentices' Library of New York City, 1820–1865," *Libraries & Culture* 34, no. 4 (Fall 1999): 347–72.

50. David M. Stewart, "Cultural Work, City Crime, Reading, Pleasure," *American Literary History* 9, no. 4 (Winter 1997): 677, 684.

51. *Quaker City Weekly*, "An Every-day Dream" (April 14, 1849): 2 [HSP Newspapers]. Lippard allowed his "Legends of Every-Day" to be collected and reprinted in the journal *The White Banner* (issue 1, 1851), which had been launched as the official quarterly organ of Lippard's labor organization, the Brotherhood of the Union. No other issue but this one ever appeared. See the following pieces: "Legend I: The First Leaf of Spring," 101–3; "Legend II: The Dollar," 104–6; "Legend III: The Destroyer of the Homestead," 106–7; "Legend IV: A Sequel to the Legend of Mexico," 107–9; "Legend V: The Dark Sabbath," 110–13; and "Legend XII: Temples Built upon Human Skulls," 122 [Library Company Periodicals].

52. George Lippard, *Life and Adventures of Charles Anderson Chester, the Notorious Leader of the Philadelphia "Killers": Who Was Murdered, While Engaged in the Destruction of the California House, on Election Night, October 11, 1849* (Philadelphia: Yates and Smith, 1849) [Library Company Printed Materials]. On Lippard's authorship of *Chester*, see David Faflik, "Authorship, Ownership, and the Case for *Charles Anderson Chester*," *Book History* (2008): 149–68.

53. Samuel Otter, *Philadelphia Stories: America's Literature of Race and Freedom* (Berkeley: University of California Press, 2010), 169.

54. Urban residence often merges with class violence in Lippard's work. In *The Quaker City*, for example, the Rev. F. A. T. Pyne tells the apocryphal tale of a Philadelphia workman who falls five stories from a scaffold, leaving his wife and children without adequate support (204). Some years later, in "Temples Built upon Human Skulls," from his "Legends of Every Day," Lippard rallies to the defense of such workmen, those responsible for constructing the "magnificent monuments of stone and mortar" that local men of wealth have commissioned as private residences. Lippard minces no words on the subject: "Why for every stone in his [the rich businessman's] building, some widow has been robbed—not an inch of mortar, from foundation stone to roof, but has been mixed with the tears of want and misery" (122). With *Chester*, the author hints at a similar instance of architectural class antagonism. Readers learn that the day-laboring father of the tale's female lead, Ophelia Thompson, died two years since in an accident that recalls the one Pyne relates. As the widow of the deceased explains, her late husband was "killed by fallin' off a building . . ." (22).

## Chapter 6

1. Nathaniel Hawthorne, *The Blithedale Romance* (1852), vol. 3 of *The Centenary Edition of the Works of Nathaniel Hawthorne*, ed. William Charvat, Roy Harvey Pearce, and Claude M. Simpson (Columbus: Ohio State University Press, 1964–).

2. John N. Miller reviews the "dramatic" commentary on Hawthorne in "Eros and Ideology: At the Heart of Hawthorne's Blithedale," *Nineteenth-Century Literature* 55, no. 1 (June 2000): 11. Included in his review is Frederick C. Crews, who had by the 1960s attached dramatic labels like "facile melodrama" and "self-critical comedy" to Hawthorne's novel (from Crews's *The Sins of the Fathers: Hawthorne's Psychological Themes* [New York: Oxford University Press, 1966], 194). More recently, Kenneth Marc Harris has insisted on theater as the "sustaining metaphor" of *Blithedale*, emphasizing its narrator's aligning himself with a Greek chorus both of and beyond the dramatic action of the tale. See Harris's *Hypocrisy and Self-Deception in Hawthorne's Fiction* (Charlottesville: University Press of Virginia, 1988), 135–36. Jonathan Auerbach, to complete this survey, extends the notion of theater as a dramatic device in Hawthorne's book to claim that same device as a basis for understanding the author's fiction generally. Refer to Auerbach's *The Romance of Failure: First-Person Fictions of Poe, Hawthorne, and James* (New York: Oxford University Press, 1989), 71–117.

3. There is no consensus on Hawthorne's status as a sentimentalist. Jane P. Tompkins contends that the author was (and remains) the critical darling of a literary community little interested in the sentimental productions of women writers. From Tompkins's *Sensational Designs*, 3–39, 127 (on "awash with feeling"), 147–85. In *Woman's Fiction*, Nina Baym similarly claims that "there is no evidence that he [Hawthorne] understood the intention of woman's fiction" (251). Ann Douglas continues this train of interpretation when she states that "serious" authors of Hawthorne's stamp "turned their sights principally on values and scenes that operated as alternatives to cultural norms." Normative in Douglas's reading is the culture of sentiment that she deems regrettable, and forgettable, in *The Feminization of American Culture*, 5. Adopting an opposing position, David S. Reynolds maintains that Hawthorne's writings forged the "conventional" morals of contemporary sentimentalism with a "subversive" urge to undercut middle-class morality in all its forms, sentimental or not. Reynolds further explains that Hawthorne experimented with different discursive styles, as called for by different rhetorical occasions. See Reynolds's *Beneath the American Renaissance*, 113–34.

4. Miller, "Eros and Ideology," 2, places the precise count (which includes both the word "heart" and derivatives like "heart-strings" and "heart-ache") at 102.

5. Theo Davis, *Formalism, Experience, and the Making of American Literature in the Nineteenth Century* (New York: Cambridge University Press, 2007), 108. Davis locates such strategic instances of "vacancy" not only at the center of *Blithedale*, but throughout the larger body of Hawthorne's work.

6. Christopher Clark, *The Communitarian Movement: The Radical Challenge of the Northampton Association* (Ithaca, N.Y.: Cornell University Press, 1995), 2.

7. Sterling Delano states that "the Farm," as it was popularly known, could be consumed in small doses by the thousand or more visitors who stopped for short-term stays in the mid-1840s: they paid $.25 for dinner, $.12 for supper,

and $.25 for one night's lodging. Semi-permanent boarders outnumbered members 55 to 15 just one year after Brook Farm opened in 1841. See Delano's *Brook Farm: The Dark Side of Utopia* (Cambridge, Mass.: Belknap Press of Harvard University Press, 2004), 65–67, and footnote page 356. Full membership in Brook Farm was conferred only after shareholding associates had admitted a candidate by majority vote.

8. The number hovers at just under one in ten by 1860, right before the start of the Civil War. Percentages rise or fall in relation to a neighborhood's proximity to Boston's boarding-rich central and south-central districts. Figures come from the Eighth Census of the United States, 1860, Boston City, Wards 1–12. See Mark Peel, "On the Margin: Lodgers and Boarders in Boston, 1860–1900," *Journal of American History* 72, no. 4 (March 1986): 816–17.

9. There has been to date no published historical account of the laboring lives of Brook Farm's workers prior to their arrival at the "Farm." I base my claims as to their boarding background on studies of Boston's urbanization. See Peel, "On the Margin," 813–34; Oscar Handlin, *Boston's Immigrants, 1790–1865: A Study in Acculturation* (1941; rept. Cambridge, Mass.: Belknap Press of Harvard University Press, 1991), 95–101; and Thernstrom, *The Other Bostonians*, 4–6. There are two final ironies associated with associationism, as the communal movement now is known. First, Brook Farm's boarders precipitated a housing shortage at the commune, recalling the residential shortages that made Boston boarding necessary in the first place. Second, Brook Farmers responded to the growing demand for housing by building new facilities, only to deepen the community's debt and damage its long-term financial prospects. It is worth noting as well that many former members eventually resided at a cooperative "combined home" on Boston's Pinckney Street, an address which in essence became Brook Farmers' preferred place of exile. From the introduction to *Letters from Brook Farm, 1844–1847*, ed. Amy L. Reed (Poughkeepsie, N.Y.: Vassar College, 1928).

10. For a parallel example, see the sometime transcendentalist Bronson Alcott. Founder of the Fruitlands community in Harvard, Massachusetts, Alcott also boarded for a short time at Mrs. Newall's Boston boardinghouse on 12 Franklin Street. From Odell Shephard, *Pedlar's Progress: The Life of Bronson Alcott* (Boston: Little, Brown, 1937), 121.

11. Upon leaving Brook Farm, Hawthorne and his wife spent three years in Concord, where they rented the Old Manse family mansion from friend Ralph Waldo Emerson. Hawthorne wrote privately of feeling finally at "home" there, "after having lived so long homeless in the world." From the author's *American Notebooks*, ed. Randall Stewart (New Haven, Conn.: Yale University Press, 1932), 322. For Emerson's residential remarks on Brook Farm, see the *Journals and Miscellaneous Notebooks of Ralph Waldo Emerson*, 16 vols., ed. William H. Gilman et al. (Cambridge, Mass.: Belknap Press of Harvard University Press, 1960–82), 7:407–8 (Oct. 17, 1840).

12. Samuel Coale, "Spiritualism and Hawthorne's Romance: The Blithedale Theater as False Consciousness," *Literature and Belief* 14 (1994): 44.

13. Halttunen, *Confidence Men and Painted Women*, 34.

14. Chai, *Romantic Foundations of the American Renaissance*, 164–65, 204.

15. Dana Brand equates Coverdale with the urban sidewalk observer, or flaneur, of European literary extraction. When not appearing out on the pavements, the flaneur played the spectator at shopping arcades, art exhibits, theaters, and, I would add, the metropolitan boardinghouse. See Brand's *Spectator and the City*, 107–37.

16. The Brook Farm staging of English playwright Douglas Jerrold's aptly chosen farce *The Rent-Day* (183–) is a case in point. See the account of a former student at Brook Farm, John Van Der Zee Sears's *My Friends at Brook Farm* (New York: Desmond Fitzgerald, 1912), 81–85. At the turn of the century, novelist Edith Wharton endowed her fated fictional boarder, Lily Bart, with Zenobia's same gift for *tableaux vivants*. Refer to Wharton's *The House of Mirth* (1905; rept. New York: Oxford University Press, 1994).

17. Hawthorne, *American Notebooks*, 28 (entry for May 11, 1838).

18. The landlady of this "tragedian" begs him "not to ruin the character of her second-best room, and the walls newly painted at that!" All involved forget about any rent due, only to repeat the performance the following week. From "White Mice," *Atlantic Monthly* 5, no. 29 (March 1860): 330.

19. Richard Francis, *Transcendental Utopias: Individual and Community at Brook Farm, Fruitlands, and Walden* (Ithaca, N.Y.: Cornell University Press, 1997), 52–60.

20. Sellers, *Market Revolution*, 237–68.

21. Carl Guarneri makes the same point about Brook Farm. See his *The Utopian Alternative: Fourierism in Nineteenth-Century America* (Ithaca, N.Y.: Cornell University Press, 1991), 178–226.

22. Benedict, "Boarding-House Experience," 103; and William Knight Northall, *Before and Behind the Curtain; or, Fifteen Years' Observations Among the Theatres of New York* (New York: W. F. Burgess, 1851), 6–7. At century's end, an English writer stated the case on boarding and feeling as follows: "Your feelings undergo an entire change when you have lived in a boarding-house; you either get thin-skinned or thick-skinned." From Juloc, *Boarding-House Reminiscences; or, The Pleasure of Living with Others* (London: T. Fisher Unwin, 1896), 28.

23. Reynolds, *Beneath the American Renaissance*, 127–32, 215.

24. Whitman's most recent biographer, David S. Reynolds, defines "adhesiveness" as same-sex love without physical expression, what we might call comradeship. Whitman borrowed the concepts of both adhesiveness and amativeness from the Manhattan phrenologists (and publishers) Orson and Lorenzo Fowler. While Whitman collapsed friendship and sexuality in the 1855 edition of *Leaves of Grass*, he thereafter inclines toward the Fowlers' view that the two were discrete categories. See Reynolds's *Walt Whitman's America: A Cultural Biography* (New York: Alfred A. Knopf, 1995), 247–50, 391–400.

25. *Blithedale*'s critical history demonstrates the continuing interest among scholars in the sexual content of Hawthorne's novel. Donald Ross marks Coverdale's fascination with Zenobia in "Dreams and Sexual Repression in *The Blithedale Romance*," *PMLA* 5, no. 86 (October 1971): 1014–17. Queer

theory shifts attention toward the other end of the sexual spectrum, namely Coverdale's feelings for Hollingsworth. David Leverenz writes of the novel's being a sex-role allegory that attacks contemporary constructions of manhood. From Leverenz's *Manhood and the American Renaissance* (Ithaca, N.Y.: Cornell University Press, 1989), 227–58. One of Hawthorne's biographers, Edwin H. Miller, speculates further in this direction in *Salem Is My Dwelling Place: A Life of Nathaniel Hawthorne* (Iowa City: University of Iowa Press, 1991), 357–58. Benjamin Scott Grossberg, meanwhile, labels *Blithedale* "a utopia of sexual desire," where homo- and heterosexual impulses both know no bounds. Refer to Grossberg's "'The Tender Passion Was Very Rife Among Us': Coverdale's Queer Utopia and *The Blithedale Romance*," *Studies in American Fiction* 28, no. 1 (Spring 2000): 3–26 (p. 6 for the quote cited). Lauren Berlant generally observes intersecting discourses of love and sexuality informing *Blithedale* as a book. She elaborates in "Fantasies of Utopia in *The Blithedale Romance*," *American Literary History* 1, no. 1 (Spring 1989): 30–62. On the critical fringe, several scholars refer *Blithedale* back to ancient Greek investigations of sexual identity. For but two examples, see Gustaaf Van Cromphout, "*Blithedale* and the Androgyne Myth: Another Look at Zenobia," *ESQ* 18 (1972): 141–45; and Nancy Ciccone, "*The Blithedale Romance*, an American Bacchae," *Classical and Modern Literature: A Quarterly* 20, no. 1 (Fall 1999): 77–100.

26. Reynolds, *Beneath the American Renaissance*.

27. For an overview of an emergent mid-nineteenth-century metropolitan underworld of recreational sexual activity, see Patricia Cline Cohen, Timothy J. Gilfoyle, and Helen Lefkowitz Horowitz, *The Flash Press: Sporting Male Weeklies in 1840s New York* (Chicago: University of Chicago Press, 2008), 18.

28. From "To the Editors of the Whip," in the *Whip and Satirist of New-York and Brooklyn* (March 26, 1842) [American Antiquarian Society].

29. "Walker," *Atlantic Monthly* 6, no. 36 (October 1860): 468; Nathaniel Hawthorne, *American Notebooks*, 250–51; Gunn, "Chapter 17," *Physiology*, 147–55; Donald Grant Mitchell, "Editor's Drawer," *Harper's Monthly* 5, no. 26 (July 1852): 275; N. P. Willis, "Cheap Boarding and True Love," *New Mirror* (Oct. 21, 1843): 34–35; Charles Dickens, "The Boarding House," 285; and Oliver Wendell Holmes, "The Professor at the Breakfast-Table," *Atlantic Monthly* 3, no. 17 (March 1859): 352.

30. "The Single Young Man Lodger," in Tony Pastor, *Tony Pastor's Complete Budget of Comic Songs* (New York: Dick and Fitzgerald, 1864), 39–40; Joseph C. Neal, "The Crooked Disciple; or, The Pride of Muscle," from *Charcoal Sketches, or, Scenes in a Metropolis* (Philadelphia: E. L. Carey and A. Hart, 1838), 203; Chudacoff, *Age of the Bachelor*, 33; and Balzac, *Le Père Goriot*, 6.

31. Victor A. Hennequin, *Love in the Phalanstery*, trans. Henry James Sr. (New York: Dewitt and Davenport, 1849), v, 25. See also Henry James, "Love and Marriage," *Harbinger* 7, no. 26 (Oct. 28, 1848): 202–3; and "The Love Question," *Harbinger* (Jan. 6, 1849): 77–78. For an overview of Fourier's writings, refer to *Design for Utopia: Selected Writings of Charles Fourier*, trans. Julia Franklin (New York: Schocken Books, 1971), 137–62.

32. Samuel Irenaeus Prime, "Marriage and Reformers," *New-York Observer* (Nov. 11, 1852): 366; and "Marriage: The Religious Views," anonymous article from ibid. (December 16, 1852): 402.

33. The reference to a "promiscuous resort" is from the *New York Sporting Whip* (Feb. 11, 1843) [AAS Periodicals]. See also Dickens, "The Boarding House," 290. On Brook Farm, see Brook Farmer Marianne Dwight Orvis's letter to friend Anna Q. T. Parsons, Dec. 30, 1844, from *Letters from Brook Farm*, 57, 84. Note, too, that it was Brook Farm's second-in-command, Charles Dana, who proposed the R. L. S. G., or "rejected lover's sympathizing group." The above-named divorcée was 35-year-old Elmira Barlow, mother of three: refer to Barlow's "Dear John" letter to Brook Farmer John Sullivan Dwight, Jan. 6, 1843, from Zoltán Haraszti, *Idyll of Brook Farm* (Boston: Trustees of the Boston Public Library, 1937), 20–21. Regarding Brook Farm's love life, see Guarneri, *Utopian Alternative*, 197. Marx Edgeworth Lazarus is the Fourierist boarder turned free lover. Lazarus alternated his residence in the late 1840s between Brook Farm and the Manhattan boarding establishment of future free lover Mary S. Gove, who, herself a divorcée, was sleeping with one of her male boarders. For more on Mary Gove's boarding past, see Jean L. Silver-Isenstadt, *Shameless: The Visionary Life of Mary Gove Nichols* (Baltimore: Johns Hopkins University Press, 2002), 79–80. With the 1852 publication of Lazarus's *Love vs. Marriage*, free love in America became national news in the wake of a furious front-page debate that followed his attack on the institution of marriage. Despite that high-water mark, historian Taylor Stoehr states that already "by 1850, Fourierism and free love were synonymous in many minds." See Stoehr's edited volume *Free Love in America: A Documentary History* (New York: AMS, 1979), 9–10, 17. It is worth noting that Lazarus issued his last will and testament on March 30, 1847, while staying at Brook Farm. The community's founder, George Ripley, signed as witness as Lazarus left his substantial estate "to the advancement of the cause of Human Redemption . . . as applied by Charles Fourier . . . in a Model Phalanx." See the G. W. Mordecai Papers [Southern Historical Collection, Wilson Library, University of North Carolina-Chapel Hill].

34. The comment on "Phalanstery-like hotels" comes from labor reformer Barbara L. S. Bodichon, *Women and Work* (New York: C. S. Francis, 1859), 19.

35. Bruce A. McConachie, *Melodramatic Formations: American Theatre and Society, 1820–1870* (Iowa City: University of Iowa Press, 1992), 200; and Chudacoff, *Age of the Bachelor*, 29, 37–38. McConachie writes that theater owners from the first half of the nineteenth century had a reliable male audience that crossed class lines. As the urban middle classes solidified at mid-century, however, and as they in turn came to insist on "proper" entertainments for ladies, theaters began catering to females as never before.

36. Scholars describe a young, unattached, and mostly male population of city-dwellers as comprising the bulk of America's antebellum boarders. See Modell and Hareven, "Urbanization and the Malleable Household," 57; and Scherzer, *Unbounded Community*, 119.

37. Berlant, "Fantasies of Utopia," 30–36.

38. "Penetrated" is how Coverdale describes friend and fellow boarder Hollingsworth's emotional hold over him, as in the following: "Had I but touched his extended hand, Hollingsworth's magnetism would perhaps have penetrated me with his own conception of these matters" (134).

39. Ned Buntline, *The Mysteries and Miseries of New York* (New York: Berford, 1848), 104–6; George G. Foster, *New York by Gas-Light,* ed. Stuart Blumin (1850; rept. Berkeley: University of California Press, 1990), 96–97; and George Thompson, *Venus in Boston* (1849), in *Venus in Boston and Other Tales of Nineteenth-Century City Life,* ed. Reynolds and Gladman. Thompson has the vicious Mrs. Franklin from his novel *City Crimes* call Hawthorne's Boston "the greatest lust-market of the Union." See Thompson's *City Crimes; or Life in New York and Boston* (1849), in *Venus in Boston and Other Tales of Nineteenth-Century City Life,* 241. On Hawthorne, refer to his *American Notebooks,* 250.

40. Peter Pendergrass, *The Magdalen Report: A Farce in Three Acts* (New York: Joshua Hardcastle, 1831). See act 2, scene 1, p. 13, for Mrs. Loosely's comments.

41. James Dawson Burn, *Three Years Among the Working-Classes in the United States During the War* (London: Smith, Elder, 1865), 9.

42. Richard Brodhead says that Priscilla's Veiled Lady public persona eclipses her female body. I would counter that Priscilla is all physicality in her status as boarder, the logistics of close-quartered boarding having made moot any distinction between public and private on the one hand, body and sentimentality on the other. From "Veiled Ladies: Toward a History of Antebellum Entertainment," in *Cultures of Letters: Scenes of Reading and Writing in Nineteenth-Century America* (Chicago: University of Chicago Press, 1993), 48–68.

43. Gilfoyle, *City of Eros,* 102, 115; Chudacoff, *The Age of the Bachelor,* 29, 37–38. Claudia Johnson writes of "third-tier" call girls at theaters in ante- and postbellum America. See "That Guilty Third Tier: Prostitution in Nineteenth-Century American Theaters," *American Quarterly* 27, no. 5 (December 1975): 575–84. William Dunlap cites the same phenomenon at Boston's Federalist-era theaters, where prostitutes appeared after the city lifted its ban on plays in the 1790s. From Dunlap's *History of the American Theatre and Anecdotes of the Principal Actors* (1797), 3 vols. (New York: Burt Franklin, 1963), 1:407–12. Actresses themselves were suspected of being promiscuous, and Hawthorne works that centuries-old stereotype into two of his early tales: "Passages from a Relinquished Work" (1834, 1854), in *Mosses from an Old Manse,* in *Centenary Edition,* vol. 10 (1974), 421; and "John Inglefield's Thanksgiving" (1840, 1852), in *The Snow-Image and Uncollected Tales,* in *Centenary Edition,* vol. 11 (1974): 184. Note that *Blithedale*'s Priscilla is doubly prostituted in her combined roles as the Veiled Lady, that sexually ambiguous mistress of the stage, and again as a city seamstress, a persona that served as nineteenth-century vernacular for the exploited, wage-laboring working girl who was just one step shy of a still-worse form of exploitation. See Amal Amireh, *The Factory Girl and the Seamstress: Imagining Gender and Class in Nineteenth-Century American Fiction* (New York: Garland, 2000), 77–110.

44. Caleb Crain, *American Sympathy: Men, Friendship, and Literature in the New Nation* (New Haven, Conn.: Yale University Press, 2001), 61. Richard H. Millington writes that *Blithedale*'s characters exemplify an unstable sense of self and so "disguise" their alleged "emptiness." He relates the book's motif of personal performance to middle-class anxiety over community watchfulness. From Millington's "American Anxiousness: Selfhood and Culture in Hawthorne's *The Blithedale Romance*," *New England Quarterly* 63, no. 4 (December 1990): 558. David Leverenz claims further that Hawthorne's short stories and novels "dramatize manhood" and thus abound with "tropes" of "losing manly self-control." Leverenz's guiding idea is that Coverdale might offset his own marginalization by dominating—violating—someone weaker than himself. See Leverenz, *Manhood and the American Renaissance*, 239.

45. Halttunen, *Confidence Men and Painted Women*, 153–90.

## Epilogue

The chapter epigraph is from Edgar Allan Poe, "The Murders in the Rue Morgue" (1841), in *Selected Poetry and Prose*, ed. T. O. Mabbott (New York: Modern Library, 1951), 171.

1. Harry L. Watson, "Slavery and Development in a Dual Economy: The South and the Market Revolution," from *The Market Revolution in America: Social, Political, and Religious Expressions, 1800–1880,* ed. Melvyn Stokes and Stephen Conway (Charlottesville: University of Virginia Press, 1996), 43–73.

2. Balzac, *Le Père Goriot*, 321; Sedgwick, *Clarence*, 1:20–21; Fanny Fern, "The Sick Bachelor," from her *Memorial Volume*, 339; Sarah Josepha Hale, *"Boarding Out,"* 106–18; and Oliver Wendell Holmes, "The Professor at the Breakfast-Table," *Atlantic Monthly* 4, no. 25 (November 1859): 632.

Added to these fictional boarders' deaths are the fates of several antebellum boarder-authors. Writer Nathaniel Hawthorne watched his friend and publisher William Ticknor die in a Philadelphia hotel. Hawthorne himself, in turn watched by the surviving half of his sometime publisher's partner, James Fields, expired in a hotel on the coast of Massachusetts not long after. There is also the case of William Apess. After what one witness called his final drunken "frolic," the Native American evangelical preacher, lecturer, and author died one April night in 1839 in a New York boardinghouse at 31 Washington Street. None of Apess's contemporaries noted his passing in print. See, respectively, James Mellow, *Nathaniel Hawthorne in His Times* (Boston: Houghton Mifflin, 1980), and the Coroner's Inquest for William Apess, April 10, 1839, New York County Coroner Inquests, Roll no. 16, July 1838–August 1840, Department of Records and Information, Municipal Archives of the City of New York, New York.

3. Edgar Allan Poe, "Dreamland" (1844), in *Selected Poetry and Prose*, 32.

4. Kevin J. Hayes, *Poe and the Printed Word* (New York: Cambridge University Press, 2000), 92–93; and William Carlos Williams, *In the American Grain* (1925; rept. New York: New Directions, 1956), 216, 219.

5. Kenneth Silverman, *Edgar A. Poe: Mournful and Never-Ending Remembrance* (New York: HarperPerennial, 1992), 172; *The Letters of Edgar Allan Poe*, 2 vols., ed. John Ward Ostrom (Cambridge, Mass.: Harvard University

Press, 1948), 1:123 (Poe to Mrs. John C. Cox, Dec. 6, 1839), 251–53 (Poe to Maria Clemm, April 7, 1844); and Richard Henry Stoddard, *Recollections, Personal and Literary*, ed. Ripley Hitchcock (New York: A. S. Barnes, 1903), 147.

6. Silverman, *Edgar A. Poe*, 173.

7. Under extraordinary circumstances recalling Poe's fiction, antebellum boarders did court danger on occasion, with an untimely death being the possible end result of their living arrangements. *Harper's* magazine provides one case in point from its March 1857 issue. The editors there make specific mention in their monthly news bulletin of one Dr. Harvey Burdell, dentist, who is discovered dead in his New York rooms. The doctor had been strangled, while the fifteen wounds on his body and other evidence of violent struggle account for the blood left covering the walls and floor of Burdell's apartment. As to blame, the news item continues, "Suspicion was at once directed toward the inmates of the house" (551). That is to say, Dr. Burdell, the owner of the two-story building in question, had been using its second floor for his office and sleeping compartment, while he rented the remainder of the house to a Mrs. Emma A. Cunningham—who, in turn, let her rented portion as a boarding-house. In a plot twist that would have made Poe proud, Mrs. Cunningham and her suspected lover, who was also one of her boarders, emerge as the leading suspects in the sensational boarder-murder case. From "Monthly Record of Current Events," *Harper's Monthly* 14, no. 82 (March 1857): 549–53. To take another example, this one closer to the time of Poe's "Murders," author Lydia Maria Child wrote for publication of a poor German immigrant for whom boarding becomes nothing short of a nightmare. While boarding with a quarrelsome native couple, the man spends his last day of freedom holding a knife shoved into his hand by the homicidal wife after she stabs her husband. Her cry of "Murder" draws a crowd before the German can react. Left with the bloody implement in his hand, and an at-best broken English for an inadequate self-defense, the unfortunate boarder watches his American dream move from boardinghouse to jailhouse to gallows in quick succession. See Lydia Maria Child, "Letter Thirty-One" (Nov. 19, 1842), from *Letters from New-York*, ed. Bruce Mills, 141–42.

8. Like many commentators at the end of the nineteenth century, Jacob Riis mistakenly conflated the boardinghouse, lodging house, and tenement house. Each for Riis seemed a haven of unmonitored antisocial behavior, often of a decidedly ethnic-immigrant kind. See Riis's *How the Other Half Lives: Studies Among the Tenements of New York* (1890; rept. New York: Dover, 1971). For a historical perspective, refer to Modell and Hareven, "Urbanization," 51–52.

9. The discussion here of nineteenth-century lodging draws on the work of historian Mark Peel. Peel adopts postbellum Boston as a case study of urban living in America from 1860 to 1900, giving lodging the central place in that study. While his data is mostly for Boston proper, Peel tentatively extends his findings to similar metropolitan areas of the northeastern United States for the decades in question. See Peel's "On the Margin," 813–34.

10. One compelling and chilling instance of the literary shift from the boardinghouse to the lodging house comes from American author Theodore Dreiser.

His hard-luck character Hurstwood pays fifteen cents for the privacy he requires to commit suicide in a flophouse lodging house in New York's Bowery. See Dreiser's *Sister Carrie* (1900; rept. New York: Penguin Books, 1986).

11. Juloc, *Boarding-House Reminiscences;* Leonard Grover, *Our Boarding House* (n.d., American play in four acts, ca. 1900); Dorothy Whipple, "Boarding-House," from *After Tea and Other Stories* (London: John Murray, 1941), 158–81; Robert Antoni, *My Grandmother's Erotic Folktales: With Stories of Adventure and Occasional Orgies in Her Boarding House for American Soldiers During the War* (New York: Grove, 2000); and Emily Arnold McCully, *Mirette on the High Wire* (New York: G. P. Putnam's Sons, 1992). One compelling instance of the boardinghouse's place in popular culture is the newspaper war that erupted over boardinghouse comics during the Great Depression. The Newspaper Enterprise Association launched its popular comic serial, "Our Boarding House," featuring the gruff Major Hoople, in 1921. Urged on by its rival's success, the King Features Syndicate launched its own boardinghouse column in 1936, hiring George Ahern—the creator of "Our Boarding House"—to write and draw its in-house strip, "Room & Board." The original serial ran until 1981; its competitor lasted until 1956, when Ahern retired.

12. Louisa May Alcott, *Little Women; or Meg, Jo, Beth, and Amy* (1869), ed. Anne K. Phillips and Gregory Eiselein (New York: W. W. Norton, 2004); Henry James, *The Portrait of a Lady* (1881; rept. New York: W. W. Norton & Co., 1995), 89; Rudyard Kipling, "The Ballad of Fisher's Boarding-House" (1888), from *Rudyard Kipling's Verse, Inclusive Edition: 1885-1918* (Garden City, N.Y.: Doubleday, Page, 1925), 45–49; Edith Wharton, *The House of Mirth* (1905; rept. New York: Oxford University Press, 1994); James Joyce, "The Boarding House," from *Dubliners* (1914; rept. New York: Cambridge University Press, 1995), 57–64; Federigo Tozzi, "The Boardinghouse" (1917), from *Love in Vain*, trans. Minna Proctor (New York: New Directions Books, 2001), 57–65; Irving Howe, *Sherwood Anderson* (Palo Alto, Calif.: Stanford University Press, 1951), 51–90; Sherwood Anderson, *Winesburg, Ohio* (1919; rept. New York: Penguin Group, 1993); William Trevor, *The Boarding House* (1965), from *Three Early Novels* (New York: Penguin Books, 2000), 167–410; and Barbara Ehrenreich, *Nickel and Dimed: On (Not) Getting By in America* (New York: Henry Holt, 2001), 51–56. Not long after Sherwood Anderson boarded among artists in Chicago, the Chicago Art Institute opened and operated during the Depression a boardinghouse for literal "starving artists" at the corner of 39th Street and Lakeside. One boarder-painter who survived the experience recorded his impressions in the 1990s. See Donald S. Vogel, *The Boardinghouse: The Artist Community House, Chicago 1936–37* (Denton, Tex.: University of North Texas Press, 1995).

Since Vogel's day, sizeable cities such as Philadelphia have continued to offer short-term, hybrid housing solutions that fall somewhere between boarding and lodging. The privately run Coles House, at 915 Clinton Street, catered until recently to single women, that residence having closed its doors in 2005 after some 140 years of operation. The Catholic Divine Tracy Hotel, meanwhile,

persists to this day at 20 South 36th Street, providing along somewhat monaste-
rial lines daily and weekly rooms for guests willing to abide by house standards
of "modesty, independence, honesty, and righteousness." See the brochures for
the "Coles House: A residence for Women since 1865" and the "Divine Tracy
Hotel" [Library Company].

13. From the orchestral work *Fisher's Boarding-House* (1899), composer
Percy Grainger. Refer to track no. 6 from *Orchestral Works: The Grainger Edi-
tion*, vol. 1, performed by the BBC Philharmonic Orchestra, conductor Richard
Hickox (Colchester, Eng.: Chandos Records, 1996). *Fultah Fisher's Boarding
House* is the silent short film by director Frank Capra, with a screen scenario by
Walter Montague and Frank Capra, producer Walter Montague (San Francisco:
Fireside Productions, 1922). For a companion piece to Capra's early boarding-
house work, consider director Clarence Brown's 1922 short *The Light of Faith*
(New York: Kino on Video, 1995 re-release), in which a sentimental thief steals
a religious relic in the hope that it will cure the ailment of a young boarder acquaintance. *The Last Command*, another silent short (with English subtitles),
is the work of director Josef von Sternberg, with a screenplay by John F. Goodrich and an associate producer in B. P. Schulberg (Hollywood: Paramount
Pictures, 1928). *The Ladykillers* is an English boardinghouse film directed by
Alexander Mackendrick. William Rose wrote the screenplay, and Seth Holt
produced (London: Ealing Studios, 1955). See the American remake of the
same film, written, directed, and produced by Joel and Ethan Coen and starring
Tom Hanks (2004). *Madame Rosa* is the French film (with English subtitles)
above named, the director and screenwriter being Moshé Mizrahi. The film is
based on the novel by Émile Afar (1977). Historian Robert Sklar argues that
the James Dean–like "Fonz," from the television program *Happy Days*, is the
working-class intruder in the Cunningham family's middle-class domestic bliss.
The Fonz also happens to board in the room above the Cunninghams' garage.
See Sklar's "The Fonz, Laverne, Shirley, and the Great American Class Struggle," from *Television: The Critical View* (1976), ed. Horace Newcomb (New
York: Oxford University Press, 1982), 77–88. "Real" TV had a big-screen ante-
cedent in the 1949 Filmmakers production *Not Wanted* (Hollywood: Emerald
Productions, 1949). There, the then-taboo topic of unwed motherhood appears
amid a series of American boardinghouses.

14. For an overview of Jewish boardinghouses in the Catskills, see Phil
Brown, "Sleeping in My Parents' Hotel: The End of a Century of the Jewish
Catskills," from *In the Catskills: A Century of the Jewish Experience in "The
Mountains*," ed. Phil Brown (New York: Columbia University Press, 2002),
9–21. Jewish writers were wise to the literary potential of Catskill boarding.
For two examples, refer to Abraham Cahan's novel *The Rise of David Levinsky* (New York: Harper, 1917) and Isaac Bashevis Singer's short story "The
Yearning Heifer" (1970), in *In the Catskills*, ed. Brown: 64–74. There would
seem to be a strong connection between the Jewish comedians who appeared
(and still appear) at Catskills resorts—which include hotels, bungalows, and
boardinghouses—and the American TV sitcom, with its recurring boarding orientation. Perhaps it is more than a coincidence, that is, that the Jewish

television producer Norman Lear has created a number of hit shows like *All in the Family* that look to boarding for laughter. Or perhaps we might locate the boardinghouse behind a string of recent programs that feature "wandering Jews" as key characters. On this latter count, several shows (not all of them sitcoms) with residentially conscious titles come to mind, including *Beverly Hills 90210, Our House, Picket Fences, Caroline in the City,* and *The Single Guy.* See the following for more on the Jewish boarding-entertainment connection: Joyce Antler, "Forty Prime-Time Shows," from *Television's Changing Image of American Jews,* ed. Neal Gabler, Frank Rich, and Joyce Antler (Los Angeles: American Jewish Committee and the Norman Lear Center, 2000), 39–42; and David Zurawik, *The Jews of Prime Time* (Hanover, N.H.: University Press of New England, 2003), 1–16.

15. Watson, "Slavery and Development," 44, argues specifically for the urban industrialization of the postwar South. Contemporary southeast Texas corroborates his claims, providing as well a nice illustration of the significance of southern boarding in the postwar boom economy. With logging companies and railroads penetrating to the Texas Gulf in the 1880s, workers arrived by the thousands at a location then known colloquially as the "Big Thicket." Most of these laborers in turn found food and shelter at the boardinghouses that arose to meet local demand, the trend intensifying after the oil boom of the turn of the century. For an overview, see Wanda A. Landrey's *Boardin' in the Thicket* (Denton, Tex.: University of North Texas Press, 1990). One can catch a glimpse of San Francisco boarding in English aristocrat Sir H. V. Huntley's travel account of the region. See his *California: Its Gold and Its Inhabitants,* 2 vols. (London: T. C. Newby, 1856), 1:iv, 2–3, 19–20. For more on historic southern boarding, refer to a series of promotional pamphlets that sold the South to a nationwide audience. "Southern Pines, N.C." (n.d.) [NCC] boasted of the town's sanitarium, pharmacy, and scores of boarding options for northern neurasthenics. There was also a circular for "Hotels and Boarding Houses. Asheville, NC" (1908) [NCC], which coincided with a period fad for vacation resorts. Asheville itself had been a designated destination for boarding tourists ever since the city linked with rail lines in the 1880s. See "Asheville Chamber of Commerce. Hotels and Boarding Houses, Asheville, N.C." (Asheville, N.C.: n.p., 192-?) [NCC] for a later survey of the same resort town. Maria Baxter's "Boarding Houses: Fact and Fiction" (Raleigh: North Carolina Sites Section of the Division of Archives and History, 1983) sets the Ashville of these advertisements in historical perspective. By the 1920s, meanwhile, the Southern Railway System had expanded on the idea of the promotional pamphlet to produce a full-blown brochure for its thirteen-state rail network. The Railway System's "Summer Resort Hotels and Boarding Houses" (1922) [NCC] provides not only an alphabetical listing, by state, of southern vacationers' boardinghouses—one might sample, for example, "The Battle House" in Mobile, Alabama, or "The Calhoun Mansion" in Charleston, South Carolina—but goes so far as to illustrate, by map, the geographic reach of its lines. The message is simple: would-be boarders might ride Southern Rail to the front door of any establishment that appeared in the pages of its materials. See also the Alice Lee Larkins

Houston Papers, 1859–77 [SHC]. Upon the death of her attorney husband in 1870, Houston ran a boardinghouse in the Atlantic beach community of Wilmington, North Carolina. By her own account, she became "a regular busy-body . . . attending to my household" and guests (Jan. 15, 1871), assisted all the while by a paid servant—that "gem of an African" (Jan. 25, 1871). On metropolitan Atlanta, see Harvey K. Newman, *Southern Hospitality: Tourism and the Growth of Atlanta* (Tuscaloosa: University of Alabama Press, 1999), 1–36.

Tourists' boarding was by no means restricted to the southern United States. Nellie Norton Coffman, along with her husband and two sons, opened the famed Desert Inn in Palm Springs, California, in 1909. Before its 1927 make-over into a modern hotel, "Nellie's Boardinghouse," as the Inn was known by area residents and visitors, announced the arrival of desert luxury boarding far to the American West. See Marjorie Belle Bright, *Nellie's Boardinghouse: A Dual Biography of Nellie Coffman and Palm Springs* (Palm Springs: ETC, 1981). The British Tourist and Holidays Board followed suit when, after the Second World War, it commenced publication of its annual guide *Hotels, Boarding Houses, and Restaurants in Great Britain & Northern Ireland* (1949–). One might say that English sympathy for the American South extended all the way to the boardinghouse, residentially speaking. On metropolitan Denver, finally, see Stephen J. Leonard and Thomas J. Noel, *Denver: Mining Camp to Metropolis* (Niwot, Colo.: University of Colorado Press, 1991), 1–114.

16. Mary Dodson Wade, *Homesteading on the Plains: Daily Life in the Land of Laura Ingalls Wilder* (Brookfield, Conn.: Milbrook, 1997), 7; Mark Twain, *Roughing It* (Hartford, Conn.: American, 1872), 163, 268; John D. Fitzgerald, *Mamma's Boarding House* (Englewood Cliffs, N.J.: Prentice-Hall, 1958); Oliver Wenlandt, *The Nigger Boarding-House: A Screaming Farce in One Act and One Scene for Six Male Burnt-Cork Characters* (New York: Dick and Fitzgerald, 1898); and Carole Marsh, "Thomas Wolfe's House," from *The Mystery of the Biltmore House* (Tyron, N.C.: Gallopade, 1982), 71–76. The real-life equivalent of Wolfe's fictional Dixieland boardinghouse was the Old Kentucky Home boardinghouse of his youth. For a description of that domi-cile, which was run by Wolfe's mother, see Stephanie Kraft, *No Castles on Main Street: American Authors and Their Homes* (Chicago: Rand McNally, 1979), 62–73; and Glynne Robinson Betts, *Writers in Residence: American Authors at Home* (New York: Viking, 1981), 102–7.

17. On the downward trend of boarding in the 1930s, see Modell and Hareven, "Urbanization," 51–68. The following is a small sample of board-inghouse tunes: "Tanner's Boarding House," from *Early Classic String Bands, vol. 3: Gid Tanner & His Skillet Lickers, featuring Riley Packett*, sound re-cording (Brighton, Mich.: Old Homestead Records, 1990); "Boarding House Blues," by Rhythm Willie and His Gang, from *Harmonica Blues, 1936–1940*, sound recording—complete recordings of Smith and Harper, George Clarke, Rhythm Willie, and Eddie Kelly's Washboard Band; and "Boarding House Bells Are Ringing Waltz," from *The Kessinger Brothers: Original Fiddle Classics, 1928–1930* (sound recording originally made 1928–31) (Cincinnati: Kanawha, 1969). It is interesting to note, furthermore, that recent old-time recordings

have kept a certain boardinghouse theme. One of the biggest-selling bluegrass albums ever, *Old and In the Way*, featured well-known recording artists like Jerry Garcia, David Grisman, and Peter Rowan performing traditional vaga-bond numbers like "Knockin' on Your Door" and "The Hobo Song." The men laid down such numbers and more on October 8, 1973, at the San Francisco recording studio The Boarding House. Finally, for an example of World War II boarding, see Nathaniel C. Browder, manuscript papers, 1930–92 [SHC]. A North Carolina man, Browder in 1943 left his job writing local histories for the Federal Writers' Project to join the Signal Corps in Arlington, Virginia. Much of Browder's correspondence for these years dwells on the frustrations he felt boarding out with his fellow patriots. On March 10, 1943, Browder wrote to his wife as follows: "I don't particularly care for my snobbish roommate—a catholic who loves negroes and Jews, and hates southerners and communists. Just don't like people who feel too strongly about controversial issues."

## Primary Sources
### Collections Consulted, and Abbreviations
American Antiquarian Society [AAS]: Manuscripts, Newspapers, and Printed Materials

Barnard College: Rare Books and Manuscripts Library

Columbia University: Rare Books and Manuscript Library

Historic New England [HNE]: Harrison Gray Otis House, Boston, Mass.

Historical Society of Pennsylvania [HSP]: Manuscripts, Philadelphia Neighborhood History

Houghton Library of the Harvard College Library: Manuscripts, Harvard Theatre Collection

Library Company of Philadelphia [Library Company]: Graphics, Manuscripts, Periodicals

Library of Congress: Rare Book and Special Collections, Title Page Deposit Records

Massachusetts Historical Society [MHS]: Manuscripts

Missouri Historical Society [MOHS]: Library Research Collection

Museum of the City of New York: Prints and Photographs Division

New-York Historical Society [NYHS]: Henry Luce III Center, Study of American Culture

New York Public Library [NYPL]: Rare Books and Manuscripts, Wallach Division of Prints

Ohio Historical Society [OHS]: Manuscripts

University of North Carolina-Chapel Hill [UNC]: North Carolina Collection [NCC], Rare Books Collection [RBC], Southern Folklore Collection [SFC], Southern Historical Collection [SHC]

Yale University: Beinecke Rare Book and Manuscript Library

### Manuscript Collections
Browder, Nathaniel C. Manuscript papers, 1930–92 [SHC].

Child, Lydia Maria. Papers. Personal Miscellaneous Correspondence [NYPL].

Coroner's Inquest for William Apess, April 10, 1839, New York County Coroner Inquests, Roll no. 16, July 1838–August 1840, Department of Records and Information, Municipal Archives of the City of New York, New York.

Drawings of English Theatres, 1790–1820, including those of the English Opera House and Drury Lane Theater by Samuel Beazley [Harvard Theatre Collection].

322                                                              Bibliography

Duyckinck Family Papers. Evert A. Duyckinck, Leases, 1855–1874 [NYPL].
Fifth Avenue Hotel Records. Market Books, 1859–1874 [NYPL].
Flint Family Papers, 1818–1876 (box 4, vol. 15, diary kept by Laura Flint Clapp in the *Unitarian Congregational Register* [Boston, 1850]) [AAS Manuscripts].
Forbes, Susan E. Parsons Brown, Mrs. Alexander Barclay, Diaries, 1841–1908 (box 1, octavo vols. 14–23, 1856–65) [AAS Manuscripts].
Gunn, Thomas Butler. Manuscript Diaries, 21 vols., July 17, 1849–April 7, 1863 [MOHS].
Holmes, Oliver Wendell. Miscellaneous and Additional Papers, 1825–94 [Houghton].
Houston, Alice Lee Larkins. Papers, 1859–77: see Folder 2, Journal, 1870–71 [SHC].
Lippard, George. Papers, 1843–1927 [AAS Manuscripts].
Mordecai, George W. Papers. [SHC].
Pierce, Henry. Family Papers, 1771–1921, Henry Pierce Diaries, 1845–1875 [MHS].
Weaver, Matthias Shirk. Papers, 1840–43 [OHS Manuscripts].
Worcester Soldiers' Relief Society, Records, 1861–1865 (folder 11 and octavo vol. 5) [AAS Manuscripts].

*Periodicals and Newspapers*
*American Whig Review*
"Passages from the Life of a Medical Eclectic" 3, no. 5 (May 1846): 469–79.
Gardiner, O. C. "Foreign Immigration—Charitable Institutions of New York City: Voluntary Associations, Almshouse, and Commission of Emigration" 7, no. 4 (April 1848): 419–32.
"Meredith Demaistre, the Pet of the Parvenus" 13, no. 74 (February 1851): 129–41.

*Atlantic Monthly*
"The Autocrat of the Breakfast-Table" serial November 1857–October 1858.
"The Professor at the Breakfast-Table" serial
3, no. 16 (February 1859): 232–41.
3, no. 17 (March 1859): 350–61.
4, no. 22 (August 1859): 232–43.
4, no. 25 (November 1859): 622–34.
4, no. 26 (December 1859): 751–70.
"Bulls and Bears" 3, no. 19 (May 1859): 585–600.
"White Mice" 5, no. 29 (March 1860): 329–38.
"Walker" 6, no. 36 (October 1860): 460–70.
Russel, Amelia. "Home Life of the Brook Farm Association, Part I" 42, no. 252 (October 1878): 458–66.
"Comment on New Books" 73, no. 435 (January 1894): 133–39.

More, Paul E. "A Hermit's Notes on Thoreau" 87, no. 524 (June 1901): 857–64.

*The Banbury Guardian* [England]
"Death of Mr. Thomas Butler Gunn, A Veteran Journalist" (Thurs., April 14, 1904).

*Brooklyn Daily Eagle*
"A Visit to Walt Whitman" (July 11, 1886): 10.

*The Christian Examiner*
Felton, C. C. "Emerson's Essays" 30 (May 1841): 253–62, in *Emerson and Thoreau: The Contemporary Reviews,* ed. Joel Myerson (New York: Cambridge University Press, 1994), 77–108.

*The Colored American*
"Gambling" (boardinghouses as gambling dens: Nov. 11, 1837).
"Boarding House in Boston" (adv. for a Boston boardinghouse: August 15, 1840).

*Democratic Review*
"The Census" 25, no. 136 (October 1849): 291–305.
"The True History of Alcibiades Scribo, Contributor, Concoctor, et cetera" 25, no. 138 (December 1849): 516–28.
"Poems by George P. Morris" 35, no. 6 (June 1855): 473–93.
"Municipal Government" 36, no. 3 (September 1855): 253–61.
June, Jennie. "Jennie June's Letters. Blessed Are They Who Have Nothing" 41, no. 1 (January 1858): 83–89.

*The Dial*
Ripley, Sophia. "Woman" 1, no. 1 (January 1841): 362–66.

*Diogenes, Hys Lantern* (a.k.a., *The Lantern*) [Library Company Periodicals]
"A New Berth," Thomas Butler Gunn illustration from vol. 1 (1852): 180.
"Fancy Sketch," Frank Bellew illustration from vol. 2 (1852): 195.
"Accounting for the Milk," anon. illustration from vol. 3 (1853): 302.

*Frank Leslie's Illustrated Newspaper*
Literary review of Thomas Butler Gunn's *The Physiology of New York Boarding-Houses* (July 11, 1857): 95.

*Frederick Douglass' Paper*
Two separate advertisements for Philadelphia boardinghouses (Nov. 9, 1855).

*Graham's Magazine*
Poe, Edgar Allan. "Marginalia" (December 1846), as cited in E. A. Poe, *Essays and Reviews* (New York: Library of America, 1984), 1415.

*The Harbinger*
Brisbane, Albert. "The Isolated Household" 1, no. 2 (June 21, 1845): 22–24.
"The Isolated Family" 1, no. 16 (Sept. 27, 1845): 251–53.
Ripley, George. "The Democratic Review and Association" 2, no. 4 (Jan. 3, 1846): 60–62.
Lazarus, Marx Edgeworth. "Society" 4, no. 1 (Dec. 12, 1846): 7–9.
James, Henry. "The Observer and Hennequin" 7, no. 25 (Oct. 21, 1848): 197.
———. "Love and Marriage" 7, no. 26 (Oct. 28, 1848): 202–3.
"The Love Question" 8, no. 10 (Jan. 6, 1849): 77–78.

*Harper's Monthly*
Mitchell, Donald Grant. "Editor's Drawer" 5, no. 26 (July 1852): 275.
Curtis, George William. "Editor's Easy Chair" 6, no. 35 (April 1853): 704
"History and Incidents of the Plague in New Orleans" 7, no. 42 (November 1853): 797–806.
Thackeray, W. M. Serial of *The Newcomes,* "Chapter 17: A School of Art" 8:48 (May 1854): 780–801.
"Infant Heir" 8, no. 48 (May 1854): 824–32.
"Day in a Lunatic Asylum" 9, no. 53 (October 1854): 653–59.
James, G.P.R. "Love and Charcoal" 10, no. 58 (March 1855): 533–38.
Curtis, George William. "Editor's Easy Chair" 10, no. 58 (March 1855): 551. Review of *Ruth Hall.*
"Duke Humphrey's Dinner" 11, no. 63 (August 1855): 352–57.
"My Neighbor's Story" 12, no. 70 (March 1856): 491–94.
"Cinderella—Not a Fairy Tale" 12, no. 70 (March 1856): 501–07.
"Negroland and the Negroes" 13, no. 74 (July 1856): 161–78.
"Board for a Lady" 13, no. 75 (August 1856): 358–59.
"Monthly Record of Current Events" 14, no. 82 (March 1857): 549–53.
"Mr. Seedy" 15, no. 88 (September 1857): 529–33.
"A Screw Loose," 15, no. 89 (October 1857): 629–34.
"The Bronze Gaiters" 15, no. 89 (October 1857): 681–86.
"Love Experiences of an Impressible Man" 16, no. 91 (December 1857): 67–72.
"Our Sons" 17, no. 97 (June 1858): 57–62.
"Costly Kiss: A New York Detective Experience" 18, no. 107 (April 1859): 620–26.
"Bored to Death" 18, no. 107 (April 1859): 658–61.
Haven, Alice B. "An Armistice" 20, no. 115 (December 1859): 53–58.
Ludlow, Fitz Hugh. "Regular Habits" 20, no. 115 (December 1859): 72–88.
Thackeray, W. M. Serial of *Lovel the Widower,* "Chapter 1: The Bachelor of Beak Street" 20, no. 117 (February 1860): 383–92.
"Editor's Table" 20, no. 117 (February 1860): 409.
M. D. Conway, "The Great Show at Paris" 35, no. 206 (July 1867): 238–53.

*Harper's Weekly*
"Horrible Murder in Bond Street" (Feb. 7, 1857): 86.
"Wanted—a Boarding-House" (Oct. 10, 1857): 652.

*Holden's Dollar Magazine*
"New American Writers" (July 1848): 421–24.

*International Magazine of Literature, Art, and Science*
"Herr Fleischmann on the Industrial and Social Life of the Americans" 4, no. 2 (September 1851): 158–64.

*Knickerbocker*
Bristed, Charles Astor. "A New Theory of Bohemians" (March 1861): 311–17.

*Lippincott's Monthly Magazine*
Sullivan, Louis H. "The Tall Office Building Artistically Considered" 339, no. 3 (March 1896): 403–09.

*The Literary World*
Carhart, Jotham. "Free-Stone for Authors" 10 (May 22, 1852): 363.
Stylus. "Our New York Letter" (Feb. 20, 1886): 64–65.
English, Thomas Dunn. "That Club at Pfaaf's" (June 12, 1886): 202.

*Living Age*
"The Reverie of an Old Maid" 31, no. 393 (Nov. 29, 1851): 385–432.
"Civilized America" 61, no. 783 (May 28, 1859): 554–77.
Channing, William Henry. "Henry Thoreau, the Poet-Naturalist" 120, no. 1553 (March 14, 1874): 643–50 [rept. from *The British Quarterly Review*].

*Lowell Offering*
Bagley, Sarah G. "Pleasures of Factory Life," Series I (1840): 25–6.
Ibid. "Tales of Factory Life, No. 2: The Orphan Sisters," vol. I (1841): 263–66.
"Editorial: Home in a Boarding-House," vol. III (1842): 69–70.
Farley, Harriet. "The Affections Illustrated in Factory Life: No. 1—The Sister," vol. IV (1843): 14–23.
Ibid. "Letters from Susan" [First through Fourth], vol. IV (1844): 145–48, 169–72, 237–40, 257–59.
Baker, Josephine L. "A Second Peep at Factory Life," vol. V (1845): 97–100.
"A Week in the Mill," vol. V (1845): 217–18.

*New Englander and Yale Review*
"The Condition, Hospitals, and Homes for Sailors" 3, no. 12 (October 1845): 481–93.

*New Mirror*
Willis, N. P. "Cheap Boarding and True Love" (Oct. 21, 1843): 33–38.

*New-York Observer*
Prime, Samuel Irenaeus. "Marriage and Reformers" 30, no. 46 (Nov. 11, 1852): 366.

"A Letter to Mr. James" (Nov. 25, 1852): 382.
"Marriage: The Religious View" (Dec. 9, 1852): 394.
Ibid. (Dec. 16, 1852): 402.

*The New York Sporting Whip* [AAS Newspapers]
Feb. 11, 1843.
Feb. 25, 1843.

*New-York Tribune*
Brisbane, Albert. "Association" (April 16, 1842): 1.
Ibid. "Association" (Nov. 4, 1842): 1.
"The Dens of Death, No. II" (June 13, 1850): 1–2.

*The Nineteenth Century* [HSP Periodicals]
Lippard, George. "The Carpenter's Son," vol. 2 (January 1848): 72–99.

*The North American Review*
Warner, Charles Dudley. "The Demand of the Industrial Spirit" 139, no. 334
    (September 1884): 209–224.

*The North Star*
J. D. "Colored Inhabitants of Philadelphia" (Feb. 2, 1849).
W. C. N. "Boston, July 15, 1849" (August 24, 1849).

*Packard's Monthly Magazine*
Benedict, Fannie. "Boarding-House Experience in New York" 1, no. 1 (1869):
    100–03.

*The Phalanx*
"Domestic Relations in a Utopian Community" 1, no. 21 (Feb. 8, 1844): 317–20.
"Condition of Women in Harmony" [translated from the French of Madame
    Gatti de Gamond] 1, no. 16 (August 10, 1844): 234–36.

*Philadelphia Home Journal* [HSP Newspapers]
Diller, Isaac Roland. "Review of the Romances of George Lippard" (Jan. 8,
    1845): 1.
"Literature Notices" (April 2, 1845): 3
"The Quaker City," Ibid.

*Public Ledger* (Philadelphia) [HSP Newspapers]
"Mercer Trial" (March 30, 1843): 1–2.
"George Lippard" (Feb. 10, 1854): 2.

*Putnam's*
Curtis, George William. "Andrew Cranberry—Attorney at Law" 1, no. 1 (Janu-
    ary 1853): 18–22.

Briggs, Charles Fredrick. "The Homes of American Authors" 1, no. 1 (January 1853): 23–30.
"Inns" 1, no. 6 (June 1853): 612–18.
Cook, Clarence. "New-York Daguerreotyped: Private Residences" 3, no. 15 (March 1854): 233–48.
"How I Live, And With Whom" 3, no. 15 (March 1854): 320–28.
"Watering-Place Worries" 4, no. 23 (November 1854): 551–59.
"Editorial Notes—American Literature: Fanny Fern's *Ruth Hall*" 5, no. 26 (February 1855): 216.

*The Quaker City* (weekly, 1848–50) [AAS Newspapers, HSP]
Lippard, George. "An Every-day Dream" (April 14, 1849): 2.
Ibid. "The Utility of Novel Writing" (May 19, 1849): 3.
Ibid. "The Killers" (Dec. 1, 1849): 3.

*Scientific American*
News item on Mike Walsh, 2, no. 17 (Jan. 16, 1847): 130.
"Lead Colic Produced by Claret" 1, no. 26 (Dec. 24, 1859): 414.

*The Spirit of the Times* [HSP Newspapers]
"Court of Oyer and Terminer" (Jan. 15, 1839): 1.
"Board Wanted" and "Boarding Wanted" (Sept. 9, 1839): 3.
"Police Reports" (Dec. 30, 1839): 3.

*The Sporting Whip* [AAS Newspapers]
"A Female Jeremy Diddler—A Specimen of Modern Financiering—A Tale of a Fashionable Boardinghouse on Greenwich between C. and D. Streets. All alive, Ho!" (Feb. 11, 1843).
"Boarding House for Kept Mistresses" (Feb. 25, 1843).

*Whip and Satirist of New-York and Brooklyn* [AAS Newspapers]
"To the Editors of the Whip" (March 26, 1842).

*The White Banner* (Vol. I, 1851; only issue of official quarterly organ of George Lippard's Brotherhood of the Union) [Library Company Periodicals]
"Legends of Every Day," 101–22.
"Editorial Department," 141–48.
"A National Literature," 148.

*Articles, Books, Films, Pamphlets, Plays,*
*Print Graphics, and Recordings*
Alcott, Louisa May. *Little Women; or Meg, Jo, Beth, and* Amy (1869), ed. Anne K. Phillips and Gregory Eiselein (New York: W. W. Norton, 2004).
Alger, Horatio, Jr. *Ragged Dick; or, Street Life in New York with the Boot Blacks* (1868) (New York: New American Library, 1990).

*The Almighty Dollar; or, the Brilliant Exploits of a Killer: A Thrilling Romance of Quakerdelphia: Dedicated to the Million* (Philadelphia: Alfred Lanore, 1847) [HSP].

Anderson, Sherwood. *Winesburg, Ohio* (1919; rept. New York: Penguin Group, 1993).

*Annual Report of the Managers of the Apprentices' Library Company of Philadelphia* (Philadelphia: Joseph Kite, 1847) [HSP].

Antoni, Robert. *My Grandmother's Erotic Folktales: With Stories of Adventure and Occasional Orgies in Her Boarding House for American Soldiers During the War* (New York: Grove, 2000).

Arfwedson, C. D. *The United States and Canada, in 1832, 1833, and 1834*, vol. 1 (London: Richard Bentley, 1834): 33–34.

Armstrong, William. *The Aristocracy of New York: Who They Are, and What They Were* (New York: New York Publishing, 1848).

Arthur, T. S. *The Lights and Shadows of Real Life* (Philadelphia: J. W. Bradley, 1851), 188.

"Asheville Chamber of Commerce. Hotels and Boarding Houses, Asheville, N.C." (Asheville, North Carolina: n.p., 192-?) [NCC].

*Autobiography of Brook Farm*, ed. Henry W. Sams (Englewood Cliffs, N.J.: Prentice-Hall, 1958).

*The Bachelor's Guide, and Widow's Manual; Containing Three Thousand One Hundred and Eighty-Six Names of Widow Ladies, and House Keepers in the Cities of New York and Brooklyn* (New York: A. G. Powell, 1842) [AAS Printed Materials].

Baker, Benjamin A. *A Glance at New York: A Local Drama in Two Acts* (1848; New York: S. French, 189-?). Axis Theater Company revival, June–July 2003 (July 19, 2003, at the Axis Theater Co., Greenwich Village, New York; Randy Sharp, director).

Balzac, Honoré de. *Le Père Goriot* (1835), trans. Burton Raffel (New York: W. W. Norton, 1994).

Baudelaire, Charles. "The Painter of Modern Life" (1859), in *The Painter of Modern Life and Other Essays*, ed. Jonathan Mayne (London: Phaidon, 1995), 1–41.

Beazley, Samuel. *The Boarding-House; or, Five Hours at Brighton; A Musical Farce in Two Acts*. Music by Charles Edward Horn (London: C. Chapple, 1811).

Bird, Robert Montgomery. *Sheppard Lee* (New York: Harper and Brothers, 1836) [Library Company].

Bodichon, Barbara L. S. *Women and Work* (New York: C. S. Francis, 1859), 18–19.

Bouton, John Bell. *The Life and Choice Writings of George Lippard* (New York: H. H. Randall, 1855), 14–27 [Library Company Printed Materials].

Brace, Charles Loring. *Short Sermons to News Boys: With a History of the Formation of the News Boys' Lodging-House* (New York: Charles Scribner, 1866), 1–66.

Briggs, Charles Frederick. *The Adventures of Harry Franco: A Tale of the Great Panic*, 2 vols. (New York: F. Saunders, 1839).

———. *The Trippings of Tom Pepper; or, the Results of Romancing* (New York: Burgess, Stringer, 1847).

Brisbane, Albert. *Association; or, A Concise Exposition of the Practical Part of Fourier's Social Science* (1843; rept. New York: AMS, 1975).

———. *Social Destiny of Man; or, Association and Reorganization of Industry* (1840; rept. New York: Augustus M. Kelley, 1969), 362–65.

Bristed, C. Astor. *The Upper Ten Thousand: Sketches of American Society* (New York: Sringer and Townsend, 1852) [NYPL].

*The British Mechanic's and Labourer's Hand Book, and True Guide to the United States* (London: Charles Knight, 1840), 47–84.

Buckingham, J. S. *America, Historical, Statistic, Descriptive*, vol. 1 (New York: Harper and Brothers, 1841), 231–33.

Bunn, Alfred. *Old England and New England, in a Series of Views Taken on the Spot* (London: Richard Bentley, 1853), 37–42.

Buntline, Ned. *The Mysteries and Miseries of New York* (New York: Berford, 1848).

Burn, James Dawson. *Three Years Among the Working-Classes in the United States During the War* (London: Smith, Elder, 1865), 6–12.

Cahan, Abraham. *The Rise of David Levinsky* (New York: Harper, 1917).

———. *Yekl: A Tale of the New York Ghetto* (1896), in *Yekl and the Imported Bridegroom and Other Stories of Yiddish New York* (New York: Dover, 1970).

*A Century After: Picturesque Glimpses of Philadelphia and Pennsylvania*, ed. Edward Strahan (Philadelphia: Allen, Lane and Scott and J. W. Lauderbach, 1875), 185 [Library Company].

Chapin, Edwin Hubbell. *Humanity in the City* (New York: DeWitt and Davenport, 1854) [NYPL].

———. *Moral Aspects of City Life* (New York: Henry Lyon, 1853) [NYPL].

Child, Lydia Maria. *Letters from New-York* (first series, 1843), ed. Bruce Mills (Athens: University of Georgia Press, 1998).

Clapp, William W. Jr. *A Record of the Boston Stage* (1853; rept. St. Clair Shores, Mich.: Scholarly, 1970).

Clark, Christopher, ed. "The Diary of an Apprentice Cabinetmaker: Edward Jenner Carpenter's 'Journal,' 1844–45," *Proceedings of the American Antiquarian Society* 98, pt. 2 (October 1988): 303–94.

Coleridge, Samuel Taylor. *Coleridge's Shakespearean Criticism*, ed. Thomas M. Raysor (Cambridge, Mass.: Harvard University Press, 1930).

*A Consideration of the Subject of the Central Passenger Railway, Being a Railway for Passengers Only, Proposed to Be Run from Second to Twenty-Third Street, Via Walnut and Chestnut Streets, in the City of Philadelphia* (Philadelphia: W. B. Zieber, 1858) [HSP].

Cooper, James Fenimore. *Home as Found* (Philadelphia: Lea and Blanchard, 1838).

Cummins, Maria. *The Lamplighter* (1854), ed. Nina Baym (New Brunswick, N.J.: Rutgers University Press, 1995).

Curtis, George William. *Early Letters of George William Curtis to John S. Dwight: Brook Farm and Concord,* ed. George Willis Cooke (Port Washington, N.Y.: Kennikat, 1971), 108–11.

Dickens, Charles. *American Notes* (1842; New York: St. Martin's, 1985).

———. "The Boarding House," in *Sketches by Boz* (1836; tale originally appeared in the *Monthly Magazine* in two installments, May and August 1834), in *Dickens' Journalism: Sketches by Boz and Other Early Papers, 1833–39,* ed. Michael Slater (London: Phoenix Giants, 1994), 273–305.

Doesticks, Q. K. Philander [Mortimer Thomson]. *Doesticks; What He Says* (New York: E. Livermore, 1855).

*Doggett's New York City Directory* (New York: John Doggett, Jr., 1841–) [NYPL].

Dreiser, Theodore. *Sister Carrie* (1900; rept. New York: Penguin Books, 1986).

Duncan, Mary G. L. *America as I Found It* (New York: Robert Carter and Brothers, 1852), 194–208.

Dunlap, William. *History of the American Theatre and Anecdotes of the Principal Actors* (1797), 3 vols. (New York: Burt Franklin, 1963), 1:407–12.

*Early Classic String Bands, vol. 3: Gid Tanner & His Skillet Lickers, featuring Riley Packett.* Sound recording (Brighton, Mich.: Old Homestead Records, 1990); see the song "Tanner's Boarding House" [SFC].

Emerson, Ralph Waldo. *Essays: First Series* (1841), from *Ralph Waldo Emerson: Essays & Poems,* ed. Joel Porte et al. (New York: Library of America, 1996). See the essays "Love," 325–38, and "Friendship," 339–54.

———. *Journals and Miscellaneous Notebooks of Ralph Waldo Emerson,* 16 vols., ed. William H. Gilman et al. (Cambridge, Mass.: Belknap Press of Harvard University Press, 1960–82).

———. *The Letters of Ralph Waldo Emerson,* ed. Ralph L. Rusk (New York: Columbia University Press, 1939).

———. *Representative Men* (1850), from *Ralph Waldo Emerson: Essays & Poems.* See the individual essay "Montaigne; or, The Skeptic," 690–709.

Engels, Friedrich. *The Condition of the Working Classes in England in 1844* (1845; New York: John W. Lovell, 1887), 17–18.

*Fast Man's Directory to the Seraglios of New York, Philadelphia, Boston, and All the Principal Cities in the Union by a Free Loveyer* (New York: 1859) [Beinecke].

Fern, Fanny. *Fanny Fern: A Memorial Volume Containing Her Select Writings and a Memoir,* ed. James Parton, illustration Athur Lumley (New York: G. W. Carleton, 1873).

———. *Rose Clark* (New York: Mason Brothers, 1856).

———. *Ruth Hall: A Domestic Tale of the Present Time* (1854; rept. New York: Penguin Books, 1997).

*First Annual Report of the Magdalen Society of New-York* (New York: J. Seymour, 1813).

Fisher, Sidney George. *A Philadelphia Perspective: The Diary of Sidney George Fisher Covering the Years, 1834–1871*, ed. Nicholas B. Wainwright (Philadelphia: Historical Society of Pennsylvania, 1967).

"Fisher's Boarding-House," from the short orchestral work *Fisher's Boarding-House* (1899), composer Percy Grainger. Track no. 6 from *Orchestral Works: The Grainger Edition*, vol. 1, performed by the BBC Philharmonic Orchestra, conductor Richard Hickox (Colchester, Eng.: Chandos Records, 1996) [based on the 1888 Rudyard Kipling poem, "The Ballad of Fisher's Boarding-House"].

Fitzgerald, John D. *Mamma's Boarding House* (Englewood Cliffs, N.J.: Prentice-Hall, 1958).

Foster, George. *New York by Gas-Light*, ed. Stuart Blumin (1850; rept. Berkeley: University of California Press, 1990).

Fourier, Charles. *Design for Utopia* (18??), from *Design for Utopia: Selected Writings of Charles Fourier*, trans. Julia Franklin (New York: Schocken Books, 1971), 137–62.

Fuller, Margaret. *The Letters of Margaret Fuller*, 6 vols., ed. Robert N. Hudspeth (Ithaca, N.Y.: Cornell University Press, 1983–94).

———. *Woman in the Nineteenth Century* (London: Clarke, 1845).

*Fultah Fisher's Boarding House*. Silent short film; director Frank Capra; screen scenario by Walter Montague and Frank Capra; producer Walter Montague (San Francisco: Fireside Productions, 1922) [based on the 1888 Rudyard Kipling poem, "The Ballad of Fisher's Boarding-House"].

Geist, J. M. W. *Recollections of George Lippard* (Philadelphia: Brotherhood of the Union, 1900), 22–28 [HSP].

Graham, Sylvester. *A Lecture on Epidemic Diseases Generally, and Peculiarly the Spasmodic Cholera . . . with an Appendix, Containing Several Testimonials,—Rules of the Graham Boarding House, &c.* (New York: Mahlon Day, 1833), 78–80 [AAS Printed Materials].

Grattan, Thomas Colley. *Civilized America*, vol. 1 (1859; rept. New York: Johnson Reprint, 1969), 109–15.

Greeley, Horace. *Recollections of a Busy Life* (New York: J. B. Ford, 1868) [NYPL].

Green, Helen. *At the Actors' Boarding House and Other Stories* (New York: Nevada, 1906).

Green, J. H. *An Exposure of the Arts and Miseries of Gambling* (Philadelphia: G. B. Zieber, 1847).

Grover, Leonard. *Our Boarding House* (n.d., American play in four acts, ca. 1900).

Grund, Francis. *Aristocracy in America*, vol. 1 (London: Richard Bentley, 1839), 125.

*A Guide to the Stranger, or Pocket Companion for the Fancy, Containing a List of the Gay Houses and Ladies of Pleasure in the City of Brotherly Love and Sisterly Affection* (Philadelphia: n.p., 1829) [Library Company].

Gunn, Thomas Butler. *The Physiology of New York Boarding-Houses* (New York: Mason Brothers, 1857) [NYPL].

Hale, Edward Everett. *Sybaris and Other Homes* (Boston: Fields, Osgood, 1869).

————. *Workingmen's Homes: Essays and Stories* (Boston: James R. Osgood, 1874): 1–28.

Hale, Sarah Josepha. *"Boarding Out": A Tale of Domestic Life* (New York: Harper and Brothers, 1846) [Barnard].

————. *Keeping House and House Keeping: A Story of Domestic Life* (New York: Harper and Brothers, 1845) [Barnard].

Hamilton, Thomas. *Men and Manners in America* (London: T. Cadell, 1833), 1:333–93 [HSP].

Hammer, J. L. *The Mysteries and Miseries of Philadelphia, as Exhibited and Illustrated by . . . a Sketch of the Condition of the Most Degraded Classes in the City* (Philadelphia: n.p., 1853) [Library Company Printed Materials].

Haraszti, Zoltán. *Idyll of Brook Farm: As Revealed by Unpublished Letters in the Boston Public Library* (Boston: Trustees of the Boston Public Library, 1937).

*Harmonica Blues, 1936–1940.* Sound recording; complete recordings of Smith & Harper, George Clarke, Rhythm Willie, Eddie Kelly's Washboard Band. See the song "Boarding House Blues," by Rhythm Willie and His Gang [SFC].

Hawthorne, Nathaniel. *The American Notebooks,* ed. Randall Stewart (New Haven: Yale University Press, 1932).

————. *The Blithedale Romance* (1852), in *Centenary Edition,* vol. 3 (1964).

————. *The Centenary Edition of the Works of Nathaniel Hawthorne,* ed. William Charvat, Roy Harvey Pearce, and Claude M. Simpson (Columbus: Ohio State University Press, 1964–).

————. *The House of the Seven Gables* (1851), in *Centenary Edition,* vol. 2 (1965).

————. "John Inglefield's Thanksgiving" (1840, 1852), in *The Snow-Image and Uncollected Tales,* in *Centenary Edition,* vol. 11 (1974), 179–85.

————. *The Letters,* ed. Thomas Woodson, L. Neal Smith, and Norman Holmes Pearson, in *Centenary Edition,* vol. 15 (1985), 575–77.

————. "Passages from a Relinquished Work" (1834, 1854), in *Mosses from an Old Manse,* in *Centenary Edition,* vol. 10 (1974), 405–21.

————. *The Scarlet Letter* (1850), in *Centenary Edition,* vol. 1 (1962).

Hennequin, Victor A. *Love in the Phalanstery,* trans. Henry James Sr. (New York: Dewitt and Davenport, 1849).

Holmes, Isaac. *An Account of the United States of America, Derived from Actual Observation, During a Residence of Four Years in That Republic* (London: Henry Fisher, 1823), 267–68.

Holmes, Oliver Wendell. *The Autocrat of the Breakfast-Table* (Boston: Phillips, Sampson, 1858).

————. "The Flâneur," from *The Complete Poetical Works of Oliver Wendell Holmes,* ed. H. E. S. (Boston: Houghton, Mifflin, 1895), 284–86.

————. *The Poet at the Breakfast Table* (1872), vol. 3 of *The Writings of Oliver Wendell Holmes* (Cambridge, Mass.: Riverside, 1891), 22–23.

Hone, Philip. *The Diary of Philip Hone, 1828–1851,* 2 vols., ed. Allan Nevins (New York: Dodd, Mead, 1936).

"Hotels and Boarding Houses. Asheville, NC" (promotional pamphlet, 1908) [NCC].

*Hotels, Boarding Houses, and Restaurants in Great Britain & Northern Ireland* (London: British Tourist and Holidays Board, 1949).

Howells, William Dean. *A Hazard of New Fortunes* (1890; rept. New York: Penguin Books, 2001).

Huntley, H. V., Sir. *California: Its Gold and Its Inhabitants,* 2 vols. (London: T. C. Newby, 1856), 1:iv, 2–3, 19–20.

Jacobs, Harriet. *Incidents in the Life of a Slave Girl* (1861), from *The Classic Slave Narratives,* ed. Henry Louis Gates, Jr. (New York: Penguin Books, 1987).

James, Henry. *The American Scene* (1907; rept. New York: Penguin Books, 1994).

———. *The Portrait of a Lady* (1881; rept. New York: W. W. Norton, 1995).

Janson, Drude Krog. *A Saloonkeeper's Daughter* (1887; rept. Baltimore: Johns Hopkins University Press, 2002).

Jones, Justin [Harry Hazel]. *Tom, Dick & Harry; or, The Boys and Girls of Boston: A Tale Founded on Metropolitan Adventures* (Boston: Star Spangled Banner Office, 1849).

Joyce, James. "The Boarding House," from *Dubliners* (1914; rept. New York: Cambridge University Press, 1995), 57–64.

Juloc. *Boarding-House Reminiscences; or, The Pleasure of Living with Others* (London: T. Fisher Unwin, 1896).

*The Kessinger Brothers: Original Fiddle Classics, 1928–1930.* Sound recording (Cincinnati, Ohio: Kanawha, 1969) [SFC].

Kipling, Rudyard. "The Ballad of Fisher's Boarding-House" (1888), from *Rudyard Kipling's Verse, Inclusive Edition: 1885–1918* (Garden City, N.Y.: Doubleday, Page, 1925), 45–49.

*Ladies of the Mission: The Old Brewery, and the New Mission House at the Five Points* (New York: Stringer and Townsend, 1854).

*The Ladykillers,* English film; director Alexander Mackendrick; screenplay William Rose; associate producer Seth Holt; starring Alec Guinness, Cecil Parker, Herbert Lom, Peter Sellers, Danny Green, Katie Johnson (London: Ealing Studios, 1955).

———. American remake; written, directed, and produced by Joel and Ethan Coen; starring Tom Hanks and Irma P. Hall (2004).

Larcom, Lucy. *A New England Girlhood, Outlined from Memory* (Boston: Houghton Mifflin, 1889), 137–61.

*The Last Command.* Silent short film with English subtitles; director Josef von Sternberg; screenplay John F. Goodrich; associate producer B. P. Schulberg; starring Emil Jennings, Evelyn Brent, William Powell, Jack Raymond (Hollywood: Paramount Pictures, 1928).

Lawrence, Amos, and William Richards Lawrence. *Extracts from the Diary and Correspondence of the Late Amos Lawrence; With a Brief Account of Some Incidents in His Life* (Boston: D. Lothrop, 1855) [NYPL].

Lazarus, Marx Edgeworth. *Love vs. Marriage* (New York: Fowler and Wells, 1852), 102–11 [SHC].

Leyda, Jay. *The Melville Log: A Documentary Life of Herman Melville, 1819–1891* (New York: Harcourt, Brace, 1951).

*Life in Town; or, The Boston Spy: Being a Series of Sketches Illustrative of Whims and Women in the "Athens of America." By an Athenian.* (Boston: Redding, 1844).

*The Light of Faith.* Silent American short film with English subtitles; director Clarence Brown (1922; New York: Kino on Video, 1995 re-release).

Lippard, George. *The Bank Director's Son, A Real and Intensely Interesting Revelation of City Life* (Philadelphia: E. E. Barclay and A. R. Orton, 1851) [Library Company].

———. *B. G. C.* (printed pamphlet, ca. 1850–52) [AAS Printed Materials].

———. *The Empire City; or, New York by Night and Day* (1850; rept. Philadelphia: T. B. Peterson and Brothers, 1864).

———. *George Lippard: Prophet of Protest: Writings of an American Radical, 1822–1854,* ed. David S. Reynolds (New York: Peter Lang, 1986).

———. *Journal of the First Annual Convocation of the Supreme Circle* (Philadelphia: n.p., 1850) [HSP].

———. *The Killers: A Narrative of Real Life in Philadelphia* (Philadelphia: Hankinson and Bartholomew, 1850) [Library Company Printed Materials].

———. *Life and Adventures of Charles Anderson Chester, the Notorious Leader of the Philadelphia "Killers": Who Was Murdered, While Engaged in the Destruction of the California House, on Election Night, October 11, 1849* (Philadelphia: Yates and Smith, 1849) [Library Company Printed Materials].

———. *The Nazarene; or, The Last of the Washingtons* (Philadelphia: G. Lippard, 1846), 166–202.

———. *New York: Its Upper Ten and Lower Million* (Cincinnati: H. M. Rulison, 1853).

———. *The Quaker City; or, The Monks of Monk-Hall: A Romance of Philadelphia Life, Mystery and Crime* (Philadelphia: G. B. Zieber, 1844) [first edition, Library Company Printed Materials].

———. *The Quaker City, or, The Monks of Monk Hall: A Romance of Philadelphia Life, Mystery, and Crime* (reprint of the Lippard edition, 1845), ed. David S. Reynolds (Amherst: University of Massachusetts Press, 1995).

*Lowell Almanac, Business Key, and Pocket Memorandum, for 1843* (Lowell, Mass.: Oliver March, Powers and Bagley, 1842) [AAS Almanacs].

*The Lowell Offering: Writings by New England Mill Women, 1840–1845,* ed. Benita Eisler (Philadelphia: J. B. Lippincott, 1977), 13–41.

Mackay, Charles. *Life and Liberty in America; or, Sketches of a Tour in the United States and Canada, in 1857–8,* vol. 1 (London: Smith, Elder, 1859), 42–45.

*Madame Rosa.* French film with English subtitles; director and screenplay Moshé Mizrahi; starring Simone Signoret, Claude Dauphin, Samy ben Youb; based on the novel by Émile Afar (1977).

*Margaret Fuller, Critic: Writings from the New-York Tribune, 1844–1846,* ed. Judith Mattson Bean and Joel Myerson (New York: Columbia University Press, 2000).

Martineau, Harriet. *Society in America,* vol. 3 (London: Saunders and Otley, 1837), 132–35.

Mathews, Charles. *The London Mathews* (Philadelphia: M'Carty and Davis, 1824).

Maury, Sarah Mytton. *An Englishwoman in America* (London: Thomas Richardson and Son, 1848), 193, 196–97.

McCabe, James D. *Lights and Shadows of New York Life; or, The Sights and Sensations of the Great City* (Philadelphia: National, 1872) [NYPL].

McCully, Emily Arnold. *Mirette on the High Wire* (New York: G. P. Putnam's Sons, 1992).

*McElroy's Philadelphia Directory* (Philadelphia: A. McElroy, 1840–50) [HSP].

Melville, Herman. "Bartleby the Scrivener," *Putnam's* (November–December 1853).

———. "Jimmy Rose" (*Harper's,* November 1855).

———. *Moby-Dick, or, The Whale* (1851), ed. Harrison Hayford, Hershel Parker, and G. Thomas Tanselle (Evanston, Ill.: Northwestern University Press and Newberry Library, 2001).

———. "The Paradise of Bachelors and The Tartarus of Maids" (*Harper's,* April 1855).

———. *Pierre; or, the Ambiguities* (1852), ed. Harrison Hayford, Hershel Parker, and G. Thomas Tanselle (Evanston, Ill.: Northwestern University Press and Newberry Library, 1995).

———. "The Two Temples" (1856), from *Great Short Works of Herman Melville,* ed. Warner Berthoff (New York: Harper and Row, 1987).

*Men of Concord and Some Others as Portrayed in the Journal of Henry David Thoreau,* ed. Francis H. Allen (Boston: Houghton Mifflin, 1936).

*Mercantile Library: Finding List for Novels* (Philadelphia: Mercantile Library Association, 1878), 76 [HSP].

Milburn, William Henry. *The Pioneer Preacher; or, Rifle, Axe, and Saddle-Bags, and Other Lectures* (New York: Derby and Jackson, 1859), 195–96.

Mitchell, Donald Grant [Ik Marvel]. *The Lorgnette, or, Studies of the Town by an Opera-Goer* (New York: H. Kernot, 1855).

Morrison, Toni. *Sula* (New York: Knopf, 1973).

Neal, Joseph C. "The Crooked Disciple; or, The Pride of Muscle," from *Charcoal Sketches, or, Scenes in a Metropolis,* with illustrations by David Claypoole Johnston (Philadelphia: E. L. Carey and A. Hart, 1838), 194–206 [University of North Carolina-Chapel Hill, Wilson Library].

———. *Peter Ploddy, and Other Oddities* (Philadelphia: Carey and Hart, 1844); illustration facing p. 60, by F. O. C. Darley.

*New England's Chattels; or, Life in the Northern Poor-House* (New York: H. Dayton, 1858).

"A New Tavern and Boarding-House . . . " (Utica, N.Y.: William Williams, 1821) [AAS Broadsides].

New York Almshouse and Bridewell Commission Records. Covering the years 1791–1797, 1822–1825 [NYPL].

*New York City As It Is* (city directory) (New York: T. R. Tanner, 1835–) [NYPL].

Northall, William Knight. *Before and Behind the Curtain; or, Fifteen Years' Observations Among the Theatres of New York* (New York: W. F. Burgess, 1851), 6–7, 52.

*Not Wanted.* Motion picture released by the independent Filmmakers group; director Ida Lupino; screenplay by Paul Jarrico, Ida Lupino; starring Sally Forrest, Keefe Brasselle, and Leo Penn (Hollywood: Emerald Productions, 1949).

*O'Brien's Commercial Intelligencer* (Philadelphia: John G. O'Brien, 1840), 57, 69 [HSP].

O'Donovan, Jeremiah. *A Brief Account of the Author's Interview with His Countrymen* . . . (1864; rept. New York: Arno, 1969): 92–93, 185.

*Old and In the Way.* Sound recording (Durham, N.C.: Sugar Hill Records, 1973); bluegrass band composed of Jerry Garcia, David Grisman, Peter Rowan, Vassar Clements, and John Kahn [SFC].

Oldmixon, R. N. *Transatlantic Wanderings: or, A Last Look at the United States* (London: Cutledge, 1855), 37.

*On Our Own Ground: The Complete Writings of William Apess, A Pequot,* ed. Barry O'Connell (Amherst: University of Massachusetts Press, 1992), intro., xiii–lxxxi.

Orvis, Marianne Dwight. *Letters from Brook Farm, 1844–1847,* ed. Amy L. Reed (Poughkeepsie, N.Y.: Vassar College, 1928).

Osgood, Samuel. *The Hearth-Stone: Thoughts upon Home-Life in Our Cities* (New York: D. Appleton, 1854) [AAS Printed Materials].

"Our Boarding House." Comic serial running from 1921 to 1981; creator Gene Ahern for the Newspaper Enterprise Association.

Parton, James. *The Life of Horace Greeley, Editor of the New York Tribune* (New York: Mason Brothers, 1855) [NYPL].

Pastor, Tony. *Tony Pastor's Complete Budget of Comic Songs* (New York: Dick and Fitzgerald, 1864).

Pendergrass, Peter. *The Magdalen Report: A Farce in Three Acts* (New York: Joshua Hardcastle, 1831).

Poe, Edgar Allan. *Essays and Reviews* (New York: Library of America, 1984).

———. *The Letters of Edgar Allan Poe,* 2 vols., ed. John Ward Ostrom (Cambridge, Mass.: Harvard University Press, 1948), 1:123, 251–53.

———. *The Poe Log: A Documentary Life of Edgar Allan Poe,* ed. Dwight Thomas and David K. Jackson (Boston: G. K. Hall, 1987).

———. *Selected Poetry and Prose,* ed. T. O. Mabbott (New York: Modern Library, 1951). See the following tales: "The Fall of the House of Usher" (1839), 115–30; "William Wilson" (1839), 131–53; "The Man of the Crowd" (1840), 154–61; "The Murders in the Rue Morgue" (1841), 162–91; and "The Masque of the Red Death" (1842), 226–30.

Porter, Katherine Anne. "Pale Horse, Pale Rider," in *Pale Horse, Pale Rider: Three Short Novels* (1939; rept. New York: Modern Library, 1949).

"Premium" (Philadelphia: Sept. 15, 1829) [AAS Broadsides].

"The Race Wars of Abolition Days," *The North American* (Philadelphia newspaper, June 20, 1915) [HSP Newspapers].

*Rae's Philadelphia Pictorial Directory & Panoramic Advertiser* (Philadelphia: Julio H. Rae, 1851) [LCP Prints, folder 12].

Reizenstein, Baron Ludwig von. *The Mysteries of New Orleans,* trans. Steven Rowan (1855; rept. Baltimore: Johns Hopkins University Press, 2002).

Riis, Jacob. *How the Other Half Lives: Studies Among the Tenements of New York* (1890; rept. New York: Dover, 1971).

Ritchie, Anna Cora Ogden Mowatt. *Evelyn; or A Heart Unmasked: A Tale of Domestic Life* (Philadelphia: G. B. Zieber, 1845).

Robinson, Harriet H. *Loom and Spindle; or, Life Among the Early Mill Girls* (1898; rept. Kailua, Hawaii: Press Pacifica, 1976).

"Room & Board." Comic serial running from 1936 to 1953; creator Gene Ahern for the King Features Syndicate.

Ross, Joel H. *What I Saw in New York; or A Bird's Eye View of City Life* (Auburn, N.Y.: Derby and Miller, 1851).

Ross, William P. M. *The Accountant's Own Book and Business Man's Manual* (Philadelphia: G. B. Zieber, 1848).

———. *A Practical System of Double Entry Book-Keeping* (Philadelphia: G. B. Zieber, 1847).

Russell, William Howard. *My Diary North and South,* ed. Fletcher Pratt (New York: Harper, 1954), 16–17.

*Scene in a Fashionable Boarding House,* No. 1 (New York: Bufford's Lithograph, ca. 1835–39) [AAS Lithographs].

Sears, John Van Der Zee. *My Friends at Brook Farm* (New York: Desmond Fitzgerald, 1912), 80–106.

Sedgwick, Catharine Maria. *Clarence: A Tale of Our Own Times* (London: Henry Colburn and Richard Bentley, 1830).

———. *Married or Single?* (New York: Harper and Brothers, 1857).

———. *The Power of Her Sympathy: The Autobiography and Journal of Catharine Maria Sedgwick,* ed. Mary Kelley (Boston: Massachusetts Historical Society, 1993).

———. *Tales of City Life* (Philadelphia: Hazard and Mitchell, 1850) [Barnard].

Sergeant, John. "An Address, Delivered at the Request of the Managers of the Apprentices' Library Company of Philadelphia, 23 November 1832" (Philadelphia: Apprentices' Library Company of Philadelphia, 1832) [HSP].

*Sheldon & Co.'s New York Directory.* City Lodging (New York: Sheldon, Lamport, and Blakeman, 1845) [NYPL].

Singer, Isaac Bashevis. "The Yearning Heifer" (1970), from *In the Catskills: A Century of the Jewish Experience in "The Mountains,"* ed. Phil Brown (New York: Columbia University Press, 2002), 64–74.

*Sixth Annual Report of the Managers of the Seaman's Aid Society of the City of Boston. Written by Mrs. S. J. Hale, and read at the Annual Meeting, Jan. 9, 1839* (Boston: James B. Dow, 1839), 17–18 [AAS Printed Materials].

"Southern Pines, N.C.: Cottages, Hotels and Boarding Houses" (promotional pamphlet, n.d.) [NCC].

Stoddard, Richard Henry. *Recollections, Personal and Literary,* ed. Ripley Hitchcock (New York: A. S. Barnes, 1903).

Stowe, Harriet Beecher. *Uncle Tom's Cabin; or, Life Among the Lowly* (1852; rept. New York: Oxford University Press, 2002).

Strong, George Templeton. *The Diary of George Templeton Strong, 1820–1875,* ed. Allan Nevins and Milton Halsey Thomas (New York: Macmillan, 1952). Vol. 1, *Young Man in New York, 1835–1849,* and vol. 2, *The Turbulent Fifties, 1850–1859.*

Sue, Eugène. *The Mysteries of Paris* (1842; rept. London: Chapman and Hall, 1845).

"Summer Resort Hotels and Boarding Houses" (Southern Railway System promotional pamphlet, 1922) [NCC].

Taylor, Bayard. *John Godfrey's Fortunes; Related by Himself: A Story of American Life* (New York: G. P. Putnam, 1865).

*Thirteenth Annual Report of the Seaman's Aid Society, of the City of Boston* (Boston: Eastburn's, 1846), 33 [AAS Printed Materials].

Thompson, George. *City Crimes; or Life in New York and Boston* (1849), in *Venus in Boston and Other Tales of Nineteenth-Century City Life,* ed. David S. Reynolds and Kimberley R. Gladman (Amherst: University of Massachusetts Press, 2002).

———. *The House Breaker; or, The Mysteries of Crime* (Boston: W. L. Bradbury, 1848).

———. *My Life; or the Adventures of George Thompson* (1854), in *Venus in Boston,* ed. Reynolds and Gladman.

———. *Venus in Boston* (1849), in *Venus in Boston,* ed. Reynolds and Gladman.

Thoreau, Henry David. *The Correspondence of Henry David Thoreau,* ed. Walter Harding and Carl Bode (New York: NYU Press, 1958).

———. *Journal,* vol. 1: 1837–1844, ed. John C. Broderick et al. (Princeton, N.J.: Princeton University Press, 1981): 1:277–78 (March 3, 1841).

———. "The Landlord," *Democratic Review* (October 1843): 427–30.

———. "Paradise (to Be) Regained," *Democratic Review* (November 1843): 451–63.

———. "Resistance to Civil Government" (1849), from *The Writings of Henry D. Thoreau: Reform Papers,* ed. Wendell Glick (Princeton, N.J.: Princeton University Press, 1973), 63–90.

———. *Walden* (1854), ed. J. Lyndon Shanley, in *The Writings of Henry D. Thoreau* (Princeton, N.J.: Princeton University Press, 1971).

Tocqueville, Alexis de. *Democracy in America,* vols. 1 (1835) and 2 (1840), ed. J. P. Mayer, trans. George Lawrence (New York: Harper and Row, 1966).

Tozzi, Federigo. "The Boardinghouse" (1917), from *Love in Vain,* trans. Minna Proctor (New York: New Directions Books, 2001), 57–65.

Trevor, William. *The Boarding House* (1965), in *Three Early Novels* (New York: Penguin Books, 2000), 167–410.

Trollope, Francis. *Domestic Manners of the Americans* (London: Whittaker, Treacher, 1832), 225–30.

Twain, Mark. *Roughing It* (Hartford: American, 1872), 163, 268.

Warner, Susan. *The Wide, Wide World* (1850), Jane P. Tompkins, afterword (New York: Feminist Press at CUNY, 1987).

*Wealth and Biography of the Wealthy Citizens of Philadelphia . . . by a Member of the Philadelphia Bar* (Philadelphia: G. B. Zieber, 1845).

Webster, Noah. *Webster's Dictionary Unabridged,* revised edition, ed. Chauncey A. Goodrich (Springfield, Mass.: G. and C. Merriam, 1859), 133, 673.

Wemyss, Francis Courtney. *Twenty-Six Years of the Life of an Actor and Manager* (New York: Burgess, Stringer, 1847), 394–97.

Wenlandt, Oliver. *The Nigger Boarding-House: A Screaming Farce in One Act and One Scene for Six Male Burnt-Cork Characters* (New York: Dick and Fitzgerald, 1898).

Wharton, Edith. *The House of Mirth* (1905; rept. New York: Oxford University Press, 1994).

Whipple, Dorothy. "Boarding-House," from *After Tea and Other Stories* (London: John Murray, 1941), 158–81.

Whitman, Walt. *Franklin Evans; or, The Inebriate; A Tale of the Times* (1842), ed. Jean Downey (New Haven, Conn.: Yale College and University Press, 1967).

———. *Leaves of Grass* (Brooklyn: Fowler and Wells, 1855), first edition reprint from, ed. J. R. LeMaster and Donald D. Kummings. *Walt Whitman: An Encyclopedia,* (New York: Garland, 1998).

———. *Walt Whitman of the New York Aurora,* ed. Joseph Jay Rubin and Charles H. Brown (State College, Pa.: Bald Eagle, 1950). See the following, all from Whitman's days at the New York *Aurora:* "New York Boarding Houses" (March 18, 1842): 22–24; "The Clerk from the Country" (March 24, 1842): 27–30; and "Snoring Made Music" (April 18, 1842): 52–53.

———. "Wicked Architecture," *Life Illustrated* (July 19, 1856), from *New York Dissected: A Sheaf of Recently Discovered Newspaper Articles by the Author of Leaves of Grass,* ed. Emory Holloway and Ralph Adimari (New York: Rufus Rockwell Wilson, 1936), 87–98.

Whitney & Annin (engravers and authors), *"Uncle Tom's Cabin" Contrasted with Buckingham Hall, the Planter's Home; or, A Fair View of Both Sides of the Slavery Question* (New York: D. Fanshaw, 1852); illustration facing p. 112, by F. O. C. Darley.

Williams, Tennessee. *This Property Is Condemned* (1952). See the 1966 film version of Williams's one-act play. Director Sydney Pollack; screenwriter Frances Ford Coppola (with others); starring Natalie Wood (as Alva Starr) and Robert Redford (as Owen Legate).

Winter, William. *Old Friends; Being Literary Recollections of Other Days* (New York: Moffat, Yard, 1909).

Wolfe, Gene. "The Haunted Boardinghouse" (1990), from *Strange Travelers* (New York: Tom Doherty Associates, 2000), 209–38.

Wolfe, Thomas. *Look Homeward, Angel: A Story of the Buried Life* (1929; New York: Charles Scribner's Sons, 1952).

## Secondary Sources
### Unpublished Works

Ackmann, Martha. "The Matrilineage of Emily Dickinson" (Ph.D. dissertation, University of Massachusetts at Amherst, 1988), 178–93.

Broderick, John C. "Thoreau's Attitude Toward Cities and City Life" (M.A. thesis, University of North Carolina-Chapel Hill, 1949).

———. "Thoreau's Principle of Simplicity as Shown in His Attitudes Toward Cities, Government, and Industrialism" (Ph.D. dissertation, University of North Carolina-Chapel Hill, 1953).

Buckley, Peter. "To the Opera House: Culture and Society in New York City, 1820–1860" (Ph.D. dissertation, State University of New York at Stony Brook, 1984), 305–12.

Erickson, Paul. "New Books, New Men: Authorship and Antebellum Sensation Fiction." A paper delivered to the McNeil Center for Early American Studies Seminar Series (Feb. 23, 2001), Winterthur Museum, Garden & Library, Winterthur, Delaware.

Pernicone, Carol Groneman. "The 'Bloody Ould Sixth,' A Social Analysis of a New York City Working-Class Community in the Mid-Nineteenth Century" (Ph.D. dissertation, University of Rochester, 1973), 62–67.

Porter, Susan L. "Making 'A Home for Some of the Finest People': The Politics of the Genteel Boarding House in Nineteenth-Century Boston." A paper delivered at the annual meeting of the Organization of American Historians (March 27, 2004), Boston, Mass.

Stott, Richard. "Workers in the Metropolis: New York City, 1820–1860" (Ph.D. dissertation, Cornell University, 1983), 273, 329–403.

Tuchinsky, Adam-Max. "Horace Greeley's Lost Book: The *New York Tribune* and the Origin of Social Democratic Liberalism in America" (Ph.D. dissertation, University of North Carolina-Chapel Hill, 2001).

### Published Works

Alter, Robert. *Imagined Cities: Urban Experience and the Language of the Novel* (New Haven, Conn.: Yale University Press, 2005).

———. *The Pleasures of Reading in an Ideological Age* (New York: Norton, 1996).

Amireh, Amal. *The Factory Girl and the Seamstress: Imagining Gender and Class in Nineteenth-Century American Fiction* (New York: Garland, 2000), 77–110.

Anderson, Douglas. *A House Undivided: Domesticity and Community in American Literature* (New York: Cambridge University Press, 1990).

Antler, Joyce. "Forty Prime-Time Shows," in *Television's Changing Image of American Jews*, ed. Neal Gabler, Frank Rich, and Joyce Antler (Los Angeles: American Jewish Committee and the Norman Lear Center, 2000), 39–42.

Auerbach, Jonathan. *The Romance of Failure: First-Person Fictions of Poe, Hawthorne, and James* (New York: Oxford University Press, 1989), 71–117.

Augst, Thomas. "The Business of Reading in Nineteenth-Century America: The New York Mercantile Library," *American Quarterly* 50, no. 2 (June 1998): 267–305.

———. *The Clerk's Tale: Young Men and Moral Life in Nineteenth-Century America* (Chicago: University of Chicago Press, 2003).

Bakhtin, Mikhail. "Forms of Time and of the Chronotope in the Novel: Notes Toward a Historical Poetics," in *The Dialogic Imagination,* ed. Michael Holquist, trans. Caryl Emerson and Holquist (1981; rept. Austin: University of Texas Press, 1994), 84–258.

Banta, Martha. *Taylored Lives: Narrative Productions in the Age of Taylor, Veblen, and Ford* (Chicago: University of Chicago Press, 1993).

———. "The Three New Yorks: Topographical Narratives and Cultural Texts," *American Literary History* 7, no. 1 (Spring 1995): 28–54.

Barth, Gunther. *City People: The Rise of Modern City Culture in Nineteenth-Century America* (New York: Oxford University Press, 1980), 28–-57.

Bauer, Dale M. *Feminist Dialogics: A Theory of Failed Community* (Albany: State University of New York Press, 1988), 117–50.

Baxter, Maria. "Boarding Houses: Fact and Fiction" (Raleigh: North Carolina Sites Section of the Division of Archives and History, 1983) [NCC].

Baym, Nina. "Hawthorne's Women: The Tyranny of Social Myths," *Centennial Review* 15, no. 3 (Summer 1971): 250–72.

———. *Woman's Fiction: A Guide to Novels by and About Women in America, 1820–1870* (1978; rept. Urbana: University of Illinois Press, 1993).

Beers, Henry A. *Nathaniel Parker Willis* (Boston: Houghton Mifflin, 1885).

Beetham, Margaret. "Towards a Theory of the Periodical as a Publishing Genre," in *Investigating Victorian Journalism,* ed. Laurel Brake et al. (New York: MacMillan, 1990), 19–32.

Bellis, Peter J. *Writing Revolution: Aesthetics and Politics in Hawthorne, Whitman, and Thoreau* (Athens: University of Georgia Press, 2003).

Bender, Thomas. *Community and Social Change in America* (New Brunswick, N.J.: Rutgers University Press, 1978), 86–94.

———. *New York Intellect: A History of Intellectual Life in New York City, from 1750 to the Beginnings of Our Own Time* (Baltimore: Johns Hopkins University Press, 1987).

———. *The Unfinished City: New York and the Metropolitan Idea* (New York: New York University Press, 2002).

Benjamin, Walter. "On Some Motifs in Baudelaire" (1939), in *Illuminations,* ed. Hannah Arendt, trans. Harry Zorn (New York: Harcourt, Brace, 1968), 157–202.

Bercovitch, Sacvan. *The Office of the Scarlet Letter* (Baltimore: Johns Hopkins University Press, 1991).

Berg, Barbara J. *The Remembered Gate: Origins of American Feminism— The Woman and the City* (New York: Oxford University Press, 1978), 96–97.

Bergmann, Hans. *God in the Street: New York Writing from the Penny Press to Melville* (Philadelphia: Temple University Press, 1995).

———. "Panoramas of New York, 1845–1860," *Prospects* 10 (1985): 119–37.

Berlant, Lauren. "Fantasies of Utopia in *The Blithedale Romance,*" *American Literary History* 1, no. 1 (Spring 1989): 30–62.

———. "The Female Woman: Fanny Fern and the Form of Sentiment," in *The Culture of Sentiment: Race, Gender, and Sentimentality in Nineteenth-Century America*, ed. Shirley Samuels (New York: Oxford University Press, 1993), 265–81.

Berman, Marshall. *All That Is Solid Melts into Air: The Experience of Modernity* (New York: Simon and Schuster, 1982), 13–36.

Betts, Glynne Robinson. *Writers in Residence: American Authors at Home* (New York: Viking, 1981), 102–7.

Bishop, Joseph Bucklin. *Theodore Roosevelt and His Time, Shown in His Letters*, 2 vols. (New York: Charles Scribner's Sons, 1920), 2:474.

Blackmar, Elizabeth. *Manhattan for Rent, 1785–1850* (Ithaca, N.Y.: Cornell University Press, 1989).

Blakemore, Peter. "Thoreau, Literature, and the Phenomenon of Inhabitation," in *Thoreau's Sense of Place: Essays in American Environmental Writing*, ed. Richard J. Schneider (Iowa City: University of Iowa Press, 2000), 115–32.

Blanck, Jacob, comp. "George Lippard," in *Bibliography of American Literature 5* (New Haven, Conn.: Yale University Press, 1969), 405–18.

Blumin, Stuart M. *The Emergence of the Middle Class: Social Experience in the American City, 1760–1900* (New York: Cambridge University Press, 1989), 138–91.

———. "Explaining the New Metropolis: Perception, Depiction, and Analysis in Mid-Nineteenth-Century New York City," *Journal of Urban History* 11, no. 1 (November 1984): 9–38.

Boyer, Paul S. *Urban Masses and Moral Order in America, 1820–1920* (Cambridge, Mass.: Harvard University Press, 1978).

Brand, Dana. *The Spectator and the City in Nineteenth-Century American Literature* (New York: Cambridge University Press, 1991).

Bremer, Sidney H. *Urban Intersections* (Urbana: University of Illinois Press, 1992).

Bridges, Amy. *A City in the Republic: Antebellum New York and the Origins of Machine Politics* (New York: Cambridge University Press, 1984), 46–56.

Bright, Marjorie Belle. *Nellie's Boardinghouse: A Dual Biography of Nellie Coffman and Palm Springs* (Palm Springs: ETC, 1981).

Brodhead, Richard. *Cultures of Letters: Scenes of Reading and Writing in Nineteenth-Century America* (Chicago: University of Chicago Press, 1993): "Sparing the Rod: Discipline and Fiction in Antebellum America," 13–47; and "Veiled Ladies: Toward a History of Antebellum Entertainment," 48–68.

———. *The School of Hawthorne* (New York: Oxford University Press, 1986).

Bromell, Nicholas K. *By the Sweat of the Brow: Literature and Labor in Antebellum America* (Chicago: University of Chicago Press, 1993).

Brooks, Peter. "The Mark of the Beast: Prostitution, Melodrama, and Narrative," *New York Literary Forum* 7 (1980): 125–40.

———. "The Text of the City," *Oppositions: A Journal for Ideas and Criticism in Architecture* 8 (1977): 7–11.

Brooks, Van Wyck. *The Flowering of New England, 1815–1865* (New York: E. P. Dutton, 1936), 343–58.

Brown, Charles H. *William Cullen Bryant* (New York: Charles Scribner's Sons, 1971), 132.

Brown, Phil. "Sleeping in My Parents' Hotel: The End of a Century of the Jewish Catskills," in *In the Catskills: A Century of the Jewish Experience in "The Mountains,"* ed. Phil Brown (New York: Columbia University Press, 2002), 9–21.

Buck-Morss, Susan. "The Flaneur, the Sandwichman and the Whore: The Politics of Loitering," *New German Critique* 39, second special issue on Walter Benjamin (Autumn 1986): 99–140.

Buell, Lawrence. "Circling the Spheres: A Dialogue," *American Literature* 70, no. 3 (special issue, *No More Separate Spheres!*, September 1998): 465–90.

———. *Emerson* (Cambridge, Mass.: Belknap Press of Harvard University Press, 2003).

———. *New England Literary Culture: From Revolution Through Renaissance* (New York: Cambridge University Press, 1986).

Bumas, E. Shaskan. "Fictions of the Panopticon: Prison, Utopia, and the Out-Penitent in the Works of Nathaniel Hawthorne," *American Literature* 73, no. 1 (March 2001): 121–45.

Burrows, Edwin, and Mike Wallace. *Gotham: A History of New York City to 1898* (New York: Oxford University Press, 1999).

Butterfield, Roger. "A Check List of the Separately Published Works of George Lippard," *Pennsylvania Magazine of History and Biography* 79, no. 3 (July 1955): 302–9.

Calhoun, Arthur W. *A Social History of the American Family, from Colonial Times to the Present—vol. 2, From Independence Through the Civil War* (Cleveland: Arthur H. Clark, 1918), 238–42.

Cavell, Stanley. *The Senses of Walden* (1972; rept. Chicago: University of Chicago Press, 1992).

Certeau, Michel de. *The Practice of Everyday Life,* trans. Steven F. Rendall (Berkeley: University of California Press, 1984), 91–114.

Chai, Leon. *The Romantic Foundations of the American Renaissance* (Ithaca, N.Y.: Cornell University Press, 1987).

Chartier, Roger. *The Order of Books: Readers, Authors, and Libraries in Europe Between the Fourteenth and Eighteenth Centuries,* ed. Lydia G. Cochrane (Stanford, Calif.: Stanford University Press, 1994), 1–23.

Charvat, William. *Literary Publishing in America, 1790–1850* (1959; rept. Amherst: University of Massachusetts Press, 1993), 1–37, 55–56.

Chauncey, George. *Gay New York: Gender, Urban Culture, and the Makings of the Gay Male World, 1890–1940* (New York: Basic Books, 1994).

Chudacoff, Howard P. *The Age of the Bachelor: Creating an American Subculture* (Princeton, N.J.: Princeton University Press, 1999), 3–44, 133.

Ciccone, Nancy. "*The Blithedale Romance,* an American Bacchae," *Classical and Modern Literature: A Quarterly* 20, no. 1 (Fall 1999): 77–100.

Clark, Christopher. *The Communitarian Movement: The Radical Challenge of the Northampton Association* (Ithaca, N.Y.: Cornell University Press, 1995), 1–14, 98–134.

Coale, Samuel. "Spiritualism and Hawthorne's Romance: The Blithedale Theater as False Consciousness," *Literature and Belief* 14 (1994): 31–56.

Cohen, Patricia Cline. *The Murder of Helen Jewett: The Life and Death of a Prostitute in Nineteenth-Century New York* (New York: Alfred A. Knopf, 1998), 90–110.

Cohen, Patricia Cline, Timothy J. Gilfoyle, and Helen Lefkowitz Horowitz. *The Flash Press: Sporting Male Weeklies in 1840s New York* (Chicago: University of Chicago Press, 2008).

Cook, James W. *The Arts of Deception: Playing with Fraud in the Age of Barnum* (Cambridge, Mass.: Harvard University Press, 2001).

Coolidge, John. *Mill and Mansion: A Study of Architecture and Society in Lowell, Massachusetts, 1820–1865* (1942; rept. New York: Russell and Russell, 1967).

Cosman, Max. "Thoreau and Staten Island," *Staten Island Historian* 6, no. 1 (January–March 1943): 1–2, 7.

Cowan, Michael H. *City of the West: Emerson, America, and Urban Metaphor* (New Haven, Conn.: Yale University Press, 1967).

Cowley, Malcolm. *Exile's Return: A Literary Odyssey of the 1920s* (1934; rept. New York: Penguin Classics, 1994).

Crain, Caleb. *American Sympathy: Men, Friendship, and Literature in the New Nation* (New Haven, Conn.: Yale University Press, 2001).

Crews, Frederick C. *The Sins of the Fathers: Hawthorne's Psychological Themes* (New York: Oxford University Press, 1966), 194–99.

Cronon, William. *Nature's Metropolis: Chicago and the Great West* (New York: W. W. Norton, 1991).

Darnton, Robert. "What Is the History of Books?" (1982), in *Reading in America*, ed. Cathy Davidson (Baltimore: Johns Hopkins University Press, 1989), 27–52.

Davidson, Cathy N. "Preface: No More Separate Spheres!" *American Literature* 70, no. 3 (special issue, *No More Separate Spheres!*, September 1998): 443–63.

———. *Revolution and the Word: The Rise of the Novel in America* (New York: Oxford University Press, 1986), 114–23.

Davis, Mike. *Planet of Slums* (London: Verso, 2006).

Davis, Theo. *Formalism, Experience, and the Making of American Literature in the Nineteenth Century* (New York: Cambridge University Press, 2007).

Day, Jared N., and Timothy J. Haggerty. "The Bachelor and the Landlady: A Tale of Gotham," *Seaport: New York's History Magazine* (Winter 2005): 14–21.

Delano, Sterling F. *Brook Farm: The Dark Side of Utopia* (Cambridge, Mass.: Belknap Press of Harvard University Press, 2004).

D'Emilio, John, and Estelle B. Freedman. *Intimate Matters: A History of Sexuality in America* (New York: Harper and Row, 1988), 123.

Demos, John. *A Little Commonwealth: Family Life in Plymouth Colony* (New York: Oxford University Press, 1970).

Denning, Michael. *Mechanic Accents: Dime Novels and Working-Class Culture in America* (London: Verso, 1987).

Derrida, Jacques. "Différance," trans. Alan Bass, in *Margins of Philosophy* (Chicago: University of Chicago Press, 1982), 3–27.

*Dictionary of Literary Biography,* vol. 49, *American Literary Publishing Houses, 1638–1899, Part 2: N–Z,* ed. Peter Dzwonkoski (Detroit: Gale Research, 1986), 502.

Dimock, Wai-chee. "Planetary Time and Global Translation: 'Context' in Literary Studies," *Common Knowledge* 9, no. 3 (2003): 488–507.

Donald, David. "An Excess of Democracy: The American Civil War and the Social Process," in *Lincoln Reconsidered: Essays on the Civil War Era* (1960; New York: Random House, 1984), 209–35.

Douglas, Ann. *The Feminization of American Culture* (New York: Noonday, 1977).

Duberman, Martin. *James Russel Lowell* (Cambridge, Mass.: Riverside, 1966), 37.

DuBois, W. E. B. *The Philadelphia Negro: A Social Study* (1899; Philadelphia: University of Pennsylvania Press, 1996).

Dunlap, William. *The Life of Charles Brockden Brown,* vol. 1 (Philadelphia: James R. Parke, 1815), 1–67.

Ehrenreich, Barbara. *Nickel and Dimed: On (Not) Getting By in America* (New York: Henry Holt, 2001), 51–56.

Ehrlich, Heyward. "The 'Mysteries' of Philadelphia: Lippard's *Quaker City* and 'Urban' Gothic Fiction," *ESQ* 18, no. 1 (1972): 50–65.

Elkins, Stanley M. *Slavery: A Problem in American Institutional and Intellectual Life* (1959; rept. Chicago: University of Chicago Press, 1976), 27–37.

Esteve, Mary. *The Aesthetics and Politics of the Crowd in American Literature* (New York: Cambridge University Press, 2003), 1–58.

Evelev, John. *Tolerable Entertainment: Herman Melville and Professionalism in Antebellum New York* (Amherst: University of Massachusetts Press, 2006).

Faflik, David. "Authorship, Ownership, and the Case for *Charles Anderson Chester,*" *Book History* (2008): 149–68.

———. "Boardinghouse Life, Boardinghouse Letters," *Studies in the Literary Imagination* 40, no. 1 (Spring 2007): 27–47.

———. "Community, Civility, Compromise: Dr. Holmes's Boston Boardinghouse," *New England Quarterly* 78, no. 4 (December 2005): 547–69.

Fanuzzi, Robert. "Thoreau's Urban Imagination," *American Literature* 68, no. 2 (June 1996): 321–46.

Fiedler, Leslie. "The Male Novel," *Partisan Review* 37, no. 1 (May 1970): 74–89.

Fink, Steven. *Prophet in the Marketplace: Thoreau's Development as a Professional Writer* (Princeton, N.J.: Princeton University Press, 1992).

Fisher, Philip. "Democratic Social Space: Whitman, Melville, and the Promise of American Transparency," *Representations* 24 (Autumn 1988): 60–101.

———. *Hard Facts: Setting and Form in the American Novel* (New York: Oxford University Press, 1985).

Foucault, Michel. "What Is an Author?" (1979), in *The Foucault Reader*, ed. Paul Rabinov, trans. Jasúe V. Harari (New York: Pantheon Books, 1984), 100–120.

Francis, Richard. *Transcendental Utopias: Individual and Community at Brook Farm, Fruitlands, and Walden* (Ithaca, N.Y.: Cornell University Press, 1997), 35–66.

Frisby, David. *Fragments of Modernity: Theories of Modernity in the Work of Simmel, Kracauer, and Benjamin* (Cambridge, Mass.: MIT Press, 1986), 1–37.

Frye, Northrop. "Approaching the Lyric," in *Lyric Poetry: Beyond New Criticism*, ed. Chavisa Hošek and Patricia Parker (Ithaca, N.Y.: Cornell University Press, 1985), 31–37.

Gable, Harvey L. Jr. "Inappeasable Longings: Hawthorne, Romance, and the Disintegration of Coverdale's Self in *The Blithedale Romance*," *New England Quarterly* 67, no. 2 (June 1994): 257–78.

Gabler, Neal. *An Empire of Their Own: How the Jews Invented Hollywood* (New York: Crown, 1988).

Gafford, Lucille. "Transcendentalist Attitudes toward Drama and Theatre," *New England Quarterly* 13, no. 3 (September 1940): 442–66.

Gamber, Wendy. *The Boardinghouse in Nineteenth-Century America* (Baltimore: Johns Hopkins University Press, 2007).

———. "Tarnished Labor: The Home, the Market, and the Boardinghouse in Antebellum America," *Journal of the Early Republic* 22, no. 2 (Summer 2002): 177–204.

Garlick, Görel. *To Serve the Purpose of the Drama: The Theatre Designs and Plays of Samuel Beazley, 1786–1851* (London: Society for Theatre Research, 2003).

Gates, Robert A. *The New York Vision* (Lanham, Md.: University Press of America, 1987).

Gibian, Peter. *Oliver Wendell Holmes and the Culture of Conversation* (New York: Cambridge University Press, 2001).

Giedion, Sigfried. *Space, Time and Architecture: The Growth of a New Tradition* (1941; rept. Cambridge, Mass.: Harvard University Press: 1965).

Gilfoyle, Timothy J. *City of Eros: New York City, Prostitution, and the Commercialization of Sex, 1820–1920* (New York: Norton, 1992).

———. "The Urban Geography of Commercial Sex: Prostitution in New York City, 1790–1860," *Journal of Urban History* 13 (August 1987): 371–93.

Gilmore, Michael T. *American Romanticism and the Marketplace* (Chicago: University of Chicago Press, 1985).

Glynn, Tom. "Books for a Reformed Republic: The Apprentices' Library of New York City, 1820–1865," *Libraries and Culture* 34, no. 4 (Fall 1999): 347–72.

Gordon, Michael. *The American Family: Past, Present, and Future* (New York: Random House, 1978).

Green, Martin. *The Problem of Boston* (New York: W. W. Norton, 1966).

Greeson, Jennifer Rae. "The 'Mysteries and Miseries' of North Carolina: New York City, Urban Gothic Fiction, and *Incidents in the Life of a Slave Girl*," *American Literature* 73, no. 2 (June 2001): 277–309.

Gross, Robert A. "Culture and Cultivation: Agriculture and Society in Thoreau's Concord," *The Journal of American History* 69, no. 1 (June 1982): 42–61.

————. "Lonesome in Eden: Dickinson, Thoreau, and the Problem of Community in Nineteenth-Century New England," *Canadian Review of American Studies* 14, no. 1 (1983): 1–17.

————. "'The Most Estimable Place in All the World': A Debate on Progress in Nineteenth-Century Concord," *Studies in the American Renaissance* (1978): 1–15.

————. "Much Instruction from Little Reading: Books and Libraries in Thoreau's Concord," *Proceedings of the American Antiquarian Society* 97, no. 1 (1987): 129–88.

————. "Transcendentalism and Urbanism: Concord, Boston, and the Wider World," *Journal of American Studies* 18, no. 3 (1984): 361–81.

Grossberg, Benjamin Scott. "'The Tender Passion Was Very Rife Among Us': Coverdale's Queer Utopia and *The Blithedale Romance*," *Studies in American Fiction* 28, no. 1 (Spring 2000): 3–26.

Guarneri, Carl. *The Utopian Alternative: Fourierism in Nineteenth-Century America* (Ithaca, N.Y.: Cornell University Press, 1991): 178–226.

Habegger, Alfred. *The Father: A Life of Henry James, Sr.* (Amherst: University of Massachusetts Press, 2001).

————. *My Wars Are Laid Away in Books: The Life of Emily Dickinson* (New York: Random House, 2001), 191–96.

Habermas, Jürgen. *The Structural Transformation of the Public Sphere: An Inquiry into a Category of Bourgeois Society* (1962), trans. Thomas Burger (Cambridge, Mass.: MIT Press, 1989).

Hall, Peter Dobkin. *The Organization of American Culture, 1700–1900: Private Institutions, Elites, and the Origins of American Nationality* (New York: NYU Press, 1982), 198–219.

Halttunen, Karen. *Confidence Men and Painted Women: A Study of Middle-Class Culture in America* (New Haven, Conn.: Yale University Press, 1982).

Handlin, Oscar. *Boston's Immigrants, 1790–1865: A Study in Acculturation* (1941; rept. Cambridge: Belknap Press of Harvard University Press, 1991), 95–101.

Harding, Walter. *The Days of Henry Thoreau: A Biography* (1962; rept. Princeton, N.J.: Princeton University Press, 1982).

Harker, Jaime. "'Pious Cant' and Blasphemy: Fanny Fern's Radicalized Sentiment," *Legacy* 18, no. 1 (2001): 52–64.

Harris, Kenneth Marc. *Hypocrisy and Self-Deception in Hawthorne's Fiction* (Charlottesville: University Press of Virginia, 1988), 135–36.

Harris, Leslie M. *In the Shadows of Slavery: African Americans in New York City, 1626–1863* (Chicago: University of Chicago Press, 2003), 76.

Harris, Neil. *Humbug: The Art of P. T. Barnum* (Boston: Little, Brown, 1973), 20, 37–38.

Harris, Susan K. "But Is It Any Good: Evaluating Nineteenth-Century Women's Fiction," *American Literature* 63, no. 1 (March 1991): 43–61.

———. "Inscribing and Defining: The Many Voices of Fanny Fern's *Ruth Hall*," *Style* 22, no. 4 (Winter 1988): 612–27.

Harvey, David. *The Condition of Postmodernity: An Enquiry into the Origins of Cultural Change* (Cambridge, Eng.: Blackwell, 1990).

Hassan, Ihab. "Cities of Mind, Urban Words: The Dematerialization of Metropolis in Contemporary American Fiction," in *Literature and the Urban Experience*, ed. Michael C. Jaye and Ann Chalmers Watts (New Brunswick, N.J.: Rutgers University Press, 1981), 93–112.

Hayes, Kevin J. *Poe and the Printed Word* (New York: Cambridge University Press, 2000).

———. "Railway Reading," *Proceedings of the American Antiquarian Society* 106, pt. 2 (October 1996): 301–26.

Henkin, David. *City Reading: Written Words and Public Spaces in Antebellum New York* (New York: Columbia University Press, 1998).

Hewitt, Elizabeth. *Correspondence and American Literature, 1770–1865* (New York: Cambridge University Press, 2004).

Hill, Marilyn Wood. *Their Sisters' Keepers: Prostitution in New York City, 1830–1870* (Berkeley: University of California Press, 1993).

Horwitz, Richard P. "Architecture and Culture: The Meaning of the Lowell Boarding House," *American Quarterly* 25, no. 1 (March 1973): 64–82.

Howe, Irving. *Sherwood Anderson* (Palo Alto, Calif.: Stanford University Press, 1951), 51–90.

Hughes, Linda K. "Turbulence in the 'Golden Stream': Chaos Theory and the Study of Periodicals," *Victorian Periodicals Review* 22 (1989): 117–25.

Hurst, Luanne Jenkins. "The Chief Employ of Her Life: Sophia Peabody Hawthorne's Contribution to Her Husband's Career," in *Hawthorne and Women: Engendering and Expanding the Hawthorne Tradition*, ed. John L. Idol, Jr. and Melinda M. Ponder (Amherst: University of Massachusetts Press, 1999), 45–54.

Jackson, Joseph. *A Bibliography of the Works of George Lippard* (1929; Philadelphia: Historical Society of Pennsylvania, reprint in pamphlet form of the earlier version appearing in the *Pennsylvania Magazine of History and Biography*, April 1930) [HSP Manuscripts, Joseph Jackson Collection, box 1, folder 14].

———. *Encyclopedia of Philadelphia*, vols. 1–4 (Harrisburg, Pa.: Telegraph, 1932) [Library Company Reference].

———. "George Lippard: Poet of the Proletariat," unpublished manuscript biography of Lippard, ca. 1930 [HSP Manuscripts, Joseph Jackson Collection, box 1, folder 12].

Jacobs, Jane. *The Death and Life of Great American Cities* (1961; rept. New York: Vintage Books, 1992).

James, Reese D. *Old Drury of Philadelphia: A History of the Philadelphia Stage* (Philadelphia: University of Pennsylvania Press, 1932), 639, 651, 677.

Johns, Elizabeth. *American Genre Painting: The Politics of Everyday Life* (New Haven, Conn.: Yale University Press, 1992).

Johnson, Claudia. "That Guilty Third Tier: Prostitution in Nineteenth-Century American Theaters," *American Quarterly* 27, no. 5 (December 1975): 575–84.

Johnson, Paul E., and Sean Wilentz. *The Kingdom of Matthias* (New York: Oxford University Press, 1994).

Kalayjian, Patricia Larson. "Disinterest as Moral Corrective in *Clarence*'s Cultural Critique," from *Catharine Maria Sedgwick: Critical Perspectives,* ed. Lucinda L. Damon-Bach and Victoria Clements (Boston: Northeastern University Press, 2003), 104–17.

Kamensky, Jane. "Our Buildings, Ourselves," *Common-Place* 2, no. 2 (January 2002).

Kaplan, Amy. "Manifest Domesticity," *American Literature* 70, no. 3 (September 1998): 581–606.

———. *The Social Construction of American Realism* (Chicago: University of Chicago Press, 1988).

Kasson, John. *Civilizing the Machine: Technology and Republican Values in America* (New York: Penguin Books, 1976), 53–106.

———. *Rudeness and Civility: Manners in Nineteenth-Century Urban America* (New York: Hill and Wang, 1990).

Kelley, Mary. *Private Woman, Public Stage: Literary Domesticity in Nineteenth-Century America* (New York: Oxford University Press, 1984).

Kelley, Wyn. *Melville's City: Literary and Urban Form in Nineteenth-Century New York* (New York: Cambridge University Press, 1996).

Klimasmith, Betsy. *At Home in the City: Urban Domesticity in American Literature and Culture, 1850–1930* (Lebanon, N.H.: University Press of New England, 2005).

Knights, Peter R. *The Plain People of Boston, 1830–1860: A Study in City Growth* (New York: Oxford University Press, 1971).

Komter, Aafke E. *The Gift: An Interdisciplinary Perspective* (University of Amsterdam Press, 1996).

Konkle, Maureen. *Writing Indian Nations: Native Intellectuals and the Politics of Historiography, 1827–1863* (Chapel Hill: University of North Carolina Press, 2004), 97–159.

Kraft, Stephanie. *No Castles on Main Street: American Authors and Their Homes* (Chicago: Rand McNally, 1979), 62–73.

Kuklick, Bruce. "Myth and Symbol in American Studies" (1972), in *Locating American Studies: The Evolution of a Discipline,* ed. Lucy Maddox (Baltimore: Johns Hopkins University Press, 1999), 71–90.

Landrey, Wanda A. *Boardin' in the Thicket* (Denton, Tex.: University of North Texas Press, 1990).

Lane, Lauriat Jr., "On the Organic Structure of *Walden,*" *College English* 21, no. 4 (1960): 195–202.

Lang, Amy Schrager. *The Syntax of Class: Writing Inequality in Nineteenth-Century America* (Princeton, N.J.: Princeton University Press, 2003).

Laurie, Bruce. *Working People of Philadelphia* (Philadelphia: Temple University Press, 1980).

Lears, T. J. Jackson. *No Place of Grace: Antimodernism and the Transformation of American Culture, 1880–1920* (Chicago: University of Chicago Press, 1981).

Leonard, Stephen J., and Thomas J. Noel. *Denver: Mining Camp to Metropolis* (Niwot, Colo.: University of Colorado Press, 1991), 1–114.

Leuchs, Fritz A. H. *The Early German Theatre in New York* (1928; rept. New York: AMS, 1966), 72–73.

Leverenz, David. *Manhood and the American Renaissance* (Ithaca, N.Y.: Cornell University Press, 1989), 227–58.

Levine, Lawrence. *Highbrow/Lowbrow: The Emergence of Cultural Hierarchy in America* (Cambridge, Mass.: Harvard University Press, 1988).

Lewis, Paul. "'Lectures or a Little Charity': Poor Visits in Antebellum Literature and Culture," *New England Quarterly* 73, no. 2 (June 2000): 246–73.

Lewis, R. W. B. *The American Adam: Innocence, Tragedy, and Tradition in the Nineteenth Century* (Chicago: University of Chicago Press, 1955).

Linde, Charlotte, and William Labov. "Spatial Networks as a Site for the Study of Language and Thought," *Language* 51, no. 4 (December 1975): 924–39.

Lockwood, Charles. *Manhattan Moves Uptown: An Illustrated History* (Boston: Houghton Mifflin, 1976).

Looby, Christopher. "George Thompson's 'Romance of the Real,'" *American Literature* 65, no. 4 (December 1993): 651–72.

Machor, James L. *Pastoral Cities: Urban Ideals and the Symbolic Landscape of America* (Madison: University of Wisconsin Press, 1987), 3–7, 121–44.

Mao, Douglas, and Rebecca Walkowitz. "The New Modernist Studies," *PMLA* 123, no. 3 (May 2008): 737–48.

Marcus, Sharon. *Apartment Stories: City and Home in Nineteenth-Century Paris and London* (Berkeley: University of California Press, 1999).

Marsh, Carole. "Thomas Wolfe's House," in *The Mystery of the Biltmore House* (Tyron, N.C.: Gallopade, 1982), 71–76 [NCC].

Martin, Edgar W. *The Standard of Living in 1860: American Consumption Levels on the Eve of the Civil War* (Chicago: University of Chicago Press, 1942), 148–80.

Marx, Leo. *The Machine in the Garden: Technology and the Pastoral Ideal in America* (New York: Oxford University Press, 1964).

Matthiessen, F. O. *The American Renaissance: Art and Expression in the Age of Emerson and Whitman* (New York: Oxford University Press, 1941).

McCall, Dan. *Citizens of Somewhere Else: Nathaniel Hawthorne and Henry James* (Ithaca, N.Y.: Cornell University Press, 1999), 71–98.

McConachie, Bruce A. *Melodramatic Formations: American Theatre and Society, 1820–1870* (Iowa City: University of Iowa Press, 1992).

McDermott, John Francis. "Whitman and the Partons: Glimpses from the Diary of Thomas Butler Gunn, 1856–1860," *American Literature* 29, no. 3 (November 1957): 316–19.

McGill, Meredith L. "The Matter of the Text: Commerce, Print Culture, and the Authority of the State in American Copyright Law," *American Literary History* 9, no. 1 (Spring 1997): 21–59.

McNamara, Kevin. *Urban Verbs: Arts and Discourses of American Cities* (Stanford, Calif.: Stanford University Press, 1996).

Meinig, D. W. *The Shaping of America: A Geographical Perspective on 500 Years of History,* Vol. 2: *Continental America, 1800–1867* (New Haven, Conn.: Yale University Press, 1986).

Mellow, James R. *Nathaniel Hawthorne in His Times* (Boston: Houghton Mifflin, 1980).

Menand, Louis. *The Metaphysical Club: A Story of Ideas in America* (New York: Farrar, Straus and Giroux, 2001), 3–69.

Merish, Lori. *Sentimental Materialism: Gender, Commodity Culture, and Nineteenth-Century American Literature* (Durham, N.C.: Duke University Press, 2000).

Merwick, Donna. *Possessing Albany, 1630–1710: The Dutch and English Experiences* (Cambridge, Eng.: Cambridge University Press, 1990).

Milder, Robert. *Reimagining Thoreau* (New York: Cambridge University Press, 1995).

Miller, Edwin Haviland. *Salem Is My Dwelling Place: A Life of Nathaniel Hawthorne* (Iowa City: University of Iowa Press, 1991), 357–58, 369.

Miller, John N. "Eros and Ideology: At the Heart of Hawthorne's Blithedale," *Nineteenth-Century Literature* 55, no. 1 (June 2000): 1–21.

Miller, Perry. *The Raven and the Whale: The War of Words and Wits in the Era of Poe and Melville* (New York: Harcourt, Brace and World, 1956).

Millington, Richard H. "American Anxiousness: Selfhood and Culture in Hawthorne's *The Blithedale Romance,*" *New England Quarterly* 63, no. 4 (December 1990): 558–83.

———. *Practicing Romance: Narrative for and Cultural Engagement in Hawthorne's Fiction* (Princeton, N.J.: Princeton University Press, 1992).

Mitchell, Thomas R. *Hawthorne's Fuller Mystery* (Amherst: University of Massachusetts Press, 1998), 1–3, 180–219.

Modell, John, and Tamara K. Hareven. "Urbanization and the Malleable Household: An Examination of Boarding and Lodging in American Families," in *The American Family in Social-Historical Perspective,* 2nd ed., ed. Michael Gordon (New York: St. Martin's, 1978), 51–68.

Monaghan, Jay. *The Great Rascal: The Life and Adventure of Ned Buntline* (Boston: Little, Brown, 1952), 114–68.

Morse, John T., Jr., *Life and Letters of Oliver Wendell Holmes,* 2 vols. (Boston: Houghton, Mifflin, 1896), 1:69–72, 73–5, 110–11, 132–36; 2:269–72.

Mott, Frank Luther. *A History of American Magazines,* 5 vols. (Cambridge, Mass.: Harvard University Press, 1938–68).

Mrozowski, Stephen A. *Living on the Boott: Historical Archaeology at the Boott Mills Boardinghouses, Lowell, Massachusetts* (Amherst: University of Massachusetts Press, 1996).

Mumford, Lewis. *City Development: Studies in Disintegration and Renewal* (New York: Harcourt, Brace, 1945).

———. *The Culture of Cities* (New York: Harcourt, Brace, 1938).

———. *Roots of Contemporary American Architecture: A Series of Thirty-Seven Essays Dating from the Mid-Nineteenth Century to the Present* (New York: Grove, 1959).

———. *Sidewalk Critic: Lewis Mumford's Writings on New York,* ed. Robert Wojtowicz (New York: Princeton Architectural Press, 1998).

———. *The Urban Prospect* (New York: Harcourt, Brace and World, 1956).

Nadel, Stanley. *Little Germany: Ethnicity, Religion, and Class in New York City, 1845–1880* (Urbana: University of Illinois Press, 1990).

Nash, Gary. *First City: Philadelphia and the Forging of Historical Memory* (Philadelphia: University of Pennsylvania Press, 2002), 144–75.

Neufeldt, Leonard N. *The Economist: Henry Thoreau and Enterprise* (New York: Oxford University Press, 1989).

Newbury, Michael. *Figuring Authorship in Antebellum America* (Stanford, Calif.: Stanford University Press, 1997), 33–35.

Newman, Harvey K. *Southern Hospitality: Tourism and the Growth of Atlanta* (Tuscaloosa: University of Alabama Press, 1999), 1–36.

Newman, Lance. "Thoreau's Natural Community and Utopian Socialism," *American Literature* 75, no. 3 (September 2003): 515–44.

*The New York Historical Society's Dictionary of Artists in America, 1564–1860* (New Haven, Conn.: Yale University Press, 1957), 165.

Nord, David Paul. "A Republican Literature: Magazine Reading and Readers in Late-Eighteenth-Century New York," in *Reading in America,* ed. Cathy N. Davidson (Baltimore: Johns Hopkins University Press, 1989), 114–39.

Nord, Deborah Epstein. *Walking the Victorian Streets: Women, Representation, and the City* (Ithaca, N.Y.: Cornell University Press, 1995).

Oberholtzer, Ellis Paxson. *The Literary History of Philadelphia* (Philadelphia: George W. Jacobs, 1906), 251–62.

O'Dell, George C. D. *Annals of the New York Stage* II (New York: Columbia University Press, 1927), 389 and III (1928), 350, 366.

Okker, Patricia. *Social Stories: The Magazine Novel in Nineteenth-Century America* (Charlottesville: University of Virginia Press, 2003).

Otter, Samuel. *Philadelphia Stories: America's Literature of Race and Freedom* (Berkeley: University of California Press, 2010).

Parker, Hershel. *Herman Melville: A Biography, vol. 1, 1819–1851* and *vol. 2, 1852–1891* (Baltimore: Johns Hopkins University Press, 1996 and 2002).

Parrington, Vernon Louis. *Main Currents in American Thought: An Interpretation of American Literature from the Beginnings to 1920,* 3 vols. (1927, 1930; New York: Harcourt, Brace and World, 1958), 2:451–59.

Parry, Albert. *Garrets and Pretenders: A History of Bohemianism in America* (1933; rept. New York: Dover, 1960).

Pattee, Fred Lewis. *The Feminine Fifties* (New York: D. Appleton-Century, 1940), 110.

Pease, Donald E. *Visionary Compacts: American Renaissance Writings in Cultural Context* (Madison: University of Wisconsin Press, 1987).

Peel, Mark. "On the Margin: Lodgers and Boarders in Boston, 1860–1900," *Journal of American History* 72, no. 4 (March 1986): 813–34.

Perry, Lewis. *Boats Against the Current: American Culture Between Revolution and Modernity, 1820–1860* (New York: Oxford University Press, 1993).

*Philadelphia: A 300-Year History,* ed. Russell F. Weigley (New York: W. W. Norton, 1982).

Pierson, George Wilson. *Tocqueville in America* (1938; rept. Gloucester, Mass.: Peter Smith, 1969), 1–59.

Post-Lauria, Sheila. *Correspondent Colorings: Melville in the Marketplace* (Amherst: University of Massachusetts Press, 1996).

Pratt, Lloyd. *Archives of American Time: Literature and Modernity in the Nineteenth Century* (Philadelphia: University of Pennsylvania Press, 2010).

Pred, Allan. *Urban Growth and City-Systems in the United States, 1840–1860* (Cambridge, Mass.: Harvard University Press, 1980), 1–12.

Raban, Jonathan. *Soft City* (New York: E. P. Dutton, 1974).

Reynolds, David S. *Beneath the American Renaissance: The Subversive Imagination in the Age of Emerson and Melville* (Cambridge, Mass.: Harvard University Press, 1988).

———. *George Lippard* (Boston: Twayne, 1982).

———. *Walt Whitman's America: A Cultural Biography* (New York: Alfred A. Knopf, 1995).

Reynolds, Larry. *European Revolutions and the American Literary Renaissance* (New York: Oxford University Press, 1988).

Richardson, Robert D. Jr. *Emerson: The Mind on Fire* (Berkeley: University of California Press, 1995).

———. *Henry D. Thoreau: A Life of the Mind* (Berkeley: University of California Press, 1986).

Robinson, Elwyn Burns. "*The Pennsylvanian:* Organ of the Democracy," *Pennsylvanian Magazine* 62 (July 1938): 350–60.

Rogin, Michael Paul. *Subversive Genealogy: The Politics and Art of Herman Melville* (New York: Knopf, 1983).

Romero, Lora. *Home Fronts: Domesticity and Its Critics in the Antebellum United States* (Durham, N.C.: Duke University Press, 1997), vii–34.

Ross, Donald. "Dreams and Sexual Repression in *The Blithedale Romance,*" *PMLA* 5, no. 86 (October 1971): 1014–17.

Rourke, Constance. *Trumpets of Jubilee: Henry Ward Beecher, Harriet Beecher Stowe, Lyman Beecher, Horace Greeley, P. T. Barnum* (New York: Harcourt, Brace, 1927).

Rowe, John Carlos. *At Emerson's Tomb: The Politics of Classic American Literature* (New York: Columbia University Press, 1997).

———. *The New American Studies* (Minneapolis: University of Minnesota Press, 2002).

———. *Through the Custom House: Nineteenth-Century American Fiction and Modern Theory* (Baltimore: Johns Hopkins University Press, 1982).

Rubin, Joan Shelley. "What Is the History of the History of Books?" *Journal of American History* 90, no. 2 (September 2003): 555–75.

Rusk, Ralph L. *The Life of Ralph Waldo Emerson* (New York: Charles Scribner's Sons, 1949).

Sattelmeyer, Robert. "The Remaking of *Walden*," in *Writing the American Classics*, ed. James Barbour and Tom Quirk (Chapel Hill: University of North Carolina Press, 1990), 53–78.

———. *Thoreau's Reading: A Study in Intellectual History, with Bibliographical Catalogue* (Princeton, N.J.: Princeton University Press, 1988).

Scherzer, Kenneth A. *The Unbounded Community: Neighborhood Life and Social Structure in New York City, 1830–1875* (Durham, N.C.: Duke University Press, 1992).

Schivelbusch, Wolfgang. *The Railway Journey: The Internalization of Time and Space in the Nineteenth Century* (1977; rept. Berkeley: University of California Press, 1986), 33–44.

Schmidt, Leigh Eric. *Consumer Rites: The Buying & Selling of American Holidays* (Princeton, N.J.: Princeton University Press, 1995), 77–85.

Schweitzer, Ivy. *The Work of Self-Representation: Lyric Poetry in Colonial New England* (Chapel Hill: University of North Carolina Press, 1991).

Scobey, David M. *Empire City: The Making and Meaning of the New York City Landscape* (Philadelphia: Temple University Press, 2002).

Scudder, Townsend. *Concord: American Town* (Boston: Little, Brown, 1947), 187, 196–98.

Sellers, Charles. *The Market Revolution: Jacksonian America, 1815–1846* (New York: Oxford University Press, 1991).

Shelton, Cynthia J. *The Mills of Manayunk: Industrialization and Social Conflict in the Philadelphia Region, 1787–1837* (Baltimore: Johns Hopkins University Press, 1986), 71–72.

Shelton, F. H. "Springs and Spas of Old-Time Philadelphians," *Pennsylvania Magazine of History and Biography* 47 (1923): 208.

Shephard, Odell. *Pedlar's Progress: The Life of Bronson Alcott* (Boston: Little, Brown, 1937), 121.

Shields, David S. *Civil Tongues & Polite Letters in British America* (Chapel Hill: University of North Carolina Press, 1997).

Siegel, Adrienne. *The Image of the American City in Popular Literature, 1820–1870* (Port Washington, N.Y.: Kennikat, 1981).

Silver-Isenstadt, Jean L. *Shameless: The Visionary Life of Mary Gove Nichols* (Baltimore: Johns Hopkins University Press, 2002), 79–80.

Silverman, Kenneth. *Edgar A. Poe: Mournful and Never-Ending Remembrance* (New York: HarperPerennial, 1992).

Simmel, Georg. "The Metropolis and Mental Life," in *The Sociology of Georg Simmel*, trans. and ed. Kurt Wolf (New York: Free, 1950), 409–24.

Sklar, Robert. "The Fonz, Laverne, Shirley, and the Great American Class Struggle," in *Television: The Critical View* (1976), ed. Horace Newcomb (New York: Oxford University Press, 1982), 77–88.

Slotkin, Richard. *Regeneration Through Violence: The Mythology of the American Frontier, 1600–1860* (Norman: University of Oklahoma Press, 1973).

Smelser, Neil J., ed. *Sociology: An Introduction*, 2nd ed. (New York: John Wiley and Sons, 1973).

Smith, Henry Nash. *Virgin Land: The American West as Myth and Symbol* (Cambridge, Mass.: Harvard University Press, 1950).

Smither, Nell. *A History of English Theatre in New Orleans* (New York: Benjamin Bloom, 1944), 328.

Soja, Edward W. *Postmodern Geographies: Reassertion of Space in Critical Social Theory* (London: Verso, 1998), 43–75.

*Southport Secrets,* compiled by Donald Knute Johnson. See "Kate Stuart Boarding House" (Southport, N.C.: Southport Historical Society, 1998), 72–75 [NCC].

Spurlock, John C. *Free Love: Marriage and Middle-Class Radicalism in America, 1825–1860* (New York: NYU Press, 1988).

Stansell, Christine. *City of Women: Sex and Class in New York City, 1789–1860* (Urbana: University of Illinois Press, 1986).

———. "Whitman at Pfaff's: Commercial Culture, Literary Life and New York Bohemia at Mid-Century," *Walt Whitman Quarterly Review* 10, no. 3 (Winter 1993): 107–26.

Starr, Louis Morris. *Bohemian Brigade: Civil War Newsmen in Action* (New York: Knopf, 1954), 367.

Stewart, David M. "Cultural Work, City Crime, Reading, Pleasure," *American Literary History* 9, no. 4 (Winter 1997): 676–701.

Stoehr, Taylor, ed. *Free Love in America: A Documentary History* (New York: AMS, 1979).

Stokes, I. N. Phelps. *The Iconography of Manhattan Island, 1498–1900,* 6 vols. (New York: Robert H. Dodd, 1915–28), 3:550–51.

Story, Ronald. *The Forging of an Aristocracy: Harvard & the Boston Upper Class, 1800–1870* (Middletown, Conn.: Wesleyan University Press, 1980), 3–23.

Stout, Janis P. *Sodoms in Eden: The City in American Fiction Before 1860* (Westport, Conn.: Greenwood, 1976).

Tansell, G. Thomas. "Copyright Records and the Bibliographer," in *Studies in Bibliography,* vol. 22, ed. Fredson Bowers (Charlottesville: Bibliographical Society of the University of Virginia, 1969), 77–124.

Teichgraeber, Richard F. III. *Sublime Thoughts/Penny Wisdom: Situating Emerson and Thoreau in the American Market* (Baltimore: Johns Hopkins University Press, 1995).

Thernstrom, Stephan. *The Other Bostonians: Poverty and Progress in the American Metropolis, 1880–1970* (Cambridge, Mass.: Harvard University Press, 1973), 4–6.

Tilton, Eleanor M. *Amiable Autocrat; A Biography of Dr. Oliver Wendell Holmes* (New York: Henry Schuman, 1947).

Tompkins, Jane P. *Sensational Designs: The Cultural Work of American Fiction, 1790–1860* (New York: Oxford University Press, 1985).

Trachtenberg, Alan. *Brooklyn Bridge: Fact and Symbol* (Chicago: University of Chicago Press, 1965).

———. *Reading American Photographs: Images as History, Mathew Brady to Walker Evans* (New York: Oxford University Press, 1989).

Tuan, Yi-Fu. *Space and Place: The Perspective of Experience* (Minneapolis: University of Minnesota Press, 1977).

———. *Topophilia: A Study of Environmental Perceptions, Attitudes, and Values* (New York: Columbia University Press, 1990).

Tucher, Andie. *Froth & Scum: Truth, Beauty, Goodness, and the Ax Murder in America's First Mass Medium* (Chapel Hill: University of North Carolina Press, 1994), 1–22.

Vale, Lawrence J. *From the Puritans to the Projects: Public Housing and Public Neighbors* (Cambridge, Mass.: Harvard University Press, 2000), 1–91.

Van Cromphout, Gustaaf. "*Blithedale* and the Androgyne Myth: Another Look at Zenobia," *ESQ* 18, no. 3 (1972): 141–45.

Vogel, Donald S. *The Boardinghouse: The Artist Community House, Chicago 1936–37* (Denton, Tex.: University of North Texas Press, 1995).

Wade, Mary Dodson. *Homesteading on the Plains: Daily Life in the Land of Laura Ingalls Wilder* (Brookfield, Conn.: Milbrook: 1997), 7.

Warner, Michael. *The Letters of the Republic: Publication and the Public Sphere in Eighteenth-Century America* (Cambridge, Mass.: Harvard University Press, 1990).

Warner, Sam Bass Jr. *The Private City: Philadelphia in Three Periods of Its Growth* (Philadelphia: University of Pennsylvania Press, 1968).

Warren, Joyce W. *Fanny Fern: An Independent Woman* (New Brunswick, N.J.: Rutgers University Press, 1992).

Watson, Harry L. "Slavery and Development in a Dual Economy: The South and the Market Revolution," in *The Market Revolution in America: Social, Political, and Religious Expressions, 1800–1880,* ed. Melvyn Stokes and Stephen Conway (Charlottesville: University of Virginia Press, 1996), 43–73.

Welter, Barbara. "The Cult of True Womanhood: 1820–1860" (1966), in *Locating American Studies: The Evolution of a Discipline,* ed. Lucy Maddox (Baltimore: Johns Hopkins University Press, 1999), 43–66.

Werner, James V. *American Flaneur: The Cosmic Physiognomy of Edgar Allan Poe* (New York: Routledge, 2004).

White, Craig. "A Utopia of 'Spheres and Sympathies': Science and Society in *The Blithedale Romance* and at Brook Farm," *Utopian Studies* 9, no. 2 (Spring 1998): 78–102.

White, Hayden. *Tropics of Discourse* (Baltimore: Johns Hopkins University Press, 1978).

White, Morton, and Lucia White. *The Intellectual Versus the City: From Thomas Jefferson to Frank Lloyd Wright* (Cambridge, Mass.: Harvard University Press, 1962).

Widmer, Edward L. *Young America: The Flowering of Democracy in New York City* (New York: Oxford University Press, 1999).

Wilentz, Sean. *Chants Democratic: New York City & the Rise of the American Working Class, 1788–1850* (New York: Oxford University Press, 1984).

Williams, Raymond. *The Country and the City* (New York: Oxford University Press, 1973).

——. *Culture and Society, 1790–1950* (1958; rept. New York: Columbia University Press: 1983), xiii–xx.

Williams, William Carlos. *In the American Grain* (1925; rept. New York: New Directions, 1956).

Wise, Gene. "'Paradigm Dramas' in American Studies: A Cultural and Institutional History of the Movement" (1979), in *Locating American Studies: The Evolution of a Discipline*, ed. Lucy Maddox (Baltimore: Johns Hopkins University Press, 1999), 71–90.

Wolff, Janet. "The Invisible *Flâneuse:* Women and the Literature of Modernity," in *The Problems of Modernity: Adorno and Benjamin*, ed. Andrew Benjamin (London: Routledge, 1989), 141–56.

Wright, Gwendolyn. *Building the Dream: A Social History of Housing in America* (New York: Pantheon Books, 1981).

Young, James Sterling. *The Washington Community, 1800–1828* (New York: Columbia University Press, 1966), 97–109.

Zboray, Ronald J. *A Fictive People: Antebellum Economic Development and the American Reading Public* (New York: Oxford University Press, 1993).

Zboray, Ronald J., and Mary Saracino Zboray. "'Have You Read . . . ?' Real Readers and Their Responses in Antebellum Boston and Its Region," *Nineteenth-Century Literature* 52, no. 2 (September 1997): 139–70.

——. "Reading and Everyday Life in Antebellum Boston: The Diary of Daniel F. and Mary D. Child," *Libraries & Culture* 32, no. 3 (Summer 1997): 285–323.

Ziff, Larzer. *Literary Democracy: The Declaration of Cultural Independence in America* (New York: Penguin Books, 1982), 87–107.

Zurawik, David. *The Jews of Prime Time* (Hanover, N.H.: University Press of New England, 2003), 1–16.

# INDEX

Page numbers in italics refer to illustrations.

## ABOUT THE AUTHOR

David Faflik is an assistant professor of English at the University of Rhode Island.